Karl Germer

Selected Letters
1928-1962

Karl Germer

Selected Letters
1928-1962

Edited by
David Shoemaker,
Andrew Ferrell
& Stefan Voss

First printing in 2016 by

The Temple of the Silver Star
P.O. Box 215483
Sacramento, California 95821, USA

First reprinting, February 2017
Revised edition with index, March 2017

Founded in Service to the A∴A∴

totss.org

© 2016-7 Temple of the Silver Star

All Rights Reserved.
Printed in the United States of America.

Cover design and Index by Gavin O'Keefe

ISBN: 0-9976686-5-2
ISBN-13: 978-0-9976686-5-0

TABLE OF CONTENTS

Acknowledgements	iv
Introduction	v
Biographical Sketch	viii

SELECTED LETTERS

1928	3
1934	16
1941	19
1942	25
1943	34
1944	66
1945	103
1946	119
1947	132
1948	152
1949	176
1950	214
1952	257
1953	303
1955	325
1956	338
1958	361
1961	369
1962	377
About the Editors	391
Organizational Contacts	393
Index	397

ACKNOWLEDGEMENTS

Many thanks to Rex Parsons, Kelli Patton, Matthew Szymanski, Jon Perry, Teresa Wiles, Gypsy Andrews, and Ayanna Hart for their assistance with transcription from the original documents, and to Gavin O'Keefe for his lovely cover design.

INTRODUCTION

Do what thou wilt shall be the whole of the Law.

[...] it is the H.G.A. Himself who will set the proper day and hour for the union. Then all will be prepared beautifully and fall in its place. The leisure, the aspiration, the Yoga, the surroundings, the silence, and all the rest. Did I not tell you that He arranged everything for me in the solitude of the Concentration Camp? Learn to abandon yourself with utter confidence to Him. Yet, as it is said: Invoke often!

--Karl Germer to Phyllis Seckler, May 5, 1952

Karl Germer was at his best, and can only be fully understood in the context of, his one-to-one relationships with other Thelemites. In these relationships—as seen in the letters here—Germer reveals himself to be a deeply devoted Thelemite, passionate about the dissemination and expansion of Thelema throughout the world. We see his obvious love for Crowley the man and, after Crowley's death, his dedication to ensuring that as many key Thelemic texts as possible were published for posterity. We also see his perpetual frustration at the foibles of Agape Lodge members in Southern California. On the surface, this would appear to support the common impression that he didn't prioritize ritual work, initiation, or the O.T.O. management tasks that fell to him, and that he simply let things fall apart. Yet underneath his annoyance and questionable managerial strategies we glimpse his real concern for the long-term viability of Thelema, even at the short-term expense of individual initiates or Agape Lodge itself.

Selecting letters to include in this volume was no easy task, as the collection here reflects just a fraction of the letters in the T.O.T.S.S. archives. To arrive at a final list for inclusion we made multiple passes through all the potential letters, making notes and ranking the files, and attempting to prioritize those which were most informative (and in many cases, the most entertaining!)

While we initially considered organizing this book around the themes discussed in the various letters, such as magical instruction or publishing, we found that too many of the letters addressed a mixed set of topics to make this a viable approach. Ultimately, we decided to arrange the letters chronologically, and let them tell their own story. This approach inevitably forced us to interrupt the back-and-forth narrative of some of the correspondence chains, but we hope what we may occasionally have sacrificed in terms of continuity we gained in depth and breadth of coverage.

A few primary topical threads reveal themselves across the years, especially from the late 1930s onward. One central thread is an extensive series of communications between Germer and Jane Wolfe pertaining to Agape Lodge, including much hand-wringing about how to deal with problematic figures such as Wilfred Smith, Jack Parsons, Oskar Schlag, and even L. Ron Hubbard. Other common themes include ongoing publishing efforts, a constant lack of money, Crowley's declining health, and later his death and legacy. Underneath all of this, however, is perhaps the most important theme of all—that of a dedicated Thelemite attempting to pass on his insights, hopes, and fears to his colleagues and students. In these letters, we can see the seeds of modern Thelema being planted in those—Phyllis Seckler, Marcelo Motta, and others—who would later cultivate the resurgence and growth of the tradition, and set the stage for the Thelemic world after Germer's death.

While we attempted to standardize certain formatting approaches across several decades' worth of letters and multiple correspondents, we intentionally left many eccentricities intact, such as idiosyncratic punctuation and archaic spellings. Germer's unique manner of communicating about arcane topics is, in our opinion, one of the most charming and instructive rewards of reading these letters.

We hope that this collection will begin to address the sizable gap in published Thelemic history that extends from Crowley's death in 1947 to the gradual resurgence of the tradition in the late

1960s and early 1970s. It is also our hope that these letters will finally shed a more favorable light on this flawed but unfairly maligned teacher and leader, who bore the torch of Thelema in the challenging days after Crowley's death forward into the modern era.

May we each do our part to aid in the further extension of that Light.

Love is the law, love under will.

David Shoemaker
Andrew Ferrell
Stefan Voss

Autumn 2016 e.v.
Anno Legis V^{ii}

BIOGRAPHICAL SKETCH

Karl Johannes Germer was born on January 22nd, 1885 e.v. in Elberfeld, Germany. He spent his childhood in Germany, and after completing his studies there, he moved to Paris to study at Sorbonne University. Afterwards, he spent several years living in London, England working as a representative of Alfred Herbert, Ltd. in East Germany and West Russia. In 1914 e.v. with the outbreak of World War I, Germer served as adjutant and machine gun officer in Belgium, France, Russia and Serbia, receiving the First and Second Class Iron Cross decorations for his service.

In the early 1920s he was living in Munich, Germany and working at the Barth Publishing House with Heinrich Traenker (Fra. Renatus), where he was involved in the publication of the "Pansophia" series, the English translation of Dr. Franz Hartmann's "Rosicrucian Lessons", and assisted in the translation of "One Star in Sight", extracts from *Liber Thisharb* and an article describing Crowley's Ordeal of the Abyss. In 1925 Germer met Crowley in Weida, Thuringia at Traenker's house. Following this meeting, Crowley moved in with Germer. Soon after, in 1926, Germer divorced his first wife, Marie Wys. In 1929, Germer married his second wife, the American Cora Eaton, in New York City, and Crowley and Germer established the Thelema Publishing Company in Leipzig, Germany. There they published *Book 4*, Parts I and II, "A Report on the Great White Brotherhood", "Science and Buddhism", "The Message of Master Therion", "The Wake World", "Berashith", "A commentary on H.P. Blavatsky's *The Voice of the Silence*", and "The Three Schools of Magic".

Between 1925-1935 e.v., Germer lived and studied with Crowley, traveling between New York and London frequently. On February 2, 1935 e.v., during a trip back to Leipzig, Germany Germer was arrested by the Gestapo with no reason given. He was transported to Alexanderplatz Prison in Berlin for ten days where, after much questioning, it was revealed that his arrest was due to his connections to "high grade Freemasons abroad". He was taken to Columbia House – the Berlin concentration camp where he was kept in solitary confinement under horrific conditions for five months. He managed to get a permit to work in the architect's office and developed a number of connections with prominent prisoners and S.S. guards and officers. For three months he was kept in strict solitary confinement following an incident in which his wife sent him a cable from New York and he was accused of being a spy. He was later transferred to Esterwegen Camp, which he described as "one of the worst of the worst camps in Nazi Germany".

During his time in solitary confinement, having no access to books, Germer recited the Holy Books and attained to the Knowledge and Conversation of the Holy Guardian Angel. In total, Germer spent six months as a prisoner in the two camps prior to being released and returning to England.

Without a permanent visa, Germer was forced to leave England and sought refuge, penniless and unable to find work. He eventually travelled to Ireland and found work as a machinist. In 1936 Germer travelled to Belgium as a representative of the machinery firm and sought to obtain a permanent visa for Ireland.

He worked in his capacity as a representative of the machinery firm for several years, until on May 10, 1940 e.v. he was arrested in Belgium and transferred to a French concentration camp. He stayed there until February 1, 1941 e.v. when he received a visa with the assistance of Cora and emigrated to the United States.

Germer assumed the office of General Grand Treasurer of Ordo Templi Orientis, and in 1942 his second wife, Cora Eaton died. In the following months, Germer married his third wife, Sascha Ernestine Andre.

Over the next two decades, Germer would spend his time administering the O.T.O. and the A∴A∴ from various locations in the United States. Germer succeeded Crowley as the Outer Head of the O.T.O. and Praemonstrator of A∴A∴ following Crowley's death in 1947, having previously been acknowledged as a Magister

Templi 8°=3□. While Germer was never particularly interested in the formalities of initiatory work, many important writings from the Thelemic corpus were published under his supervision, setting the stage for the resurgence of Thelema in the late 1960s and beyond.

Karl Germer died on October 25, 1962 e.v. at the age of 81 years. He was survived by his third wife, Sascha.

SELECTED LETTERS

206 Lincoln Place
Brooklyn, N.Y.

Feb. 2, 1928

Dear Jane,

93

I am sure you are a little sore at me for not having written earlier. The fact is I have not at all been in a mood to write. Yet, must I say that I have not been thinking of you all the time? Can one for a day forget that such a soul as Jane Wolfe[1] lives and suffers?

I don't know to what extent you are in communication with Beast. So I should like to tell you that as much as I can about the situation, even if it is no news to you.

The finances are, of course, as usual. No need to emphasize that. But really very great things are in the making. I mean magically. Beast is magically ready for a very, very great injunction in AL[2]. I do not know to what extent I am permitted to talk, so you know best, why I shut up. But I want you to be glad and hopeful in the certainty that the ship is just waiting for the wind to come up in order to sail on to the open sea.

Did I tell you that Dorothy is through her terrible state of the past years?

What did Jan. 25 bring you? Anything good? If he failed to show up, then I am sure, the coming months will certainly not disappoint you. Saturn is ready to pass over and stays on your Mars for quite a while and he doesn't bring candies. However, what can a 30 mile wind do to an old experienced seaworthy ship that has often successfully and defiantly skipped through 100 mile tornadoes?

---

[1] Jane Wolfe was a long-time member (and eventual Master) of Agape Lodge of O.T.O. in Southern California, an A∴A∴ student of Aleister Crowley, and a key resident of the Abbey of Thelema in Cefalu, Sicily.

[2] *Liber AL vel Legis (The Book of the Law)*

More seriously is your health. You have a friend here who is worrying quite a lot and often inquiring about you. I mean Cora Eaton[3]. She told me yesterday that she was going to send you a little note to find out how you were. Then my bad conscience struck me and I decided to write to you as quickly as possible. C.E. has a heart of gold and worries more about others than about herself. (Except Beast: I believe she thinks he should take a writer's job. And as to her finances she believes in safety first.) Should you write her at all it would certainly not be bad if you could somehow mention that the experiences and your life around Beast have not been the misfortune of your life. And that you do not feel as though you had now safely escaped that hell. (A short remark suffices: Wasn't I glad to get back and help the Work!)

I still have my old job and I have discovered a rather significant meaning in it. So I don't think that I will be given a better one for the present. Things look so different, once one learns to read the signs which the Gods so wisely prepare, those almost insignificant signs in whose interpretation Beast is such an unsurpassable master. But I am sure I am safely on the road and wait for things to come and the day when I will be ready for a bigger job.

And you, dear, faithful, helpful, courageous, brave etc. etc. Jane? All my best wishes with you.

As a surprise I had a short note from Smith[4] in Los Angeles last week trying to take up a connection with me. It is his first letter to me. Last year, then I sent him the Word of the Equinox, he did not even confirm the receipt. What kind of man is he?

93 93/93

Ever fraternally,

Karl

---

[3] Cora Eaton was eventually to become Germer's second wife.

[4] Wilfred T. Smith (born Frank Wenham), an O.T.O. member who was to become the Master of Agape Lodge of O.T.O.

[Handwritten marginalia:] If you have nothing else to do why don't you take up [*Liber*] *LXV* again and learn some other chapters besides IV by heart and recite them daily, or, better, the complete *LXV*? It might help you a lot. You will probably discover many new things -- practically.

I recite since 6 months daily *LXV* and *AL* and in addition to that since 3 or 4 months, VII. Do not forget that Beast (cp. Solomon the King) recited at one time every day certain invocations for 10 months before he got what he wanted. This reciting will give you a lot of spiritual force in any difficult phases to come.

♄

Lincoln Place
Brooklyn, N.Y.

February 14, 1928

Dear Jane,

93

    I had your letter (without date, as usual; when will Jane Wolfe learn to mark the date? Don't you put dates in your diary?) this morning.

    No reply from Smith. I feel myself always unable to say anything as soon as such topics as O.T.O. as distinguished from the A∴A∴ is brought up. Also I don't know what the oath of the Abyss really means, though I have heard the term frequently. If this Abyss refers to the crossing between $7°=4^{\square}$ and $8°=3^{\square}$; then I believe Monsieur Smith is less inspired by his H.G.A. than by vanity, ambition etc., in short by instinkations [sic] (excuse my

English) of his evil Persona. This was my immediate reaction, and the day has not changed it. Of course, I know that I am absolutely unable to feel in terms of individual human beings with the exception of some very few for whom I have genuine affection. I am only capable of thinking and reacting to conceptions of humanity as a whole. So I say: what's the use of preventing him from going to hell? I do not say that no effort should be made to make him reconsider his idea. If you feel inclined to do something, I am of the opinion you should not restrict yourself. Naturally, Beast is the supreme judge. But as his reply may take a long time (provided He has not acted on the magical plane) I thought it right at least to tell you my opinion of the case. My view is: he should think and occupy himself with his next step, which is to reach the next grade. He should do the little things: have a shoeshine, a shave, a haircut, his suit pressed, a bath etc. etc. in order to be able to appear before his God. It is, I believe, a blasphemy to do otherwise and the punishment will be accordingly.

The very fact that he "seems to be dissatisfied since he has been regularly seeing you" appears to show that you are having a definite magical influence on people. All the more important for you to watch yourself very carefully, lest the influence be detrimental. Everything may be perfectly allright; really nothing can happen unless it is in some subtle way the intention of the Gods. But the aim should be to be the conscious tool of Them. Or, in Beast's terminology: to do things in accordance with one's H.G.A.

Dorothy is still in Chicago. I think you can rely on her now to take in everything solely the point of view of: how can I help the Work? With utter forgetfulness of her own personal interests. I believe she is "saved", as you say in English. I did not know about the Polish Bride.

Your question about *AL*. You ought to know all the dire punishments which came in the first 22 years from the fact that Beast and all around Him discussed certain passages of *AL* freely. He himself openly connected certain passages with definite persons. Achad[5], Mudd[6], Leah[7] followed Him. Leah evidently did it though she had had the Comment. Many of Beast's attributions seem to have been erroneous and created terrible harm. Achad fell. Mudd became practically obsessed and insane (though this was probably his own fault). It is so hard for anyone to resist the temptation to consider himself one or the other in AL. Why, don't you remember the punishment I got in 1926 for writing that stupid letter to Beast, though I should have remembered the Comment? --

The comment was inspired actually after Beast got one of those insane letters by Mudd; He got wild and into Samadhi. I think one has to keep this in mind. It makes one understand a lot. Beast erred so long himself and was punished terribly, just that he should be able to tell others about the same punishments.

Then also things should not be discussed for argument's sake. It is magically bad: if a man does not understand, and you think you do, it is absolutely no use to argue: you can only try and teach him, and even this probably only on a higher plane. (Compare what the free discussion of the Bible etc. has lead to in the past. Nothing but controversies; innumerable sects based all on one Book. And everybody thinks he or she is right in the interpretation.) Argumentation falls under the heading: Because, who is damned for a dog. But that main thing is you weaken your magical force and point of view. If you want to help, try and teach in a round about way. Suppose you tell a savage or a child the Earth is round and says: now that is positively absurd, the Earth is flat, can't you see it? You must be insane! What's the use of arguing? Don't say a word; at the first opportunity (which will positively come, if you really have the will to help him) take him by the hand to a plain and make him explain the fact that in the far distance no tree is visible: the, as you approach with your car, etc.,

---

[5] Charles Stansfield Jones (aka Frater Achad), a historically important, and eventually controversial, A∴A∴ student of Aleister Crowley.

[6] Normal Mudd, an A∴A∴ student of Aleister Crowley who later committed suicide.

[7] Leah Hirsig, an A∴A∴ student, romantic partner, and "Scarlet Woman" of Aleister Crowley.

first a roof of a house is visible, or the top of a hill, or on the sea the smoke of a ship and very gradually the whole. Let him draw his own conclusions. Later give him further food for thought. In the end he will come and clasp your feet and say: what a fool I was. He will have implicit confidence from then on.

So also with *AL*. (You see I know these things fairly well, yet I never act by this wisdom.) -- However, I don't see a need for showing somebody your copy of *AL*, though I equally don't see why it should do any harm. It is a well known fact that if there was a publisher it would be immediately distributed all over the world in the reproduction with the Comment. And if you can show a man in the meantime the Comment, I think you are only doing him a great help.

Why should it be wrong to quote *AL*? Does not Beast quote it daily in His greetings? There will probably be some day a preacher or preachers all over the world who will popularise and explain the Law. Unless I may be mistaken. Just how it would have to be done I cannot see at the present.

I know that these remarks leave many questions and raise new ones. I believe everybody has in this early stage to guide himself or herself by his own judgment.

I don't know if you know that Viator, or Schneider,[8] has broken off diplomatic connections with me some time ago. I wanted you to be informed about it. He considered my definite request to contribute in finances as an imposition and an interference with his True Will. Beast, whom he sent the correspondence, let him down. I believe he is in critical state and either conquers his money-complex or becomes stagnant.

No progress with C.E. I believe it is an "ordeal" or a "test" for me to get her to contribute. If the Gods don't help me I don't see how I am going to succeed. These women!!

I am glad that "you have rounded the corner". I hope it means more.

93 93/93

---

[8] Max Schneider, an O.T.O. member who was later active at Agape Lodge.

With fraternal greetings,

Karl

May 7, 1928

Dear Jane,

93

    I have sent off my application for the extension of my visa to-day. Let us hope it will be granted. Otherwise I would have to leave Jesus's Country June 1 or soon after, probably by steerage.
    I had your letter of April 24 Saturday, when I was in N.Y.
    The fourth copy of *777* had better be sent to Martha[9]. In her last letter she asked me for two copies, to give one to a man in Berlin, who is going to edit it.
    I intended to mail you the *Little Essays*[10], but had my head full & will mail them when I am back in N.Y. If possible, I will also send *Heart of the Master* & Master Therion & the Dossier along. But I suppose you have those? I should like to get everything back as soon as possible.
    Your remarks were highly interesting, clears up a lot for me which I did not know. You say: "Is it Smith? or [illegible]? or Estai[11]??" Why not all of them? I wish Estai a whole lot. However, the Gods choose their own time for what they want to be done just when it suits them & that is quite intriguing for us.

---

[9] Martha Kuntzel, a member of O.T.O. and A∴A∴ who assisted Germer with his early publication efforts.

[10] *Little Essays Toward Truth* by Aleister Crowley.

[11] Soror Estai was Jane Wolfe's magical motto.

You might be able to do something for me. Ever since I have been with the crowd of 93ers I have heard a lot about the "Abyss". I have -- from whatever I read about it in the Books -- placed this "crossing of the A[byss]" in between the $7°=4^{\square}$ and $8°=3^{\square}$. Again from the way the thing is actually used it seems to be somewhere else, say lower down on the Tree. Furthermore, I remember Leah saying once: one had to cross it often (i.e. on many planes).

Now you refer to it in connection with Smith. You say: he is approaching his [Abyss experience] etc.. If such periods of fights & disagreeable times is the Abyss, why he would be on his way to $8°=3^{\square}$ or Master of Temple. Is that not absurd? Furthermore: if that were so simple I ought to be a 10 fold M.T. for I have had such periods I don't know how often (at least 3 six month wars with Marie were high explosive, Big Berthas, poison gas etc. etc. all the modern appliance, were used). I don't think they were followed by anything extraordinary. I haven't even reached the $5°=6^{\square}$ stage.

This brings me to another point, just this K. & C. which is supposed to take place in $5°=6^{\square}$. He's variously said that the H.G.A. leads one to the Abyss & helps one to cross over it, or prepares one so that one can succeed in it. Now here is the contradiction! If a man or woman goes through the Abyss -- ought he [be] insane anyhow -- the usual things, [illegible], lack of money, etc., etc., [illegible] -- every business man has to face similar and worse things, every few years. Actually I would have crossed then at least 10 Abysses and am still living, but got nothing from them. It seems so bombastic, so exaggerated, show offy, to use a special term for a commonplace thing. Besides it seems [illegible].

Yet, I put my above question again. If you were the woman capable of putting me wise on the various subjects referred to above, I would be grateful indeed.

Of course I realize that as long as you don't know this [illegible] H.G.A. it's all mere talk. But then it's also mere talk to call some hard time the Abyss. It seems to be like this American tendency to apply words with a definite meaning to something much more [illegible]. For instance, you say "High School" to something which in Germany would be a very low kind of a school. What we call "High School" (*hoch schule*) is practically the same as University (like Oxford or Cambridge). Again the term University is applied here [in the U.S.] to forms of schools an educated German would be ashamed of. "Officer" is a Cop. Lindbergh is a "Colonel" etc. etc. A Colonel in Germany must have a definite amount of military and scientific knowledge, strategic and tactic experience to lead at least a regiment of infantry with artillery, machine guns, and the other units, so that he can command actually a small army in case of need. This different organization of the American brain in the use of words may account for you and Leah using "Abyss" so often for commonplace things. Still, I would like to hear what you have to say about it.

Take your time for your reply. Don't hurry. The clearer you put it the better. I want at last to get some understanding of the subject.

All good wishes.

93 93/93

Yours fraternally,

Karl

PS Beast wrote me last, that *Book 4*, iii, is being printed in London! The price is $10, or for subscription. Just what that means I don't know. He does not say when it is going to come out of press. But he has been busy revising the [manuscript] for the press so it's serious. Can you get subscriptions out there?

June 17, 1928

Dear Jane,

93

    Your letter of June 10. My visa has been extended to June 1, 1929, as I heard yesterday. So you can send the various MSS. along.

    I haven't much to reply to your letter as you seem to agree with mine. You ask "why do you kick a man when he is down" (referring to Mudd).

    In the first place, I don't kick him, but it has always seemed to me as though Mudd occupied and still occupies a positive place in your heart and soul, whichever you prefer. I doubt whether your attitude towards what the name Mudd stands for is entirely impartial or better, unattached. This may unconsciously account for the form of my remarks. For if I am right, there is probably danger.

    But there is another angle. Mudd, like Achad, has undoubtedly fallen. Now, who falls, is in my opinion, not only lost to the G.W.[12], he is not only indifferent to it, but he becomes its opponent, its antagonist, its enemy. For, fallen means, to be obsessed by some particular idea or demon. This is a general remark. But there seems to be in in this case a direct proof for it with regard to Mudd. Tränker,[13] a dangerous occult criminal, boasts that those who formerly were the closest cooperators of the Beast had now gone over to his camp and were working with him. This, as appears from the context, refers to Mudd and Leah, probably also Achad. Now, we know that Tränker is fighting the G.W., and particular in Germany with all means, directly and indirectly, and most unscrupulously, with lies, and calumnies. So there is the reason: If you keep even the slightest magical, subtle

---

[12] "The Great Work"

[13] Heinrich Tränker, O.T.O. member and X° (National Grand Master) for Germany under Theodor Reuss.

connection with Mudd, or he with you on the magical plane, you might wake up some day with an unpleasant surprise.

Here is another remark. It always strikes me that all you people ought to take up a much more selfish, or if you prefer independent, attitude towards the Beast. Your remarks about the "pencil", a "sheet of paper", a "horse" are all quite right. But don't forget there are no one-sided relations possible in the universe. If A. is the "pencil" to the Beast, then it is equally true that from the point of view of the Star A. the Beast is the necessary complement: paper. Both are necessary to each other. After the "pencil" A. has written its story on the paper "beast" (in other words: fulfilled its mission and severed its connection with Him) he goes on writing on other paper. All you seem always to look at the Beast with hypnotised eyes. To continue the parable of the poor pencil: as though he might reflect: now, after I have served the sheet of paper faithfully and made my marks on it and used myself up on it and given my very soul to it, this ungrateful paper simply leaves me, throws itself into the arms of the damned envelop to be posted and go on to other destinations. What a fine time it has, this unfaithful paper. Suppose for a moment the paper would argue in a similar way about the unfaithful pencil, having finished with its present concubine, this sheet of paper, leaving it immediately to flirt with another sheet? Don't you see the flaw in this attitude? There is no law beyond Do what thou wilt!

93 93/93

Yours fraternally,

Karl

P.S. I hope to get the London Case of books from Pickfords Colonial during the coming week. Shall I send some of the books to you? Do you think you or Smith could sell some of them? Please write this Dorothy direct. I am too much out of town & I think she ought to take care of all the book matters & keep record. I will send away wherever she asks me to.

May 28, 1928

Dear Jane,

93

    Your letter; I received it only Saturday (May 26) as I am out of town during the week.
    1) Dorothy had written me about "Abyss".
    2) You said "chasen", which, not knowing the word, I considered one of your usual special words.
    3) In the following sentence in your [illegible] letter you then said (about) "Smith is getting into his (chasm=abyss) this Summer, etc."
    So I wrote you to explain. I understand now from your letter that you did not want to say that Smith is on the travel from $7°=4°$ thru abyss to $8°=3°$. In order to nail down one these frequent abuses in an unscientific way of the term abyss - by all that have been connected with the "Cefalu crowd" I wrote.
    Yet your letter gave me perhaps some new light - I can't say. I also showed it to Cora to read who is slowly, very slowly getting ready to swallow the bait. She is a fine woman.
    No news about my visa. I expect to get it one of these days.
    Did I write you about my brother in Los Angeles? I just heard that he is leaving June 2 from Galveston for Germany, probably with his family.
    What you say about Smith is interesting. I should like to hear more. (Is he still sending money to Paris? I, being a European & thus materialistic am mostly interested in finances.) What do you mean by "he is sexually free"?
    By the way, this you have made clear to me: You say: "the Angel reappears after $8°=3°$." I could never make about what the $5°=6°$, the H.G.A., the Abramelin operation, John St. John etc. that one loses one's H.G.A. and yet makes John St. John afterwards. Now I see clearer.
    Certain of your conceptions I consider wrong. Not only unclear. (is it Mudd-slime still clinging to your soul? He had put a lot of rot into mine. Leah, in this respect, was not so dangerous;

she kept her mouth shut. But he considered his duty to teach & put his ideas over others, conceited as he was with his marvellous brain, and, I am sure with the illusion to be what Achad was not. He--I am sure--gave Leah the death blow. Get rid of the mud!)

93 93/93

With fraternal love,

Karl

PS Of course the woman in you is curious to know (I flatter myself) where I disagree. Here are some ideas.

The Law is: 93. The Law is not: to attain grades. Everybody has to do his Will. All else is immaterial. One man has to write dramas as Shakespeare is to teach humanity. Another as a philosopher. Another has to conquer the world like Napoleon. In order to put some American values in: there are Washington, Franklin, Lincoln. It is quite immaterial what grade they attain (at least it ought to be to them and to the whole world). If they had known anything about this Hierarchy, which is quite possible, and had constantly stared hypnotized at the grade they had and the next higher, they would probably have forgotten their job or Will, while the path is climbed by forgetting the path in the Work. Mudd and I am sure Leah forgot or never thought of their Will but thought of grades. My idea is that the True Will of all these "failures" has -- paradoxical as it may may sound to you -- been wonderfully accomplished: to teach the Beast object lessons. They suffer now. But has not the Beast perhaps suffered more? For His mistakes that caused the failures? If this grade business were open before the public and the newspapers, Lindbergh would long ago have been rated as $10°=1°$. I mean in this country. Because he is, as was written, "the greatest Hero of all times." "He is Parsifal." And similar things. -- No, let's forget the grades & think of nothing but our Will.

Perhaps you may argue: where are the passages in your letter that stir me to these remarks? It would be hard to indicate. It is the atmosphere of certain passages which smell to me like Cefalu crowd.

♄

1746 N. Winona Boulevard[14]
Los Angeles, California

January 7, 1934

Dear Karl,

I can't tell you how glad I am to hear from you again! I got all pepped up over the note received by Smith, with its signature. But Wilfred was sure the envelope was addressed by Yorke[15], and an examination of your former signatures never revealed 2 dots as did this one. Yes, we did get the Mass going and numbers of people have witnessed the ceremony. Some few have taken communion. And the spectators have noised the Mass round about; we hear remarks from all sorts of places, some quite unexpected and surprising. But beginning November our audiences began melting away; two or three faithfuls only have shown up in December. So Regina[16] is brainstorming the highways and by-ways once more, seeing and being seen, and she has a commanding personality; no one would ever pass her by.

---

[14] The address of Agape Lodge at the time.

[15] Gerald Yorke, A∴A∴ student of Crowley, and an important conservator of Crowley's archives, which he later donated to the Warburg Institute in London.

[16] Regina Kahl, a member of Agape Lodge, and its primary Gnostic Mass Priestess in the late 1930s and early 1940s.

Meantime she is performing *Liber V vel Reguli* for 93 days. Leota[17] is meditating [on] things putrid and rotten, and I am nearing the conclusion of *Liber Astarte*. If all this doesn't "knock 'em cold", what will?!

Outside of this work, a few earthquakes, devastating fires, floods and other little oddments, life flows serenely on.

Your letter, received yesterday. "Starting a sort of business" is highly unsatisfactory. I hope you realize that, Mr. Germer! There are heaps of other unsatisfactory items, too, I might mention. For instance, What is the lawsuit about? And who are "we"?
Where is Regardie[18]? Where is Gabriel Dee? Where is Yorke? Are they the "we", or are there others included in that "we?" Please remember that I am a female, earthy, and bursting with curiosity. Also, that my appetite is ravenous -- in case I need remind you of the fact.

I yield you the occasion for answering these questions, but nothing more. Be ye warned, for have I not a potent little wanga in my belt? A female wanga! And she has a way with her.

Leota asks to be remembered to you. You know our hearts are with you, all the time. May good good Fortune attend you.

Fraternally,

Jane

---

[17] Leota Schneider, wife of Max Schneider

[18] Francis Israel Regardie, who was at one time a student and secretary of Aleister Crowley, and later a noted writer and popularizer of the Golden Dawn tradition.

Exchange House,
Old Change
London. E.C.4.

February 20, 1934

Dear Jane,

I did not get a chance to reply to your letter before. I was sick for about 6 weeks, have been down with pneumonia, but thank God, am better now.

Your letter, in its beginning, was quite a puzzle to me, as a matter of fact, to A.C. too. What the hell do you mean by that signature, the two dots and all that? I have not sent any other signature than just my letter to you. Well, I suppose, it's not so important, so let's drop it.

There is nothing new here. 666's lawsuits have a hearing on the G[reat] W[ork] and their outcome may therefore be of importance. But the delays in the English law courts are almost as bad as in Germany, and possibly, everywhere.

What is the situation over there? The only people I know personally of your circle, is yourself, Max, Leota. I wonder what the other members are like, and whether there is really good material among them.

The business has been handicapped in its development by my and my partner's disease. So we stand to-day where we should have stood on Jan. 1. We keep being optimistic.

I hope you are all right and that your practice of which you wrote, will be profitable spiritually. Beware of lust of result when undertaking it! And thousand other things. The proper conditions seem to be so subtly difficult.

Yours fraternally,

Karl

1007 Lexington Ave
New York City

April 14, 1941

Dear Jane,
　　Your letter came duly and the first thing I did was to write A.C. to the address you gave me. Do not overlook the fact that I have been cut off from the world, from the whole of Thelema developments for almost a year, I don't know what has happened anywhere.
　　It is true that I do not expect anything to have happened of importance to productive Thelema work. That period is not yet due: "Now let it be first understood, that I am a God of war and of vengeance". I think we have to await or better make ready for the phase that is to follow. The best thing in my opinion is by first pulling out a few fortunes somehow, by finding the rich bloke or what. I have nothing in view for the moment, I don't know as yet how I can get a start.
　　As for myself, I was arrested by the Belgians the day the Germans marched into Belgium, i.e. May 10th 1940. As the latter advanced we were transferred to the French authorities on May 14th and held in French Concentration Camps ever since. I have been in the Camps of Le Vijean, and just before the Germans advanced there, sent to the Camp of St. Cyprien on the Mediterranean near the Pyrenees of Spanish ill repute, and from there ultimately transferred to the worst Camp in France: Gurs, in the Pyrenees, where conditions were so primitive, so horrible that even very mild descriptions of the actual conditions in the American press shocked and bewildered people over here. And there are still 15,000 men women and children, held there in that Camp alone.
　　I got out finally on February 1st 1941 after a non-quota immigration visa had been anew procured by Cora as long ago as September last, out the French only gave me permission to go to Marseille to see the Consul four months after he had asked me to call urgently for the visa. It's just their complete incapacity for doing anything, for making progress, for organisation, that made it

impossible to obtain the permit before, despite all kinds of urgent steps that were undertaken by Cora, others and myself with the various French authorities and the American Ambassador and Consul. We in the Camps have come to understand thoroughly the basic reasons for the rapid break-up of French resistance both militarily and administratively. Most, 95%, of the prisoners in the Camps were Jews, all violently hostile to the Nazis, violently friendly to the French, many offering spontaneously to fight on their sides actively, who have now more or less become hostile to the French due to the unsanitary conditions in the Camps, the dirt, the ridiculously poor food, causing scurvy, various diseases, the unhealthy water, and their incapacity and unwillingness to improve conditions, until at long last attacks in the American Press – based on reports smuggled out by devious and dangerous means – forced the French to pretend to do something. Believe me, I am glad to be out of that hell. Fortunately, my health and general conditions do not seem to have suffered very much, and that is really a miracle which the French did their best to defeat.

If we had been prisoners of war, if we had been enemies of the French, if we had been young and vigorous, if we had been nothing but men, if we had shown the least sign of revolt on occasion – one could perhaps excuse the French. But most of us were over forty (up to 70), several thousands were women (of whom perhaps 35% over 65 and up to 95 years of age), 10% children and babies. And yet all those atrocities. There is no reasonable excuse or even explanation. No wonder that the death rate was horrible, and that the blind sympathy for the French and their cause in those Camps has turned to the complete opposite.

As regards things in California, I was under the impression from a report by A.C. some two years ago, that you had definitely established a farm in some valley – not having access to my files and books, which have remained behind and are somewhere in Belgium – I cannot check up on anything. But I am sorry that all those plans have dropped into the water. Let me know what actual and active positive work is being done there now – I am sorry too that Max Schneider has severed relations with all of you. It had all sounded so promising some years ago. Can't you procure his address for me? I just must get in touch with him.

Well, Jane, I am glad that I was successful in locating you and that you personally seem still to be fit as a fiddle. It seems such a long time since when I saw you last.

Give my love to all and I hope to be seeing you some day. I wonder whether we will be able to fix something up for A.C. to come over as long as the going is possible. I personally do not think though, that the Germans will actually be able to land in Great Britain. Still one can never know.

All the best.

Fraternally,

Karl

1746 N. Winona Boulevard
Los Angeles, California

April 20, 1941

Dear Karl:

93

P.O. Box 231, Altadena, California, will reach Max. This attractive little rambling city adjoins Pasadena on the North.

Wilfred wrote A.C.: "We have the valley in the bag." When the property had not been passed, no agreement decided upon, etc., etc. His wishful thinking saw it as a fact; and while some of us sat back, and regretfully watched the performance, he announced here on two or three occasions: "We have the valley." So dear to his heart was this project.

And the Leffingwells[19]-- people who had to be helped more or less all their lives, and who left the Order disgruntled--swapped their commercial acre in El Monte with a good house and chicken-raising apparatus, for 130 acres up toward Barstow with 2 houses, water, etc. Reclaimed desert, I understand. This was a bit of a blow to Wilfred, who said: "I talk--Leffingwell goes out and accomplishes." Max lived out there for a time, and could give you more information about them, if you wish.

Here at Winona we have kept the Mass going since its inception March 1933. Also Thursday nights we have a study class, which has brought two of our suckling babes to adolescence, anyway; and John Eller, a tractor driver for the County in its road building, and his wife Thelma, are excellent people.

In Pasadena Jack Parsons is holding his bi-weekly discussion groups, and last night we had a "board meeting", so to say, regarding subjects for continuing these groups, etc. Also what each individual member of the Order can do to further its progress.

Now 8 years ago Jack was writing matters Thelemic, and looked forward to giving a series of radio talks, at the end of which he intended to announce the Word of the Aeon! He was thoroughly surprised, if not a bit shocked, to learn on coming to Winona some 2 years ago, that the word had been pronounced. All of which he promptly accepted. I tell you this that you may have some idea of him.

Education: University of Southern Cal., California Institute of Technology. His teachers all said, "Literature for you." No sir; said he; "Science!" And this he now works on -- although the literature will follow more or less shortly. His talks are rattling good, but hampered with poor delivery. He can talk with scientist, physicist, mathematician in their own language -- all 3 of which W[ilfred Smith] lacks. Writes good poetry, too. 26 years of age, 6'2" in height, dark hair & eyes, fine looking; passionate & a warrior; boyish, simple, shy, hierarchical in belief but proper sense of equality as a result of his mystic experiences, he says. Born in him, no doubt. And this sense of equality gives him a poise I have

---

[19] Roy and Rhea Leffingwell, Agape Lodge members.

found lacking in many places. Not the least bit pretentious. Altogether most fortunate in his birth and general set-up.

You now see why I likened his general attainment with Crowley's original make-up.

Heretofore I refused to go into any detail about things out here -- wrong impressions can so easily be given -- and I know what difficulties arose because Max indulged in what I consider "scribbling" from this end.

Letters are dangerous, and we some times fail to see the strength and good points if weaknesses are brought out through a momentary peeve or - worse - unrecognized jealousies. I know I would just chatter away by the hour, my European connections and love for you all affording a kind of intimacy that would/might make you slam and bar the doors.

After posting my last to you, I realized that it was Cora, of course, who was a prime mover in your release, etc. Please give her my love. I think, too, it would be rather scrumptious if you folks were out here. Perhaps you are more needed in New York but... how about it? I don't know anything about the job market here, however; but assume one piece is as good as another for that.

93 93/93

Fraternally,

Jane

K. J. GERMER
1007 Lexington Ave
New York, N. Y.

December 26, 1941

Dear Jane,

    I feel I ought to have written you personally long before, but with all kinds of personal, business, and Order matters cropping up, I just did not get the proper chance. But please do not think for a moment that I have neglected and taken to heart what you said in your letters. Also for quite a while I felt positive that I would come out to California myself and that all could wait till then. There must be much which requires personal attention.

    As it is, you are the only one in your group whom I know and in whom I have confidence. As you are aware, 666 has vested quite a lot of authority in me, and to tell you the truth, I feel utterly inadequate to the task. I have always disliked the technical part of everything which goes with the Order, though I realise that it is the way that appeals to many people, and is possibly their only path to achieve. But it is a fact that I feel lost in the grades, rituals, dignities, offices, rights and what not. Also I dislike the crowd of people who hang around and never get anywhere, who do nothing but talk, jabber, ask questions and would not understand your answers anyway.

    I am still hoping to turn up some day together with 666, though his last letter to me was very very pessimistic. His asthma is giving him serious trouble and he has made preparations for his death and says so quite openly. It almost sounded like a letter of farewell. However, I can't make myself believe that he will be allowed to die yet, I have the conviction that he still has to do things, so I am hoping for the best and that some miracle will permit him to get through another winter. Also, he mentions that if he can't get the visa at once, he would like to get to some place like Bermuda where the climate would be easier for his asthma.

    Fighting against red tape in Washington seems so hopeless. I have seen the crowd at the Refugee Committee and they refuse to handle A.C.'s case, because, as an Englishman, he is not a refugee at all but an ordinary immigrant and advise me to make the application direct, which I will have to do. As your biography is not quite complete, I am waiting for A.C.'s reply to a cable to give me the required data so that you can fill out the form B fully. There is one more thing: I was told that the two affidavits were extremely weak and they did not consider the chances for a success too great. They suggest that I try to get somebody to make out at least one affidavit who is of better financial standing, to replace 132's[20]. Is there really nobody in all your crowd who could be made to do it? Leffingwell's is at least better than 132's because he has real property. – All good wishes for yourself and for a happy New Year.

Fraternally yours,

Karl

K. J. GERMER
1007 Lexington Ave
New York, N. Y.

March 12, 1942

My dear Jane,

Thanks very much for yours of March 10th and the copy of the letters to 666. All your analyses of people are very good and illuminating and helpful.

In the meantime I've heard from Max. There was no cause for worry on my part. As you know, M. never took out papers to become a citizen, as he should have done. Now there has been so much clamour in the newspapers, at least in the East, stories of

---

[20] 132 was the enumeration of Wilfred Smith's magical motto.

how people on the west coast were demanding the evacuation of aliens, that I feared it had struck M. All the more so as I had the FBI agents in the house who asked a lot of searching questions and ransacked every nook for almost four hours. All my letters – and Cora's as well – were read, every book was opened and its pages searched, really I've never seen anything like it, though I have some experience with Scotland Yard and the Gestapo. In the end they were satisfied and tried to be sweet. That really caused my postcard to you, and I am glad my fears were unfounded and I hope will remain so.

You are a great dear and I am very grateful to you for the frank transmission of what I consider some sort of a vision. * It encourages me somewhat in all the worries I am having at the moment, not the least of which is how to scrape together the cash, or some cash, to cable to 666 on the 15th. There has been a crisis all round, it appears, and everybody seems to think that I can manage alone. But I can't. Besides, to fall down and interrupt the regularity of the promised contributions, would have very very grave magical consequences for those concerned. Help impress this.

Who exactly is Helen[21]? Is it Jack's sister and at present Wilfred's partner? I have never been quite clear on that. You asked some time ago what I thought of Parsons' horoscope. I have written him my view on it, and I suppose he has let you know. He has a pure and powerful aspiration and much help by favorable aspects. It should help him to pull through. But he needs a Guru, especially as he lives in Los Angeles' spiritual atmosphere which does not have a good reputation; if he is scientifically inclined, all the better. Let him use most of all common sense and go by his own inner light.

I think this is about all for to-day.

Love and best wishes,

Karl

---

[21] Helen Parsons Smith, a member of Agape Lodge, wife of Jack Parsons and later Wilfred Smith.

*

a) 6 horse power is my de Soto car;
b) "sorrel-bay" – the color of the car is grey-ivory
c) who was the woman? Cora? Another, that has yet to turn up?

K. J. GERMER
1007 Lexington Ave
New York, N. Y.

September 15, 1942

Dear Jane,

Yours of Sept. 9. The certificate looks bad. I'm glad I have it with A.C.'s letter to Max. A.C. likes to keep things like that away from me, possibly not to let me worry too much.

As to your questions re A∴A∴. I really don't know how to answer adequately. A.C., I think, started out with drawing it up with outer degrees similar to other outer Orders. He possibly found out that it just didn't work. How are you going about if you want to assign degrees to people like Lincoln, Beethoven, Shakespeare and all such Masters who all are in the A∴A∴? A.C., if you read his Comment to *The Voice of the Silence*, gave Blavatsky the $8°=3°$. Don't for a moment think that Blavatsky herself thought along such terms. Growth in the A∴A∴, well, it's just growth. Of course, you can take a tree, say an oak, and tell him, you are now in the $7°=4°$ and all such things. He will, if he is wise, probably nod and say, well, it's O.K. with me, as long as you say so. But it really doesn't make any difference either to him or to anybody else, as long as he keeps growing.

So with us. I have never, in an outer formality, been initiated either into the A∴A∴, nor the O.T.O. for that matter. It seemed to make a difference to me years ago; but no longer. You really initiate yourself as you grow, if you do grow; most people become stagnant and accept the rewards (read "The Wake World"). You can trace your growth yourself by listening with your inmost ears to the subtle signs that will be given to you. He who knows the Tree of Life and its attributions, will find indications strewn across his path which will correspond to paths and Sephiroth; or to descriptions in the Wake World or other books. It's like following progress on a map, you know where you are, but that's really all. There is no reception committee in any outer sense, no diplomas and similar stuff. A.C. has never told me where I am in the A∴A∴. Yet I believe to know. The messages you get are in my case sometimes quite striking. It may be a change of occupation or activity or job; or change of surrounding; it may be the colour of a dress or hat or car you buy; the messages may be visible in millions of ways. The Voice of the Silence is speaking and trying to tell you all the time. It's you who has got to learn to hear or listen to it, and understand its language.

My path is different from most others, therefore I cannot very well teach in the academic sense. I possibly need personal contact to inflame, inspire and encourage. I dislike words and conceptions like chela and the relation it alludes to. You yourself are advanced enough to help people along. You have lived with A.C., you know the substance of what it is all about. Have confidence in your own self and nature; speak YOURSELF, I mean EXPRESS yourself. Every Star is independent and has his own language; so find your own and work accordingly. If A.C. is a Sunflower, and you are a Rose, learn to smell, grow and blossom like one and forget to stare at the other, whose life, nature and self-expression, whose laws are different from your own. Don't be afraid to make mistakes. What does it matter? Only don't try to make another Rose out of a Star-soul that may represent a thistle.

I really don't know what else to say or suggest. A.C.'s writings are fairly universal in scope (there are a few things for which I have an adequate sense, one is music) and he gives instructions in his books where a great variety of people can find their suitable method. There are some essentials which everybody has got to master: learn control (Yoga and all the rest); learn the magical language (by becoming familiar with general literature as outlined in the various Reading Courses); strengthen the Will; keep a diary. Etc. etc. etc. Which are just means to understand the magical language and to carry out your T[rue W[ill].

You may remember A.C. from years way back. Don't imagine that he has stood still in that time. Cefalu for instance was an experience, necessary, perhaps, but one on which he looks back as an attempt carried out in a childish way. At that time he probably still thought along literal lines in carrying out *AL* and some of the instructions. Since then he has learned to understand *AL* in a deeper way; and so with many other things.

Many people who lived through those former years with him have got their outlook spoiled. There is no better advice but to be yourself, use your own common sense, be simple and natural, and – if you've got to have a chela – learn patience.

Good luck to you.

Fraternally,

Karl

Write any time you've a problem. It gives me pleasure to answer.

K. J. GERMER
133 West 71
New York, N. Y.

December 4, 1942

Dear Jane,

Yours of December 1st requires immediate answer.

The more I see the more do I realise the importance of your personal role in the machinery of the present ordeal, and it would be a shame if you would fail, from weakness or lack of confidence in yourself. You have a great gift of seeing persons and things clearly, and then you fail to act up on that insight.

When Tull was here he mentioned that he had had only two interviews with Smith, but came away with the impression that Smith was a Master of the Temple. Who gave it to him? For, what does he himself know about such things? Now you tell me that phantastic story about the Chokmah Grey Cat! It is revealing enough on the state of minds generally around there and explains the awe in which you all seem to live with regard to the person Wilfred. Now you yourself also show signs of a particular delusion.

It seems to me that you still cling to some phases of the Cefalu life which were prior to the revelation of the Comment to *AL*. I don't know much about that. But I presume that certain subtle ways were different after the Comment was obtained and when you lived in La Marsa in 1926. Anyway, it seems to me it were better to forget completely about the $8°=3°$, $9°=2°$, the Scarlet Woman and similar things. 132 should have the example of Jones; but no; he wants to go one better even! Why can't anybody be just what he or she is?

Smith, realising his outer failure, apparently seeks a compensation on some higher plane: Smith is nobody; ah, but 132! You poor fish have no idea that he is a $9°=2°$; so he's got to hint at it! Don't you see how morbid all this is? The next thing will be that he is an Ipsissimus like Mudd – and end there. Being such a good judge, how can you fail to see this then? How can you fail to see the real motives behind 666's steps? Can't you rise to a plane where you see the deep concern, pure matter-of-fact motives, instead of assuming all kinds of personal spite and wicked things in what 666 does? You should have learned and matured since 1926!

666's instructions were very clear, yet he leaves the final decision to you. The question is not that of a three weeks Retirement for Smith, but of putting him temporarily outside the Order until such time that he has proved his worth for reinstatement. The Retirement is for you, so as to come to a clear decision in which you can act with complete authority. I will fully back you up; so far I have not seen any sign on your part that there is even a basis for a clear decision. It was for that reason that I suggested a Retirement away from Pasadena where the morbid atmosphere no longer influences you. I understand your reasons for not choosing Roy [Leffingwell]'s ranch. Very well, choose another spot, but act, and quickly. And let me know.

Jack sent me a very nondescript letter which again shows to me his dependence. If he hasn't shown that letter to Smith before, there are signs that its contents was first discussed, or that Smith's influence prevented Jack's real nature to express itself. All his protestations that he is not a rubber stamp of Smith's are unconvincing. And we won't make any real headway until some drastic action has been taken.

That I wrote you at the time that it was allright to show Smith my letters to you, was camouflage. If 132 were really where he supposes, or pretends, to be, things would be different. But he is a man still under test, thrown by accident into a position for which, very probably, he has not succeeded in making himself ripe spiritually. On the contrary: the position has gone to his head.

Thanks for the details about Regina which throws light on the situation. I do hope we will be able to trace her when her person and her qualities might become useful again.

With fraternal love,

Karl

1003 S. Orange Grove Avenue,
Pasadena, California

September 9, 1942

Dear Karl:

Enclosed copy of A.C.'s to Max, with the certificate.

I do not think Dawson would be the publisher, but I hope to get his mailing list -- rather, some names from it, who might be interested in contributing toward the publication, if nothing more. Dawson himself has become a Christian Scientist. I shall most certainly keep you promptly informed if anything at all turns up re Tarot. I would have to in any event, as I know nothing whatever of what "publishing the tarot" would involve.

In bed last night the A∴A∴ crept into my mind. Some few years ago I had a chela -- out of town -- and I wished to inform myself regarding this chela when my Probationer period was over. I wrote A.C. He wrote, "Good Lord, you were passed into the Order long ago."[22] I was not informed at the time, nor do I know the Word of the Neophyte, etc., etc. Wilfred is no help because every thought, every ounce of energy is to go into the O.T.O. (I understood later he feared lest I would take the Oath of the Abyss too soon.)

I ask now because I have another chela[23], [a] Probationer for 3 years come next Spring, when she hopes I will admit her. She is an O.T.O. member, but would like the A∴A∴ as well. What, if anything, can be done about this. Also who will carry this on? You? People at a distance can be handled more adequately in this way, can they not? Let me know how you feel about this, will you?

All my best that the "big things" mature to your heart's desire.

---

[22] i.e. Crowley was confirming that Wolfe had in fact already passed to the grade of Neophyte, in spite of the absence of formalities, and was therefore qualified to admit the prospective Probationer.

[23] Phyllis Seckler

Love,

Jane

K. J. GERMER
133 West 71
New York, N. Y.

December 4, 1942

Dear Jane,

 I wrote you yesterday in reply to yours of Dec. 1 and now I have yours of Dec. 2. Let me point out some inconsistencies.
 First you write A.C. giving some magical aspects without realising their import and consequences. Again you tell me in yours of Dec. 1 some events – which only confirm my suspicions – and a day later you fall down again to a place where you wish to avoid their conclusions. Magically, you seem to perceive quite well that there is something wrong and on a lower plane you are afraid that something should be done about it. I know it isn't easy because of the habit-forming surroundings. That's why I suggested to get away completely for a while so that you may become firm in your vision and be yourself again.
 The fact that you "don't push ahead. We know it" only proves that there is something basically wrong on the magical side. Smith for years has lived in some subtle delusions which make him incapable of actual progress and proper leadership. The tragic fact is that you all have become under their spell to the extent that you are convinced Smith is right, or almost right, and whoever wants to interfere is wrong, or has a personal grudge, or doesn't see the facts. Distance usually gives you a truer picture and correct proportions. So, again, get away, completely out of touch from your present surroundings.

I have really said all I have to say. It's now up to you and I am waiting.

And don't console yourself with your conviction on Roy Leffingwell, and others. May-be he did not see certain things the way you did. But in the case of Max, he positively saw the deeper magical implications; and Roy very probably, though he may not have been able to make this clear to himself and express it properly.

Love,

Karl

K. J. GERMER
133 W. 71
New York, N. Y.

January 11, 1943

Dear Jane,

I have your two letters of Jan. 4 and 5. I have not yet received the monthly contribution, and despite a recent letter from 132, I do hope it will not be less than the last.

In the last week or so I have been extremely busy and I have not been able to devote much thought to the Californian matters. But I must say that I was much relieved when I received your letter of Jan. 4. I had known that you had gone to Roy's ranch, and that you had also met Max there. I had asked Roy specifically not to influence you in any way, and I had, of course, not told either Roy nor Max what it was all about, except that you had been charged by A.C. to come an independent decision in an important matter.

You are not very specific about your decision, but I take it that you are fully carrying out the suggestion, or rather instruction the way 666 charged you. I understood this to mean that 132 will be completely relieved, for the time being, from his function in the Lodge, and that he will by this time have left the Community House at 1003[24]. I have had the intention of sending him a letter, but it is a fact, I have not had the leisure to concentrate on this these last few days. If my hands run over this keyboard properly, I may yet write to-night. I do not wish him to feel anything that looks in the least like hostility. He is a Brother, and as such we have to help him, in his own interest as well as in that of the Order. Never lose this out of sight.

I also take it that you have fully informed 666 by this time. The best would have been to have nightlettered him, as a lot of correspondence, which nowadays takes so long, is going back and forth, and your cable would not only relieve him of any strain, but also enable him to send you further advice, and, if necessary, instructions. As the charge to you was from 666 direct, it is hard for me to do anything positive. I would also have to know how this new development has worked out in practice, or whether there have been any consequences or difficulties.

Let me point out to you one characteristic: you have the habit of writing a, let me say, positive letter, and follow this up by the next mail by a negative letter. I suffer from the same defect, perhaps no longer as much as formerly, and I believe it is a general fealty of human nature. Steps which often have to be carried out from observations on the magical plane, are usually in conflict with habits, wishes, inclinations etc. on the human side and relation. It is similar with the lover who knows inside that the time has come to depart, and yet cannot make up his mind when he sees the tears and the (apparent) suffering it will cause to his beloved. Yet from a higher insight it has got to be done, otherwise there will be the curse of the relations of two people with exhausted love. 132 has the stuff to greatness; but he has got to be pushed into it, so it seems to me; and you should know that the birth of the Crowned Child is preceded by pangs and throes. "If he is a King thou canst

---

[24] The street address of Agape Lodge.

not hurt him" applies. Haven't you lived long enough with A.C. to have seen this time and again?

The decisive thing, the last straw, was for me that Master of the Temple and the Chokmah-Magus matter. It's so wrong magically, and I don't see how you don't see this. It is like a searchlight thrown on the whole problem that has puzzled me (and I suppose, A.C.) so long. There is absolutely nothing in the whole of 132's correspondence with me that indicates that he is a M[agister T[empli]. Quite on the contrary! A M.T. has given up all that he is. A M.T. who still has such spiteful, hateful and hostile personal reactions as Smith expressed on many occasions openly in his letters to me and A.C., is a very funny M.T. indeed. I know that Smith aspired to the grade a long time ago, obsessed by Jones'[25] example. But the demonic forces that lie in wait for such a one, are too formidable to be tackled easily. You know the literature on this well enough yourself. I have never quite lost the suspicion that Smith was somehow obsessed by such demons. To deal hardly with him is in my opinion the only help he can be given.

You have misunderstood those passages in my letter of Dec. 4th which you quote on Jan. 5th. I have no objection to magical names at all. I only pointed to Smith's severe inferiority complexes which turn up right and left and make him incapable for any real work and success. They must be broken, or got rid of else he will never push through the veil.

And, don't fear for the Order. Better none, or one that is dormant for a while, than one which has defective leaders. As somebody said to me: "How can your Law of Thelema be any good when such things as have happened the last two years – of which I am more or less a witness – in California exist?" The whole trouble is that Smith has not been under personal tuition by A.C. They don't know each other personally and Smith fell into the job of leading the Lodge and getting the IX° conferred by a desperate situation in Europe when A.C. (perhaps) lost hope for a moment, thought he might die, and needed somebody, and Smith was the only one in sight, those that had the training having

---

[25] Charles Stansfield Jones, aka Frater Achad.

dropped out for good or temporarily. But anyway, Smith was appointed, it inflated him beyond measure, and he proved that it was premature, to say the least.

Let me soon hear, and if I can help you in your difficult position, I will gladly do so.

Love,

Karl

K. J. GERMER
133 West 71st Street
New York, N. Y.

January 25, 1943

Dear Jane,

I had the copy of your letter to A.C. of Jan. 20th which you sent me. I am glad you had cabled him, so that he is fully informed. I am having difficulties with the Censor out here; for some reason or other they question me every time I get a cable or send a cable to London (AC. or somebody else, my solicitors) not only about every matter or person that is mentioned, but also their addresses, activities etc., the OTO, the Agape Lodge, but also about my business, the office address, how I run it and all the rest. If I get a cable I can be sure to be called up by the censor the next day. So I consider it wise to cable as little as possible.

You may remember that So-and-so Greene had ordered 9 vols. of the Equ[inox] for $35.00, on which she gave $10.00 as a deposit. I don't think I can hold this any longer, and the deposit would have to go by default unless she pays up at once as she had promised. Have you any means of contacting her or do you know her address? Is there any body else in the Lodge who would care to take these 9 vols. for the balance due, i.e. $25.00?

Your references to me in your letter to AC were interesting, I refer to the remarks by 132 and Jack. If I can speak frankly to you, I would say that 132 acted like a little boy in his childish hatred, his vile remarks about everybody else in California, about A.C. himself, in many of his letters to me, which showed me too clearly over a year ago where he stood magically and spiritually. I forced myself to be very patient, used diplomacy where it was indicated, but did not refrain from being outspoken on some occasions. Jack, when visiting here, was treated by Cora and myself in the most hospitable way. He did not open up in the slightest, and kept shut up like a clam, but snooped the atmosphere like a detective who has to report to a superior. Yet I did my utmost, met him enthusiastically, as some of my earlier letters to him showed. My antennae sensed the root of the trouble, and made some outspoken remarks to him. Alas! He was and still is too young, immature, and unfree for the position I then hoped for him.

He went back, reported to 132 what he had seen and heard, and now, I feel acutely from several signs, will finally fall under the dreadful spell to which he yielded.

Do understand: I feel very intensely for yourself and the grave decision you had to take, and that you took it, that you affirmed your attachment once again to the OTO itself, its heads and what it stands for and shook yourself loose from the shadows that had hung over you. I feel intensely the difficult situation you are in which may torture you in its daily connections. Do remain firm; you have weathered storms in London in 1923 (was it?) and elsewhere that were worse. You will get help.

Why, for goodness' sake can't you find the way to Max and open up in a talk between brother and sister? It seems to me you have some distorted vision of Max's soul. I know him very well; I know that he had to go through hard times and ordeals these last 12 years. But everything, every act of his during these last one or almost two years proves that he has come through. It was Max's heroic efforts that were the main help to me. I wish Agape Lodge had shown similar devotion to the Work.

Our Order judges by inherent qualities. The feather of Maat must be unstirred by even the slightest breath of falsehood. No fake, no powderpuff make-up can fool the Supreme Heads. I have a suspicion that you yourself have permitted yourself to lose sight of this when judging others. We want much: utter devotion, perfect purity of soul and aspiration, and all the rest on top of that. The tests are severe and unfailing. If anybody has the littlest impurity left, the best is to push him into the water if he doesn't want to go wash himself. And for God's sake let everybody leave aside the thought as though anybody acted for personal ambition, to get somebody else's position, to take something away or what not. We need hundreds of people. But none that isn't tested to the marrow of his bones.

With fraternal love,

Karl

K. J. GERMER
133 West 71st Street
New York, N. Y.
ENDICOTT 2-6799

February 25, 1943

Care Frater 132[26],

Do what thou wilt shall be the whole of the Law.

Your letter: it was a good thing that you read my letter to Jane. You should consider my remarks as a reply in kind to remarks by you behind my back. Your game is playing one against the other, establishing and maintaining your position by dividing;

---

[26] The letter is addressed to Wilfred Smith.

minimising others instead of lifting them to higher planes; what your letters show is 90% Smith and 10% 132. May-be, and I would be happy, the actual facts are different, but you forced this impression on my by your dealings with me.

Go back over my letters, there are plenty of attempts at reconciliation with the other California groups; to make you see your defects in so far as they hamper the Work. For me nothing counts but that 93 should have apostles in California who represent it truly and efficiently.

Instead of that I had seen very soon in 1941 that there was too much squabbling, gossiping, personal rivalries and jealousies, which are very contrary to the expression of the thelemic freedom of doing one's Will and nothing but that. I have often been reminded of the disgusting atmosphere in Theosophic Societies.

Your job ought to be to help others to become independent and free. Instead of that there are indications that you try to restrict people. The root is plain: you are afraid of your position, which again stems from the subconscious knowledge of your incompleteness which engenders fear. You are afraid of and criticise me for writing to Jack or Jane.

666 formally made me his representative in the USA, with jurisdiction over the Agape Lodge – quite against my wishes and inclinations. It took me endless letters and superhuman patience to extract some – unwillingly given – report from you. I even planned in 1941 to spend cash and time to go to California to see for myself, until A.C. dissuaded me from going, and stopping my Work in N.Y.

Then Jack Parsons came here and there would have been a chance to improve matters. What residue that visit left you know from my frank letter to Jane; except that it confirmed my opinions on the state of affairs more strongly.

What have you given me? Some inadequate contributions to the Work. If you knew how insignificant they were compared with others you would be ashamed. Agape Lodge ought to have seen its pride in financing, let us say, the production of the Tarot. Outside of a few hundred dollars (and those probably through Jane's personal efforts alone, (and against your wish), and beyond your small monthly contribution, you accomplish nothing. The thousands you left A.C. to worry about. There was a small flicker of greater enthusiasm last Fall, but it dies down and was no more. It was as if all of you out there were thinking: Let Germer worry his head off and carry the burden for the Order; he is good enough for that; he may do the sacrificing – with some others – we'll play at Grand Master; we'll distribute the books they print, for which others have sweated: We'll go to Pasadena. (This may sound hard and bitter; but I yet have to learn why an organisation of ten or more cannot sacrifice as much as single people who just have their weekly job.)

I tried to give you instructions in the IX° in 1941, I believe spontaneously, a grade you have incompletely. I don't think I ever got acknowledgement, (probably from fear that you, the Grand Master, could be indebted to plain ordinary Karl Germer) Result: I stopped attempts at initiating you further.

You scorn advice, call it preaching. Part of your soul is so distorted that everything seems so hopeless. Yet we all know that there is a chance for greatness in you if only it could be set free. It is characteristic of you to think you could create a diversion by pointing out a contradiction between such a statement, and the wish to see you as a shining Head of the Lodge, with and severe criticism of you. We want a big 132, but don't want twisted, bloody Smith to interfere with the former. Either you want to misunderstand this deliberately – or you just haven't got the proper initiation.

Your perverted brain, enslaved by reason, which you have not mastered to any extent, and which chases you around like a squirrel in a cage, goes to the Holy Books and finds excuses for justifying yourself, and discrediting advice: all your letters to me are argumentative. "A curse on Because and his kin".

You complain about good manners, you of all people! These nigh two years have often made me disgusted at not receiving reports, information or even replies from you; at your secretiveness; often enough your low and vile niggardly jealousy of others, not to speak of undisguised attacks on me and vicious letters. But quite apart from myself, one would at least expect display of good manners from you towards A.C. whom you owe everything. What then is one to say if he complains about your bad manners? You often do not reply to letters of his; you, a Rex Summus Sanctissimus, sent him *AL* and *Liber II* with a curt note on a torn off scrap of paper! – I could disregard all this if there had been spiritual integrity, enthusiastic cooperation and subordination to right authority. What I have received from you had to be obtained by constant fighting and worrying.

You are not even true. Take your last note to me: you quote 666's cable congratulations in order to create the impression of disunion, or a discrepancy between 666 and me about you – always your way of trying to create division. But you make the mistake of supposing that I do not have a copy of that cable, which indeed I have!!! You just wouldn't have dared giving me that cable verbatim. Poor dignity.

You find comfort in the support of your camp, Jack, Helen and Jane, for your actions. They have always appeared to me to be overawed by your much vaunted and advertised IX°, and by your open claim to supreme grades in the A∴A∴. How can they judge what is true of this? I was shocked when I heard of the latter claims from various sources. Only those who know what those grades imply can judge whether the claims can be genuine, or to what extent they are ridiculous. Meanwhile they think you are the big "IT"; they are led astray and get the queerest ideas of the O.T.O. and A∴A∴. It doesn't harm the latter really, but it harms them. See Jack's letter to 666 of November 24. You cannot possibly have given him a true realisation of the prime thelemic factors.

Yet you have done so much in all these years for the Work (So have others!) which nobody wants to deny, forget, or disclaim and minimise; that is definitely to your credit. But the situation in the Agape Lodge has for a long time driven towards a climax. It led to 666's decision whose execution has been much bungled so that now the affairs are utterly unsatisfactory as I can see despite the haze around all of you people, as nobody seems to have the gift of sending a clear, concise, cohesive report.

The last I heard was from an outsider, Roy, and he suggested that he invite you to stay at his ranch for a while. I wholly agreed. And should he decide to invite you and you accept, this certainly seems a good solution in many ways. It would also give me time to make up my mind as to how to handle the compromised situation. (This is, of course, a sinister trap of Germer's scheming brain.)

Love is the law, love under will.

Fraternally,

Karl

P.S. Feb. 27, 1943

It could all be so different, viz. that you had been sitting enthroned in California using Smith all the time to tease Germer, keep him on tenterhooks, testing his patience and other magical qualities, while 132 looks on serenely, benevolently and aloof. Then you would have acted as the Master you claim to be. But nothing sustains this view. It seems even that you have no conception of a real Master.
    If, however, there should be any misstatement in this letter, or a distortion, or a wrong vision of my part, or if I should show to be misinformed or have misinterpreted certain facts, I shall be pleased to hear from you within a reasonable time.

K. J. GERMER
133 West 71st Street
New York, N. Y.

February 28, 1943

Dear Jane,

  I have decided to send you copy of my letter to 132 in reply to one I received Monday. I want you to read it carefully, meditate on it, then let Jack read it. I have restricted myself to matters from my own experience in 1941 and 1942.

  The affairs in the Lodge are disappointing to the nth degree. Some move will have to be made and 666 gives me instruction to make it according to my judgment of the situation. You possibly know or have felt that when 666 in 1941 after my arrival appointed me his personal representative and special appointee of the Order with jurisdiction over Agape Lodge, I first remonstrated, and accepted that position very unwillingly.

  When finally I had to accept and obey, and notified 132, I soon found a situation of opposition and reluctant cooperation and help. I knew the cause: 132 was mad that he, the Grand Master, had been put under what he considered a newcomer, especially so far as the U.S.A. are concerned. The further developments are more or less referred to in my letter to 132. – I asked to get full reports: it took ages, repeated letters – often unanswered – before I obtained something at all. However it was, I felt great disappointment.

  When it came to signs of devotion to the Work, it became worse. Innumerable letters dealt with finances. Yet, devotion should be a free gift, a burning passion and flame. It never came from Agape. I felt that Agape Lodge had, let me say, the isolationist spirit: it thought rather in terms of development in California, independent, instead of seeing that under its present leadership and constitution, it will just drop flat if G.H.Q. should succumb.

I must blame myself for losing too easily the necessary interest and becoming disgusted. This was weakness. The Gods always force you back into their chosen path. The fact is that for almost a year the silent and open hostility from your camp, covered periodically by phases of formal politeness and apparent collaboration, made me lost interest. Never in any way have I been offered the spirit of wholehearted devotion and cooperation as it should be.

What conclusion was there for me to draw, but that the cause of the disappointing state of things was the leader? Smith very early began attempts which I can but call intrigue against me; but also against others.

What I want from you, as well as from Jack is

(a) a criticism of my letter to Smith, matter-of-fact, detached, after elimination of personal prejudice and passion. Sentimental loyalty will not help the Order.

(b) a report on the situation in the Lodge; financial; and present situation generally. How have members shown their devotion to the Work.

(c) What plan is there to carry matters forward in Smith's absence

(d) Smith, it appears, is still at 1003. Your orders to him in that respect were clear. They came from the O.H.O.[27] Why were they disobeyed? Is this recalcitrance or are there circumstances which excuse?

In other words I want that "clear, concise, cohesive report" which helps me form a judgment so that I can act.

Smith – not 132! – wrote in a biting aggressive way. I have no objection to frank and balanced criticism of anything I do, I even invite it, because only that can help the Work. But TRUTH

---

[27] The "Outer Head of the Order" of O.T.O.

and selfless devotion to the Work should be the basis of anybody who criticizes.

666 also sent a 3 page letter for Jack, but said a duplicate had gone direct, asking me to send a copy to Jack, if the other had failed to arrive. I hope it has.

I think Smith should go to Roy's ranch, if he invites him. I want to come to some decision and his absence from Pasadena for a while would be more correct, diplomatically, politically, and magically, apart from the fact that it might help him clear his mind.

Love,

Karl

K. J. GERMER
113 West 71st Street
New York, N. Y.

March 16, 1943

Dear Jane,

I am frightfully overworked; there is no Sunday, I have no time for leisure, and this has been going on for the last few months. It is difficult for me to find the time to concentrate on matters of the Order.

Yesterday I had your letter; last Saturday a letter from 666. He asked me to forward to you a copy of his letter to you of Feb. 16. I presume you have an original; but here is a copy.

All you people, I almost copy A.C.'s words, remain a puzzle to me. Your last letter to me proves it again. What is one to do or make out of you? I often think the best is to drop a block buster. May-be your Horus Ritual will have that effect anyway. He always comes as the avenger and destroyer first.

As an Hors d'Oeuvre I am sending you herewith 6 copies, signed by me, formally of a letter which has got to be seen by every single member of the Lodge (except Max or Roy should they be in some way considered as such). Please make some copies of the declaration they are supposed to sign and send either to me direct; or if easier, you can collect them and send them to me. I wish to state a time limit: do you think March 31 will be all right? I do not know all the names of the members. I would have preferred to sign a letter for each one; but to save time, please give one copy to the more important members, and have one copy left on which those who can't get an original, sign their names that they have seen it and taken cognizance. You will have to make, however, a number of copies of the declaration, and give every one a copy. Now, there is no prevarication: neither Smith, nor anyone else will be given a chance to say: Oh, I'm in touch with 666 myself; I'll write him first. Please get this clear: I am exercising my authority for the first time clearly, definitely and without a flicker.

I might add a warning: it would be good to admonish every one that the Heads of the Order do not look favourably on conspiration: each one for himself has to make up his mind as to whether he wants to sign or not; we want individuals; we don't want signatures from people with rubber backbone. The time has come to purge the Order, if there is anything left to purge. Needless to say: only those who sign will get the Vernal Word[28].

I hope my style and wording of the letter are correct; English is always difficult for me in formal documents. If there are mistakes, please correct without changing the stern meaning.

I'll answer your letter as briefly as possible.

I don't understand your second par[agraph]. What is the instance where all the fact etc. etc.?

Third par. "against your wish": it was clearly in my memory that you had said in one of your letters of 132 being an obstacle. Looking through my files I find your letter of May 20, 1942, par. 5.

---

[28] i.e. The "Word" of the Vernal Equinox.

Who are the Long Beach group? I had heard the name, but never was told plainly who they are?

Your last paragraph just baffles me completely. What do you mean? On this lowest physical plane, if somebody hits me, I as a non-Christian strike back, just to settle that score and leave no residue to rankle on that plane.

You still take the side of Smith and try to excuse him. I had said all you people are 'overawed', 666 says it better: Smith vampirises you, and as is usual, the vampirised never sees it. That's why everything is so hopeless. You do not know much of my spiritual development before 1926. So I will assure you that I for years lived with a man, under him, in a similar way as 666 was under McGregor Mathers; both had to be destroyed; both went foul. So I have personal experience of the problems that arise, how they arise and all that. I am convinced the situation in California has shown a similar trend. There has been an evil air blowing from Agape Lodge for quite some time.

Where is that other side of Smith? Make it clear to me; show me the ACTS of that side, then let us purge the man so that his beauty becomes visible in acts of pure devotion to the Order. The funny thing is that there is always another side, including McGregor Mathers and others.

No: personal defects, character, manners, etc. do not as such deprecate a man. What counts is his magical nature which always shows in his Work. Where is Smith's proper discipline? I sent him in 1941 my Charter, or at least a copy of it, of my appointment to be his chief. He was modest enough for a month or two, then, when I began to exercise my authority, asked for reports, financial statements and so forth, the obstacles put in my way became regular traffic jams; there was bad will, there was insincerity; there was fear for position; jealousy and all the rest. He ultimately became aggressive against me; and very insulting. I recall a particular piece of impudence when Jack was here. A.C. and I had asked Smith to send me copies of the O.T.O. rituals, such as he had. He instructed Jack to hand them to me, quite evidently with the injunction to give them only after having passed me through some test!!! The fact is that Jack gave them to me not at once, but on the occasion of his last visit. – I considered Jack immature at the time, though I had met him with much love and enthusiasm (vide my first exchange of letters, as long as Smith permitted it). After later reflection I saw the basis of it all. I can vividly recall the almost automaton-like face of Jack's; as though he were in a straight-jacket put on him by Smith.

An acquaintance of mine is an outstanding astrologer. I showed her Smith's horoscope once. She studied it deeply, and said: do you have any dealings with him? Beware; that man is dishonest. She had no idea who S. was. You see, there is always just one serious defect in the make-up for those McGregor Mathers [29]types; they don't purify it; they transplant it to the higher planes, and through those special defects the demonic forces work, and bring about the magical downfall. Enough of this.

I had a financial report from Helen which was a joke. I disregard it for the moment, because it was evidently written under obsession. But I must have some idea how 1003 [Orange Grove] is run. I have said time and again that the thing that baffled me most was the inadequacy of the Agape contribution. I heard once that there were 11 people living at 1003. Deduct a few children; also two to run the house. There must surely be 7 who earn at least $35.00 a week as an average. If each one would give 10% of that income for Grand Lodge it would make over $100 alone per month. To this would have to be added contributions from those who live outside and are members. I have given some 40%, perhaps 50% of my income these last two years, because I was forced to. Somebody else is doing the same. If Grand Lodge would have had to depend on Agape contributions nothing would have been accomplished in 1942 and 1941.

Tell me exactly how much Smith is making per week? I understood at the time that he gave up his Gas job; what other job has he now and is he making more? How much do the other inhabitants of 1003 make? With present war wages it should be easy to make much better contributions.

---

[29] Samuel Liddell "McGregor" Mathers, co-founder and mainstay of the Hermetic Order of the Golden Dawn and its offshoot, the Alpha et Omega, and later a bitter legal opponent of Crowley.

I wrote a letter to Jack a few days ago asking him to collect a sum of money for the Order in Hollywood. There is no record that the letter was actually posted; yet the letter cannot be found. Did he get it? please let me know, sure.

Love,

Karl

K. J. GERMER
133 West 71st Street
New York, N. Y.
ENDICOTT 2-6799

April 1, 1943

Dear Jane,

I still have to answer your letter of March 20. Since that time Jack has been here and we had a number of pleasant talks. As he is fully informed about the general position, there is no need of going into all the details.

You are, of course, wrong about the signing of the pledges. They are not to be signed when handing out the Word. What 666 wrote you is just that whoever does not sign it, won't get the Word; that's all. But the idea is not that you can buy the Word by signing of the pledge. This is entirely a matter of discipline and separating the chaff from the corn. Also the fact that some members seemed to support Smith in his stand; furthermore that you wrote that Smith thought he could get away with it. If there is to be authority in the Order, well, let him prove it.

The only point which Jack raised was Helen's pregnancy. I am fully with him in waiting for drastic action until after the event. But the signing of the pledges is not any drastic act. So there is definitely no reason for delaying this. Please go on with this, after discussing this with Jack.

There is the point of the set of 9 vols. Of the Equinox which Miss Graham ordered and paid a deposit of $10.00. There is a balance of $25.00 and Jack said the Lodge would buy this and pay the balance. I do not wish to delay this much longer, so please remind Jack and let me know what you want to do. I think the Volumes are still there, though January 1 was supposed to be the deadline.

I am glad you went over your diaries and that this – as is always – cleared your mind and made you see matters in perspective.

I dislike conversing on the subject of "Authority is absolute in the Order". I don't quite see what *Liber OZ* has to do with it. It's like going into the army: a private can never know all the issues; he has got to obey his corporal, who knows more; or his captain who gives him a tactical order; he in turn depends on the orders of the Major, the Colonel, the general etc. If the general finds that a Colonel is incapable, he is discharged, else he would endanger the safety of his regiment; and he bloody well has to obey. Isn't all that very much commonsense? Why should it be different in any business or organisation or for that matter in our Order? There is no fight; there hasn't been any. There has been dissatisfaction with Smith's leadership right along. This has been expressed time and again. Too many reports have been received at G.H.Q.[30] of Smith's inadequate way of conducting affairs.

There is another analogy with life in an army. All units have to cooperate under a supreme command. It can't be that, say, one regiment fights another of the same army while this army is engaged in fighting a battle. But this is the very thing that has been going on in California for a long time.

The plans and activities of the Order are much vaster than you people seems to think or guess. Of all the various groups it is not too much to sat that Agape, instead of being the most creative and the greatest asset as a single unit, has been the one that these last years has possibly done less than most, if not all others. No

---

[30] Grand Headquarters of O.T.O., i.e. Crowley and Germer.

wonder, if you eat yourself up in internal bickering and strife. There is not enthusiasm among the members; there is not the slightest idea rampant among all of you that we are doing something, and that we are making wonderful progress. Only: Agape almost seems outside, and doesn't seem to take part in it. It is very tragic indeed.

All you have is Jack and his friends; HE is the great asset of Agape; and left to himself would probably have been freer. Yet these experiences are very good for him.

Authority is allright; discipline too. But orthodox autocratic tyranny is the greatest evil. We want free men and women, Kings who discipline themselves and undergo the necessary hardships selected freely. Slaves, dominated by a tyrant or dictator may just as well go to Hitler. The proper ruler inspires those under him; creates enthusiasm; is glad if he seems the bud of the T.W.[31] blooming; and will rejoice and feast if it blossoms out to full development. Instead of that we have seen too much that stifles others and restricts them.

Another angle of this topic: Every man and every woman is a Star. This star is not the particular body, not the physical. This body should be the tool, or if you will, the slave of the Star. The Stars are free in their orbit; they go their way out of their own True Wills. It is the work of the leader to set these T.W.s free. If he only clings to the physical – where are we?

All this is really very boring, and I will stop on this subject. You should really think any problem out for yourself. – Anyway, I have asked A.C. to elucidate the matter to you.

I hope you will let me have those pledges back some time next week after discussing it with Jack.

With fraternal love to you,

Karl

---

[31] True Will

K. J. GERMER
133 West 71st Street
New York, N. Y.
ENDICOTT 2-6799

April 24, 1943

Dear Jane,

Do what thou wilt shall be the whole of the Law.

    I enclose several copies of the Word. One of them is for yourself, one for Jack. I want each one to keep his copy for himself. Wilfred must not receive the Word (see instructions by 666 to you in regard to this matter of last year.) Pledges have been received from

Grady McMurtry
Frederic Mellinger
Ray G. Burlingame
Phyllis Seckler
Helen Parsons
Mildred C. Graham
G.E. Northrup
Joseph D. Miller
Jane Wolfe
Wilfred T. Smith
Regina Kahl
John W. Parsons

There are three people who have raised objections:

    E.S. Forman makes the reservation at the end of the ordinary pledge: "Provided the officers of Grand Lodge are as they are represented to be".
    Richard B. Canright says: "The pledge sent me will not be signed because of the insistence upon the "personal pledge of loyalty to the Officers of Grand Lodge, whom I do not even know

my name as such, with the exception of yourself. Since I know none of you personally, I do not feel free to give you my personal pledge of loyalty. I think you will agree with me that no intelligent individual will pledge loyalty to another unless that other is very well known to him. – However, I herewith renew my allegiance to the principals and constitution of the O.T.O."

Barbara W. Canright: "I am writing to explain to you why I do not choose to sign the enclosed document as this time. I am perfectly willing to sign the part alluding to the principles and constitution of the O.T.O., but I do not feel that I care to give a personal pledge of loyalty to the officers of the Grand Lodge when I do not know them, or, for the most part, who they are. In a time of war, when our organisation in international in scope, there may be some among the officers who are at this time considered enemies of our country, and I do not wish to pledge loyalty to any such there may be. I have no national or racial hatred or prejudice of any kind, but in time of war, I believe that it is best to be cautious. I hope that you will understand my viewpoint, and if you can give me further enlightenment on the subject, I would welcome it."

I have been wishing for some time that the day had 48 hours: I just have to steal the few minutes that I can spare for the business of the Order.

I will have to answer those three letters some time, but to-day I just cannot force it. I must attend to the pressing matters. But please tell those three that I will answer them shortly.

All those who have signed the pledge unconditionally – really only with the exception of Wilfred; and I hate to withhold it from him – are entitled to receive a copy of the Word. But I want to leave it to your discretion, or to handle the issuance of the Word according to your habitual ways. The best, in opinion is to wait with this (except Jack, who should have the Word at once) until Wilfred has left 1003.

This brings me to Wilfred. On Monday I received a letter for Smith written by 666, to send on with my comments. I have done this April 21, asking S. to let me know positively when he is going to leave 1003.

This morning I received a letter from Wilfred, of April 21, which shows a completely changed spiritual attitude. I have answered him to-day congratulating him, to this, as well as to the happy event. I think he will not make any trouble, and suppose I will hear from him this week that he has left.

This demands a decision about the further running of the Lodge. Formally, according to 666's instructions, you are to run the Lodge for the time being. Please read your instructions again carefully. 666 has not changed these, so I wish to keep them in force. (By the way, Jack wrote me that according to his knowledge Smith still was the head of the Lodge. I want to remind you that you wrote me on January 16 that you had formally given 132 666's instructions, and, of course, I had not any doubt that at least Jack had been aware of this. And it was this fact that there were no signs that 132 was obeying them, which put him in such a bad light.)

I have written 666 about the matter, and I do not think that your present general condition makes you very enthusiastic about handling the job. I have, of course, discussed the matter with Jack, and despite his youth, I think he is really the best man and the only one who can temporarily succeed 132. I cannot, and I do not wish to supersede 666's authority he has conferred upon you. I have asked 666 to agree to nominate Jack and notify you accordingly. But on the strength of the charter I hold from 666 I am entitled to nominate Jack temporarily as your assistant or adjutant, who can run matters (until 666's authorisation arrives) on the strength of your instructions to him. This would, in fact as far as I know your opinions on Jack and Jack's personality, mean that Jack already now would have the run of the Lodge. I hope you will agree to this general plan. (handwritten notes to the side of this paragraph say: on re-reading and reconsidering everything I've made Jack's appointment more definite; but I can't re-write all of these letters.

I am writing Jack – if possible by this same mail – in that sense.

As to Helen? I will write Jack about this too. – Write me soon whether you agree with what I have written. I am quite prepared to listen to advice.

Love, Yours,

Karl

April 24, 1943

P.S. There is one more letter with a pledge and a reservation:

Phyllis J. Forman writes: - "I herewith renew my allegiance to the principles and the Constitution of the O.T.O. as I understand them at this time. I do not care to sign the pledge of loyalty to the Officers of Grand Lodge for I do not wish to pledge any allegiance to people, only what they stand for. I have not had the pleasure of making your acquaintance and aside from you I do not even know what people, or what kind of people make up the Grand Lodge to which I am asked to pledge (in my mind) blind allegiance. This answer is late but I have considered the issue for some time and believe this is my stand. I shall give my wholehearted cooperation and assistance to the O.T.O. until such time as I do not feel it lives up to its principles and Constitution."

(Is Phyllis J. Forman E.S. Forman's wife?)

Please show Jack this letter to you, and discuss it with him. He ought to be fully informed.

On reading over once again 666's instructions to you of September 1942 I find that there is some possibility of doubt as to the real appointment of you as Head of the Lodge. But this doubt seems merely implied, unless you have some other letter by 666 which makes the appointment more formal and definite. Please enlighten me on this.

In any case 666 had expressed clearly to me that he wanted you to take over the running of the Lodge temporarily during 132's absence. Understand clearly, that Wilfred is not expected to be finally discharged; there is far too much recognition of his work. But he has to eliminate certain defects; and we all wish that he should come through his ordeal with flying colours. And it may take some time.

A FEW GENERAL OBSERVATIONS ON THE QUESTION OF ALLEGIANCE.

The questions has been raised by some members of the AGAPE Lodge of the justification of giving a personal pledge of loyalty and allegiance to the Officers of Grand Lodge. Some point out the fact that they do not know them personally; it has been said that only "allegiance to the principles themselves" can be given. Somebody states that he (or she) will give this "until such time as I do not feel it lives up to its principles and Constitution". The reservation has been made "Provided that the Officers of Grand Lodge are as they are represented to be". Even the problem of nationality has been raised.

I wish to reply *in toto*, as the general line of objection is the same.

"THE METHOD OF SCIENCE, THE AIM OF RELIGION" is valid for the O.T.O. This aim constitutes a long and arduous path, in which grade and falsehood have to be rediscovered from grade to grade. What is Truth to Neophyte is Falsehood to the Zelator, and so on. How is any one in a lower grade to judge a superior? His truth is different, of a different order, and his truth again is falsehood to the one above him.

So then the principles and Constitution may mean something quite different to Baphomet than to the Minerval or to the Sovereign Price of Rose Croix. How is any one in the lower grades to know whether Grand Lodge is "living up to them"? It is in itself an absurdity. Is a catholic priest to judge whether the Pope in Rome and the Rota live up to the dogma of the Catholic Church? None of the priests – as a rule – knows the Pope personally – yet he accepts him. (Even on a lower plane, in the political field very few of the citizens of the United States know the President personally, and even if they do, not intimately. Is he for that matter not accepted as the Head of the Government? This applies in a way to the Judges of the Supreme Court who interpret the Constitution: they are hardly known personally, yet their judgment is accepted.)

The aim being religious, the question of race or nationality does not enter. Religion has nothing to do with nationality, it is above it, of a different plane all together. The O.T.O. is worldwide, petty national, local and temporary quarrels do not reach up to it. If any Officer of the O.T.O. would permit himself – in that quality – to become prejudiced by them, he would betray the very foundation of the principles of the O.T.O., that has accepted the law Do what thou wilt!

Again the system of the Catholic Church may serve as an example. The Pope and many Cardinals and Bishops are enemy aliens, Italian, German, Austrian, Hungarian, or what not. Yet, in spiritual matters their authority remains independent of the country involved. We would stoop down to the level of Hitler and the Gestapo if we would mix politics with affairs of the O.T.O. They dissolved the O.T.O. in their countries, suppressed the teachings of Thelema, because for our Orders (O.T.O. and A∴A∴) the Head is God Himself, who is not confined to any single country or race, while they do not permit the allegiance to any one outside of Hitler.

There is a subtle fallacy of thinking involved, and I warn against its pitfalls. There is also a great wave of totalitarianism abroad, whether in Europe, Russia, or even the U.S.A., despite all democratic institutions. It is the totalitarian way of thinking. We, who have accepted the Law of Thelema, should beware of contamination.

Now, as to the personal acquaintance with the Officers. It is well known that Aleister Crowley is Rex Summus Sanctissimus, the Baphomet XI° of the O.T.O. He should be sufficiently known to all members of the O.T.O. by his writings, his rituals, which form the very backbone of our Order. His personality should be familiar to any one who seeks by the published volumes of the "Confessions", the "Temple of Solomon the King", etc. But what is much more important: his Soul, his Spirit, his Genius should be recognised by his works.

Furthermore, whoever accepts *The Book of the Law*, should see that he has been appointed by Those who uttered it. This appointment has been won by Attainment, it is not merely honorary. Either one accepts him after studying his works, or one rejects him – it is no odds. But those who accept him should logically also accept those he has appointed under him.

It had been considered necessary to remove Frater V.O.V.N.[32] temporarily from his Office as Head of Agape Lodge. There is no-one in the Lodge who can judge the reasons or implications for this step. It was in order to see whether members of Agape Lodge in a critical phase considered themselves bound to the Order itself or by allegiance to a local Head, that the signing of the pledge was asked.

New York, May 15, 1943

KARL GERMER X° O.T.O.

K. J. GERMER
133 West 71st Street
New York, N. Y.
ENDICOTT 2-6799

Nov. 12, 1943

Dear Jane,

    93

You are a wonder! I certainly did not expect a $20 M.O. from you. As it is every dollar counts, as there have been several defections. Thanks from all my heart.

Re your student: This "psychic" stuff is in most cases a defect people have no idea to make out of this an asset. They become influenced by every force or intelligence that approaches them – see Jack. However – all, ALL Yoga practices should lead

---

[32] Wilfred Smith

to stop thinking, P.Y.[33] is just a preliminary. (As you know: Asana[34] gives control of the body; P.Y. that of the breath, Dharana[35] that of Mind; and only then can you approach the real goal: to attain Dhyana[36], etc.) Do you remember that I started with Asana and P.Y. at Cefalu[37] very intensely and regularly, and had to stop it because I ran into an accident. The thing was that I went after it with too much violence. I have used P.Y. often in my life as an exercise in walking, but cannot advise on the real practice.

You should know about the genuine phenomena that accompany success from the literature: a certain kind of perspiration; later hopping about; and of course, a wonderful purification of the system, body and mind. (I know a woman here in N.Y. who has confirmed all the phenomena that A.C. describes.) But all these are irrelevant. They are no goal in itself. What the man should begin is Dharana – provided some success has been achieved with Asana. And he should keep a record of every practice, and not go off the handle. All these outer results are temptations to lure you off the true track. – I loathe to give my view on these matters, as I have not trod that path and have no personal experience. I can only say: let the student never, never forget to apply his commonsense. But let him persevere, and not stop his zeal. I don't know whether visions are wrong? May-be. Let him write them down immediately afterwards in detail. A.C. can check and comment.

No word from [Paul] Seckler yet. Can you not give me some data on your student? What is his occupation, age, circumstances, (also birth data: time, and place of birth?)

One word more: I have great admiration for your work, and I think the only trouble is that you cannot see yourself, your T.W., as a thing apart, so that you maybe perfectly sure of yourself; also

---

[33] Pranayama, i.e. control of breath

[34] Yoga "postures", i.e. bodily stillness.

[35] Meditation practices

[36] The Union of Subject and Object, a major milestone in meditation practices.

[37] Cefalu, Sicily, where the Abbey of Thelema was located.

you have probably not the faculty of expressing in the outer what is in your inmost. The light is there, but it has often not the medium to express itself in words, art, or deeds of which you are yourself conscious. You have been all the time Smith's superior in spiritual development and in purity in particular – yet you cannot discern where he rules you magically. You do not seem to have the assurance and certainty of your own self. If you could acquire a vision of it, I would be happy indeed.

93 93/93.

All my love

Karl

K. J. GERMER
133 West 71st Street   260 W. 72
New York, N. Y.
ENDICOTT 2-6799

December 2, 1943

Dear Jane,

93

    Your letter of Nov. 27 with the copy of the one to A.C. have given me much joy. I hope you are conscious of it yourself, that you have quite changed in the last few months, every letter that comes from you proves it more and more. – I wish I could say the same thing about Frederic; not only I, but also Sascha feel it acutely, that the Smith atmosphere is still clinging to him. But I have hopes. In his case it seems to me that of the female soul in the male body that has not much interest in females, but searches for the real male, and wants to love. Evidently in Smith he has satisfied his urge - I am not speaking of any physical relations, no need for that - - and he has not been able to replace it and find the 'love' of another man. (I am about the worst subject he could pick; also there is a subtle but noticeable jealousy on his part toward Sascha[38] – all quite natural. But he should see it and trace the urge and place it in right relation.)

Paul has not written. Is there any need for it? Unlike A.C. or others, I dislike people confiding in me. (I never wanted children; I suppose I dislike responsibility generally.) I will ask Frederic[39] to comment on Paul's chart and send it to you. I do hope he shows his right spirit to help the Work first by contributing regularly.

I will ask Frederic to comment on Hugh[40]'s chart which I have drawn up.

I understand your reaction to Miller.[41] He succeeded in bluffing me. Also, he sent me a $10 contribution and said larger ones were to follow. Later he repudiated to ever have written that. He fooled Max too, it appears because he made a good impression on him and it was due to that that I agreed that Max give him the IX° document. Since that he's independent and does not sent a cent. He should do just the opposite to show his recognition of what the Order had given to him. I had a letter from A.C. about him: he says all his qabalistic stuff is pure bunk. Yet, I am going to write him some stern note about contributions.

About yourself: you know the fact that if any living being has missed some vital phase in childhood or the appropriate experiences at the later stages of his or her development, the crave becomes dormant and craves for satisfaction. A child, for instance wants to play. If that need is thwarted in childhood, it will

---

[38] Germer's wife at the time, and until his death.

[39] Frederic Mellinger, a member of Agape Lodge who was an expert in astrology.

[40] Hugh Christopher (born Max Rosenau), a member of Agape Lodge.

[41] Joe Miller, a member of Agape Lodge.

continuously break out, perhaps in ridiculous ways, at a grown-up stage and looks silly. If a boy needed a girl during his teen-age and in the twenties, and was thwarted, this will have its consequences later. In other words every natural urge corresponding to any phase of growth should be satisfied and not repressed, else it will persecute one later. – What Frederic evidently meant about you, that some natural need was thwarted by environment or education when you were 15 or thereabouts, the unsatisfied urge has remained, and whenever placed in the proper environment, comes out. I think this is just one of the tragedies, and you can't change the facts of your life – but, you can understand them.

Dec. 5.

All the above is very incoherent, but I haven't the time to re-write it. – One more word about the end paragraphs of your letter to me: You see, you don't need advice, you can find it all in yourself. I think that those so-called visible experiences are not the vital ones – at least not for all. The essential thing is the gradual, unnoticeable transformation of the human being on the magical planes, and, as you say, then the personality 'must radiate and convince others more subtly than by speech.' As the old German mystics said: "you must leave the images behind" and reach those spheres where where there is no more form, and where, I think, spiritual truths are no longer conveyed by visible experiences. Though I may be mistaken on this. But I myself have – to my knowledge never had any visible spiritual or magical experience.

I am sending you herewith copy of a letter from A.C. to Phyllis. Please find out whether she has received the original. If not, let her copy this copy and return A.C.'s copy to me.

I am also sending you copy of a V-mail letter I had from Grady McMurtry. Some of the passages were indecipherable. You can keep this. I want you fully informed.

Furthermore: copy of a letter from A.C. to Smith. Please return this to me.

Then I am sending you copy of A.C.'s letter to Jack Parsons. Please return this immediately, I would copy it, but haven't the time.

A.C. wrote me a long letter, and agrees with all my suggestions. In particular to dissolve the Agape Lodge. No, I better send you A.C.'s letter in original. Please return this to me also at once. I will have to sit down and steal the time soon to carry out A.C.'s instructions with regard to notifying the members of Agape Lodge that it is dissolved; give them GHQ's reasons for it to some extent; then ask them to communicate with me if they wish to give some new pledge (a thing I hate to ask, because it appears so silly after the past experiences.); and to either contact me or Max, or Roy, or you, if they wish to continue Work in some form. Then the main thing is to inspire them with a new enthusiasm.

When you have the time, please give me your views and comments on the best methods to continue and build some thing new. How do you stand now with Max? If A.C.'s interpretation of the phase in which Max is now, corresponds with mine, Max would not be the most suitable focus for quite some time to come.

I think this is all for to-day, you have enough to digest anyway.

Love and all best wishes.

93 93/93

Yours ever,

Karl

P.S. As to Betty[42], please understand quite plainly that both A.C. and I counted her the vampire, always sent to Neophytes as a test. Unless Jack succeeds in passing the test, he'll be useless. But it's no use telling him in plain words, as I did. It doesn't help it only harms. K.

---

[42] Betty (Sara) Northrup, sister of Helen Parsons Smith, and later the wife of L. Ron Hubbard.

PPS. What are your relations with the Burlingames[43]? He and Mildred have shown very great and constant devotion in the last months so I contacted them. Ray has quite a group of people who had been active, but the group is somewhat dispersed. They wrote me asking me to contact them and get them to work and send regular contributions. They thought several of those people would be glad to do something.

Now Ray and Mildred have the greatest admiration for you. Would you not have the time and chance – as they also live in Los Angeles – 4424-1/2 Sunset Boulevard – to contact first them and keep up some closer relations – and then gradually draw some of the others into a group which you could loosely form? I don't see why you should not become the focus for quite a group which you could rule subtly and discretely, without their being even conscious or aware of it? This is just a thought, let it brood in your brain and let me know.

The tragedy of isolated groups is often that if they don't see some visible progress, that they are liable to lose hope and confidence and gradually begin to stray away. If however they get some news from or about GHQ occasionally, it is like being directly connected with the blood and life current and stream of the Order, and it may help them to push their efforts.

Please let me know about this. I find it so difficult to contact all those people of Ray's group at this distance when I don't know them personally, what they are doing, thinking or what their situation in life is.

K.

---

[43] Ray and Mildred Burlingame, members of Agape Lodge. Mildred Burlingame later worked with Phyllis Seckler and Grady McMurtry in the late 1960s to conduct the first legitimate O.T.O. initiations in the post-Germer era.

5169 ¼ Fountain Avenue
Los Angeles, 27, California.

January 7, 1944

Dear Karl:

Do what thou wilt shall be the whole of the Law!

I enclose M.O. for $45 – my $20, plus $25 from Jack. He and Betty dined with me Tuesday night. He was delighted to get over, misses the Order activities, and, answering Aleister's letter, outlined ideas regarding the Order when re-established. He has asked A.C. if a copy should go to you. This will take time, of course.

We talked of nothing else than Order, and during the talk he said that Betty cared nothing for the Order, but that if and when it was started again, she hoped to remain in it, she would have to take a job for a stated period – say 4 or 6 months – and donate every cent of her salary to the Order. The statement struck me, because of your saying she wouldn't do an honest day's work for the Order. Jack is weak, as you know – the future will tell the tale: but the isolation is doing him good.

He also brought with him all correspondence between Aleister and himself, McMurtry[44], et. al. This includes "ARTEMIS".

He said, too, that Smith <u>seems</u> about at the breaking point, and ready to go ahead with the ordeal. ???

Group Work. I have asked the Burlingames if they would like to hold an <u>informal</u> meeting, if George would hold an informal meeting, Jane to hold one – taking turns. This would develop the various chairmen, each one to formulate his or her program and develop his or her subject. I have not asked Max as I understand he is on some sort of retirement (?), but as he and Jean invited a few people – including myself – to a New Year's Eve "housewarming" in Beverly Hills, perhaps <u>he</u> would be free to take

---

[44] Grady Louis McMurtry, who later assumed leadership of O.T.O.

an evening. This would give the four time for preparation of the next talk.

In this way, each chairman could make an appeal to friend's or acquaintances to come and <u>hear him</u>, as an opening wedge. Then God help him if he failed to interest the friends. The Group might overlook mistakes, weakness, or whatever. Outsiders wouldn't be so lenient. It might be a way to interest others in the Order – or at least in Thelema. Would this meet with your approval? And have you further ideas?

I am sorry about your difficulties with Amexco. I thought their Orders could be cashed anywhere – their office is 2 blocks from me. But P.O. Orders it shall be hereafter.

I want to thank you for Hugh's chart. Maym Kelso immediately pounced upon those Leos and asked if the man had throat trouble, or stammered? "He is seething inside, consumed with a great desire – Messiah complex – in his eagerness to pour forth he gets enmeshed in speech because he is not a clear thinker – intellect in abeyance because soul qualities must first be developed – intellect might now draw him away from his Desire – speech freedom will start when he enters Libra." I give this much of her short reading that you may know her line of approach. We shall progress the chart and go over it more carefully. She thinks it quite interesting.

He and I are still making progress.

While writing this letter, Joe Miller phoned to thank me again for copy of the *Vision and The Voice* and *ARARITA*, given him shortly before I left Pasadena. The word I used was teetering – meaning a doubt about his continuing. I have naught but hearsay, (poor authority) from Phyllis and Georgia[45]: Phyllis expressed the doubt, Georgia later told me Joe had decided to follow Buddha's command (?), that man fulfill his obligations to wife and family. Whatever was meant by that.

Just at the moment I cannot think of an opening re O.T.O. Publication Fund, but I will mull over the matter. Jack thought a drive for a total of $200 from all the members might work if he were given permission to approach them. Perhaps he has written

---

[45] Georgia Schneider, a member of Agape Lodge.

you. But the Pasadena group, at least, were quite lukewarm about publications, which they viewed only from the personal angle: – "Maybe we wouldn't like the book when it is published"! This P. group – with but one exception – wanted the social angle uppermost.

I shall be writing Aleister shortly, and will of course enclose your copy.

Love is the law, love under will.

With love,

Jane

K. J. GERMER
260 West 72
Zone 23

January 12, 1944

Dear Jane,

93

Your interesting letter with M.O. For $45 received. Let me answer point by point.

I am glad Jack and Betty dined with you and that he keeps on proving his interest. That is the vital thing. If he sticks to it, he may get over the problems that confront him. I am also glad he is in direct touch with A.C. and gets his advice from him direct: to tell you the truth, I have not very many ideas for any new organization of Order activities. Either I am not ripe for that angle, or it is my complete lack of interest in the Lodge work which makes me in some spot of my soul obdurate against it and prevents my having any practical ideas. However, Jack may me cast for some role in that line. I wish he were, and I wish that he would make some progress in his magical growth. As A.C. said: he is now, or was until recently a straw blown by every breeze.

As to his Betty problem, I enclose a little note A.C. sent me some time ago. Please keep this to yourself and return it to me soon. I have some theory that Jack is in a phase through which I passed around 1923 to 1924. It was for me terrible legal intricacies, and ended with breaking up all I had, with the exception of Maria with whom I broke finally 1926-27. Will it help you, if I say that her image still haunts me in some subtle way, occasionally at least, and if I conjure it, to understand the subtleness of the Kundry problem? And so to get a clearer perception of the proper attitude to take for you with regard to Betty? Because I think you are having some doubt about the accuracy of mine, or A.C.'s diagnosis in that respect. You are a woman, and a man who has gone through that phase sees more clearly what is involved. My mistake was that when I perceived Jack's situation that I barked like a Prussian what I thought. It had just the opposite effect. If Jack should succeed in solving his problem, then he may understand many years later his own case. - What is ultimately comes to is that nobody can intervene in an ordeal set by the Gods. Jack has to solve it and find the strength all by himself. As a matter of fact I don't understand A.C.'s remark "If I were on the spot."

The essay "ARTEMIS" is really for people who have been given the IX. I enclose a copy for yourself.

The devotion of the Burlingames is admirable. They sent me three days ago: $30 annual OTO fees for Ray & Mildred; $10 AC fund; $5 *Liber Aleph*; and $25 from little Laylah as her first contribution (an amount given by Ray's boss) $70 in all. I was deeply moved. Is Mildred behind all this, and is she inspiring Ray? I'd like to know.

Go ahead with your plans of initiating informal meetings. It can only work our to the best. Only see that mere go sip doesn't develop too much and overgrow the genuine shoots. - As to Max I wouldn't put it too formal: he may be in a critical phase. But it would be best not to show it in any way. Keep up with him as usual; but make your observations and let me know what you think.

I don't like the way Miller is behaving at all. If he is still in the poor old phase where he has got to solve the family problem which, I think Buddha meant for the very beginners, who intend to tread the path, but have not karmically ridded themselves of physical ties, - that is either poor excuse for not contributing, or, I don't know what.

If you see Jack again: there is no reason why he should not tackle members for a $200 drive. Your passage, that the Pasadena group were lukewarm about publications, etc. and were more interested in social activities, is quite illuminating. I had always feared it was like that. Why??? If they are members of the Order, it is up to the Heads to determine what is essential to produce at any given moment. - However, if he can get a share of $200 together, I won't ask how he got them together. A.C. wants Jack to continue and considered his resignation as "off the record". He has my blessing as long as the spirit of devotion to the Order itself, and not to some local Lodge or so, is right.

93 93/93

All my love in the New Year to you,

Karl

P.S. The fact that Ray and Mildred thought it right to send the annual fee has made me consider whether it would not be possible to get some cash together from all those who are formally members of the OTO and who have not made any contribution otherwise. This would be probably best up to Jack to collect all the fees and either thereby get the money for a publication share and transfer it to A.C. What is your opinion? Naturally, I would never expect anybody who is making his or her monthly contribution anyway, to make the formal payment of the OTO fee in addition to that, as Ray and Mildred have done. Do let me know your opinion on this.

5169 ¼ Fountain Avenue
Los Angeles, 27, California

January, 16, 1944

Dear Karl:

Do what thou wilt shall be the whole of the Law!

The enclosures speak for themselves.

I phoned Max last evening, to put my group proposition before him. I doubt he cared for the idea, since he is preparing to open classes in Qabalah, and Thelema, too, if I understood correctly. Classes to be held in Beverly Hills, starting some time in February. However, he might come to Hollywood if necessary. But we are to discuss the matter at a later date.

Personally, I would like some activity by a few of the members. People should learn to get out of the nest, and assume a responsibility which will be of value in contacting others – formulating ideas in a 15-minute talk, say – or even 5 minutes – and then accepting the analysis of the group re presentation, content, interest, worth, etc., etc. We started this type of work in Pasadena, but hadn't gone very far when Smith left. After which, for some reason, we got onto something else.

As you realize, no doubt, my interest is a personal one as well. I have sat on the side lines for years – I was forced there by Wilfred & Regina, after which I calmly stayed there! Now I have a strong desire to get on my feet and say something. Gathering material, formulating the talk, won't be easy; but I want to do it.

Max doesn't want "personal" groups – whatever he means by that. I surprised him, no doubt; he must have considered himself alone in the matter of the classes. I have considered attempting an opening elsewhere, if necessary. I am not unmindful that there is danger in such an undertaking – that it might cause a split. (Perhaps I am at the point where split-offs could occur?) But more of this later, after talking things over with others.

Ray needs no inspiration – he has always been generous with money, and was the only one we ever had who could make people feel it a privilege to give. I always felt it a pity he wasn't turned loose in Pasadena. Still it was too late for that after he recovered from the L.B. smash-up occasioned by his union with Mildred. She phoned me about a week ago, telling me about the $25 Laylah contribution, and asked me what I thought about collecting dues from the 3 remaining at Long Beach. She and Ray have kept in personal touch with them, going to L.B., or phoning. Two of them also came to Hollywood occasionally.

Under those circumstances I suggested that she go ahead, let me know the results, after which the correct head could be notified – in this case Jack, according to your last letter. I will also let him know about starting the drive, and also tell him that L.B. has been taken care of – if and when it is so taken care of. Two of the three did not pay dues last year, I think.

Since leaving 1003 I have a clearer perception of many things, I think including Betty. I find, too, I don't like her as well as I did – in fact not at all, but I can be friendly, and she is happy to see me again. I expect to have them over again near the end of January. Another thing; my attitude toward Jack has taken on some authority since coming here. I don't know how or why. It is better so.

Love is the law, love under will.

With love and all best wishes,

Jane

Jan 17. I did not get this posted last evening, so I add an item which I jotted down this a.m.

Something to do – something definite – is drawing near. It may not be talking to groups at all. In fact, I believe it is something of more importance than that. And I believe further, that Jack may come into this picture, or be implicated. I also feel that Max has little to do – nay, nothing to do in this particular matter. Somehow he has become remote.

While I am about it, I will pass along my analysis of Georgia.

"Could be a beautiful and effective woman and so accomplish much. But she can't rely on Herself at any point. It has to be a Max, or Thelema, or Crowley, or Germer, what she is doing, or intends to do. So she is affected to the deepest layers of her mind, and bluffs in her attempts to create the proper expression or atmosphere. But I think this 'bluff' is somewhere known to herself.

"She has a deficiency Regina had – based on the above analysis: They want to be the boss to convince themselves they are something, and so strive for a personal following, even to the extent of depreciating others in this effort."

She, then Max following after, made what we at 1003 considered a blunder in the case of Miller, for this very reason. She went off the tracks entirely, and Max got heady, over at last getting their fingers on Agape Lodge. I feel them both ran amok. They did not make a single inquiry of us regarding him.

Thanks so much for your enclosure, returned herewith. It is a privilege to read such things, and I am in complete agreement with you and Aleister.

K. J. GERMER
260 West 72
New York, N. Y.

January 24, 1944

Dear Jane,

93

Your letter of Jan. 16th with the copy of yours to Aleister came last week.

First: re that little confidential Note from A.C., please calm my mind, that I have your promise never to discuss this with anybody, whoever it may be; and, second: that you have not made a copy of it; should you have done it, please destroy it.

In this connection, can you tell me who this Jeannette Hayes was in relation to Norman Mudd? I don't think I ever heard her name?

Now your letter. What do you mean by "attempting an opening elsewhere"? (in par. 5 of your letter).

I don't think Jack's position has as yet been fully confirmed. I am waiting for news from Aleister about this. So, meanwhile, I think it would be quite correct if members pay their dues to me, or to anybody who knows the fees and is prepared to collect them and send them on to me. I have confidence in you and Ray to do this. However, I don't wish to cause confusion. Therefore, if you have already contacted Jack in this matter and told him that dues would be paid to him, I won't interfere any more, but just wait what happens. I have sent Ray's and Mildred's fees to London.

Thanks for your analysis of Georgia. Very interesting.

Re your letter to A.C. No need my going into this, though it was very illuminating. But A.C. will write you himself. Only this point about the S.W.[46]: I stick to what I had written to you and others. Don't you see that there had been very much talk and gossip at Cefalu and elsewhere about not only the S.W. but all kinds of other verses in *AL*. I will only recall Mudd. Most everyone identified him-or herself with something or other in *AL* or other Holy Books. It is so sweet to be able to do so. And the demons that inspire those thoughts are so tender, alluring and make it so easy and self-evident. A.C., I suppose, joined in the game to some extent, until a particularly violent obsession by Mudd embodied in possibly 50 pages of his close writing, worked out at my house in Weida, and mailed to A.C. in Tunis in 1925, worked the miracle: A.C. wrote the Comment, driven to agonies thru Mudd's ravings. He realised the source of the danger. The better and more complete you eradicate any such and similar thoughts, and forget all

---

[46] Scarlet Woman

speculation and rumination, the better for all concerned. I am afraid the old habit has been carried on to some extent in Agape Lodge?

I think this is all for the moment, so will close.

93 93/93

Love as always,

Karl

5169 ½ Fountain Avenue
Los Angeles, 27, California

February 10, 1944

Dear Karl:

Do what thou wilt shall be the whole of the Law!

Re note. I shall not discuss it with any one; I do not have a copy of it, nor do I know of Jeannette Hayes. And I very much appreciate your letting me read it.

"attempting an opening elsewhere" Meaning that, in case there was no place for me from the talk angle in the proposed group work, I might see what I could do outside the Order group. The danger in this case, as I see it, might consist in building up one's own little pile. Jones is Chicago, for instance, with his Psychomagian Society. I am of the opinion that there must come a time in the travels of the aspirant when he wants to get out on his own. However, nothing has been done so far because of the Pasadena situation.

Incidentally – and I am not looking for an answer – my mind has considered Max – from a statement made by you in a letter to me, also from Aleister's statement he had a feeling that the whole movement in California was in danger (if I remember correctly), followed by the P.S. re the packet Max to Karl.

One thing I should like to know – but again I leave it to your judgment to tell me or no – is the meaning of Selah. This word came up at intervals in my early life, coming from a Bible reading family and community, and no one knew what it meant – even those fathers of the Church to whom I appealed.

Yes, Jack has had a cable from A.C. to make a start, but to "build slowly", and that the performance of The Mass is of prime importance. We have talked things over, and he plans to write Aleister this week, fully outlining his plan proposed plan, and await the London reply.

It will be a tough assignment. And Jack will need help in the house, and who is available? I have a horror of going back – 11 years of communal life, with jarring personalities and strenuous physical work, etc., etc. I feel at times I have not the fortitude to undertake it again. I can't at present, in any event, due to some necessary medical attention; which, of course, should not continue indefinitely.

The unhappy part of it is that people have to combine because there are not enough funds to carry on otherwise, nor people to do the work. And there are not enough members willing to love in from whom to make a proper selection.

However, time enough for all these matters when the hour arrives.

Thanks for much for your interesting letter. I shall get off this at once or there may come another interruption.

Love is the law, love under will.

Love ever,

Jane

K. J. GERMER
260 West 72nd St.
New York, N.Y.

February 14, 1944

Dear Jane,

93

    Yours of February 10 came to-day with the M.O. for which many thanks.
    I don't know what Selah means. The dictionary says its real meaning is unknown. I take it to have the same root as Salaam which means some sort of salute or 'Hail' in Arabic. However, I don't think to attach any particular meaning to its use by A.C. in that little note.
    Furthermore: you may perhaps misunderstand the reference to Max in that note if you take it as criticising Max. It mentioned merely that A.C. had the premonition that something was impending about the movement in California. Then he received that package of letters I sent A.C. among them some letters between Max and myself, which threw light on developments at Pasadena. And the danger was not from Max's part, but from other influences. There was not enough purity and magical maturity in the parties involved at Pasadena to withstand the attacks by certain demonic forces.
    Why should you of all persons have to take a hand again at heavy physical work in the community life? Would it not be enough for you to show up at evenings occasionally and radiate atmosphere? I think if activities are to be built up again there should be younger hands available to do the work. That should be part of the plan. By the way: is W.T. Smith still there? and Helen? I just can't see how that could work. A.C. recently reiterated the stern injunction that no member must have anything to do with Smith.
    Another thing: since the dissolution of Agape Lodge the contributions I have been sent by various individual members have

enabled me to make a decent transfer to London monthly. I am much afraid that if those individuals would rejoin the new Lodge at 1003 their contributions would fall off, and that would be a catastrophe to the Work. Nobody at Agape saw that the maintenance of A.C. in the first place; of the activities of the Order in the second, were of prime importance; the activities of a local lodge are of tertiary weight. Agape's policy was always that their matters came first, second and third; A.C. and the rest came after. This must not develop again. And I shall ask all those members who have so kindly sent me their contributions in the last months with so much devotion, to continue doing so. I will not let any new Lodge jeopardise the Work. Almost everyone: Jack, Smith, Helen, Betty have written me time and again that I was only out for money. Well, I am, because without it A.C. would hardly be alive to-day or in the state of health and creative capacity he is in now. You yourself will have to be very firm on this point.

93 93/93

All my love to you,

Karl

5169¼ Fountain Avenue
Los Angeles, 27, California

February 21, 1944

Dear Karl:

93

    Enclosed is a re-typed copy of my letter to Aleister. I was much engrossed when I wrote the letter, I suppose, for I completely forgot to make an additional copy for you.

Jack and Betty were over last night: they took me to dinner, and from there to the Paramount in Hollywood to see "Lady in the Dark". The following are his present plans:

Will abandon the idea of establishing the Order at this time, and will do A∴ A∴ work, sending diaries to Aleister.

He considers three of the members worth working with as students – Fred Ewing, Dick Canright and Paul Seckler. Fred and Dick have some stability; esoterically Paul could be valuable if and when he becomes stabilized, and he is far from that now.

Also Jack has carried out a determination expressed some time ago, that Betty would have to get a job, work at it six months, say, and contribute toward the Work. She is so working, and it is her money that is going to London. I don't know just how much, but Jack said he expected to send $40 or $50 "this month".

Wilfred and Helen are still at 1003, but expect to get out before long. Their being there Jack knows would not work, and he said that if it became necessary he would throw Wilfred out. Also in this way he could not have an excuse to come back at any time.

By the way, have you copies of "The City of God" for sale to a dealer? Jack and I plan to get together an exhibit for Dorson's, the largest place in town for occult lore, consisting of the Tarot cards we have here, a copy of "The City of God", and one or two other items -- if they will take it. My reason for this was and is to interest money: Jack's reason is not quite clear to me. But I will tell you of this if, and when, the exhibit is arranged. How many copies were struck off for this issue would also be desirable information – if there are any copies for sale.

My love to you,

93 93/93

Jane

K. J. GERMER
260 West 72
New York, N. Y.

March 7, 1944

Dear Jane,

93,

I haven't replied yet to yours of Feb. 21 with copy of your letter to 666.

I note that Jack proposes to work in a small group rather than start regular lodge activities. Personally I think this plan is better, though even so he lacks magical and spiritual training. May-be he will learn in teaching as one always does.

I do hope he will be able to transfer at least $50 per month direct to A.C. Contributions have been meager the last month and will be for the next months as some people have dropped out, I hope only temporarily, and it throws most of the burden again on me.

I do hope Jack will find the resolution and strength to have Smith part from 1003. I believe I told you that A.C. has reiterated his warning against any relations whatsoever with Smith. And I see signs that the injunction is wise and that those who disregard it are finding themselves in trouble, even though their intentions appear to be 'good'.

I have no copies of the 'City of God' for sale, except one which is at your disposal if you can find a buyer. Nor do I know the edition that was printed, probably only a few hundred copies. This also applies to *The Fun of the Fair* of which I have no copy to spare.

The plan of that exhibition might be good. As to the Tarot, the last A.C. wrote me was that the Chiswick Press had been sold to a gang of people who wish to disregard the arrangements he had made with the former people. This means that he may have to find another printing house. In any case it seems to make for delays. A.C. wanted to send me the complete proofs of the text of the Tarot ahead with the plates for the cards so that I could look around for a firm that would be willing to issue an American edition. I have not received this yet. He suggested McCoy's but I saw them a year or so ago and they seem to have gone out of that field. May-be there is more interest for such a scheme on the Pacific coast? Please discuss it and let me know.

Your remark in the letter to A.C. about his note to Phyllis about Jack: This - in my view - has nothing to do with the Third Degree injunction but comes from the relation of Hierophant to pupil. The pupil showed a defect in his make-up by making a silly remark about a member of the Order and the Hierophant simply gave him a slap back in kind. There is nothing more complicated in this – so I think. That the remark should go back to Jack was probably the very intention and purpose of A.C.'s.

93 93/93

All good luck to you and love.

Karl

[Handwritten in the margin next to the final paragraph above:]
A practical understanding and application of Thelema (*AL* I).

5169 ¼ Fountain Avenue
Los Angeles, 27, Cal.

March 11, 1944

Dear Karl:

93

    Just a short note to enclose the contribution, that it may reach you in time.
    The post card, signed by the dear New York Threesome, received, as well as your letter, which came this morning.
    A.C. cabled, then confirmed by letter, his request that Jack start the Order; so the first official meeting will take place the 18th of March. Frederic will receive a notification. I will write you next week of these things. Somehow I do not like it. But then A.C. ordered that it be done!

93 93/93.

With love,

Jane

K. J. GERMER
260 W. 72
New York, N.Y.

March 14, 1944

Dear Jane,

93

Thanks for your M.O. The $ this month very much reduced – transfer was cabled to London to-day. I think most everybody reduced, or defaulted altogether, because of the tax.

My dear Jane, you should learn to have confidence in Aleister's plans. They should have the full support of all of us. Don't you realise that only if this full confidence exists and is manifested (with, shall I say, enthusiasm?) can there be any success. There must be confidence, but also discipline. And it has always been the lack of both that has led to failures. (I know arguments you can raise: my experience tells me that they do not apply from a deeper point of insight.)

I am completely out of touch with Jack, and this may be best. Ray wrote me that he has been asked to 1003 for a discussion, and so have probably been the others which is allright. I shall advise Ray to attend – then it is up to him to choose Max's circle or 1003. The angle that interests and concerns me is contributions. You and Ray have been most wonderful and if you join the new lodge I suppose it would be only fair to pay contributions to Jack for the collection of a regular transfer through him to A.C. Naturally, after two years experiences with Agape, I am doubtful about the results. I will, however, give Jack the benefit of any doubt and hope he will be able to make a substantial transfer to A.C. regularly and that the forming of a new lodge and payments to him which hitherto were sent to me, will not prove detrimental to the support of the G.W. I would quite understand an interim phase where expenses might be high. But, if the activities are started right, the end might be able to support the G.W. Much better than was formerly or is now the case.

In all of this, you can entirely choose your own path. Let me soon hear from you.

93 93/93

Love,

Karl

P.S. I wish to stress a recent repetition of the injunction by A.C. in an emphatic way: that any intercourse with W.T. Smith means expulsion. As the situation at 1003 is not quite clear to me, and if W.T.S. should still be there, there might be danger of contact. Please warn anybody that there is no change in that respect in the policy of Grand Lodge. I have only written this to Ray and Mildred.

Karl

5169¼ Fountain Avenue
Los Angeles, 27, California

March 20, 1944 e.v.

Dear Karl:

93

    I thought Roy would notify you that 132 is under way at Rancho Roy-AL. The place of sojourn is the immediate work – building the cell, shall I say – out of railway ties. There are books, etc., to be taken from 1003 when everything is ready and it is ascertained what will be wanted; as well as the magical implements designed and made up by 132 during the past few months. Perhaps Max or Georgia has given you particulars? Roy had us together at Beverly Hills, that "no garbled reports" got to our ears. But those of us who knew anything have not opened our mouths. I would have written but Jack suggested the notifying was properly up to 132. I write now, as I consider Roy unsealed my lips where you are concerned. But I can't understand why Roy did not write you.
    Yes, that remark, "something I don't like" sounds strange, standing alone. My sole thought was Jack and Betty, who had just left, after Jack told me about re-opening Lodge. The atmosphere,

for a time after they left, seemed sinister, which was never the case when they had been here before. It was this condition that was at the root of my remark. Again, maybe they had nothing at all to do with it?

Does one have to make a choice between Max's circle and 1003? Mildred is enjoying work on Tree of Life with Max, and she also goes to 1003. I want to say here that I again went to Beverly Hills, and this second time found Max more interesting. Possibly his opening night he felt ill at ease, and therefore unable to assemble his ideas with assurance.

It pleased me no end to be able to take the Burlingames over to Pasadena Saturday night. It was the first night Mildred had been out since the birth of Laylah. There little fellows were on hand; Helen's boy, of course, a beautiful, interesting child of 11 months; Barbara Cartwright's son of 5½ mos. And Laylah, about 3 months. Not a whimper out of one of them.

I am Secretary-Treasurer in the new set-up, and would like to know about the transference of money to London, in case it is sent direct from here. Cabling, of course, is more expensive from our Coast, and uses up money at best. Could an order be given to a Pasadena Back to credit its associate in New York – New York, in turn, issuing credit on a London Bank? Would money be saved this way? Or is straight cabling simpler for A.C. ? I shall inquire, of course. Also, I will take minutes of the monthly meeting and forward copy to Aleister.

93 93/93

With love,

Jane

K. J. GERMER
260 West 72nd St.
New York, N. Y.

March 27, 1944

Dear Jane,

93

Yours of March 20th was a surprise with the news about Wilfred. It is only to-day that I received Roy's letter on the subject of the same date (but with false address, therefore the delay.) I am really glad about this. Firstly, because of Wilfred himself, to whom Frederick sticks unflinchingly, secondly, because this should give Jack a greater sense of responsibility, and independence. Let him show what he can do.

I am glad you are Secretary-Treasurer. I have not the faintest idea on what sum you will be able to collect and transfer per month, nor am I curious. I know well enough that this financial angle has in the past been the great point of friction in my dealings with Agape. I have had many a conversation with Frederick on that point and I would really love Jack to have the feeling and conviction that I do want him to act in the transfers without knowing that I am or wish to stick my nose in, and I have written A.C. to-day in that sense.

I transfer monthly, as you know, and the fee of my bank is $2.59 for any sum up to $200. For sums cabled above that it is $2.84. The fee is so low because these cables go by Night Letter to London. I feel sure that the banks in California have a similar service. I don't think there is any possibility for you to mail to a bank in New York, and then have them transfer by cable from here. However, this is a matter to find out there. I transfer through the National City Bank. They have an office in London, know A.C. and telephone him when a cable has arrived. This cuts down delays. Please find out whether that bank has an office in Los Angeles and discuss the matter with them. May-be they could then mail your payment to N.Y. and have it cabled at their usual rate from here. Should this not be possible, and if the direct cabling charges be too high, it would, of course, cause much unnecessary expense.

If, after maturely thinking this matter over and discussing it with Jack, you should wish to decide to mail the transfer to me to include with mine, I'll of course, comply – though I do not ask for it. There is the other possibility: to mail to Frederick and ask him to go thru the required formalities. But again: he is tied to his job from 8 to 5 p.m. and would not be able to go to the bank except at lunch time. I want you all to act entirely on your own decision in this whole matter.

No, I don't think there need be any conflict between Max's courses and Agape. No reason why they should not supplement Agape, if members of both would avoid all kinds of gossip carried back and forth.

Here's wishing you all the best success in the world.

93 93/93

Love from both Sascha and myself,

Karl

P.S. A word on Joe Miller and Ray Burlingame and Mildred. I take it that they all want to join Agape as good members. I think you should take a firm stand with Joe. Outside of his $10 which he sent me 9 months ago with the unrestricted promise to send more and monthly, I have not received one cent from him, and my letter about this to him evoked very nasty replies. Georgia has talked to him on the subject and I am of opinion that he has to learn to complete a very serious defect in his nature. A member who has been given the IX° should feel the gratitude to his Order that gave it to him, quite apart from usual considerations.

I have found Ray as well as Mildred the most generous people I have ever met. Is it that their knowing that every cent they gave went to A.C. boosted their enthusiasm? Please avoid damping this. It is too fine a quality to be treated lightly. I would like them to know that they continue just the same with Agape as they did when writing me direct, and will, if I find the time, tell them so.

K.

Frederick told me that he informed Jack on March 19 or 20, never mentioning his intention to me before. I think he did it on the spur of the moment.

K.

5169½ Fountain Avenue
Los Angeles, 27, California

March 29, 1944 e.v.

Karl:

93

    The enclosed is Jack's contribution for March. He gave me this but recently, and asked that I send it you. In the present set-up there will be no doubt about contributions going forward; and I see no reason why it should make any difference in the amount Jack sends: He told me $50 the month of February: $15 now because of income tax.
    My living in Hollywood, with restricted gas, will not be convenient. Helen could be more suitable for the Secretary-Treasurer is Jack would use her. I did not want the job; habit constrained me, and Jack said he would close up again if people did not support him.
    I have not been asked to move back to Pasadena, but in any event I shall remain in Hollywood. I have things to work out; fragments of strange and subtle nature, which are slowly seeping

through – and resultant equilibrium to a degree. Something I usually lacked – if, indeed not always – and this should have a bearing on my physical state, not too good at present. The sins of omission and commission have overtaken me.

Aleister has not seen fit to answer my somewhat lengthy letter of January 15 re S.T. and Phyllis. I assume he received it. But I do wish he had answered about Phyllis. She has just had returned to her a letter written Aleister by her, and addressed to 93 Jermyn. Is the A∴A∴ in abeyance? Phyllis is First Degree O.T.O. and could, of course, carry on her studies; but her imagination was stirred by it at Winona when Wilfred was signing Probationers, etc. Let me know about this, will you?

93 93/93

Jane

K. J. GERMER
260 West 72
New York, N. Y.

April 1, 1944

Dear Jane,

93

Yours of March 29th with the M.O. Thanks. - If this M.O. from Jack means that you prefer to remit to me in future for me to include with the rest, this will be quite all right. It would save expenses in any case.

My opinion is that it would be better for you to be Treasurer. It will avoid possible friction and ease personal relations. I had a talk with Frederick and it seems to me that your age should preclude you from taking up household or other work which in the past has put too much strain on you. After all you have to take care of yourself.

As to your last passage let me say first this: no need to be impatient for A.C.'s reply to yours of Jan. 15th. Only if he would have replied at once could you have expected his letter for sure by now. But it is unlikely that he should sit down and reply immediately. He is preoccupied with other urgent matters, one of them being his personal safety and comfort. (I have seen from a letter to Roy that a bomb hit within 250 yards from his place and smashed up everything. After all, "there is a war on" in England.) Second, he has no secretarial help, and I have been waiting for letters from him for quite some time.

But, perhaps, you will allow me to say a few things to your problem. A.C. has never talked to me on any degree in the A∴A∴ that I might have, though I remember that there were times when I was extremely impatient to hear from him just where I stood.

It seems to me that A.C. has somewhat come away from the point of view of where he stood back in the Cefalu days or before. I know of no case in the last 15 years or so where A.C. has conferred any A∴A∴ degree to anyone in the formal outward way. I know of no "pledges", diplomas or similar written documents issued or signed by prospective members of the A∴A∴. I know that this used to be different. Is it because A.C. has realised that the A∴A∴ is an invisible Order where checks are automatic and on a different plane of bookkeeping and records than here where people demand outer visible diplomas? If so, the change must have taken place before 1925 because I recall the case of Traenker who had the IX° OTO and when A.C. turned up signing himself as $9°=2^\square$ he insisted on being told just what degree he held in the A∴A∴ system. A.C. never satisfied his desire.

I believe the best thing is to forget about this urge of the lower self to be told 'oh, you are this and that' or 'you have risen above so and so' or, what not. I think this feeling of uncertainty was very much at the bottom of Wilfred's troubles. The proof of attainment, in my view, is in the Work. Compare *Liber LXI*, 20-28. If that great reward which, since A.C. especially, everybody is waiting for is to come to somebody, it will come in a certain subtle passive state when the bride, the soul, has become without patience or impatience, and has learned the lesson to WAIT. See all those passages in the Holy Books that stress that point: *LXV*, ii, 55-62; iii, 30-37; 63, 65; iv, 29, and lots of others. Also *Liber VII*, v. 46 and 47 where the stress is on "await", and on "passive love".

All this searching for it is poison. In Turgenieff's 'Fathers and Sons' somebody says: "There are three states of the soul: one, in which time flows too fast, one where time passes too slowly; and one where you do not notice time at all." It seems to me that this is the proper mental attitude. One must lose oneself in the Work in hand, no matter what it is at the moment. - You know the Holy Books well. I have always found that in difficult stages the reciting of these Books are soothing and calming and purifying. May-be you have another method. There are many roads that lead to Rome, and I would wish yours will lead you there.

As to Wilfred handing out diplomas (of the A∴A∴) or setting A∴A∴ tasks, this seemed to me a presumption. I heard first about it when Perry Tull gave me the tasks Wilfred had set him – and was astounded. Frederick has told me his own case which shows that W. set tasks which he certainly was incapable of judging, or criticising or examining himself. Does this not remind one of the A∴A∴ rule that nobody is to set tasks who is not entitled to it? Remember Captain (now General) Fuller[47] who was thrown out of the A∴A∴ because of that very reason.

We have a Hierophant, and that is A.C. People who wanted to make progress in the A∴A∴ should have sent, or rather should have been encouraged to send their records to A.C. for advice and examination. But this was never done. Why? From the above you will see the obvious answer. Wilfred apparently never asked members to do this, but seemed to want to keep that job to himself, with the results we know. Even such intelligent people like Frederick have got a very wrong idea of the A∴A∴ What then should simpler minds think? I could write ages about all this,

---

[47] J.F.C. Fuller, an A∴A∴ student under Crowley who was at one point the Order's Cancellarius.

because I have seen the tragic results of these initial and vital failings for more than a year.

Good luck to you and write me whenever you feel like it.

93 93/93

Love, yours,

Karl

5169¼ Fountain Avenue
Los Angeles, 27, California

April 22, 1944 e.v.

Dear Karl:

93

    Enclosed M.O. is from my sister, "Mary K.", who wants to buy a "Book of the Tarot": then come what may she will have a copy of her own, to consult or loan. I typed Jack's letter to you, so know of his contribution; Ray told me of his good work. So something has been achieved, and I hope more than this known amount has flowed in to you or to A.C.
    Hugh Christopher is now passing through a state I experience at Cefalu, and never had clarified. I copy a paragraph from his diary, and underscore my own experience. I shall be very glad to understand this 'blackness'.
    "I've always worried about obsessions, as to whether or not I at times take on obsessions. Experiences stand out so clear & defined as to their starting & ending that it seems like obsession, or am I just cultivating the ability to separate & define 'experience'. At times there is a black astral object appears in flashes; is that an

outsider or my own soul body picturizing an experience about to happen or take form? Is it good or bad? Am I becoming aware of a split consciousness which I have had to overcome? Taking the idea of obsession out & looking at it, takes away the fear."

My 'blackness' was not in flashes; it stayed by me like a cloud – some times very close. It ceased all together before I left Cefalu.

Hugh was very badly messed up when I got hold of him, a feminine interior and masculine exterior; occasionally going at each other, hammer and tongs, like any man and woman. But he has improved tremendously, and the stammering ceased entirely except when he gets emotionally entangled.

I shall appreciate a little information about Frederic. You wrote some one he is very busy, and I would not want to disturb him, but he is doing a work more to his liking, to his betterment? I am sure he is learning much from his association with you, so I do not inquire in that direction. I have not heard from him since beginning of the year.

93 93/93

With love,

Jane

K. J. GERMER
260 West 72
New York, N. Y.

April 26, 1944

Dear Jane,

93

You and Jack have both made me very happy with your special effort, and I am sure A.C. will appreciate your help very much, and warmly. Nothing else has come in so far. No word from Mildred or Ray. Georgia has written me that she was willing to take a loan, but that in that case she would have to forego her monthly contributions, and I dissuaded her. Roy seems in a hell of a mess and about his problem and WTS later. I cannot expect anything from Max: he is the mainstay of the monthly contributions, and has been so for the last few years. I do not think he has any reserves, as I noticed when the March tax was due. So I hate to ask him for anything special and thereby possibly endanger the regular contributions. - I had been able to make a special contributions on April 15th – but then the Feb. and March transfers had been unusually small. Still, if I can get something from Ray, as you indicate, the total should be enough for A.C. to pay up the most important dues on the Tarot and put the volume on sale.

I have had some extended correspondence with Rhea and Roy on the subject of WTS. A full letter is now on the way to A.C. and Roy asks a definite reply by cable how to act with regard to WTS and *Liber 132*[48]. Meanwhile he had asked for my advice and I have given it to him.

I have also touched this point of WTS in my last to Jack and sent him copy of Roy's last letter to me. It might be as well for you to ask Jack to give it to you to read, as I think you should know what is developing. Anything I say about the problem WTS

---

[48] *Liber 132,* or *Liber* Apotheosis, was a set of instructions for W.T. Smith's magical retirement.

is, of course, personal, and not authoritative. – Now: I have not lost, and never did lose, my skepticism about WTS despite all the wonderful loyalty with which Frederick stuck up and tried to explain WTS. All this just does not count, at least not with me. I have had too many forcing magical symptoms to make me change my attitude easily.

My view is that WTS is in the same hole in which Achad, Mudd and several others found themselves. Any amount of attainment or merit does not count when you have to face certain demonic forces, it is there where "success is your proof". As I wrote to Jack: we all are servants of the Order. It has seemed to me for a long time that WTS was not pure in this aspiration. That he has some spot in his make-up where he thinks the Order has to feed, shelter and maintain such a high person as WTS – with his woman and child thrown in plus his car. My view has been that long ago he should have taken a job (Helen too) and, instead of drawing on the scant resources of the Order, to assist contributing. Had he done so, the Tarot would have been out long ago, and two or three other books, which A.C. trembles to get printed, too. I have felt that Jack was being sucked dry by the demands of WTS and Helen all the time. I had been sure that WTS was being kept at 1003, and, if so, that his presence would be of the greatest danger – magically speaking, (same as his presence at Roy's ranch, as I warned him in January.)[49] I now have the proof in Roy's letters as well as in Jack's. It is so utterly incomprehensible to me that all you people have not learned certain simple magical lessons.

There is the old story that if you put a rotten apple in the midst of healthy apples, it is not the latter who will cure the former, but the latter ones will rot too. If you permit yourself to have intercourse with a person who is in the phase where he is the object of violent attacks by malignant demons, and shows that he has not the maturity nor power nor purity to eliminate them instantly and continuously, the result will be that where this person resides, or where he contacts healthy people, these will be under the stress too. (Remember the period when A.C. - too early – attempted the

---

[49] Written in the margin in Germer's hand: "This was the subject of A.C.'s injunction not to have any relations with W.T.S. apart from Liber 132."

Abramelin operation: both at Boleskine and in his London Temple all kinds of sinister forces manifested.) In the same way, Roy has been troubled for some time by visitations, evil astral forces and what not which he has the greatest difficulty in exorcising. I have warned him of the danger he runs in keeping contact with WTS as early, I think, as December 1943. - I cannot see how Jack can possibly succeed when WTS still lives – even only temporary - at 1003. However, I was doubly, trebly happy when he wrote me of the transfer of his $300: it's such acts more than anything else that may help him overcome the enemy. It also seems to show the attainment of a degree of independence from Smith's influence. It will be easier to get along.

Still, it may well be that A.C. will take a different attitude. It is his cable to Roy that will decide the issue and further action. -

I can't advise on "obsessions". I have no astral experiences whatever, I have always left the astral behind and tried to pierce straight through. We all are subjected to phases of blackness. I don't think you are exempt on any plane, where dualism exists, and this is practically everywhere. I think the goal for everyone is to realise the state where duality has been dissolved, a state where you can always take refuge in the midst of conflicts. – If you have cured the stammering in Hugh, I congratulate you. He should further improve. The man and woman part of his make-up do not seem to be bad: remember the passage of the androgyne and gynander in *LXV*, chapter 5.

Frederick has a government job, on which he is not allowed to write or speak. The work is indeed more to his liking, though he would probably not mind if the pay were better. We both like him very much. He will probably have written you in the meantime himself.

Don't worry too much about details such as lodge dues: pay them by deducting them from your monthly contributions. I know perfectly well that you are going the limit with the little you have. I also wish to thank your sister very warmly for paying for a copy of the Tarot in advance. And I thank you for making this possible.

Let me close now. I think I have mentioned all I have on my mind.

93 93/93

Yours ever,

Karl

Give me your sister's correct name, for me to write A.C. to send her her copy direct with an inscription. Or, will you write A.C. yourself?

5169 ¼ Fountain Avenue
Los Angeles, 27 California

May 10, 1944 e v.

Dear Karl:

93

    I shall be writing Aleister shortly, but I would rather you mentioned to him the Book of the Tarot for "Mary K. Wolfe."
    I am enclosing the usual $20, but June I may have to cut it by $5. My teeth are in a bad way, and for this I shall have to pay $10 a month until the bill is met. I am building up physically, what with one thing and another, and when the teeth are in shape I hope to get me a part-time job of some sort, and all to the exchequer.
    Your news re WTS is no more than I expected: i.e.
1) The time for the Retirement had passed.
2) The undertaking of the Retirement lacked sincerity.
I knew – a) of 2 return trips to 1003, though I never saw Smith after leaving 1003 last October; -- b) of Helen and the baby – Helen who did not want to go to the ranch but who was, as thought, being railroaded there, to be gotten rid of.

Smith has left Rancho RoyAL, as you no doubt know. Jack came over to tell me (though I had your letter first), and says: "Smith will get a job, save his money and in two years make the Retirement at his own expense." He also said Smith would be out by the latter part of May. But I have heard all these promises before. However, Jack has been notified by the agent that the owner intends to post the property for sale, as it may be Jack will have to move.

I will not write of my feelings in this whole matter at the time, as I know I am not infallible. Also, the experiment had to be made, no doubt: and for Roy as well. He was so enthusiastic about his arrangements and plans.

I say "time for the Retirement had passed." I felt the train had come to a stop at the station, WTS did not board it, and that it went on its way – constituting one of those "only once does the Great Order knock at any one door." Progress can be made, always; but not the Great Attainment offered.

Before leaving 1003 last October I told Smith, on his questioning me, that as I saw it he had but one chance, and that was to get a job and humbly ask A.C. if he might be permitted to assist with the publication of his books.

What I don't like is Jack's saying he intends to keep on seeing Smith.

93 93/93

Love, a heap,

Jane

May 31, 1944

Dear Karl,

93

Forgive me for not writing earlier. Frankly, I have had no heart to write anyone. In your case this was coupled with waiting for some word from A.C. - word that hasn't come up until now.

From such an introduction you can easily deduct that all has not been going well here at the ranch. That is putting it mildly. All has been definitely going NOT well, dating back to the beginning of the WTS fiasco.

First to answer your question. Smith left here right after I wrote you last. He decided not to wait for A.C.'s cable. (Thank God he didn't – it hasn't come yet!) Helen, except for the two short two or three day trips she made here in February, has never been out here. When Smith left, Culling[50] of course went with him, promising to come back whenever I wanted him to do any carpenter work for me.

WTS tried hard to get us to change our viewpoint before he left. Tried hard, that is to sell us his viewpoint, and having Helen here, and all the rest of it. We were adamant, and so we have neither seen nor heard of him since the day he left.

Perhaps I had better amend that. His mark, or the mark of the forces he has attracted to himself, have definitely made themselves felt. Consider this:

While he was still here, coyotes came in one night, killed three valuable goats, nearly a year old, although said goats have been in the same spot for all their lives without ever being molested before. Goats mind you.

Next, my engine and pumping plant went completely haywire. Piston through a cylinder wall, then $25 of belting ripped to ribbons, then a pulley flying apart and all but wrecking my whole engine frame – all within the space of one week.

---

[50] Louis Culling, a member of Agape Lodge.

Three turkey hens, setting on eggs, killed another night, inside a run where they were supposed to be safe from marauding animals.

Add to all that very serious financial difficulties, so serious that I may have to sell part of the ranch to straighten myself out – my daughter and son-in-law leaving the ranch for the city, partly because, so Ruthie claims, they couldn't stand the psychic pressure which they attributed to WTS, leaving me all alone to handle ever increasing work, pile on to this the forces we have had to combat ourselves - - and you can understand, I am sure, why I have had no heart to write!

I do wish I would hear something from A.C. It might help my viewpoint a little to get his viewpoint. I am sure I did right in the matter of the ordeal he never intended to play it square, and he did intend to play me to gain a soft berth for Helen (and himself), but these material annoyances, plus the magical monkeyshines, is not so easy to take. However, ten times as much wouldn't make me alter the decision, so he might as well call off his dogs!

Roy [Leffingwell]

K. J. GERMER
260 W. 72
New York, N. Y.

June 19, 1944

Dear Jane,

93

Thanks for your M.O. and letter. I hope your dental work will be a success. It is curious that so many have had their teeth attended to: A.C., Max, yourself, I and Sascha, Georgia.

No, Ray did not write me his impressions on the last meeting. I do not hear from Jack at all, and I don't think he is acting wisely in that. But I hope he is at least writing A.C. regularly with full reports and requests for advice.

The most tragic thing is that he keeps WTS at 1003 – with Helen I presume and the baby. How terrible the disregard of a magical injunction by A.C., given in a formal way, reacts upon the disobedient, can be seen from the letter I received from Roy some weeks ago and of which I enclose a copy for your personal instruction. No need to show it to others. In his case there was the purity of motive, the belief to be acting in the interest of the Order, and probably in the line of A.C.'s thoughts, that attenuated the circumstances. But still, not being magically or spiritually mature enough, he was incapable of seeing the subtle workings of the poison of the demonic forces, until Rhea asserted herself and wrote me. He himself was already too ensnared to see and act with sufficient clarity and strength.

I do wish somebody would write A.C. fully on details as far as they are available concerning 1003. It's the only way of obtaining help. The only one out there who has understanding in a clearer way on such magical matters – apart from yourself, but you seem to lack clearness of insight into causes, and therefore strength and surety to assert your convictions – is Max. And he has been outmatched not only by the hold that WTS has on 1003, but also by WTS' subtlety, and mostly Jack's weakness and the latter's utter ignorance in magical matters. - In the absence of other reports I do wish you would keep me posted on details as much as you can.

93 93/93

All my love to you,

Karl

Let me know when the Tarot copies arrive.
The greetings of the Solstice.

5169¼ Fountain Avenue
Los Angeles, 27, Cal.

October 1, 1944 e.v.

Dear Karl:

93

    The enclosed carries my news.
    But I want to mention a book recently come into my hands: *The Psychology of Jung* by Jolande Jacobi, Yale Terry Lectures 1943. It started my mind speculating about "Matter in its deepest metaphysical sense." I could get on the fringe of "The Wise Old Man", the "Magna Mater" - the second break from father & mother, that expression new to me. I pondered his diagrams: I traveled in and out and round about his circles, hoping to find an entrance. The upper half is a bit of a blank. Did I find the 'dark' so much more interesting, or is it simpler to grasp?
    It took me back to a London mystic experience, when I drew near to what I called the Ego. This I likened to a bundle of sticks held together by the will, each stick representing a given quality; that when the will was withdrawn the bundle fell apart and each stick returned to its particular source – that nothing was lost.
    Jung did enlighten me regarding the matter I mentioned in mine of February 16, speaking of 'running together along the edges', and 'objectifying' you and A.C. It is to be found in his analysis of "Projections". I mention this because I am happy to find myself corroborated: also to clarify my bungling efforts at interpretation.

93 93/93

Oodles of love,

Jane

P.S. Cooper and I received letters from you the same morning. He promptly phoned me -- being nearer than any one else -- for an appointment that day. But it was the next that I joined him at lunch. I hope to see him again the coming week, and may then have more to say. I would not see him a second time until he had seen Max, and this he has done, as you no doubt know from Max.

Regina wrote Jack about him, but so far they have not met. Pasadena difficult for Cooper, Jack will not call on him. If he really wants the work, he will go after it, says Jack, who himself is a very busy man these days.

260 West 72nd St.

February 14, 1945

Dear Jack,

Do what thou wilt shall be the whole of the Law.

Your very welcome letter of January duly arrived and I must apologise for not answering earlier – I have been too busy. I think your choice of Ray for his particular office is an excellent one.

As to the IX°: I wonder whether ultimate mastery of this art can ever be achieved. It is really a long path of discovery to first find out how and when it works, its conditions and phases. The fact that you received the formal instructions is really enough. That it may take years of training to master its prerequisites is up to you. I believe A.C. once told me that each one has to work out his own rules and contribute with the results of his personal experiences some day to the total wisdom and knowledge of the members of the Sanctuary.

I wonder whether it is correct to deduct 25% from your IX° fee. My view is that this is a due to Grand Lodge. It is not particularly important at this moment, and I'll take it up with A.C. – If I were I wouldn't worry too much about a formal charter for the time being. (I don't have one either.) Look at the case of WTS who had one and discredited himself and the Order by showing the Photostat copy around.

I have become a little wary of granting the IX° or revealing the secrets. I know that I've made mistakes. As to Ray Burlingame he has really given ample proofs of his worth, reliability and sincerity. Yet, let's wait a few weeks and I'll consult A.C. (Let me here mention that it appears that the copy of the 'Emblems' you made here, seems to contain some errors; these should not be perpetuated and I'll have this corrected one of these days.) The same remarks apply to Betty. I'll write A.C. Meanwhile he should have the copy of your letter forwarded to him.

Re 1003: it was news to me that you had bought 1003. If the price was right, I would say, it was an excellent idea, as from all I have heard about it it is a desirable property. I can't see how under prevailing housing shortages on the West Coast it can't be easily put on a paying basis.

I'm glad you made Georgia treasurer. Her proven full devotion may be contagious. I quite agree with your P.P.S. remarks. Don't pay any attention to outside groups. There is room for many forms of manifestation in the Body of Nuit. I am not quite clear on your statement of payments. If I take March 21st 1943 as the date from which to count, the following are amounts I received from Agape Lodge:

1943			1944	
April	$50		January	$25
May	75		April	25
June	75			
July	85			
Aug	75			
Sept	70			

To this are to be added $50 which you handed me personally in March 1943.

What I want to have from you is a statement of the sums you have cabled apart from the above to A.C. direct, sums which are personal contributions. Also how much of the above stated sums are to be credited to you personally.

Re Statement of Lodge Receipts and Expenditures: - You give total Lodge Receipts in 1944 (9 months) as $ 167.00 and Expenses as $62.71. This would leave a balance of $104.29, plus the Petty Cash balance of $4.84. Please let me know whether this is correct, or ask Sister Georgia to write me.

I hate all this tedious bookkeeping, but I just have to make an effort to put everything on the square once and for all, and my records should tally with those of everybody concerned.

I think I have covered every point. Let me soon hear about my letter to you of Feb. 4th.

All the best to you and all members of the Lodge, both from myself and Sascha.

Love is the law, love under will.

Fraternally,

Karl

P.S. I enclose A.C.'s original letter to me of Jan. 16th as it should interest you. The expenses involved seem to be about $50 to $60 per month. It is most desirable that A.C. should have this assistance without worry and I'll take it up with him. If the ten copies of the Tarot arrive and you can sell some and I can dispose of some at this end, the problem should be solved. Please return the letter without fail.

K.

K. J. GERMER
133 West 71st Street
New York, N.Y.
ENDICOTT 2-6799

260 West 72

February 15, 1945

Dear Jane,

93

Yours of Monday came this morning – as a shock if this were possible.

I agree with most of your remarks and I hope by this time you will have received a cable in reply to yours or Jack's. The only trouble is you may not have A.C.'s present address. He wrote me some time ago that he would move to

                c/o Vernon Symond, Esq.
                Nether Wood
                The Ridge
                Hastings, Sussex.

But immediately after I got the letter which I mailed Jack y'day.

Let me state my personal views.

If Smith has left Rainbow Valley Is this due to notice from Culling? If so, is it because Culling saw 132 was not serious about *Liber 132*? There was some talk of Culling asking Smith to leave if he did not start working seriously.

However it is, I don't like it, and I don't think this development speaks in favor of Smith. Still, I'd have to know more facts. But it is significant that the very moment that Jack is beginning to work with a new and promising wave of enthusiasm, this disturbance sets in. He must know and realise that he has the sole responsibility; he is the only Head at Agape Lodge; that he must be firm and not tolerate interference of any kind. He should not weaken. Especially the injunction still holds good about personal relations with Smith as long as Liber 132 has not been accomplished.

I don't like this idea of Georgia's taking in Smith in her small apartment. You put the idea very clearly in your letter where you say 'you are united...'

Please show this to Jack and let him arm himself.

I'll send a copy of this to A.C.

93 93/93

With love,

Karl

K. J. GERMER
133 West 71st Street
New York, N.Y.

ENDICOTT 2-6799

February 17, 1945

Dear Jane,

93

Yours of Feb. 14th hardly came as a surprise after your preceding letter. The more I see of it the more I am convinced of the serious test involved for all of you people. The hell! what does 'Brother' mean? Brother of what? If of the O.T.O. the 'Brother' has to abide strictly by the Constitution and the rules, and he has to show Holy Obedience to the appointed Head.

Of course, you know well enough that there have been other 'Brothers', who partly had risen higher than 132 and who fell subsequently. This is no black mark in a higher sense. Who knows but that certain experiences may not be vital for any particular incarnation? But if so is not the corresponding treatment by the Order just as vital? In fact vital to his avoiding a pitfall or a crash.

All this neglect to abiding by the clear injunctions of the Book of the Law will always lead to catastrophe. 'As Brothers fight ye!' applies not only to the Heads of the Order but also to the 'brother' that claims mild treatment. But it says again 'If he is a King thou canst not hurt him'. We are no sob sister family of softie old wimmin. The aim of Thelemites is Strength and Force and Joy.

I've been sending Aleister parcels regularly monthly. As you know Aleister's nature requires sugar. This being short can I appeal to help from the members of the West Coast? I don't know whether anybody has kept up sending A.C. parcels. If not, you know the type of products A.C. wants. I send him as a rule red caviar, chocolate, dates, figs, or dried fruit, sardines, and sugar. However, the one parcel I was allowed to mail every month, is not very much, and his health is not of the best. He hates any of the 'improved', scientific, artificial products. Please talk to the others about this. Let this be all for to-day. Lots of love.

93 93/93

Karl

METAL WORKING MACHINERY
260 West 72nd Street
New York 23, N.Y.
TEL. ENDICOTT 2-6799

260 West 72nd St.

March 1, 1945

Dear Jane,

93

Yours of Feb. 24 with the enclosures received with thanks. I'll first reply to some points in yours.

I am sending pure Perique tobacco regularly, and have been doing so for the last three or almost four years. No use doing anything at your end. The matter came up because last year he had too large a supply and asked me to stop or rather skip a shipment. Then possibly due to war conditions, there was a considerable delay and he got a little short. But if he gets the parcels that are on the way he should be well supplied.

Yes, it would be wonderful if you would mutually send three or four parcels to Aleister per month. Don't forget: they must be marked 'Unsolicited Gift'. You know perhaps best what kind of things A.C. likes: natural food, not 'scientifically improved' on nature; dried fruit, figs, dates, apricots; red caviar, which he likes very much and is not expensive; chocolate. I sent some genuine Portuguese sardines lately – they might be of great value because of the olive oil (I know from experience how much the body suffers from a lack of fats and oils). (The caviar should be well packed separately: one of my parcels arrived with the jars of honey and caviar broken and all messed up.) I think sweets are allright.

Aleister said the atmosphere in his new place at Hastings is very good and he likes it very much; the air is more bracing. Otherwise I don't know much more.

Of course, Jack is at the same time repulsed and fascinated by Smith. I have seen that for years. I wonder whether Jack has access to the planes where he perceives Smith's magical workings? You should have had a reply from A.C. before this and I hope it has arrived or will so soon. I can't imagine A.C. taking and other stand than mine, as expressed in recent letters. Smith, as a brother, has been given a task. Upon fulfillment of that task depends his reinstatement in the Order, in one function or another, which remains to be decided according to the outcome of the ordeal, which in itself is given to clarify the T.W. of 132.

If Smith runs away from the ordeal; or if he does not undertake it seriously with all his heart; he will just find himself out. But there is more: he will find himself the enemy of the Work and the Order, and will use all his stagnated, bottled up, distorted forces to operate in hostile ways to the Work, instead of concentrating them upon the accomplishment of that personal G.W. which alone would make him fit for a larger role, and for the accomplishment of his T.W. It is because of the putrid vapors which contaminate the pure air of its surroundings, that A.C. has always insisted upon spiritual quarantine in that phase, the necessity of which appears as unreasonable to the uninitiate, and seems almost as dictated by petty spite.

I think you should make this train of thoughts a theme for your discussions among members of the Lodge.

I might further add that, when it comes to the stage of the destruction of the Ego there are two forces at work: the H.G.A. and the Evil Persona. It's like a tug of war. Both will manifest in succeeding stages. If the latter wins – you know the outcome. It is only when the side of the H.G.A. has reached a complete and final victory, visible by definite proofs (a phase which may take years) that the candidate can gradually be welcomed back into the fold. The decision on whether this success has been reached can only rest with the Heads, or rather Baphomet.

I dislike from the bottom of my convictions that Smith should stay on the same grounds as the Lodge. Some sort of contact cannot be avoided; the atmosphere is bound to be contaminated; and Jack is no match for Smith's infinitely wider experience and knowledge in arts magical and control of their forces.

I do hope Jack will soon take a firm and categorical stand and carry out to the letter the instructions that A.C. may send, provided he does so at all, having given clear enough instructions long ago. It is a supreme test for Jack, and he just has to prove himself. These are the sort of phases when daily recital of the Holy Books – provided one knows them by heart – prove of such a great value. It makes for the creation of an amour which the emanations of the Evil Persona of a disintegrating soul has no power to pierce. It is never too late.

I think Helen, with her strong magical link with Smith, should be out of the Council for the time being.

I have said all, it's nothing but repetitions of things said time and again.

93 93/93

My love to you and good luck. You have a valiant fight to fight.

Karl

5169 ¼ Fountain Avenue
Los Angeles, 27, California

April 8, 1945

Dear Karl:

93

Have you met Ayn Rand, author of *The Fountainhead*? And have you read that book, over 700 pages? She was born in Russia, educated at University of Leningrad, and came here 1926. In this book she argues vehemently for Man: Man the Individual, and against any collective society, any kind of paternalism, which she calls slave society. She has her hero say, "The world is perishing from an orgy of self-sacrifice." I'm sending her copy of AL and Liber Oz. She is Mrs. Frank O'Connor and lives somewhere in the East Thirties. Hugh handed me the book, saying "She is one of us!"

Will you give me a definition of Ego? The dictionary leaves me cold. Functions of the Ego I can grasp, can I get a hold of the idea of "Ego"? It came up at 1003 a month or so ago, how Hugh asked if "Completeness of being in outward action" would cover it; Which in turn would seem to depend on definition of 'outward action'.

Beginning this year I gave Hugh my copy of *Psychology of Jung* by Jolande Jacobi. This book has revolutionized some of his concepts, thank heaven: Jewish, as well as "Metaphysical" to which he exposed himself for years. He is using a Tarot Trump each time he comes for discussion. I asked him to do this and accept it more for the ferment than knowledge. Later I shall start him on Liber Aleph, 2 or 3 sheets a lesson. I don't know about this word 'lesson'; he keeps me humping, and is delighted when he adds to my information, as he does – more perhaps than he realizes or I do myself. But I always let him know when I notice it at the time.

I was quite pleased with a recent dream by him. Picture of broken down and collapsing structures, images, etc.; then a regrouping & new formation in most beautiful & brilliant coloring. He analysed this as his past ideas, teachings, etc., and the new structural work he is receiving through my agency.

His need is to step outside the family circle, a bond of steel when I first met him. The past 2 years have softened that bond enough to bend, and two weeks ago he finally tackled the situation – but where his wife is too well known and liked, and so the attempt was unsuccessful. However, getting that far is a big step for our Hugh.

I have not heard from Cooper since the death of Regina.

Frederic has likely told you of my letter to him. So let me state the present picture. Jack has recovered, and with that recovery Ed is back in the Order, and was present the Second Degree initiation last Friday, when Dick Canright, Barbara and Paul Seckler officiated, with Jack as orator. Dick not only knew his lines, which was a relief, but he had Paul marching along with him. Barbara is always O.K. for whatever job she undertakes. She is now Secretary for these Degrees, and I am glad to be relieved. Barbara has the making of an excellent woman. Dick likes & responds to Ritual; his climb may be through that if at all. His Cal-Tech training will not permit him to admit things – as yet, at least. Ritual may nab him unawares.

Ray Burlingame. He really was pathetic as S[51]; no memory at all, and could not follow a script, losing his reading place, and had to be told. Jack did not memorize, true, but was not so bad because he has a quality I used to have, that is, taking a complete line at a single glance. Ray used to go on periodical binges of days or weeks duration, and this may have damaged the memory, for he is but fifty.

So you see the ship did not go on the rocks so god knows it may be be-calmed; and some one could snort "Hysteria!" at me. So I have jotted down an admonition not to jump at conclusions when 1003 begins to itch and squirm and called things funny names.

I am writing Aleister, but shall not post until I get together his second box from Wolfes, which I shall do this afternoon or to-morrow. Ray sent a box late in March, but forgot chocolate. I shall get a pound of that into my next cartoon. When that letter is written, I will forward you a copy, as well as a copy of what I write Ayn Rand, as I mentioned you in that letter. But there has been a lapse since my last to you, and the very nice letter you wrote in return, that I think it well not to hold this up longer.

93 93/93

With love,

Jane

---

[51] Title of O.T.O. ritual officer redacted. -Eds.

260 West 72

April 20, 1945

Dear Jane,

93

    Let me quickly jot down a few paragraphs in answer to your recent letters before I forget.

    The Word has not come in as yet. Aleister only cabled me at the Equinox that the Word itself is ASTARTE. The formal thing has not arrived yet and will be mailed at once.

    I'm surprised about all the difficulties with parcels. Over here a few ounces over don't matter, they accept and pass the package anyway. Still, I always add up the individual things and let them not exceed four pounds, figuring one pound for packaging. Also, there is always the grocer around to weigh the complete parcel before going unnecessarily to the Post office.

    Chocolate: I think it should be bar chocolate, which is the purest and most concentrated form.

    I have not heard from Miss Rand, nor have I read her book. If I get a chance, I'll read it.

    The Ego? I don't think I can give an adequate definition. I also believe the meaning changes with the authors, same as 'God' who for some is a man with blue eyes, a long white beard, sitting on a beautiful throne (pardon me, with a capital T) looking (only) benevolently down upon human beings and fulfilling ALL their wishes however contradictory they are. For others, as you know, God is Zero. So with the Ego. I believe in the highest sense it is Hadit. In the lower sense that which makes for separateness, egotism, the feeling that one is something which closer inspection reveals one is not. (Compare and use the Buddhist meditations on this subject.) – Generally, definitions are interesting but usually lead to discussions, differences of opinion, to 'Reason' and 'Because'.

Why must people like Ray be appointed to tasks for which they are not fitted? Ray has qualities unrivaled by any out there. But it is silly to appoint a snake to a bird's role or vice versa.
I do wish I would soon get the MSS back with the copies I need. Some people are waiting. Will Roy get a set of the 'Letters'? If not I wish he would be given the Letter on Family.

Do I understand aright: Mary K. has received her copy of the Tarot? I'd be happy. Frederick got his last week. I hope the Burlingames will soon get theirs.

I think this is all for the moment. All the best to you and yours. This letter is a bit in a hurry, I'm still very busy answering arrears.

93 93/93

As ever, Love,

Karl

METAL WORKING MACHINERY
260 West 72ND Street
New York 23, N.Y.

October 22, 1945

Dear Jane,

93

I have an idea that I owe you several letters. But I had yours of Oct. 18th with the copies to A.C. and want to send a few lines at least at once.

There is something strange going on, and I don't like it. First, Sascha's case has been serious, has had serious consequences; somebody else connected with the Work reports on peculiar attacks too. 1003 has first delayed the usual contribution for over a week and then reduced the contribution of $ 100,(only recently pledged by Jack in a letter to A.C. as the minimum for the future) to $75. This came as a blow, because I had made my transfer to A.C. on the dot, and not having the one from 1003, but counting on it, had taken the required money from other sources, and now I am short of it.

Jack's idea of getting a group together and inspiring it with fresh and young enthusiasm, is perfectly fine. But will it work if the plan is to free them from adherence to Crowley?

It smells of Smith! And there is danger. Jack, in a recent letter to A.C. said he was praying for Smith. I am afraid he has been injected some Smith poison again. And that bodes ill for the Order, and himself, but may also explain the series of magical attacks.

The burden is always thrown back on my shoulders of all those silly mistakes that some of the people who should know better, insist on making, despite every kind of formal warning, and the strictest of injunctions! Well, we'll see.

Good for you, that you stick to your allegiance, and remain the silent light, in all that youthful turmoil! I think I will have to mail you those !Letters! in which Jane Wolfe is set up as a shining example - when I find the time.

93 93/93

My love to you as ever,

Karl

5169 ¼ Fountain Avenue
Los Angeles, 27, California

October 25, 1945 e.v.

Dear Karl:

Do what thou wilt shall be the whole of the Law!

Yours of the 22nd in yesterday. I thank you for giving me your precious time.

I cannot divert more than $65 by sending to you direct --- bless me, not even that. I made the mistake of including Jack's $14. Georgia's $14, Ray's $22, my $15. As he is sending $75 I can do nothing to increase the sum. He is at the end of the year when contributions are flowing. There should be a system whereby dues – paid January-March – could be spread over the year; or – well, that will need some thinking over.

There is something strange going on, quite apart from Smith. There is always Betty, remember; who thoroughly hates Smith. But our Jack is enamored of witchcraft, the houmfort, voodoo. From the start he always wanted to evoke something – No matter what I am inclined to think, long as he got a result.

According to Meeka[52] yesterday, he has had a result; an elemental he doesn't know what to do with. From that statement of hers, it must bother him – somewhat at least.

There was a time, at least, when Jack resented you – the Smith, Betty letters. Without in the least meaning to cause trouble, could he, while doing this evoking, etc., have thought of you? have thought of what he considers holds him back, or want to "interfere" in his preferences?

Fred thinks Jack should stop "his invoking". Meeka told me also that Fred was always banishing around 1003.

---

[52] Meeka Aldrich, a member of Agape Lodge.

Margot[53] found the place impossible when she moved there, the top floor the most grievous place, and finally located the hand wrought silver ring back of the bathtub which seemed to be the focus. With that removed the house cleared; She in the meantime purified and consecrated the ring, and has it with her. I shall ask to see it the next time I go there.

Love is the law, love under will.

All love to you and Sascha,

Jane

October 31, 1945

Cara Soror Meeka,

Do what thou wilt shall be the whole of the Law.

Thanks for your letter with statement and enclosures.
As usual, you have answered your problem yourself, as one always does. "Because" is the enemy. Yet, let me say a few words. Somewhere it is said that the defunct religion taught: "Not mine but Thy Will be done", as the human being speaking to God. *AL* has it the other way around; The Gods tell every man and woman; "Do what thou wilt." thus giving Man his full dignity as a Star; as well as putting him on his feet with full responsibility for his actions. Fuller realization of any verse of AL, however, comes only by initiation, and that is a long process. The danger is to discuss it. "Argue not", as is repeated time and again.
The case with the Tarot copies has at last arrived, and I will certainly send you a copy as soon as I find the time, probably Saturday.

---

[53] Margot (Margaret) Gwynn, a member of Agape Lodge.

Please tell Jack that I will at the same time send him two of the Tarot copies, and I would be happy if he could sell them, as he promised, for $50 each. I need some cash.

Love is the law, love under will.

Fraternally,

Karl

5169 ½ Fountain Avenue
Los Angeles, 27, California

January 11, 1946

Dear Karl:

Do what thou wilt shall be the whole of the Law!

I should have been close to you the within copy, at the time it was written! I feel in a sort of stupor, and writing seems futile. I revive when with people; but let Jane pass for the time being, well I meander around "1003".

Pasadena has been in a most upset – chaotic state, really, but now it seems to be shaping up once more. You could easily be given more information and possibly more accurate news. Nonetheless I enter here that the Big House, and the front half of the 3-acre tract on which it stands, is now in escrow. Jack plans to move into the garage apartment, and the living room there, which is quite large, will be used for Lodge meetings, gatherings, etc. only Minervals to be taken in, after Spring Equinox, and these to be inducted on the desert, at night.

I hope for better conditions after jacket settled, with the big house harassed and upset him considerably. He likes living with a number of people, but has not the capacity for handling them.

A small library has been given the Lodge by Mary Green, a one time GBG[54] [member] who had been the Leader of a group in L.A. She joined Agape at Winona in its beginnings, and a few years later dropped out. Mary made her living all these years "telling fortunes with cards, plus astrology", and several times during these years at Winona she sent $100 to Aleister.

Vols I-X, and Blue *Equinox*, *Eight Lectures on Yoga*, *Little Essays*, *Book 4*, Parts 1 & 2, *Book of Lies*, *Goetia*; most of Regardie; all of Vivekananda; 3 vols, incl. Yi, of *Sacred Books of the East*, two copies *Book of the Dead*; the usual East Indian books, and many others.

Mary is recovering (she thought she was dying and wanted the books in good hands) but does not want her books back – indeed she is disappointed she did not die. She sees no way of making her living (about 60 years of age) and says she cannot touch another card – it fills her with horror.

Georgia phoned me at the Winter Solstice, when she emerged for a day, to go once more into seclusion, so far as Agape members are concerned, I would not have seen her then except that I had typed copy of *Tao Teh King* to give her.

Last fall, I'm going over Phyllis's diary, I kept out two pages to copy for you. The occasion for doing so has passed, no doubt; still I send it because she was disappointed that I did not do so. The quotation follows:

> Why is it? For all Smith's drawbacks & failings, I was enthusiastic about his projects. I can't seem to get interested in Jack's.
>
> Is it because Smith had stamina and stuck to his workings, so that's something (at least) arose out of them? And that Jack has not & you know that whatever he starts will be forgotten shortly?
>
> Jack attempt seems like drifting. Smith's attempt was something solid. The man had principles and stuck by them. I was in accord with W.T. over many matters. I also agree greatly with Jack on some of his attitudes. Now what? Does

---

[54] Great Brotherhood of God

the above attempt really explain my disinterest; perhaps I had better make a list – see if I can clarify this.

Why I don't care to go to Orange Grove now:

-I feel no man of great spiritual strength there.
-Projects drift along & no one seems to stick long enough to make them come to something.
-No purpose stays still very long.
-Don't care to see Paul, and more deeply personal am tired of seeing him and Barbara being lovey-dovey in public.
-Same crowd & mostly all mated – feel left out.
-Reminded to the deeply of Joe – heartache.
-Shop talk – Who has anything very interesting to stay on the subject most interesting (or should be) to us all – the progress of the soul? (Or occult matters.)
-Why I was drawn to Smith's projects.
-Didn't really felt here was a fountainhead of life-giving water.
-Spirit felt its thirst was being slaked.
-Here was at least an organization which for all its glaring faults, had a purpose and a way of life which deeply appealed to me.
-There were always new people around.
-Interesting talks on the occult things. Crowley one felt to be with us because he was mentioned much.
-Regina had her moments, was a good drawing agent for people. She got their attention & Smith winnowed & somehow got some of them interested. Of course Regina's & W.T.'s joint action often threw them off again – but at least they came & saw Jack has prejudices against certain types of people, & so a certain type or two never shows up at the Orange Grove.

I have a funny little thought popping around in my head. It was after the 'Holy Obedience Week', that Jackson adjusted, that Smith went haywire. Almost immediately after.

Was it due to Jack's suggestion that Smith fell through? Or, on the other hand, did a woman master him?

Regina loves Smith in now to put backbone to some of his doings. I think Helen tore down & Regina built up.

Phyllis, by the way, is maturing. The child-voice, the child-actions, are dropping away and the woman is emerging – she is 32, I think. And she has finally released Paul – is willing to accept him as he is, and as an expression of Adonai. Heretofore she scorned some of him, and look down on most of him, as being beneath her. Funny, how some women insist on marrying men they think so far beneath them – and it was Phyllis that married Paul.

If and when Paul finds a house near his place of work, in Ventura Valley, off on a hillside, because of the dangerous type of work – Hormones – They will live together again. Then Phyllis can improve her growth.

Let me add that item following the above quotations :

> How delightful is domesticity at times. Joy to see a shining surface or an arrangement long sought after. Sometimes I feel I could do any kind of work anyhow just to enable me to complete several long-planned & long-awaited domestic arrangements.

Love is the law, love under will.

All love to you,

Jane

P.S. Jan 23. The entire property has been sold for $25,000 (I do not know the terms) and Jack is given a 5-year lease on the G. apartment, rent free. The big house is to be wrecked, eventually; the inmates have been given 60 days to locate elsewhere.

5169 ¼ Fountain Avenue
Los Angeles, 27, California

January 23, 1946

Dear Karl:

Do what thou wilt shall be the whole of the Law!

I met Grady McMurtry the 17th, at which time he, Jack, Burlingame and myself assembled at 1003. Roy could not be there, but he had previously discussed matters with Grady & Jack), and Dick Canright had that day come down with the Flu.
The result of this meeting was another entirely new program – which may or may not have been posted as of yet.
Grady also interviewed the members separately – his notes to go to Headquarters. The notes of my interview – read back to me and which I signed – seemed rather mixed, but Grady put certain questions and these only were answered.
But he put in my mouth the statement that Jack's efforts were always sabotaged.
I don't doubt that Jack looks on it that way – in fact, I am quite sure he does – but one cannot always overlook Jack's sappyness. He has a truly fine side, but that weather-vane mind is difficult to take. He writes tip-top letters, says Thus! And So! And it gets no farther than paper and ink.
Everybody at 1003 – so I have been told to-day – has to dance to Betty's whims. This I have known for some time; but I just learned yesterday that the damn fool has just recently executed a will making Betty his sole heir.
She, by the way, has transferred her emotional life into the hands of one Ron Hubbard[55], a very likeable Irishman, who lives there, and Jack is the platonic friend accompanying the 2 lovers here and there – the genial older brother. I would rather he got as mad as hell, accomplished something in the way of getting rid of

---

[55] L. Ron Hubbard, science fiction author, magical colleague of Jack Parsons, and eventual founder of Scientology.

Betty. For it could so easily be that he hopes to get her back. Meantime, they are "excellent friends", with brotherly and sisterly embraces; and Betty will continue to be custodian of the property and hostess of the menage.

The proposed set-up after 60 days; Jack & Betty in the G-apartment, Ron to have Roy's bailiwick (mind you!) for his studio. (He writes.)

But Betty & Jack rented the G.-Apt. – November I think – to a Navy officer and his wife at $125 a month, accepting a deposit therefor and signing an agreement. And these 2 youngsters thought all they had to do was return the deposit! Plus a little conniving & dirty work.

But they reckoned without the wife, who is a fighter, and the Navy man, who is a lawyer. So those 2 are in. Jack served notice that he would want the apartment in 60 days. The Navy man shut his jaw and said we will see!

Ron is now the go-between.

So there is the dirt. Will Jack & Betty get in at all?

We have a new Treasurer: Marie Prescott. She came to me with Meeka Aldrich's 3-months book-keeping, and it is sad indeed. Of course, this is a matter for Agape to handle, I mentioned it in connection with the amounts sent you recently. Plus this additional information.

December 22, at a Fourth Degree Council meeting, attended by Jack, Dick, Roy, Ray B., Betty and Jane, Jack presented his demand for 50% of Lodge dues and contributions. The other members agreed as stated. I added: "If you exclude from the amount the IX° dues: they cannot be paid into a IV° Lodge and must go to Headquarters." Jack countered with the statement that he would institute Ninth Degree activities, which would take care of that.

* * *

How often have I come up against Jane's thumping ignorance, stupidity and egotism, since the organization of Agape Lodge! I, too, Knew so much in Cefalu.

Love is the law, love under will.

Love to you,

Jane

P.S. I have made an extra copy of these two letters. Do you think Aleister should have them? I would spare him if you think it better so.

April 13, 1946

Dear Jane,

93

    Thanks for your letter of April 9th and copy of yours to Aleister.
    As to the 777, for which preparations had been made to issue an expanded and vastly improved edition, nothing further has been done, unfortunately. I don't know whether the nearly 80 drawings made by an artist in Thuringia, are still in existence. With the ascent of the Nazis all outer work in Germany was, of course, stopped. All thelemic books were banned, and Martha Kuentzel, who was an ardent Nazi - even when I came back from the Concentration Camp, and when I tried to hint vaguely at some of their methods - had to learn by personal bitter experience how right my warnings to her were. (You must not judge her Nazi leanings from the present-day knowledge. Germans of the educated classes always despised everything connected with politics. Women in particular had no political experience, insight or understanding in Germany. So, naturally, she took all that Nazi propaganda at its face value. She believed they were actually out to cleanse the Augian stable the foul developments of a

'democracy' imposed by the Allies who kept it corrupt to further their own selfish ends.)

It is all very sad and tragic and Martha Kuentzel has paid dearly enough for her errors. M.K. back in 1935 still saw Hitler and the Nazi development as an end in itself for the best of humanity. She did not see that from the thelemic point of view he was but a means to an end. However, she may have become enlightened later: I have not heard from her again since I last saw her in 1935.

No, 'OLLA' is not the 'Book of Oaths'. From what 666 wrote me it is a compilation of poems selected over a period of years. He wrote me he had sent me a typescript which has not arrived yet.

As promised, I am enclosing Frederic's letter after his return from his visit with A.C. and some photos he made. One is earlier, must be a year ago. Please return all at your convenience.

You received a copy of Jack's letter to 666 of March 6th. I would like to have your judgment on the value of that 'vision', or any additional personal information or observation of yours.

Love is the law, love under will.

My love as always, and all the best,

Yours ever,

Karl

5169 ¼ Fountain Avenue
Los Angeles, 27, California

May 16, 1946

Dear Karl:

Do what thou wilt shall be the whole of the Law!

Thanks for you letter of April 23, with its news of Frederic's activities and improved business status – how he will love that theatre job! And your statements re Jack.

I so wanted this materialization to take place, I acted as though it had, if not though Jack's efforts, then surely through the work of some one else: accepting the statement that there was One seeking incarnation.

"a beating" - I see that now as an exaggeration from your point of view, so careful of language. I knew by his eyes that he felt a bit guilty, at least; but I must not fall into Roy's love of dramatization.

I also see Jack as "the most promising at present". One feels Life & Light with him, but the undisciplined personality is disturbing to the little ones who still want a father to lean upon, and who in turn bore him beyond endurance, if it be but once a month.

His handling of money is altogether wrong. For himself as well as for the Work. I have heard...at secondhand. From Marie Prescott, who still lives at 1003...that he has been pretty thoroughly milked by Ron Hubbard and Betty, who have been floating along the Atlantic Seaboard, from New York to Miami, on some boat proposition. And I am wondering if Ron is another Smith?

Secondhand information can be harmful, and deviate from the real thing in hand; and I am not unmindful of that fact, and yet I pass this along. Why?

Now for the Hitler incident.

I used *Liber Samekh* daily for one month, then twice a day for the second month, 3 times a day for the final month, during which month the following took place. I quote from my diary.

1940 May 12:45 p.m.

Something terrible happened! While reciting Section Aa, the name "Hitler", "Hitler", was repeated. Going from the centre of the Circle to the East I thought it strange that his name should come to me and put it down to a world-thought drifting across my consciousness. I said Section B with more fervor than for some time. Invoking Fire, I did so with a feeling of great need of invoking and throwing in Power where it was badly needed. I was full of this Power, the Hitler business being still faintly in my consciousness. Indeed it was almost as though it was he who needed power.

At the West solemnity confronted me. I intoned the words solemnly and with a weight, as though something of tremendous import was about to take place. And starting "Come thou forth", I felt sobs rising out of the center of my being. It was with difficulty that I controlled myself though I steadily finished the invocation.

Beginning the Section G, the sobs took possession of me, tears streamed down my cheeks, and I could only brokenly get through -- with a some times whispered word -- to the finish of the Ritual.

There was a distinct feeling that something of vital importance to Thelema was lost.

Evening. I am wondering if all this refers to Jane only, and that the tricky mind went racing around looking for a reason?

One thing I omitted in the above account! That there was considerable exhilaration...in some subtle way I was in the thick of things and enjoying it. Then followed the reaction of sobs and tears. There was nothing in the slightest way resembling orgasm, however.

I repeated this experience to Frederic from memory. On going over the entry at this moment I note the "Evening" entry as something new and strange. It had gone completely from my memory and had, therefore, no place in my talk with Frederic.

And see that I have omitted in the diary what may be the crux of the whole thing: That there was a funeral dirge (At the West), faintly permeating that recital, and there was a casket wherein lay a body, which I assumed to be that of Hitler. But I was afraid to look!

I shall be glad of any comment, 'good, bad, or indifferent', as this experience puzzled me. Still does.

Love is the law, love under will.

The love of the High Gods be with you & Sascha,

Jane

P.S. I feel minded - for reasons unknown to Jane - to add a few of the closing days of this Ritual.

> 1940   May 22   12:45 p.m.   .... I say - with hesitation - that Harpocrates in the Egg came into Manipura. Did my mind put it there, for it first appeared in a lower centre. Also Force flowed to my head and played about Ajna - at least, between the eyes and around the eyes. There was gold at Boleskine.

> May 23   12:50   Discovered myself crowned, as an Egyptian goddess: i.e. with Uraeus Serpent.

> May 23 At the West Phyllis came vividly before me (I have been going over her diary for Probationer), and I realized her as one of the chosen, the sacredness and holiness of her Yoni, and that she must regard herself as the custodian of a trust.
> ....

> May 26   12:45   Toward the end of the Ritual the Tree of Life came before me. I saw Beast's star sapphire with the serpent setting -- then a figure came onto the Tree, the head in Kether, the arms stretched out to Chokmah and Binah. Afterwards the figure was crowned with thorns, which may be association.

The Ritual has re-established my center. I feel dignified and more at ease than ever in my life, while there permeates me a desire to forge ahead along a line not altogether clear, but some intellectual attainment is a necessary part of it.

... "so do thou bind together the words and the deeds, so that in all is one Thought of Me thy delight Adonai.

On going over my Winona diaries, I feel a ferment was working, but what have I done about it? I have given up the past, with all its dreams and possibilities, its potentialities; and am now content (?) to take a few crumbs that come my way, with gratitude. I mean, opportunities for doing things.

There are days when I can rest in eternity, but often enough there are days when I wonder, without depressive thoughts, what I am sitting around for. I miss the Profess House, or Community House living. Even with that one needs congenial people, and I found two or three in both Winona and 1003.

93 93/93

Love,

Jane

October 20, 1946

Dear Jane,

93

I owe you a letter in reply to yours of Sept. 9, I think, and Oct. 6. Please excuse the delay, but I am too busy just now.

I have no news from Aleister about the Commentary to *AL*, if you have, please let me know. Meanwhile, I should keep these typescripts. They are too valuable. They were naturally sent to Jack

Parsons as head of the lodge, and as a member of the Order. He has withdrawn from both. He has even offered for sale unique MSS. Why should he not do the same with this one? A.C. may take a different view, however, but do not act without instructions.

Sometimes, I think there are attacks; on the whole I do not like that way of looking at it. Possibly my being in Concentration Camps were magical attacks. But they also were the means for rather interesting initiations. So what? Are 'attacks' induced by the 'Lord initiating' in order to bring about conditions that make initiation possible?

The fact is that while Sascha had her fracture, I had two accidents with the car (first in 10 or 15 years); my nervous condition was bad; and Aleister wrote me that approximately during this period he also felt a severe strain. He says that the high tension is the world with its complicated strain and utter confusion has an effect on our aura. My condition, by the way, has improved very considerably, I actually feel back to normal. But certainly not through the help of doctors.

I do feel sorry about the breakdown of your car. I know how it must affect you, and my sincere wish is that you may soon be able to find some second-hand gears.

Let this be all. Sascha asks me to send you and Mary K. her love and, of course, here is mine.

93 93/93

Ever yours,

Karl

5169 ¼ Fountain Avenue
Los Angeles, 27, California

January 30, 1947

Dear Karl:

Do what thou wilt shall be the whole of the Law!

Will you kindly accept a belated thank you for your letter of December 16, enclosing the Pentagram notes. These Notes were copied and sent all members.

Notwithstanding these latest instructions re the Pentagram, some questioning and argument arose in one or two places because these instructions were different from those given in *Collected Works*, page 265, first volume. Let me say – as you must know – in Cefalu we used Netzach for Michael. In *Collected Works* Michael is placed in Hod.

And like the stupidest of the stupid I passed along this stuff, and I'm still annoyed with Jane. This is so you understand my remarks in the copy of letter to Aleister enclosed herewith. And this, too, is so unnecessary!

I want to thank you and Sascha for your seasonal greetings. This includes Mary K. She and I, by the way, decided some years ago to eliminate these greeting cards, and this is the first year since then that I regretted I did not make up some personal Solstice greetings for the Group. Hearing from so many of them, as I did, I felt on the sidelines.

I sent Aleister such cards (in which I enclosed the handkies) as I never did think to send him; he must have gnashed his teeth at the first one. And to insure these envelopes going through as greeting cards, I pasted on the envelopes gobs of gay red bells a-ringing.

I wish you two dears might be with us now, when we are having such wonderful days; cold nights, but warm sunshiny days. Latterly Mary K and I started gardening, laying out our tiny beds as best we know how with the many things we will plant instead of being content with 3 or 4 varieties. Past that are the cyclamen and azalea; bilbergias, those exotic flowers that breathe of Persia or old Egypt, started blooming 2 weeks ago. The carnations have stood by all winter with a few scattered blooms. In another month they will be full of blossoms and the pansies will be showing happy faces.

We were glad to hear Sascha was dispensing with her cane, and hope she is her own good self once more.

Love is the law, love under will.

All love to you both,

Jane

K. J. GERMER
260 West 72nd Street
New York, N. Y.

March 26, 1947

Dear Jane,

Do what thou wilt shall be the whole of the Law.

The Greetings of the Equinox of Spring!
A short while ago we had a long letter from A.C. addressed to Sascha in which he gave some details about the awful conditions he has had to live through the shortages of coal etc. in England. I copied out some parts and asked Max to pass them along to the members of the Lodge.
A few days ago I had a letter from 666 of which I'll make a few excerpts, because I know you can understand and visualise more than anybody else from things between the lines.

Summer Time begins: heavy snow last night: ½ England flooded. . . . . Electricity cuts have made printing of any kind impossible . . . .

Problem: can you get *Liber Aleph* printed in U.S.A.? Local Estimate for *Liber Aleph* complete about 250 pounds. . . . .

For all that, I had a close shave a week ago. Thus. The heat in my bedroom goes off at 9 A.M. till noon. Hence I must be downstairs by fire before 9.

About 8:30 tried to get up and take an injection to wake properly. Syringe got clogged; fagged & went to sleep again – half dressed, half frozen by 11 A.M. Then my H.G.A. sent my hostess to ask about lunch. I looked so ill it scared her, & she sent a man across the road (all telephones up here are down) to fetch my henchman. He pushed me into bed & got a hot water bottle; then cleaned syringe & tramped a mile or more through deep snow to get my doctor. Luckily he made the contact. When he arrived he found my heart just ticking over. He gave me the injection, and 2 minutes later I came round. Had he been ½ hour later, or if another doctor who didn't know what was wanted, I should have been dead.

Moral: trust the H.G.A.

Please tell all the BB & SS this and ask them to write me, apologizing for not having answered many letters. I will answer yours, too, as soon as my secretary can resume her work.

The Spring Equinox Word has not yet come; I'll send it on at once.

At the moment I am trying to get Estimates from U.S.A. printers for *Liber Aleph*. What I have got so far is very much higher than quotations from England. And those consulted so far can't take work before the fall or next year. Does somebody know a printer in California? – Please inform everybody concerned.

Love is the law, love under will.

Ever yours,

Karl

K. J. GERMER
260 West 72nd Street
New York, N. Y.

May 29, 1947

Dear Jane,

Do what thou wilt shall be the whole of the Law.

I am answering your letter of May 26, received this morning, at once. Your letter shows Jane at her best. It gives the sort of information I need, and what I need more is advice in the present tangle of contradicting views and opinions. As a matter of fact, after the latest letters from Rhea, Roy, Georgia, etc. I have written A.C. rather comprehensively and asked for his views.

Frederic is at this moment with A.C. He seems to have arrived a few days ago, and I just had a letter from F. saying that he has to be back at his job June 1 or 2 at the latest. F. hopes he can meet me some time this year in Brussels, as he wants to see me. Aleister writes he wants to see me, or rather, he would be happy if Sascha and I could visit him after September 13 when the summer guests are gone. A.C. has had a pleasant news last week: Aleister Ataturk, his son born May 2, 1937, is alive, after an odyssey of travels with his mother through Egypt, Switzerland, Yugoslavia, Palestine, etc. etc., dodging from place to place. He pins great hopes on the boy and is very happy he is alive. In fact the news seems to have pepped him considerably. He had feared they were dead, when he had not heard from them for many years during the war.

Aleister is preparing for his death. I am not so sure that he will be allowed to die yet. But living in his condition is, it seems, agony. His lungs are too far gone, and death would be a relief. So we have to face the facts. I am not sure whether you should tell everybody as fully as I'm writing to you. I leave this to your judgment. It is, however, in my mind to make the journey to London, if it can be managed.

This is a matter of finance. For the remainder of this year I have enough income to pay for my expenses while staying in London. The problem is the journey. It costs at least $600 both ways to go by plane, with taxes, possibly more. A seat can be procured, I hear, within a short time. I'd prefer to go by boat, which is cheaper, but to get accommodation is a problem.

The reason why I'm writing to you about this is: do you think I could count of any substantial assistance towards ticket expenses from Lodge members? I would like to know before I could settle down to serious thinking and planning.

Another thing is that we are leaving for two months June 28th for Canada. Sascha has worked so hard, she needs a well deserved rest. And her health is not any too good. Once in Canada I plan to visit several Brethren in Ontario, Detroit, as well as Perry Tull in Chicago. My journey to London can only come after that, because A.C. prefers it in September, and Sascha, who would have liked to go along, must be back on her job Sept. 1st.

I cannot write in detail about this to others, and I leave it to you to use this letter to the extent and at the time you see fit.

Now then the matter of the Ranch, which is also a problem of Roy, and the Lodge. I am writing you frankly, because I am confused and need advice. I thought it best after your sending me the extensive data to mail you a copy of my letter to Roy of May 2, and his letter to me of May 19th which is his reply. I have not answered yet.

What happened before is all in the few weeks between Roy's letter of April 9th (after 2 months' silence) and April 20th. I had approved of his plan to develop the house, and had offered financial help to the maximum. But I was so shocked when I heard that he owed over $3000 – almost $3500, that I withdrew my offer and suggested he bury all dreams which were not based on facts. He sent several frantic wires, but I saw no way to help keep the main ranch, and it was sold. When this was decided, I suggested that the barren land be not further developed, time wasted, but that everybody, Ree, Harold, Ruthie, build up a new and independent life, and thus be more happy, content, and prosperous.

As an alternative, I said, I could only see it this way: that the barren land of 120 acres be used for that 5000 turkey plan as a basis to recuperate financially; this would mean to rough it until water was got and some living quarters built. But my conviction was that without that turkey project there was no financial background.

I have not heard from Roy in reply to any of my vital, basic questions. I don't know how he is expecting to pay as he goes along. All I realise is that he has embarked on what I called the #2 Plan.

But – about ten days ago I got a letter from Rhea they had decided to detach the lower part of the 120 acres in order to sell it as an independent ranch. That was something new again, I replied, I agreed, but that I in that case insisted on an accounting from the sale of the main ranch and of turning the money they had received to Grand Lodge. Roy's enclosed letter changed that situation.
(I had written Roy – No: I'll enclose copy of my letter to Roy of April 24th also, then you see better)

Now I come to my main, puzzling problem, and that is where I hope for your advice: The Gods urge one sometimes to things in Their queer way, which are ill-understood by outsiders. My – let me call it – vision when Roy insisted on the development of the ranch, was quite strong. I wrote him, when I first heard about the 5000 turkey offer, that that seemed a God-send and indication to keep the Ranch and develop it. I even mentioned that I foresaw a crash when it would be nice to have a place available. This referred to A.C.'s desired flight from England. My views have since matured in that respect. The "crash" may be different in type; but I do expect some grave events in the not too distant future. After all the conflicting news I don't know what to advise: my feeling is that now that Roy has definitely undertaken the development of the ranch, that he go on; that he must not listen to criticism from anyone; that wavering spells failure. That everybody should pitch in and help to the best of their ability.

Now here is another problem:

I am sending you herewith a list containing the titles of 72 "Letters" constituting the proposed book *Magick Without Tears*. There are a few more that have come later. I have mailed all of these Letters in the original, as received from 666, at one time or another, to Max. The idea was to make all of them available to the members of the Lodge.

Max returned the majority to me; there are some which I have not got back. My question – and the matter is very serious to me – is: have all the Letters been made available? If Max has not done the necessary to get them copied and distributed to members, please give me the titles of those that you do not have, and I will mail them again.

I feel very strongly on this: there is so much devotion and the Work has been made possible solely by the support of All, that the least we can do is to give them without delay access to such light as HQ. receives. Naturally, I want these valuable MSS. treated with care, and not lying around loose. For that reason I asked for their return when I thought they had been loaned long enough.

Georgia mentioned in her last that Rhea has repeatedly told her, that Roy had taken the Oath of the Abyss. In connection with your remark that "you thought you saw a bit of Smith" (in Roy) makes me ponder. I had bawled out Georgia long ago that there was too much loose talk about the "Abyss", and she recently asked me some pertinent questions. That is how it came out. Since Achad, so it seems to me, there is a certain fascination among members of aspiring to the M.T. grade, without their realising the awful chances involved. Choronzon and those demons that form the protection of the Supernals, have mouths bigger than a hippo; they don't even notice a small fish when they swallow, except the aspiration to such a grade comes from high necessity; yet the candidate, though prepared and properly fortified, has a hell of a time to withstand the onslaught. Does this throw light on some of the events happening? I like you to keep me informed.

I did not know Roy's motto was "Being, not seeming". Perhaps it is the realisation of his main deficit, and his need to strive ever more toward the first.

Do not bother to return any MSS. to me now, but keep all in a safe place – unless I can get it back here before I leave for Canada. I may want to read the 4 vols. of the *Confessions* there.

Please return the correspondence I am enclosing at your earliest. But take your time to reply, I want your considered opinions.

Love is the law, love under will.

Yours ever,

Karl

P.S. I may send your letter which is so informative to 666 as it completes my letter to him of y'day.

P.P.S. You might make a copy of your answer & send it either to me or to 666.

June 24, 1947

Dear Roy,

Do what thou wilt shall be the whole of the Law.

I had to delay answering your letter of May 19th, because every time I tried to do so some new versions of what was happening with or on the ranch turned up. The whole matter left me confused. Also I had been waiting for a clear financial statement about the sale from you. (Rhea in her letter of last week has given this to some extent.)
You say: "You dedicated the ranch solemnly in 1940 to 'The Great Work, To Mega Therion, and the Crowned and Conquering Child'. Those that supervise such matters take such an act in the cleanest sense of the word. If you try to withhold one iota, if there is a mental reservation, or if you even try to quibble,

saying 'it was only Temple Hill that was vowed, not the ranch', They simply take by force. They laugh at tricks of an American lawyer or politician. You of all people had ample warning.

My view is that ever since you made that 'dedication' the ranch no longer belonged to you. The Chiefs accepted it, and what you should have done, was to put the act at once in simple legal form. Lofty vows or intentions must be completed by the final seal, and one must be prepared to face the possibly bitter consequences of all that is involved. The inherent vice of 'clinging' must be torn from its subtlest roots.

In retrospect it seems to me that the Masters saw flaws in the purity of your act; They put you through a purgatory; They first got you into debts and frustrated all your plans. When – so I think – you continued in your errors, the vital part of the ranch was wiped out and sold, and the 'gift' has lost its value. May-be They have given you one more chance?

However it may be, you cannot expect me to take too much cognizance of details of the ranch land that remains, while basic factors remain as they are.

You write at length about Georgia (and Joe), and why you designate Rhea as "Head of the Abbey of Thelema", instead of Georgia. In view of the above remarks, and the fact that the place, which you call "Abbey", looks now as a mere settlement of the family Leffingwell, it might not have been such a bad idea to emphasize the inner truth of the dedication by placing Georgia in charge after settling the formal transfer first.

Rhea, whom I like, sent me a long letter last week to which I have not replied yet. Her, as well as your, letters show resentment to Georgia. She has been blamed for 'bad' influences, and partly for the failure. I cannot believe this to be true. It is always wiser to look into one's own failings, and search one's own soul. If it has a silver armour there is no hostile influence that can hurt it.

There is nothing else that I have to say, except that I have just received word that I have been able to get a place on a boat to England on September 26th. Sascha and I are leaving for our vacation about July 8th, and I will be more or less inaccessible from then on for the next six weeks.

Love is the law, love under will.

Fraternally yours,

Karl

Copy to
666
Jane
Max
Georgia

K. J. GERMER
260 West 72nd Street
New York, N. Y.

November 11, 1947

Dear Jane,

Do what thou wilt shall be the whole of the Law.

    In the first place: here is the copy of your letter of Nov. 4: you sent it to me, and I tore it up.
    I never knew that Aleister had a stroke in 1919! Was this just this Bell's Palsy, or was it more general? Are you sure it was in 1919? Or was it a few years earlier?
    About parcels for A.C.: I have not sent anything apart from the usual packages of Perique, and the last time I sent him 5 lbs of a very fine honey along. – What are "outing" flannel pyjamas? I had planned to take one or two ordinary flannel pyjamas with me to give him – had I gone to England. In judging the case, you must remember that England is no longer what it was. A respectable Briton may have scoffed at flannel pyjamas some years ago. But

the eternal cold, unrelieved by heating, the dampness, and all the rest of the enforced austerity have made Britons more human, I think, so that any Briton will now probably take flannel instead of silk – provided he would have the choice, which austerity won't even give him. One or two more years of this, and, I am inclined to think, the English will begin to consider Continentals as almost equal human beings. If I were Mildred I would send anything to A.C. – food or clothing – that she feels like. The more time passes, the more I'm raring to sail.

Contrary to former plans I would even consider a visit to Germany of a week or so, if I could get the military permit. We have quite a few really first rate men there who were very distressed when I told them I was not going to visit them. I'm sending them parcels, but that is all I can do. But what they need too, is some spiritual encouragement and facts. If we only had some people of their calibre in California! I am enclosing a letterhead from one of the men, who is Martha Kuntzel's magical heir, and has kept the flag flying despite Nazi persecution, and probably censure by the military authorities now. (Please return the enclosed.) All these people have gone through quite a lot. One has been, and still is, for 5 years in Russian captivity. He may return soon, what is left of him – he is a medical Doctor. And if he does it would make me all the more intent on visiting various places in Germany, as they are not allowed to leave the Zone in which they live.

But undergoing hardships is just the means of melting out the gold, whether in an individual or a nation. If they live too easily they forget their God.

I'm chatting to you a little about these matter in order to show you that 93 is not dead, and that there are people, trained partly by IWE[56], who are only waiting for the word "Go".

I am not very happy about Agape Lodge, and I can't make suggestions or advise. You know that I know nothing about lodge affairs, initiations and formalities, so cannot comment on robes etc. What must be done is to keep the little faithful group together, and not let them despair or become despondent, because there are no

---

[56] Soror I.W.E., i.e. Martha Küntzel

outward signs of growth. I feel that the Work, the Work of Thelema, is heading towards a crucial period, and that important events are not too far off. May-be a 'dry spell' has to precede it? Who knows.

You mention Culling. What is he doing? What is his connection with the lodge now?

I wanted your advice on Ray Burlingame whom I would more than anyone like to reward with the IX°. I have been burnt on two or three occasions and become wary. Still, I have seen Ray (and Mildred)'s devotion and loyalty and wonder whether he is ripe for the IX°? Do you think he has an inkling of its meaning, which should really precede the conferring of the grade? My opinion is that a man or woman can be intellectually simple and yet have the qualities of the soul that entitle him to the secret. Can he keep silence? Can he make proper use of it? Do let me know your views!

I have a soft spot for Rhea. When the main ranch was sold, she came with the plan to sell what was left instead of sinking more money into uncertain adventures, discussed it with Ruthie and Harold who agreed wholeheartedly. Then Roy got mad, went out and talked them all out of it. Under pressure they acquiesced, but I believe, against their better judgment and will. I am afraid Roy's obsession by his wish-dream will only lead to further trouble and disaster, divert money, work and enthusiasm from 93, and lead astray.

I for myself have buried any thought of the matter completely. But I have learned how persuasive the devil can become once he starts whispering into willing ears.

I presume Candida's[57] call on 666 is mainly spying. I do not agree with your optimism re Jack Parsons. He always struck me as lacking in a peculiar kind of background which Europeans take for granted. And as he has this ridiculous pride of his, he won't develop that subtle kind of humility so necessary to true growth that Caesar taught us. (I presume your know the facts? Whenever

---

[57] Marjorie Cameron, aka Candida or "Candy" in these letters, was a magical partner of Jack Parsons, and went on to become a prominent artist. She also appeared in Kenneth Anger's film "The Inauguration of the Pleasure Dome".

he gained an important victory or success that was liable to flush his ego he had himself used by a negro slave. That was his magical gesture to assert that no matter what victory that would turn any one else's head: he showed in that very hour he was but the servant of the Gods.)

Sascha is passing through some poor aspects these weeks and has to put up with some ailments. – However, last week, I think, she happened to visit 666 (or he visited her) and had a chat with him; she said he was smoking his pipe and looked better. I hope it's true.

I return the copy of your letter to Roy for your files. I think it is very good, but see my above paragraphs re this matter.

There are still a number of "Letters"[58] out there. When can they be returned to me? I'd like to go through them again.

There is not much else that I can think of and I believe I have answered your letters point by point as far as I can. Jean[59] and Georgia have been writing me several letters. Max is a little better, but must be still very very sick, as he can't read or move. I have not the least experience in this matter, as I have never seen anyone in a similar condition, nor do I know a thing about strokes except the state I was in last year which extended more or less over a period of 9 months.

Sascha sends her love, I suppose you know that she has a great admiration and respect for you – which, of course, you deserve.

Once again, before I close: if the spirit moves any one to send a parcel to A.C., do so by all means. Since October 1st conditions in England have become very much worse, and we have got to keep Aleister at least in decent physical conditions.

Love is the law, love under will.

As ever yours,
Karl

---

[58] This is essentially the working title of the collection of correspondence which would later be published as *Magick Without Tears*.

[59] Jean Sihvonen and her husband Ero were members of Agape Lodge.

K. J. GERMER
260 West 72nd Street
New York, N. Y.

November 12, 1947

Dear Jane,

93

After receiving yours of Nov. 9, and one from Mildred of same date: I thought I should add to mine mailed last night.

My view on Roy has rather hardened during the last six months. I am still convinced that his pledge of the ranch to the Order was a magical act on which he has gradually defaulted and on which he is still defaulting. You are no doubt aware of the danger of such an act: the temptations will follow instantly and it takes all the purity and strength of the candidate to survive.

I think I ought to have been more on the alert both in the case of Jack and now in Roy's case and strictly insisted on their following up their pledges with acts. In that way I might have helped them. A.C. with his experience and his quick insight might have been successful: with me reactions are so slow that both problems dawned fully when it was too late.

The results (as in the case of Smith, which is similar) will show unfailingly, and progressively worse as time goes on. The state of Roy's mental condition is an index. I will await Roy's announced letter, if it comes. But on no account must there be deflection of monies given for A.C. or the publication fund for other purposes, and I'm glad you and Ray will firmly safeguard this. I cannot let A.C. down. My monthly transfer had been cut for the last 4 or 5 months; I had tentatively increased it again to the former level as I saw A.C. getting worried (mostly due to Sasha's help) and I want to do my best to continue this. With Max out it makes it hard.

For years Roy has not paid his dues except a few times. Yet he should have set a shining example. He should be the last to try to reduce contributions.

I have just read again the letter I wrote to Roy June 24th of which I mailed a copy to you. I really have said everything there and gives my views as they are to-day. Roy's irritation and objection to what he calls 'criticism' is merely bad conscience, the conflict between his true self which still speaks veiledly on occasion, and his lower self that is taking over more and more. I think none of us can do a thing about this. It is the risk that every candidate takes when he makes a claim for initiation: "Refuse none".. The laws of nature or of magick have automatic reactions.

I think it is wise to see clear and be prepared, and not let the handful of trusted members run danger of harm.

You can show this letter in case of need to anyone to whom you think necessary. Yet be careful as I am doubtful whether it is legitimate to speak of such magical implications so openly. In other words, if you show it, do it only to one or two who are sufficiently mature.

I am glad you notice the effect of the Sun Ritual. I have never used it. 666 tried repeatedly but it did not appeal to me. I use other methods, alas! far too irregularly.

I had a fine letter from Mildred, and also from Gene. I am glad little Gene is showing up so wonderful and I regret that I did not get closer to her when I was on the West coast. But then, I don't get close to anybody. I am not human. My contacts seem to be on an invisible plane. What is Meeka's status? She was a bit distrusted last year and I was rather curt with her because I heard also those money wangling doubts. May-be that was all wrong? Also I had nothing against Culling, except that Roy was rather definite in his stand.

I think from some letters received that Max's payments from the Union or Insurance are now starting so that he should not be in any further financial need of assistance from the Order.

Is Meeka the owner of that house?

Love is the law, love under will.

With love yours,

Karl

Dec. 5, 1947

Dear Ray, dear Mildred,

Do what thou wilt shall be the whole of the Law.

    Words are too weak to express the grief that has been upon me since the fatal news arrived by cable Tuesday morning. It is not so much the sorrow about Aleister's death. On that I feel rather a relief that His suffering, the suffering of his body, and his unfathomable loneliness during these last years has been ended at last. This loneliness has been deeper than possibly at any time during the many, many years since he has been awake. (I mean that in the sense of the "Wake World" etc.) This loneliness is over, and as I see it, the very condition for his final attainment which He expressed in His cable to me of Nov. 18th. After that, it seems, there was nothing left to keep Him here.
    But what grieves me so insufferably is that in retrospect I see how often, how very often during the years – over 22 now – that I have known Aleister, I placed obstacles in his path, I obstructed, and sometimes made his life hell for the man A.C. I thought I could make good during the months I thought I could stay with him from September to early December of this year. But the British who have crucified their greatest son, and who persecuted him with their hatred, have remained true to form to the very last by refusing me a visa, and though A.C. knew that the visit was not to be, and must not be, he felt the cancellation of my journey as a deep blow.
    There is no secret about it that our relation had been from the start close and intense, closer than men generally can judge. His Work, that was His Life, must and will continue and be brought gradually to the success and glorification that he should have seen during His earthly life. Seen from that point I am deeply grateful to you both for the fine words in which you express this very idea in yours of December 3rd.
    I'll add some further remarks: the last letter I have from 666 is dated Nov. 5; it was typewritten and had a long postscript in his own hand, written as of old in a firm hand and showed him at his

best. However, the letter was mailed by someone who saved airmail postage, and it arrived here Nov. 24th! I answered at once because he was worried about the printer, and now I wonder whether the letter reached him in time. I hope it did because I tried to relieve all the worries connected with that, and *Liber Aleph*.

On Dec. 2nd I received two cables: One from Lady Harris announcing the death, asking me to communicate with her as I am joint executor with her of A.C.'s Will.

The second cable was from a Brother who had contacted Thelema through an eminent Brother in Berlin when he was there on military duty for the British. I do not know when this Brother first went to see A.C.; it may have been a few months ago. However, all I know so far is from his cable which reads:

"DEAR BROTHER: OUR MASTER PASSED AWAY PEACEFULLY TODAY ELEVEN AM DECEMBER FIRST. MY WIFE AND I ARRIVED NETHERWOOD YESTERDAY. WRITING"

The word "yesterday" would then mean Nov. 30th. I am extremely glad that at least someone in the Order has been with A.C. in the hour of his parting.

This is all I know so far. I have not had any communication yet. I expect this soon.

It may be of interest that, not having heard from the British on my detailed statement for the need of my visa, and making a new application, I asked them by letter about it on Dec. 1st. The reply came this morning. "We regret to inform you that the authorities in the United Kingdom are unable to accede to your request for a visa".

In an emergency I will ask Frederick to go to Hastings and secure all files, MSS., papers, etc. etc., and, bar a clause to the contrary in A.C.'s Will, to ship everything here. That would raise the problem of having an office or storeroom where one could work to catalogue the vast mass of material.

So far I have only seen the event mentioned in The New York Times of Dec. 2nd, very brief. I suppose I will have to give an order to a newspaper clipping bureau to get all notices pertaining to A.C. after his death.

Now a word in reply to your two letters of Nov. 14th and your Treasury Report. Thanks for both! Also for the M.O. for $100.00. I wish I could ease this amount for awhile. But these contributions had already gone to A.C. early in November, because I cabled the Nov. contribution in advance with the Dec. contribution to ease matters. I paid it out from my last balance.

A brother in Germany asked me if a copy of the *Equinox of the Gods*, especially the facsimile of the *The Book of the Law* section was available. Do you by any chance have a spare copy?

This letter has been rather an effort due to the overwork under present circumstances. What I wanted to do was to send some sort of circular letter to every member in order to give as much information as I have on this tremendous event. As your letter received to-day demanded an immediate answer, my thoughts almost naturally ranged themselves around that intention. I am not in a position to write about the matter to everyone. Would you be so good to ask Gene to make some copies of the pertinent passages of general interest, and mail copies to Agape members? Please include Max, Georgia, and Grady among these, whom I have not written yet.

Love is the law, love under will.

Sascha sends her warmest wishes to all of you with mine.

Fraternally,

Karl

K. J. GERMER
260 West 72nd Street
New York, N. Y.

December 16, 1947

Dear Jane,

Do what thou wilt shall be the whole of the Law.

    The Greetings of the Solstice of Winter.
    Yours of Dec. 13th. Do you remember last year when, commenting on *LXV* you asked me a positive question concerning the passage of at the end of *LXV*/IV? When I said we should beware of speculation?
    All the Holy Books contain passages which have intrigued students. Every one of us has sinned against the rule laid down in the Comment of *AL*: A.C., perhaps most of all, but then of those whom I know personally, Leah, Mudd, I.W.E., Smith, Jack, etc. etc. Some lost the balance of their mind completely and went insane. Achad is still pursuing his insane dreams. I have strong indications that A.C. up to almost his end had not rid himself of old interpretations of certain passages. "Be ready to fly or to smite", may be one of them.
    The trouble is that no one knows from what plane these books or some particular verses have to be interpreted. I believe that all prophetic passages in the Holy Books are realised or understood after the event has taken place. To interpret them before, leads invariably to obsession.
    A.C. wrote the Comment in a rage of despair at renewed proofs of Mudd's insane obsessions about his interpretations of passages of *AL*. As long as we are human, and live on this plane, the constitution of our minds is bound to keep making us err. I even don't think there is anything wrong with that, except that we ought to train our mind to doubt, doubt, and continue to doubt, and with its help develop a method to check and balance the activities of that mind; and remain detached, distant, from all our conclusions. A.C., of course, has preached this constantly, and

practiced it. With a vivid, imaginative, brilliant mind like his he was always in greater danger than others.

I think it is excellent to recite and/or meditate on *AL* daily. I am doing this with all H[oly] B[ooks]. I have found that apart from flashes of meanings (possible meanings) that sometimes spring up, the main thing is that this reciting operates like a mantra, or like the "prayer mills" of the Chinese, or the monotonous handling of the rosary by the Catholics, or a similar practice of the Mohammedans. (A Turkish friend of mine handled their form of rosary continually.)

A vital thing is to step up the practice to "inflame thyself in prayer". The flame must be aroused to lit up the inner recesses of the soul. But there again we must remember *LXV*: "thou strivest ever" . . . . "then yield". That is the point: to be able to yield. The soul must be ready to receive Adonai. May-be to attain to this condition of the soul is a grace?

I will shortly pass on to you some information that has arrived about the funeral, etc. etc. Briefly, the problem is to get the Will probated. Difficult, because A.C. was an undischarged bankrupt, and the creditors might step in to seize all valuables or assets. All the papers are safe. They may now be with Wilkinson and Symonds, to be listed. Money for the funeral and local debts and I hope for the legal expenses was found. *Liber Aleph* seems complete, also the Golden Twigs. The printer claims, as far I heard, over one hundred pounds. Whether this includes the binder, I don't know. The legal problem is whether A.C. as an undischarged bankrupt can make a Will at all the way he has made it.

Lady Harris writes: ". . . it is so sad to bear, I was so fond of him. Luckily during the last few months I have seen quite a lot of him, and after finding him in a really deplorable state, was able to ensure in fact that he had a daily nurse and Watson, who was waiting on him incessantly. I went down the day he died & found, altho I don't think he recognised me, that he had everything & got a night nurse, as I did not think he ought to be alone. Mrs. McAlpine (Pat) was there with the child who is a strange little thing, and Pat was with him when he died. She says he just went to sleep, no struggle thank goodness. He was a bit confused the day before and said he did not know where he was. I think *Liber Aleph* was complete but I can tell you more after Tuesday, when, if the cases come to London by then, we hope to make a serious effort to sort them & a list will be made, & sent to you. What a pity you can't come over, it would be such a help but I am sure you can trust Louis Wilkinson & John Symonds to do their level best to carry out not only the letter but the spirit of his wishes. . . . the press here is unbearable not a decent word said tho James Laver & Bax have tried. There are 2 books at Hastings printers *Liber Aleph* & another. For *Liber Aleph* 104 pounds is owing. We told the printers to wait. . . . The cremation was most impressive & dignified. Louis Wilkinson read the poem & *The Book of the Law*, excerpts of the Gnostic Collects magnificently. Even that could not stop the mouth of the foul reporters."

This, so far, is all I have heard. Would you mind to get the pertinent parts of the above copied and mail to those entitled including Max and Grady? I have too much to write.

Love is the law, love under will.

Ever yours,

Karl

K. J. GERMER
260 West 72nd Street
New York, N. Y.

January 27, 1948

Dear Jane,

93

The enclosed came to-day, they were sent by Mr. Louis Wilkinson on the understanding that I either send them, or copies of them, to Mr. W.'s daughter:

Mrs. Vernon Kirchner
215 Fairbanks Road
Dedham, Mass.

I think we should keep the originals. But we must make copies, complete with all references as to the name of the paper, and date. I know this means much work. Who of the members can help? Please let me know if the work proceeds.

We must make at the same time a number of copies to be able to pass them on to out-of-town members. In short I want a copy to go to

>   Agape Lodge itself
>   Max and the people living there
>   Grady
>   one for myself, and
>   I'd like to have two or three for Frederic
>   and two brethren in Germany, if possible.

I've received a most interesting letter from Buenos Aires from a brother who has known something of A.C.'s work for many years and can be considered a high initiate. He has lived among other things with "wild" Indian tribes in the Andes, from whom he learnt the most astounding occult things, which he knows to place in their proper position in regard to our occult tradition. I had written him to find out something about K.-H[60]. and his organisation. Well, to make it short, he acknowledges that K.-H. has built up a powerful organisation in the various S[outh] A[merican] countries, but he also said that he is a charlatan. The law "Do what thou wilt" is being taken in those lodges as "do as

---

[60] Arnoldo Krumm-Heller, founder of Fraternitas Rosicruciana Antiqua (F.R.A.), and holder of an (unused) O.T.O. charter from Theodor Reuss.

you like" – license. I suggest to be careful with that messenger from K.-H.

Did I mention to you that I had a letter from Bayley?

Can the set of copies made for Mrs. Vernon Kirchner be mailed direct to her to save time? I'd appreciate it.

93 93/93

Love,

Karl

February 26, 1948

New York

For Soror ESTAI,

The following paragraph from a Document in A.C.'s papers are of interest: –

"In the event of our death or disability a General Council of the Order shall be summoned within a year and a day of that event by Fra. Saturnus, or such other as we may by subsequent appointment designate. The Council shall discuss the existing conditions of the Order (i.e. A∴A∴) freely for 11 days; after hearing the same the members of the A∴A∴ highest in rank (and then in seniority) shall assume our present functions and govern the Order in our place."

[Comment by Fra. Saturnus:] This is only a preliminary notice. It will take months before the complete document will be available in New York. The above paragraph was copied out in view of the short time that may be available to summon distant members, and it was deemed advisable to send out this notice ahead.

This went also to E.Q.V. For Roy & Agape Lodge & to Max, Grady.

K. J. GERMER
260 West 72nd Street
New York, N. Y.

March 5, 1948

Dear Jane,

Do what thou wilt shall be the whole of the Law.

    Please understand that there is plenty of time for the Yorke papers. Take a rest, whenever required and don't strain your eyes! We need them!
    Do you need photostats of the sigils? I'll have them done here if you have difficulty. But send your typescript on even without them; I can send them later. I believe I told you, if I have them done here, I want to get about 25 for later copies; we cannot think of a reprint for quite a while.
    Re Paul[61]: May-be I'll meet him when I get out there. I now plan to leave (by bus, if it is not too strenuous) March 29, take in a call on Brethren in Ontario, Can., and Chicago, and arrive April 4th at Barstow. I hope by that time legal matters will be in shape.
    When there, I want to arrange for Grady and yourself to come up for a general discussion of A∴A∴ matters amongst us. There are things to be prepared as a sort of preliminary to the clause # 14 of which I sent you a copy. And I want you, Georgia, Grady and Max to be present. Nobody else, so far. I have not mailed Roy a copy of that Notice yet. I am still doubting whether I should at all notify him and the other brethren, unless I do so much

---

[61] Mentions of "Paul" from this letter onwards refer to Paul Millikin--a business partner of Germer's with an interest in occultism--not Paul Seckler.

later, after I have had a chance to study the original, and other papers.

I am enclosing a letter which came to-day from Frederic. Forget his three lines in the address; he didn't know any better, then. I have no time to copy it; please return the original; I thought it would interest you. A.C. before his death predicted a rise and success to Frederic's work. He has been working hard during the last months at the production of the German version of the well-known play "Our Town" by Thornton Wilder at the Bremen Theater (in German theater never means a movie house). And he played the leading role himself. This letter must have been written after the first production. Believe me, I as well as Sascha (who loves F. dearly) are very happy about F.'s rise from the depth of his years of tribulation from 1933 to when he came to New York. And we hope he will keep on Going. – I am sending this letter primarily for yourself; but leave it to your discretion to show it to others. F. is a very sensitive soul; may-be he would not like it ?

Love is the law, love under will.

Ever yours,

Karl

K. J. GERMER
260 West 72nd Street
New York, N. Y.

March 8, 1948

Dear Jane,

93

Yours of March 4th arrived to-day. – I tell you frankly that if we had Rancho RoyAL, or what remains of it, for us, I would prefer it. Those 50 acres seem indeed barren land; Georgia says it has the well on it, and not hearing a word or a whisper from Roy, I have had no other place to consider for the proposed H.Q. – for the whole Order, not merely for a local Lodge. I have to have a place where I can collect all the valuable property of the Order (mostly A∴A∴ material, but also O.T.O.), and where I cannot be in danger of claims by members who might contest property rights, once material has been stored, buildings erected. I must stand on clear legal grounds.

The 50 acres at Mrs. Miller's are deeded in my name (I wanted it as Treasurer of the Order). Here then I can put my whole weight into developing the property and making within a reasonable time a H.Q. out of it where members and visitors can stay and work.

Roy's place is unsafe legally ("all must be done well and with business way") and that is the point I have stressed. He has done nothing to redeem his original pledge – neither to A.C., as long as he lived, nor to me, though I gave him all the rope. He has shown himself unreliable: A.C. kept complaining about it, in respect to Roy not writing promised letters, not doing pledged things, not stating frankly the full facts about his Ranch, and leading me by the nose for years, (and A.C.); not writing certain music for which A.C. had been waiting. He has been in arrears for years with his IX° dues.

As a result Roy has not been able to pass on to a certain vital grade in the A∴A∴.

Again, to develop his ranch and bring water and electricity there would demand capital investment. I could not assume responsibility, even if I wanted to, without a clear legal basis, as far as I see. I would not be prepared to recommend his 'ranch' on the basis of mere further 'pledges'. A year ago 666 wrote to me (and to Roy) that he was suffering from "swelled head"; that he considered himself as a head of an order instead of being but the head of a local lodge. He seems to be under similar illusions even to-day.

I expect to see him as soon as possible, in fact, I am not starting work on Lenwood before I have not seen it myself. – The trouble is that Agape Lodge has not produced anyone with the Tiphereth stage or beyond (5°=6□ of the A∴A∴) it seems.

The O.T.O. Constitution is fairly clear. I believe a new O.H.O. ought to be elected. What I am concerned with is the A∴A∴ material etc. for which I want a safe place, over which I have some sort of control, so that I need not worry constantly that it might be falling under control of people who have not even a faint glimpse of the lofty higher grades.

I feel sorry for Rhea – and very much sympathy; in fact one of my first calls when arriving at Lenwood will be to see her. I have the highest respect for Sascha's crystal clear vision; she likes Rhea too, and sized up Roy, whom she likes, very shrewdly. In fact she remained skeptical about his glowing promises for the G.W. and the ranch, until the bubble broke, and proved her right. While I always expect others to act like myself and accept their words and acts in that sense – and then, when it doesn't come off, am very disappointed & surprised!

Very interesting what you say of this Mary Gardner. I believe I told you months ago that I liked her poems which you sent me, very much. I like the quality, and the contents, and the mood. I can't imagine that Agape Lodge inspired her much. If she would enter the Catholic Church of all churches, she'd probably be doomed. May-be the Gods have a hand in this?

To come back to Roy's letter: I don't quite see what your par. (4) means. What is 'third man out' (that he follows WTS and Jack as the third? What means Baphomet's letter puts him 'on the spot'??? I am fully aware of 666's dealings and views on him. Naturally, he as (one of many) IX° members has a right to be fully informed on O.T.O. matters, and will be. But I myself have only the vaguest idea myself as to what's what. I know that my T.W. has to do with the "establishment of 93". At the moment, however, we all are living in a sort of vacuum or interregnum, and we must be patient until the salient material bearing on some of the matters of the A∴A∴ and O.T.O. have arrived, and are sifted and studied by me. More about this when I have arrived.

I may now send Roy a copy of those Notes that I sent you and which you apparently showed Roy. I should not have mailed them out at all at this time. Matters are not ripe enough. Also I have to deal or contend with some intrigues, of which I have heard, and will know more soon.

Love is the law, love under will.

Fraternally, as ever,

Karl

5169 ¼ Fountain Avenue
Los Angeles, 27, California.

July 19, 1948

Dear Karl:

Do what thou wilt shall be the whole of the Law.

I return herewith duplicates of your letters to C.S. Jones of April 22 and May 18, 1948. Roy read naught to me but a copy of his letter to you, acknowledging receipt by him of this letter of May 18, for he stated: Karl asked me to make available a copy of his letter to Jones; but Jane, I am not doing so because I am tired of these personalities that have been going on ever since the organization of the O.T.O., and that he was writing you to this effect. I thank you for mailing me these duplicates; they are informative and instructive.

O that I could read German – for many reasons. Ishrah[62]'s advent in my life makes it still more desirable. Your news of him is indeed interesting. I shall, of course, be glad for any news you may see fit to pass on to me. His last to me is of April 10. I answered this letter May 28, and have been promising myself to write him again during the last 2 or 3 weeks. I wondered if the post out of Germany – or into it, for that matter – was interrupted. Mary K. sent 2 or 3 CARE'S during this June-July period; one always gets a receipt from the recipient or a refund of the money in case of non-delivery. So we will know eventually.

There has been, possibly still is, a current abroad near enough for me to encounter. For instance: In the elevator of a Department Store some time in June, I became "aware" first of the women in this elevator as a group – then as vibration – and we all flowed together in this pulsating vibration. I have in the past experiencing a flowing with a room, or things in a room, the life of trees, things seen on the street; but never have I got so close to the human. But none of these things are vital enough to illuminate the mind... Of course! In my case it is the accepting and living of these states when they occur – without thought intruding – so that one becomes stabilized in the knowing, that the knowing can be turned into doing automatically when needed; and thereafter comes the understanding? – after the automatic use? Have I analysed this correctly?

I noticed at times in the class that ideas and words flowed out of me which had not occurred to me previously – the group evoked them. As a result I am having more confidence in myself. Inarticulateness of speech ordinarily has always been my stumbling block – it gave me a feeling of insecurity, and therefore lack of confidence. Conversation in many cases puts me to rout. I have no difficulty with individuals who come to me "to talk things over".

In this connection, let me say that a short while back I had a slight, slight realization of the dynamic militant aspect of Thelema. But here all is darkness once more.

---

[62] AKA Herbert Schmolke, an astrologer whom Jane Wolfe admired, and an important contact of Crowley and Germer's in post-war Germany.

July 21.

I did not finish this Monday, here is Wednesday, and yesterday came a letter from Ishrah, postmarked 10th of June – written the 8th. He acknowledges a CARE sent 31st March, nothing in April, CARE in May with two weeks of each other!

Regarding his experience of which you write, he adds: "In the days from the 24th May to the late June of this year I wrote a great poem with the title: 'The Aeon of Horus'. Contents: In poetic form without any name (so was the inspiration) – not: so was the strict order – the myths of Osiris, Isis, Horus and Seth, particularly the fight between Horus and Seth. I was inspired to write it in great haste and to make a threefold commentary, because the aspects of the poem are threefold: historical, personal and spiritual-psychological. The commentary has a volume of 10 pages of the size of this letter and was written within 5 hours. The next day I sent a copy to Frater Saturnus. It is a pity that you don't know German but for me it is impossible to translate it into English because it is to difficult for me the translation in poetic form."

I did not expect him to write me about it, but I cannot help but be pleased that he did so. Of course, I hold this and your information in trust – members with a little knowledge prattle and prattle, while those more mature some times indulge in jealousy – neither of which amuse me

He set me up a horoscope which is a work of art in its blue and red tracings, with other blue figures, and the natal with red and green tracings. Never have I seen a chart with such a variety and number of figures, letters, and little lines. I am quite sure Roy will not know it, but I shall show it to him, and also ask the meaning of MC or M.G. – that he should know.

In any event I can't read horoscopes, but I do find it interesting that he brings in Neptune/Uranus in my "Irruption of the unconscious" and the Vision I had of Aleister January 11, 1919, which took me the Cefalu eventually, and which Aleister linked with Leah. Frederic placed the Irruption with Sun-Uranus – I did not mention the Vision to him.

Georgia was in for dinner last week one evening. We had an enjoyable 3 hours alone – Mary K. at the Hospital, Allene in a nursing home.

Oh, for the first time, Aleister was in and out of dreams last night, and some where along the line I came smack up against the fear which accounts for the lack of confidence. I will analyse this later and then write up my deductions.

Love is the law, love under will,

Bestest love to you and Sascha,

Jane

K. J. GERMER
260 West 72nd Street
New York, N. Y.

October 4, 1948

Dear Jane,

Do what thou wilt shall be the whole of the Law.

 Yours of Sept. 28.
 Do not hold it against Mrs. Sherrill if she "is averse to emotional approaches" – 'Rituals comes under this head'. There is an infinite variety of stars and human beings, and they must not all follow one path. If she has studied so much, she may have a capacity for reading and studying. Let her now try to get a grasp of where A.C.'s teachings are so fundamentally different. They demand that students do actual work: start with training the mind, do Yoga to get control of the various functions of the body, mind, etc. Then, on this fundament, build up the superstructure. A.C. has

far too much taken for granted that people who call themselves students go ahead and do work of this kind seriously, passionately, with vigour. Unfortunately, the whole group around Agape Lodge do not show any signs of progress along these lines; therefore all that stagnation and frustration.

I am afraid some day somebody will have to wake up and make all of them wake up, and forget about gossip and charlatanism. A.C. was always impelled to make allowances and accept things as they were for the single reason to keep the spark glimmering, however weak, on the West Coast. Smith probably was the only one of any stature out there – apart from Max, of course. Nobody has been able to follow this up, so far. I would like to think that out of your womb may yet spring someone to fan the spark to white hot heat.

I don't like that part of your description of the 'Man' on the ranch, that he is a bachelor and lives with his mother. How very American! Motherlove; Mother is always right; the American Mother, how different from and how much higher and holier than any other!!! How often have I not heard all that slimy bunk! – Still, may-be that man is a Man after all?

It is certainly no weakness on your part to keep certain things to yourself and not communicate them to others. As you know, I've long had some doubts about Roy and his family fetters and grip which I think is at the basis of his magical stagnation. Some 4 or 8 weeks ago he wrote me about his plan to sell most of his land on the ranch and use it to get *Liber Aleph* out. I now hear he wants Lodge members to put up the money to buy land etc.! I have not heard from him again. But I don't like all that.

I wish Paul Milliken would turn up here. I have not heard from him. What he should have done was to commit all his spiritual experience with all details to his magical diary, whose importance he does not seem to have grasped.

I want to talk to him suggesting to put up some case for either the production of *Liber Aleph* or the Headquarters, or both. I may have a man to do at least a little toward this. And with Paul's help we may get somewhere.

Liber Aleph and *Golden Twigs* demand another $2000. There is something peculiar about the Hastings printer. I have corrected the galley proofs, sent them back for a final check to Yorke and Grant, and Symonds, asking them not to return them to the printer before I do not give the green light. The fact is that the printer is unbelievably unbusinesslike; they do not answer letters. I have written them three letters since July or August, and no reply!

The H.Q. We have lost that house in Penna. It was the funniest combination of circumstances. Anyway, we could have paid for that house, but would have had to build a road to get access to it, and water, and electricity, total about $3000 on top of the price of the house. It now has been taken over by one of the heirs himself.

But we are driving around every week-end looking at other properties. We want seclusion; conveniences; some acreage to retain the privacy on which too close neighbours would encroach with their radios, juke-boxes, gossip, check-up on where one goes to church, and all that inquisitiveness which is unknown in Continental Europe. One thing is certain: real estate prices have gone up considerably since Spring, and we have pay much more than we figured. But it has to be done.

Sascha is even more behind the thing than I myself have been for some time; she is really driving, and on her would be the main financial responsibility; so we are perfectly unified in this undertaking. (I believe I wrote you once that I did an Op. on March 26, and am wondering whether it will have to run a nine months' course, as certain more important ops. seem to do.) – My old Belgian stuff has at last arrived and I am having it sent to my apartment. I am very anxious to see what the cases contain, and whether my important thelemic files have been rescued, and what of my books are there. It had to be packed by a shipping agency who in turn had to pick the various files up in cartons at three addresses in Brussels, and pack the lot in two cases!

Again: beware of Culling. Do not reveal anything to him which would only go on to others. – Can you let me have some copies of AL? – I congratulate your old Studey on its performance; but even more you yourself; for I myself am getting tired now when driving 200 miles in heavy traffic around New York.

Love is the law, love under will.

Love from Sascha and yours ever,

Karl

My love to Mary K.!

5169 ¼ Fountain Avenue
Los Angeles, 27, California

October 5, 1948

Dear Karl:

Do what thou wilt shall be the whole of the Law.

    Mrs. Sherrill: At present she has "Little Essays", "Sammasatti – Analysis of the Mind", "The Qabalah – Best Training" and Magick & Yoga Confronted." Her only Yoga experience, Pranayama some years ago.

    I see I did not tell you that she lived a few years at "Krotona", here in Hollywood, the then Headquarters in U.S.A. of the T.S.[63]; that she studied music and dancing at this time, and wrote a few newspaper articles. She and I crossed each other's path at this time: I quit T.S. 1917, and Krotona definitely 1918 – I kept going occasionally because I liked some of the people. She had made a toe-hold there by this period.

    As I told you she wrote me about Magick. I think she connected this with healing, as that seemed her big desire when I was there. And prayer: prayer that really meant something. I told her what I know of a Golden Dawn woman, who had some healing

---

[63] Theosophical Society

power: she cured, they thrived, but some few years later the same sickness was back because the sickness lay deep, deep within. Also I quoted Aleister: Spiritual means for spiritual ends, mental for mental, material means for material ends.

I am now prompted to ask: If one had the power to use spiritual means for healing, and performed that healing on the spiritual plane (where no doubt the real weakness lies and not in the material) would not one fulfill "Spiritual means for Spiritual ends"? If you have time, please mention this when next you write.

Paul. He was in Guatemala 1st October, as I had from there my first communication from him since he left. This signifies a change of his itinerary. He must be here the 20th, so will surely be in N.Y. before long.

So far as I know, he just would not keep a diary – I spoke of it several times. Ero[64] started one and then quit. But Paul did jot down on bits of paper carried for the purpose, some unexpected thought, a rhythmic couplet, etc.

Ergo:

> I can be crystal clear
> And even jeer
> As what I fear comes near.
>
> O give me the power through tools of fire
> To be near Thee in this sacred hour –
> The hour of tension, dissension, contention –
> Even through this retching comes God to my attention.

Yes, I can give you 3 copies of *AL*. Culling gave me 4! Truth to tell, I forgot about sending them, and I am glad you reminded me at this time. No, I will send the 4. My copy of that blue edition has my name in gold lettering on the cover, and this I can give or loan to Santa B. if, if, etc. At Pasadena, whenever one was initiated he or she received a copy of this blue *AL* with his or her name written in gold ink on the cover. The "Pen" etc., was

---

[64] Ero Sihvonen, with his wife Jean, was a member of Agape Lodge.

borrowed from Aerojet the evening of the initiation and returned the next a.m.

Roy has some wild and enthusiastic notions about "the Ranch". These two lots, Dr. Montenegro and John Eller[65], are worthless without water – the 'well' does not produce, and $500 of the sale price is to be used to go farther down into the hole already dug.

Roy has another set-back. Montenegro hurt his back, in bed for three weeks, Frances sick; before that the man who made the well was laid up for weeks. Also he did not make this article strong enough, more ply board had to be added. Just one damn thing after another.

A note re Phyllis, lest you forget she exists. Recently I questioned her isolation (Did you know she was my chela for a number of years?) thinking Roy might have wished it. She tells me she has achieved somewhat of "it will be to him as silver"; likewise "come unto me!" She has given up, for the present, any and all book work, Lodge attendance, etc., and is exploring first hand. This accounts for what was, to me, a state of purdah. She has dedicated herself to 111.

Let me go back to my diary of 1940, when I was performing Liber Samekh three times daily.

> At the West Phyllis came vividly before me (I have been going over her Diary for Probationer), and I realized her as one of The Chosen, the sacredness and holiness of her Yoni, and that she must regard herself as the custodian of a trust. (This is not a correct description; It was not Phyllis I saw, but this radiating Yoni.)

I wrote Aleister while at Winona I wanted Phyllis to go on from where I left off. Maybe something will yet come out of California?

I thank you for all the information contained in your letter re H.Q., the Brussells shipment, Hastings printer, etc.

---

[65] Dr. Gabriel Montenegro and John Eller were members of Agape Lodge.

Oh, a big, big item! Two days ago the heaviness of the summer, my weariness, dropped off my shoulders like a cloak! Strange, strange. I have had this sort of thing happen before, but never for three or four months.

Hugh returned a month ago, and his contribution will keep my contribution to H.Q. At $25 a month.

Love is the law, love under will.

Jane

May you find The Right Spot shortly!

K. J. GERMER
260 West 72nd Street
New York, N. Y.

October 15, 1948

Dear Jane,

93

In a hurry a few lines. I have just received a letter from one of A.C.'s attorneys in London back from the times of the suit Crowley vs. Constable in 1934. In the course of that action A.C. pawned to his attorney a lot of MSS. and books. I have received a list of the books which this man holds and he asks me for an offer on all or some of the items.

I wish I could buy the whole lot. As it is this is impossible. I am writing to him to give me details as to the various numbers of the Equinox and of *Book 4* parts 1 and 2. In the meantime I am sending you a copy of the list with the numbers given to me and one without.

Personally, I am interested in the *Winged Beetle* which does not appear on the market here any more, and *Book 4*, also a copy of *Rodin in Rime* which I do not have. I would like to have a copy of the *Sword of Song*, provided it is that large edition as I remember on excellent paper, the cover marked all over with 666's.

You might take this up with Ray who seems the only one who would be able to buy anything, and particularly with Paul Milliken who should return next week. I always wanted to have a set of the three 'Rasa's' again (with each one a drawing by Rodin), but the stuff from Belgium that just arrived contains a set. But I'm sure Paul would like a set and also a *Rodin in Rime*. Would it be possible to get Paul to go into the book interests, buy the whole lot get it over here, and gradually distribute it to dealers on the West Coast? I'll try to get full details on the stock.

Incidentally, I have not talked to Paul on financial help for either the printing of *Liber Aleph* etc. or the H.Q. The reason is simply that I am without any news whatever from the printer in Hastings and do not know where I stand.

One more word about Paul, as I failed to mention it in my last letter to you. What Paul experienced appears to me as a Tiphereth illumination; he told me some details which sound like the Beatific (lower beatific) Trance, and also the Universal Joke. If my assumption is correct he should pursue the important work of finding out how the H.G.A. speaks to his soul, increase his understanding of his language and communications, progress his intimacy with him so that at long last he may be able to face the higher ordeals.

93 93/93

Love to you, fraternally,

Karl

K. J. GERMER
260 West 72nd Street
New York, N. Y.

November 23, 1948

Dear Jane,

Do what thou wilt shall be the whole of the Law.

Re Ishrah: I think he should in any case make a formal application for a visa. Even if it takes 9 months, at least he has a quota number and from what I know the available visas take their turn. May-be by some chance a sponsor or two may be found in the meantime. Once we have the H.Q. definitely established I could perhaps give a pledge to house him or them when they arrive. We know well enough how hard it is for intellectuals to get placed unless they have connections, and try hard at any job, not their intellectual ones. We find as a general rule that the wife took a job in a factory (there are innumerable such cases in our Jewish acquaintanceship here) and supported the household, until the husband could establish himself. But Mrs. Schmolke is a dentist, and there is no reason why she could not work as a helper or assistant or some such thing to a dentist.

The two books I sent are a small payment for your devotion and spirit.

Paul: Of course, he'll come to you; give him what you can. We have met his wife and were not impressed; she could never understand his spiritual aspiration. Wait: you'll soon find how serious conflicts will develop because of incompatibility. Then is the time for him to watch and listen to the voice of his H.G.A.

What Paul could do is to give me some assistance for the H.Q., either as a temporary loan, or outright. After you have read my letter to Mildred of to-day you'll see my situation. A few hundred dollars would be of great help. – His job is to find out first the subtle whisperings of his H.G.A. Then learn his language and in what way He speaks to his soul – not to his brain! Then to follow him.

"The Wake World" is in *Konx Om Pax* which I thought you had? If not, Paul will oblige.

No word from Roy at all. I'll write him soon, too busy now, have been for many months. I don't like Phyllis' relations with Roy. I wish you'd have a talk with Jean who gives indications that the Rancho Royal camp is toying with Achad; perhaps already bound. I'll have to clarify that and see how Roy stands.

Please send me those things by Ishrah: the poem, astrological figures, sheets on Fire and War. I expect much from him, despite Frederic's opinion. – This is all, you'll see more from my letter to Mildred.

Love is the law, love under will.

With love, yours,

Karl

K. J. GERMER
260 West 72nd Street
New York, N. Y.

December 13, 1948

Mr. Ray Burlingame
4422 ½ Sunset Boulevard
Los Angeles, 27, Cal.

Care Frater,

Dear Ray,

Do what thou wilt shall be the whole of the Law.

Ever since that bad bubble broke concerning Lekve[66] and yours and Mildred's actions in the matter, I wanted to write you. I must tell you that this affair has deeply distressed me. much more than I can make clear to you in writing. You and Mildred have acted wrongly, much more so, however, Lekve. You two brought your usual fine and pure intentions into this, so that I acknowledge this gladly; yet you were rash, and without thinking your step over properly.

In the case of Lekve is it bad manners, and, worse dishonest thinking, and scheming. In fact, I have become convinced that he is temporarily somewhat insane in the strict sense as applied to such delicate magical and spiritual matters by the Master Therion. Lekve is in a severe magical crisis, and in a definite ordeal. There is no Thelemic literature about such cases in English. We have a very important and significant document in German which I have not yet taken steps to translate. Otherwise you would get an idea of what it is all about. Enough to say only that in such crises of a candidate certain steps are usually taken by the Order, and I may yet have to resort to them.

Soror Mildred in her last letter adds that 'it is not for me to understand'. True! How could she? Outside of Jane – and after the death of Max – and possibly Fra.:. E.Q.V., there is nobody in Agape Lodge who could. Nor can you. It has taken me a full year to wake up to the true situation from the magical point of view.

Here are a few plain facts: –

1. I am X° O.T.O. with a special Charter for all the Free German speaking countries.

2. I contacted Lekve immediately I heard his address from Ishrah almost 2 years ago.

3. I asked him immediately his standing in the A∴A∴ and O.T.O. He said he wanted to have nothing to do with the O.T.O. I came back to the matter in almost every letter during these two years.

---

[66] Friedrich Lekve, a correspondent of Germer living in Germany.

I went very far in all that I said; in fact I wanted to advance him quickly; I urged him a year ago to visit Frederic Mellinger in Bremen (only a distance of 80 miles from Hildesheim); I had prepared matters for Frederic to give him wisdom quickly if he found him right-minded; he refused and did not do anything. I despaired; the more so as he had all the Thelemic material, while Ishrah has not so much; yet Ishrah was fully acknowledged by the Master Therion in the Order, while he wrote about Levke that he had only appointed L. as 'his personal representative' which did not signify anything in matters of the Order, and thus was not curtailing Israh's position, or mine, or that of others in the Order. I kept on urging Levke, and finally told him plainly that the O.T.O. was not a plaything like other Orders, but had genuine knowledge and that he was only depriving himself of a vital part of the thelemic work. My last statement to him about this was mailed October 18, 1948.

4. He received this Oct. 22 or 23. Instantly he writes you by Airmail his long letter of Oct. 24, acknowledging to you in a distorted – to him flattering – way a phrase of mine. He says that it had been you (or Mildred) who had opened his eyes!!! in a recent letter – when I have done nothing else in the last 18 months! This is plain dishonesty, in order to camouflage his application to you.

5. I received no reply and so wrote to you both on Nov. 13th. At last I received a letter from him dated Nov. 5th, sent Ordinary Mail which came Dec. 10.

6. His action is all the more despicable as he had known for all this time that I was the Grand Master for Germany.

7. During my correspondence with him I tried to put at his disposal vital thelemic material which he did not have; I sent him copies; I promised him a set of the "Letters" on condition that he make them available to Ishrah – which you sent in part. (He has so far not sent Ishrah either the *Blue Equinox* which I need badly, nor any of the "Letters". Ishrah complained to me about L.'s

prevarication.) I tried to be, and was, as liberal and generous as possible and gave him all possible physical and spiritual help.

8. The fact is that he has the Achad-Smith-Mudd craze. He not only considers himself way beyond the Abyss, but also the coming great Establisher of Thelema, and the "child that is to be mightier than all the Kings of the Earth." It is tragic. And my flattery that I expect him to play a great role in Germany for Thelema fell – quite unconscious to me – on a ground that had been fertile for years for crazy illusions. He is jealous of me and shows it in many ways – which I unfortunately detected too late. He thinks he is the Big It, therefore his refusal to see a Brother of whom I had written to him that he was in the special high confidence of Therion, and one of the highest in the Order, which is the truth. Frederic with his deep and penetrating mind would have seen through the sham at once and called his bluff. Lekve is all right for the little girls and men with whom he has surrounded himself. He with his brass sword would have been bowled over instantly by the Steel blade of Frederic's. He felt and feared this instinctively.

Now, having torn down, let me build up.

Every candidate who aspires to a certain grade arrives – if it be his Will – at a certain critical point where he was to make up his mind to make the last sacrifice. This is described in several thelemic books. This decision is so terrific that there is none who does not falter, and if he persists and plunges on, has needs to become the prey of all the insane-making forces of the Universe. Only his past Karma, and the purity of his aspiration steeled by his clean living, and the strength of his Will can get him through. There is no possible appeal for help to his H.G.A. or to any entity whatever.

The candidate has to be left alone. In such cases Therion has always forbidden all contact with the candidate on penalty of expulsion from the Order. He himself gave the signal for the resumption of relations should the candidate have passed successfully; if not – well, good-bye!

If my theory is correct. And it has grown to conviction, all of Lekve's work will have to be destroyed; to be resurrected again after his passing, in a purified form fortified by the light – the True Light – obtained in the process. During my long exchange of letters I've seen many false conceptions of Thelema in Lekve's presentation; I corrected them; he argued; and, of course, resented my criticism, ascribed it to petty thoughts, and would rather keep in touch with you, drew you out, get the names of all other members of the Lodge, etc., etc. – all because he has this delusion that it is HE who will have to establish Thelema all over the world! But all this will fall by the wayside once a new Brother is born.

I am writing this via Jane who will understand better, and who will have to be informed, and pass the letter on to you personally. The letter is primarily addressed to you in your position in the O.T.O. I leave it to you to convey the matter to Mildred in the form you deem best, after careful consideration of all points. Mildred is peculiarly woman; she is attached to this German connection, obtained through me; she is alleviating suffering and hardships; always the fine prerogative of her sex. Its defect, however, among other things is that she is incapable of seeing or understanding the greater, Solar, point of view. I want to help Lekve. A woman wants to do so too. But a woman is incapable of knowing when her path would lead to disaster.

For the time being, continue by all means with food parcels but in a restricted way, as I suggested before. And in letters confine yourself to personal matters; you can explain to L. that this affair had led me to issue strict injunctions.

Love is the law, love under will.

Fraternally yours,

Karl
X° O.T.O.

Through Soror ESTAI.

5169 ¼ Fountain Avenue
Los Angeles, 27, California

January 1, 1949

Dear Karl:

Do what thou wilt shall be the whole of the Law.

I am sorry no end there has been so much delay in writing you, and that when I saw a letter was impossible, I did not forward a card of Solstice Greetings for you and Sascha. The comings and goings of this holiday season were most unusual and tiring.

During this time I kept a sort of diary for you and jotted down a few items as the days went by – explanatory notes re Ray and Mildred – only to discover to-day that what I was told in the first place by Ray, will not be fulfilled: i.e. that his insurance, his union dues, plus the needful clothing made it impossible to send the full amount, but from now on he would shoot through (his words) his usual contributions. Mildred now tells me that henceforth Ray will contribute only his dues.

Also: Mildred has resigned as Treasurer-Secretary pro tem, and will not assume any further Lodge duties. She is taking outside sewing to make some extra money, and "will be too busy" for these activities.

Rhea, who is spending the Holidays near Pomona with her daughter and family, spent a couple of hours with me Wednesday. During the conversation she scoffed at organization, but also remarked she had thought of joining the Mormons but found them too restrictive. No coffee, no cigarettes, etc., I mention this in connection with my last, in which Roy insisted that the family were staunchly for you.

So, you see things have been unfolding! And I wondered if you might not be unduly concerned about Jones!! I favor the O.T.O. rather than a new Order without A.C.'s Rituals? But I also speculate about the folding up of Agape Lodge, which trails so much with it: and make a fresh start. But how? where? with what people? Paul had one of pendulum swings lately, and decided to join. Mind you, it was Dorothy who had asked him to do so – she it was who telephoned me about the matter. But when Paul found she was not prepared to join with him, he said No, not at this time.

However, that is the first swing the Order direction. He will eventually come around I feel sure: he it is I would like to see eventually installed as Lodge Master. Or as a good Right Hand Bower. until he learns more.

Some time ago I copied *Ararita*. Would a copy be suitable for Ishrah?

Meanwhile Hugh Christopher (born Max Rosenau) has a big question mark in the picture. Before going east to Pa. to settle his mother's estate, he decided to take up *Liber Astarte* on this return: so wrote a sketchy ritual last summer. After his return he fumbled around during the Fall, but by latter part of October or early November he was under way – invoking Ra Hoor Khuit! "How can you approach Him?" Hugh: "He is defined through action. I have a healthy respect for That Fellow!" Through the following conversation, for the first time I achieved some understanding of "Fear of God is the beginning of wisdom" a statement which always puzzled me. Also, through this same conversation, I felt more in touch with the activities of R.H.K. Something to make one think!

Also, Hugh is set to raise the Beast – sensed some 2 or 3 years back, which experience kept our Hugh quiet for some time, for just that bit of power scared him.

I have looked for "The Pulse of Life" by Dane Rudhyar, but cannot find a copy, so I will send you mine next week, and meantime will order a copy for you as my name is in this one. For the season, Paul presented me with a copy of "Psychic Energy" by Dr. M. Esther Harding, pupil of Jung, this I will share with Hugh, as he is tiring of two hours steady work on Qabalah. I will continue a smaller content, say one hour, and finish the evening with "Psychic Energy".

One morning I read: "These two world spirits, which Greek philosophy called 'the growing' and 'the burning' stand in mortal combat, and we cannot foretell the outcome." Walking along the street later, thinking of this statement, I consciously lined myself up with R.H.K., heretofore an acceptance only. Something is becoming objectified in me? Jung's objective psyche? I may find out just what he means by this. "I am a black and terrible God; with courage conquering fear shall ye approach Me." Not in vain have I been working on *Liber Tzaddi* lo these several weeks. At least I am moving from my 'suspension in space' down into Jane, a source of considerable satisfaction, though a yawning abyss may lie before me.

Is it possible that this work may have somewhat to do with the reactions of lodge members, or former members? At present I feel (do let me say it!) like Christ driving out the money changers. I am beginning to get mad. And here I want to add an item, in case it has any value: I once told Mildred Russia and Communism meant more to her than Thelema. We will see.

Love is the law, love under will.

With all love and greetings to you both,

Jane

P.S. I feel we have pregnant months before us.

K. J. GERMER
260 West 72nd Street
New York, N.Y.

January 3, 1949

Dear Jane,

93

You would do me a favour by answering the enclosed letter received from Lekve to-day. I have made some marginal notes. I also enclose copy of his letter which he mailed to Mildred-Ray (which please give to them). I wonder what your opinion will be after you have gone through the letters. I'd appreciate your views.

I would suggest writing somewhat like this: –

"Fra. Saturnus has sent me your letter to him of Dec. 27 and yours to Mildred-Ray of Oct. 24, asking me to reply. Having been the Master Therion's chela, his personal secretary for many years, and in the closest possible touch with him for a quarter of a century, as well as a high-grade O.T.O. member, I may be somewhat qualified in pointing out certain things to you.

"What would you say in the German army if the general excites your interest in, and asks you to become an officer, takes a personal interest in you, and you try to sneak into the army by the back door by applying to the sergeant for admittance?

"Your letter to him, and yours to the Burlingames show discrepancies. In (2) of your letter you say that not in a single case were you invited to join the Order, while on p. 3 of your letter to Burlingame you say the very contrary! Fra. [Saturnus] told me that you kept writing him emphatically that you refused to become a member of the O.T.O., or in fact, of any Order.

"Fra. [Saturnus] asked all of us a year ago to come to the help of the German brethren and it was so arranged that the Burlingames undertook to send you parcels. When you misunderstood this gesture and tried to take up closer magical relations with them, Fra. [Saturnus] pointed out to you that this was inadmissible, and you promised not to continue efforts along such lines. Your application for membership in the way you made it shows how little you keep your word.

"We all of us have been connected with the efforts of establishing the Law of Thelema for years; many of us have had to suffer for it acutely. Let me tell you as the senior member of the Order that we will never be able to carry out our high goal if we would show such lack of discipline and due subordination to just authority, tact and good manners, as you do in such crucial cases. In your best interest I hope you will take this experience to heart."

Sign with your magical Motto, without giving your name.

I am hurrying this off before I leave on a business trip tomorrow. Use your own judgment in wording your letter and return his letter to me with a copy of your letter to him. I cannot think of another way to deal with this case. (I am in correspondence with him for other thelemic matters.) Do not let yourself be drawn into further letters to him.

93 93/93

Ever yours,

Karl

K. J. GERMER
260 West 72nd Street
New York, N. Y.

January 3, 1949

Dear Jane,

93

    I think I still have not answered yours of Dec. 11, and now comes yours of Jan. 1st at the moment when I'll have to go away on a business trip. Generally speaking I have to neglect my correspondence until I'll get some sort of secretary. That, in turn depends on the H.Q. being ready for living; and that, I hope, will be by the end of this month. Until then I'm handicapped all around.
    No letter from Roy to two, I think, of mine.
    No word from Mildred re resignation as Treasurer. It might be necessary to go back to the old system of each one to send M.O. direct to me?
    What is so bad is gossip and unnecessary talk. I believe that Rhea is O.K. for Thelema at the bottom of her mind. But seen from

this distance, several remarks made from various members of the Rancho camp, make one feel sit up, and watch. I wish all of the isolated members or former members would talk to you from time to time.

Is there any word from Jean Cooper? I've sometimes been thinking of her. I suspect that her in-laws are devout catholics; and that would put her to severe tests. Is there any way to help her? She started so well.

Still, I feel that the only one among all Agape Lodge members who is doing work regularly is Jean. And she is the only one of whom I can say that she shows signs of making progress on the path. There must be an insistence on Work; otherwise nothing moves, but stagnates!!

I agree with what you say about O.T.O. vs. a new Order. However, A.C.'s Constitution is for the 'Order of Thelemites'. No importance now. It'll have to be discussed at the proper time and with leisure. Some sort of foundation for a new start of Organisation of an Order will have to be made. May-be this year? May-be 1950, which the Pope calls the 'Holy Year'; of which I have long been expecting something important.

Yes, by all means, send Ishrah copy of *Ararita*; also if you have the time, of *Liber Trigrammaton*.

Hugh: – R.H.K.: let him not forget *The Heart of the Master* which contains aspects of the complex problem of diving deeper. – What do you mean when you say: "Hugh is set to raise the Beast, etc." I'd like to know more about this. Never forget that *The Book of the Law* always speaks of "The Beast", and the Thou always means this generally. Aleister Crowley has no place in this scheme of things. Thus the death of the mortal body of the tool used by the author of *The Book of the Law* has no bearing whatever on the teachings of *Liber AL*. The Beast is a four-dimensional being, who did not die (excuse me for being so trite!), but which is active and very much alive, and operative all the time.

Re your paragraph at the end of "Two world spirits": – Why not? Study A.C.'s poem "The Twins" in *The Winged Beetle* (I recommended it to Ishrah some time ago); but there are many other passages in A.C.'s writings bearing on the matter of what I always used to call the ball players scheme of the Universe. If you want to play ball you have to have two. So also in the Universe. And in *The Book of the Law* we have the Beast and the Scarlet Woman; in nature: female and male; Nu and Had; *LXV* and *VII* are replete with this fact that there must be two who create Adonai: the Heart and the Serpent (I tried to show this up in my two lectures in L.A.) And Nuit says "None and two", "for I am divided for love's sake", etc. – I am not quite clear myself when it says "The half of the Word of Heru-ra-ha, called Hoor-pa-kraat and Ra-Hoor-Khut", which means, I think, a twin division of the central conception which unites the two. Somewhere, I can't remember at the moment, A.C. has more on this subject.

I'm sure Patricia MacAlpine[67] would take second-hand clothes and shoes. Anything. She is very poor.

Your remarks about the circumstances of Max-Jean-Georgia-the Ranch, do not cover the facts. But I'm too busy. Jean knows all about that phase, may have the day by day facts in her diary. I remember that Max refused point blank to be moved to Rhea; for one thing.

I've just taken steps to get the cases of A.C.'s material shipped to the H.Q., though it is too early, but I was to impatient.

Love is the law, love under will.

I thought I did send you the Greetings of the Solstice, but it seems now it was done only in my mind. Let us forget such formalisms as Xmas and New Year!

Give my love from both of us to Mary K. and there is lots of it for you!

Karl

---

[67] Patricia ("Deirdre") MacAlpine was Aleister Crowley's final companion, and the mother of his son Aleister Ataturk.

K. J. GERMER
260 West 72nd Street
New York, N. Y.

January 22, 1949

Dear Jane,

Do what thou wilt shall be the whole of the Law.

Thanks for yours of Jan. 19 with M.O. for $25.00.
The arrangement was that 50% of dues at Agape Lodge go to Grand Lodge. This means that you should have sent me $7.50 instead of $11.00, thus $3.50 too much. Please deduct from next.
Montenegro: – March 21, 1904 began An I, 1. 1926 began An II,1. Thus 1948 should have begun An III, 1. The fact is that A.C. does not seem to have kept a correct tab on the counting. His counting varies. The Fall 1947 Word carries An I, xxl while it should have been II, xxll. – Again, I have only some 'Words' going back to 1926 and 1929 which carry II, 1, 2, etc. A.C. seems often to have either made a mistake or neglected to count systematically, or accurately. May-be when I get his diaries and other papers it'll throw further light on this matter. Meanwhile, I suggest to disregard this matter, at least for the time being. It is quite possible that A.C. finally decided to call 1904 1, 2, 3, etc. That he began 1926 with I, 1, 2, 3, etc., which would make 1947 I, 22, the way I count. 22 is of course the number of the Hebrew etc, alphabet, and has other connotations.
Ra Hoor Khuit? Roy's calling him the Representative of the Sun is quite correct. It is possible that the precession of the Zodiac gives a ruler of the affairs of the Earth once in 2000 years. That the Gods choose a God to represent Them during such a period. That in 1904 the job fell on Ra Hoor Khuit. According to *The Book of the Law* He would be the child of a conjunction of Nuit and Hadit. His qualities are explained on several occasions of A.C.'s works: Force and Fire, etc. but read *Equinox of the Gods* p. 70 sq. – *The Heart of the Master* can also be used for throwing light. Sorry I cannot be more helpful. I think the nature of RHK will only

gradually unfold as He shows Himself in the management of the affairs of the planet.

Love is the law, love under will.

I enclose three photos of the house and barn. It'll give a general idea. I wish you'd circularize them, or show them, including Jean and Ero when they are in town. The young infant is giving plenty of headaches, and I'm thinking of nothing else.

Love to you,

Karl

The lone figure shivering on the Porch or Patio to the right of the one of the photos is Sascha. There are 5 beautiful tall pines in front of the House which are not visible.

Los Angeles

February 3, 1949

Dear Karl:

Do what thou wilt shall be the whole of the Law.

    I thank you for yours of the 20th, 22nd, and 27th January, with the enclosed 3 snapshots of H.Q. and the two examples of Ataturk's work. These I will return when all have seen them.
    Also M.O. for $39 is enclosed. At present Ray is sending his dues only.
    Yes, the 6 copies of the Stele of Revealing arrived safely. Paul, Hugh and Jane so far. Lekve sent the B's 11, which they are

keeping for "new members", Montenegro being one such. Some 2 years ago Ray had the Stele reproduced, and the various members got copies from him.

A sewing job came Mildred's way which paid her $10, and with this she sent a Care parcel to Scotland. I am getting together a box of clothing to go Friday or Saturday.

Enclosed are further charts by Ishrah, one (or possibly two) a duplicate. And I mailed him last week a copy each of *Ararita* and *Liber Trigrammaton*. If you wish copies please let me know. I would like to type *Liber LXV,* as I have never done so, but that is beyond me at present. Some day, perhaps, spreading it over the weeks.

Now for Hugh. Thursday, the 27th, he came for his study and discussion period. First he unburdened himself of some things at his home, but seeing them as tests which he needs; after that in a talk about the Heart of the Master – especially "The Sensibility of the Universe is the Triumph of thine Imagination", he gradually passed into a state of –

> To-and-fro pulsation" moving his body with the rhythm –"where everything that is to happen has already happened" – "strange, there is neither Time nor Space!" – "take your hands off unfoldment, let it unfold" – become aware of where you are headed" – "If the observer I enjoy the action, if one-with I am part of the to-and-fro."

His mood was strong enough to cause me to partake, slightly, and for just a moment, of this one-with – that sensibility that is active participation.

'Take your hands off' recalls Jung's interpretation of Wu-Wei – not doing, letting be. The positive aspect of inertia, non-doing. Whereas it reminded me strongly of Laotze, what I said notwithstanding was "This sounds like the Hindu Nirvana." Hugh said, "I must put it on the Tree of Life." I then asked whether it might not be the core of each Sephira, the Paths being the attainment (which he had said was meaningless). I can now see my use of 'attainment' was careless, that I should have said, the Paths consisted of the going.

I hope this doesn't take too much of your precious time, but I would like you to keep in touch with the doings of these folks.

Paul's mind is interesting to me as I see him using it in various situations. Wednesday evening, the 26th Jan., he brought in a man to see me and have a talk. He has another in tow with a list of questions (!!) He discusses Crowley writings whenever he can get an audience, and now has three copies of *Little Essays*, which he uses to loan.

Hugh's angle as I now see it is a release of considerable power. For what? When he first comes he speaks rather steadily, as he tires – after an hour, say – the stuttering begins. But some day he will quit it entirely I feel sure.

By the way, Hugh said when he came, "All day I have been spiritually hot." Before leaving he said, "I'm getting afraid of myself." He didn't want to go home but finally picked up his papers, magazines, etc. and took his leave.

I will set up the Treasurer's report shortly, I hope, and send it along. The books, etc., are still with Roy in Temple City. He was to have been over a week ago, but had a bad stomach upset which kept him at home.

Tell Sascha I was delighted to see the back anyhow of the shivering figure on the porch.

Love is the law, love under will.

Best of love to you both.

Jane

K. J. GERMER
260 West 72nd Street
New York, N. Y.

February 21, 1949

Dear Jane,

Do what thou wilt shall be the whole of the Law.

We spent the first weekend at the House and though Sascha was shocked to tears of despair when she saw the place of desolation, we stayed with a minimum of comfort. But it was warm at least. No furniture yet. The workmen are still not finished.

But I opened the cases and unpacked and stored the books and MSS. etc. in the separate room by the barn, setting up boards to serve as some sort of shelves. Naturally, I have only had time to take a peek at the contents. It is vast, and will take months to even start listing the material. I should have a helper, a good Thelemite who knows the literature – published and unpublished – and a typist. When the time is ripe, which it is not – I'm sure the proper assistants will be there.

There is a peculiar co-incidence – if you like to call it that – Last week I was notified that the Urn and little casket with A.C.'s ashes had arrived. After some delays and formalities with the Customs I was able to pick up the box last Friday. Saturday morning we went for our first week-end at the house, and I set up the Urn in the little room where I have put A.C.'s material in the midst of A.C.'s works! Sascha marveled at the 'co-incidence' and said: Aleister did not want to let us go and sleep in the house – for which he had wished so ardently and so long – without him. Incidentally, my plans, or shall I say our plans are to transform the barn into the real H.Q. at some time after the house itself has been made habitable and the funds are available. I say 'our plans' because Sascha has pledged herself to help me do it. She did it in a formal, or magical way and I told her that such a formal act given to the Gods and accepted by Them is an altogether different kind of a pledge than a simple promise or resolution. I warned, or forewarned her that instantly the obstacles would arise to make her weaken or swerve; make it seem crazy or impossible; but if she would overcome these hindrances and fight through to the end, her very wish would not only be accomplished but the the Gods who put the obstacles in her path would help her in the end and give her on top, and plenty.

I am mentioning this in connection with Paul. You wrote recently in a letter when Paul gave you that $50 check that he phoned you a day or so later that he did not want to bind himself by that for the future or words to that effect. May-be he is afraid that he tie himself down by that act and is afraid of future consequences. I had seen the same trait in Max often. He did not want to give a positive pledge as to monthly regular contributions. All he allowed himself to do was to say that he wanted to give as much as he could. He had not understood what I have mentioned above. That, once he would have given the definite pledge, and, instead of weakening the moment the first hurdle appeared on the horizon (which automatically come when a magical pledge is given), he would set his teeth and with tremble, fear and apprehension think and worry of nothing but how he can overcome the difficulty, the Gods would have rushed in to help him. All They look at is: "how does the candidate behave at the first obstacle We set up?" They are out to test the grit of the patient, and nothing else.

The problem of magical responsibility comes in here too. One must run forward spontaneously in an emergency. I hope you understand the magical basis of these my considerations. It applies also to such other planes as "making reports". I had some correspondence with Jean lately about this point. She wrote it was better to keep one's mouth shut, because always one is let down if one tried to report on a given situation (her experience was Rhea, Georgia, Roy, Ruthie, etc. but she recalled Max's reports on W.T.S., Jack, etc. I tried to point out to her what is spiritually involved. One should not let one's deeper urge be frustrated by any considerations. "That is sin to hold thy Holy Spirit in". The rule is simply: is one judging situations with a pure heart and motive? All the rest is unimportant. Courage, moral courage, is one of prerequisites of any Magician.

If somebody who is being reported on is angry, he or she simply shows that they are not true Thelemites, who are sworn to be truthful to themselves. They should consider the report, when they learn of it, as a message from the H.G.A. to mend their ways, to study the complaint, if any, and be ultimately grateful to the reporter, for having by their action called their attention to a defect in their physical, mental, moral, spiritual or magical make-up. The H.G.A. is all the time around a candidate and sends him messages. If He sees that his beloved is too dense to react to his impulses, He uses others to use means that will penetrate. Somebody who does his practices regularly prepares the aura in such a way that it is pure, clean, and permits rays from above to penetrate easily and directly without the need for an outsider to be used as a medium.

Now Paul's fear of committing himself definitely to something well defined and pledged, is weakness on some plane or planes. He is now accepted by his H.G.A. and he must learn to live up to his calling, and go on!

I wrote Paul to-day, sending him a copy of de luxe ed. of

OLLA
Fun of the Fair
The City of God
The Heart of the Master
Pamphlet by the Compte de Fenix (pseudonym of A.C.'s)

which I have been able to pick out for him. I'm sending them to him as a compliment, of course.

The above magical thoughts which came spontaneously into the typewriter, might be good; may-be you can use them, for they do not seem to be understood by many. Roy's problem falls under this heading too!

Love is the law, love under will.

Ever yours,
Karl

March 21, 1949

Dear Roy,

The Greetings of the Equinox of Spring!

Do what thou wilt shall be the whole of the Law.

Thanks for yours of March 17th. – First, let me say: if you quote scriptures, quote correctly; but if you quote *Liber Legis* quote it super-duper, or not at all! "Change not as much as the style of a letter!" I refer to your quotation on page 2. – Let me go immediately *in medias res*.

The crucial point that strikes me, and from which stem so many false conceptions, is this: Nu says in Verse 28 "None . . . and two" "For I am divided for love's sake, for the chance of union", while you emphasize the heresy of the Old Aeon of the "One", or the "I, that is God"; (you do not seem to say this in such words, but the idea seems to pervade your thought). "My prophet is a fool with his one, one, one . . . and none by the Book"? This "none" is attained in the union of two. A.C. wrote on this extensively and repeatedly (see the Letter on Zero equals 2).

This is where we are fundamentally different from all old religious teachings, so it seems to me. I tried to go into this particularly when giving my talks on *LXV* in L.A. The division into two separate entities is there shown as the "Heart" and the "Serpent". They two unite and what remains? Nought or Adonai, or what you wish to call it for the argument's sake, but not "God" or "I". It is this state of Nothingness which is the goal to attain, and is attained in Samadhi, or further still in the higher states.

Study *LXV* and *VII* carefully on that point, I pray you. It recurs again and again in every chapter, mostly many times in every chapter. The emphasis then, and the focus of A.C.'s message has been "Attain to the Knowledge and Conversation of the (Perhaps better "Thy") H.G.A." This H.G.A. is a separate entity from your own Star Soul. It is almost as if each one of us had a twin Star-Soul (Dante: Beatrice; Goethe: Gretchen) who is riding his or her twin in the human flesh, loving it, teaching and guarding it, preventing it from making too gross mistakes, whispering into its ear and despairing if the manifested twin will not listen, or learn to hearken to the voice that speaks to the very depth of its soul.

In the 20th Aethyr this guide is given to the soul for the first time more or less closely. From that Aethyr on the intimacy of the communion between the two entities will increase to inconceivable heights, if the incarnated soul is chosen. That 20th Aethyr seems to correspond more or less with the attainment of the $5°=6°$). It is the lowest form. The path from there, even as far as the 18th, 19th, 17th, 16th is tremendous; for it is said that the farther one advances in the Aethyrs, the longer and harder it takes from one to the next.

The whole object of our system is then to learn to know, and then to learn the language of, and then to intensify the intimacy with, the H.G.A., who is a thing that really exists on some 4th dimension, and may be incarnated, but unknown to the twin as such. That is the vital fact to get into one's blood: that this incarnated existence is only an image of the existence on the higher planes. That is where the actual life is, where wars are fought, etc., etc., etc., where Life and events on this planet are prepared and planned from possibly thousands of years ago. We should train ourselves to live on those planes and grow to partake of it.

These considerations will also answer some of your other points. "Gods", Secret Chiefs, the "Devil" and all the rest can only be experienced by such trainings of the mind as Yoga, etc. (I, personally like the Devil; don't forget: I never was a Christian; I never read the bible; I never understood what "Sin", "original Sin" etc. was) On the Gods, Secret Chiefs, etc. but also on the H.G.A. A.C. took pains to write at length in his "Letters". They all actually exist, and are different from each other. They have infinitely more power than for instance the H.G.A., who may be himself advanced as a soul or not. Your bus driver's H.G.A. will possibly be less advanced than that of, say. a true artist, who may have gone through thousands of previous incarnations. But read and study the "Letters" on that.

I also refer you to a passage in the Equinox, No. 1, 2 or 3, I think, where the adept advances up the mountain, up the snows, and finally it turns out that the devil who kept seducing him, was

God Himself! This is really basically the idea that has been with me from my reading of the old German Mystics.

The "Gods", "Secret Chiefs" that you mention on p. 2, are then actually doing Their stuff; They have plans, in which poor little Saturnus, or Roy are expected to do some job; if we don't, They rap us over the knuckles. As Above, so below! Isn't all that very natural? Wouldn't you do the same thing if you are a good voice teacher? But there is no mystery about it? – What you say in the third last par. on page 2, seems very good. Still, I believe it would be wise to assimilate the thought that there are Powers in the Universe with consciousness who are directing and supervising events with vigilance and planfully. So as on this plane there are minds from the lowest savage to the finest flowers of art, science, and thought, so does it rise higher and higher on unmanifested planes. Don't forget, even Adonai, such a vast entity, says in *LXV*, I, v.8: "I who am the Image of an Image say this". – Yes: "Bother the Gods!" Why not? But learn first to understand who They are; sometimes They don't care if you say or think that: sometimes They DO! It depends on the frame of your mind.

Glad to hear what you say about the loyalty of the Rancho group! Even more if you can finish the house which I remember well. And for initiations it seems ideal! Keep me informed on the progress. I remember that it was 32' x 16'. I took the measurements at the time.

April 4, 1949

I was interrupted, and will now continue, if I can.

I wish you would give me again a clear statement on the Rancho property. You have given this several time, and 666 was often worried about how serious you took it. Believe me: I am not personally interested in that angle. But the situation should be unmistakably clear from the point of view of the Order.

The Rancho place would be valuable as a second storage room for books MSS. and papers; secondary to the H.Q. here. We have had the warning example of 1923 when all of A.C.'s diaries, books, and papers were seized by the Customs in London (ask Jane!). We have had two examples in Germany when my stuff was seized; and later when I.W.E.'s books and MSS., and all translations – her work of a lifetime – in short all her thelemic material was seized and destroyed by the Gestapo. The same happened to some other brethren in Germany. Who knows but that the same might not happen again.

We are already guarding against this. One set of all of 666's books, MSS., copies of diaries and papers, are being concentrated each in two separate places – in USA and in Europe. The way the hostility to Thelema will explode some day (soon?) makes it advisable to have my place here not as the only collection. I have been thinking of sending you or to some one else on the West Coast a part of the stock that has arrived so far. In case of fire or incendiary at my end, for example, a secondary collection of duplicates should be safe elsewhere. What is your view? What facilities could you offer?

Do I possess a complete list of your (personal) books and MSS.? I think you promised it but did not send it. (I have the list of what is the property of the Order (Agape Lodge)).

See what you can do about the IV° by the help of Jane.

I am all in accord with what you say about initiations on the Desert. I hope this need not long be delayed now. – I hear you are getting water?

Aleister Ataturk's[68] education keeps worrying me. After my appeal some months ago I received $22 from Agape Lodge on Feb. 18. Since then nothing. I have managed to scrape the $200 together needed for the early February payment. I have just heard that the remaining payments of $200 each will become due early May and the last in September. I must have help for them! Sacha and I are and will be tied up with obligations for the H.Q. to the breaking point. My attempt to open up other avenues for A.A. have only been partly successful. The main burden should be borne by members of the Order! (Can we not sell some books to get some cash in? I have 'Hearts of the Master', 'City of God', 'The Fun of the Fair'; one or two sets of "Magick in Theory and Practice"; several copies of the 'Tarot'; 'Olla', and 'Little Essays'

---

[68] Aleister Crowley's son with Patricia MacAlpine, who was later in the care of Germer and other members of O.T.O.

some other books. You have still a lot of copies of 'Eight Lectures', and 'Little Essay'. Do try and sell a few!

I am waiting for your report on Monte and Phyllis.

Thanks for your good wishes! We both reciprocate them for yourself and your Rancho camp.

Love is the law, love under will.

Karl

Just had a letter from Georgia. She (with Joe) is making good progress in developing the Miller property into a self-sustaining thing. Is there no bridge across?

K. J. GERMER
260 West 72nd Street
New York, N. Y.

May 11, 1949

Dear Jane,

Do what thou wilt shall be the whole of the Law.

Address of Hollander: I wrote him to-day asking him for a suggestion to get over the difficulties of sending the books back and forth and the long time I'd be without them.

Yours of May 5th: Thank you for M.O. of $53.00. With this, and Jean-Ero's special contribution, plus the announced school fund, I should be able to transfer the May school fees for A.A.[69] Thanks to all of you.

---

[69] Germer is here referring to Aleister Ataturk, not the Order A∴A∴.

I do hope Montenegro's health will improve. I notice that Madera is up north, probably closer to the mountains, and he may be able to build up a new practice. He might also be able to keep in touch with Grady when he visits San Francisco which seems to be nearer than L.A.

Whenever you should need any books write me.

I am sorry to hear about your health, but hope you feel better now. Sascha gets frequent messages from 666, intended for herself and me. There has been some sort of a warning as though there was a phase of magical attacks. But they must be expected, faced, passed, and taken in stride. We must have the firm confidence that our Work is in the hands of the Gods. The Secret Chiefs are watching it, and those who live in this Work without deviating from the lines laid down, and doing the practices regularly, will have automatic protection. Those who fall down and do not live up to their Work will feel it soon enough.

But do take care of yourself! I don't know what would happen without you to the Work on the West Coast. The more months go by the more I realise what Max's loss has been. His work is living after him, it is true, but his stature has not been equalled, and we badly need someone who has his deep understanding, his devotion, and his knowledge of A.C.'s teachings.

The last paragraph of your letter: No, I don't quite know what you refer to in your 'subtle breathing'. Don't forget that I am awfully dumb in the understanding of the technical outer, conscious, side of the magical-spiritual training system. I am there, but there is a veil, a thick veil, that hides my real knowledge from my outer consciousness.

All our – Sascha and mine – best wishes to your speedy complete recovery!

Love is the law, love under will.

Karl

The H.Q. is a lonely place. How I wish you could live there for a few months & take a complete rest! K

5169 ¼ Fountain Avenue
Los Angeles, 27, California

May 22, 1949

Dear Karl:

Do what thou wilt shall be the whole of the Law.

    I thank you for yours of the 11th.

    The School Fund. Roy tells me Monty[70] is not in a position to continue his contribution: the house bought in Madera, which, fortunately provides both living and office accommodations, and various expenses connected with the move north. Madera is nearer San Francisco, and I hope Monty will see Grady. He did not meet him here.

    I thank you for what you say about 666. I accept the fact of attacks; also that the weakest spot is the one to give way, and the state of my health lies at my own door. Long years of physical abuse and neglect, plus emotional unbalance, cash in sooner or later. I am one of those folks who never liked himself or herself. I should not say 'never' for it may have taken root after I went to New York.

    But be that as it may, I have had interesting experiences and acquired some knowledge during the period which shall both fortify and ease me, I am sure. If and when I get around to typing, my diary might be of some interest.

    Breath. I cannot explain, now at least, just what is back of my sensing of 'breath' beyond the human breath: I thought you might know what I was talking about. That I sensed it would seem to indicate that the knowledge can be attained? That it is important to attain it?

    Again, the word "substance" bounced from the page when reading something about Space. This word fastened itself in my mind; I use it in pranayama.

---

[70] Gabriel Montenegro

Also, when reading *The Heart of the Master* I came upon "The Voice of the Vulture". Came upon, because it stopped me short; I got no further. It, too, fastened itself in my mind.

Is this not an open pathway for me to follow? So I practise pranayama with Substance as the key. Unattainable, no doubt, but – as Aleister would say – the practise, the delving, the concentration will exercise the will at least.

Let me add one other item. During my G.M.R.[71] I attained and kept for quite a time what Aleister described as the "spirit breath". There was no consciousness of its meaning.

And yet, I frequently forget the work!

I hope to write next time about the Group and Roy; I have a report from Hugh, I want what Paul and Bud have to say, as I am trying to get hold of Roy – get more facts.

Love is the law, love under will.

All love to you and Sascha,

Jane

K. J. GERMER
260 West 72nd Street
New York, N. Y.

August 17, 1949

Dear Jane,

Do what thou wilt shall be the whole of the Law.

Yours of Aug. 11, 12, and 15. Thanks for the M.O. for $45.00!

---

[71] Great Magical Retirement

The news about Roy hit us both deeply. I hardly know what to say. If it is true what Mildred wrote that he had a stroke, I can only hope that he will recover completely and quickly and then go at it with renewed vigour. Who knows but that this has been lingering for some time? It would solve the riddle that has puzzled me for five months, that he wrapped himself up in complete silence since I wrote him last on March 21. I enclose copy of this. Please read it, return it, and give me any comment if you have any. Do you notice anything in my letter to which he could have taken exception?

I enclose a letter to Roy from me and Sascha; I'm sure you'll have means of transmitting it to him.

Dion Fortune[72] has been in fairly close relations with A.C. over the years. There is quite a file of letters at H.Q. which, when I have the time, I will look at more closely. All the recent books of A.C.'s as well as unpublished ones, such as "Aleister Explains..."[73] were the subjects of discussions. I have not seen a single book of hers as yet. Considering the correspondence between them it is hard to imagine that she should not have visited him frequently. – Regardie was in her outfit at one time back in 1930 or so as the files show; there are letters of his to her; I have not read a single book of his, but have an idea that there is more to this.

As for your continuing your group, I think you should do this as best, and with as much vigour, as you can, without lust of result, and keep a circle of Thelemites, if only budding Thelemites, as it were like glowing ashes under the fire. As long as there are live ashes extant on the West Coast, there is always the chance that by the grace of God some wind might blow it into a roaring flame. I cannot do much in this phase; I, or shall I say we – Sascha and I – are too much and too exclusively absorbed by our work at H.Q. – Jean wrote me recently of her thought of seriously coming to H.Q. During her vacation of three weeks. I wish she'd come and stay

---

[72] Violet Firth (aka Dion Fortune) was a prominent occultist, author, and correspondent of Aleister Crowley.

[73] "Aleister Explains Everything" was the original working title of *Magick Without Tears*.

with us. When she is back she can give you all a better pictures of the place and what we are doing.

My thoughts come always back to Roy's case. The second case in two years after Max! I hope it will not become as serious. His loss is still felt by me as irreplaceable. Roy must very much take care of himself to avoid a relapse after his recovery!

Love is the law, love under will.

Karl

P.S. I'll send you a set of the Holy Books; and, when ready, a copy of that "Preliminary Analysis" of *LXV*. I will have copies for sale.

5169 ¼ Fountain Avenue
Los Angeles, 27, California

September 1, 1949

Dear Karl:

Do what thou wilt shall be the whole of the Law.

First, let me say I was wrong in saying Roy maintained something about the "one god". Paul said my interpretation was wrong: that Roy held to 'no God'. Now, *Liber VII* is full of "My God". If you have the time, would you please give me an explanation of this?

Also, is your H.G.A. the same as Jung's "Anima"? I think Jung would so designate Beatrice and Gretchen? According to him, the Anima eventually abides with the attained man.

Now then, Roy: I was over Tuesday for the first time. Frances said in the beginning, "No visitors. I will let you know when you may come over." Monty spent 3 nights there and was shocked that Frances and her sister were carrying on alone. Roy is so uncooperative, he wants Frances and Frances only, morning, noon, and night. And she refuses to, or cannot, lay down the law to him. Her sister can do this nicely and effectually, but she has her husband and her own duties, and, too, no doubt thinks Roy is not her particular job. So the burden falls on Frances, who lets Roy get away with murder.

Illustration: He refuses the bed pan, will not use a bedside substitute, and insists on going to the toilet – an arm over the shoulder of either woman, they an arm under each leg, to carry him there. No sedatives, because of de-hydration; so he "cat-naps". He is in pain with his throat and cannot understand why the pain cannot be stopped, etc., etc.

I took on for half an hour only when there. Frances asked me to go to the studio to separate the books, his and those of the Lodge, and look over other things there preparatory to vacating it. I was there from 10 to half-past 4, and got home utterly exhausted, tumbled into bed at seven or a little after, and slept 11 hours.

The Leffingwell family will not – nor indeed can! – do a thing – beyond paying the doctor bills by the daughter in the North, for Roy won't have Rhea near him! It's a mess all round.

But enough of this. I was shocked when I saw him. The doctors say there should be a change in about 2 weeks. ? ? ? ? Frances meantime wonders why "the Order can't do something for him". Poor girl, she doesn't realize everything involved in Roy's case. My sympathies are with her, but you know how we stand here. Paul gave $10 and I gave $10.

Schmolke. Mary K. reached her limit some few months ago, about $300 up to that time, so I send him, once a month, 2 lbs of coffee, some tea, a tin of shortening, etc., about $3 worth of food, plus transportation. According to their letters, they have their eyes on California, but this may be solely to flatter Jane. You will know.

Love is the law, love under will.

My best to your and Sascha,

Jane

K. J. GERMER
260 West 72nd Street
New York, N. Y.

September 6, 1949

Dear Jane,

Do what thou wilt shall be the whole of the Law.

 Yours of Sept. 1. Meanwhile you should have received my letter of Aug. 31st through Jean. – It answers part of yours of Sept. 1. We cannot be responsible for messes created by people themselves. I myself consider the ranch the best place to recover if that is possible. We all have had to make concessions. –
 Re Jung. I don't know anything about Jung's philosophy. I just cannot imagine that he can reach up to insights given by 93. – But we have a very interesting recent case. Our leading brother in Germany, the one appointed by I.W.E. as her successor, Lekve, who has built up an "Abbey of Thelema"; who has quite a following and is preaching the Law actively, was a strict follower of Jung. In fact he misinterpreted the H.G.A. conception in such a way that I had to write him some pretty harsh letters, with the result that he tried to turn to Mildred-Ray, etc. etc. One eminent man in Germany who was in touch with Lekve, a scholar, wrote me that he had to drop L. because L. was too exclusively sold on Jung, while he thought that certainly a man like Crowley must have a deeper philosophy and one that could not be squeezed into that of a man like Jung –
 I was not a little surprised that Lekve wrote me in his last letter (3 weeks ago) very humbly (after having been quite cocky before) that he had had an illumination in which among other things a voice shook him and told him "I AM, not YOU"! In a blinding flash he realized that his former conception that the H.G.A. was but a function of the Psyche in the sense of Jung, was wrong, and that mine was right. I.e. (in his words) "that the H.G.A. is a living Being of such ineffable qualities compared to which the conception of the 'Self' shrinks to a mere phantom". Etc.etc. – But

do read *LXV* and *VII*. 'Also I beheld my God and the countenance of Him...' Chapter IV, *LXV*. *Liber VII* is the love song from one God to another. – (Who create Zero).

I had thought that A.C. in "Aleister Explains Everything" had made all this abundantly clear. There are 'Secret Chiefs', 'Gods', etc. and also the H.G.A., all described under different headings. He also uses the term 'The Masters'. It is a matter of initiation to understand all these things from the inside out.

In fact, Lekve has now to drop all the 'Lections' he had had printed. I had told him that his conception was unthelemic. But I hold nothing against him. We all of us have to GROW through mistakes and false early conception. If you reach those silent cold higher planes: how much have not A.C.'s conceptions changed since you knew him! All we want is that we do GROW, and reach through fog and cloud the fount of Light. 'Come up through the creeks to the fresh water, I shall be waiting for you with my kisses.' The trouble begins when one like Jones, and others, set up a false God, and are led to disaster.

Agape Books at Roy's. I wrote about this Aug. 31. Yours of Sept. answers much about this and makes it easier. But I realise the amount of physical work it has meant for you. Do please enlist the help of Mildred in such cases, or whom else you can find. I am very eager to hear more about this angle. Especially also about the 'Rituals and paper' that Rhea wrote me she took away and to the ranch. I presume there are also a lot of Lodge books at the ranch? In my letter to Jean I said it might be wise to take and store anything she picks up at the ranch with Georgia's. That was meant only for convenience's sake, as I thought Jean's & Ero's quarters are too cramped.

Please make a complete and exact list of all the papers you collect. We must act businesslike. Even in such trifles. And whatever you have collected (and Jean) hang on to it and don't hand anything over to anybody without my o.k. I'll be glad, and it may be necessary anyway, to appoint you as temporary Head of Agape Lodge and direct representative of Grand Lodge during the phase of Roy's incapacitation.

I'm afraid I can't do much for Ishrah. I'd love to and may send him another parcel. But I have so many obligations that I have to concentrate strictly on the first call. Please tell me if you or anyone else is still sending parcels to others, such as Aleister Ataturk? I've got yo send parcels to Ruth Schneckenburger (Lekve's friend) as she had made copies of Vol. III of the Confessions with great devotion. She asked for shoes size 5 ½ and 6! No one in our circle has such Lilliputian feet. Ask Mildred if she has sent her shoes, and whether she has traced somebody who can spare a few pair. That would save me expense, as we cannot afford to buy new ones.

Love is the law, love under will.

Should you come to visit us with Jean, and if you pump me sufficiently, I'll be happy to try and make as many thing clear to you as I am able to.

All the best to you, and all our love from Sascha and yours,

Karl

K. J. GERMER
260 West 72nd Street
New York, N. Y.

October 17, 1949

Dear Jane,

Do what thou wilt shall be the whole of the Law.

    Thanks for yours of Oct. 11th with the M.O. for $59. I think this is the best way to wind up financial matters of Agape Lodge. I suppose you know that Orders, Lodge, etc. have never appealed to me. I feel in that atmosphere as a fish on land. Yet it is doubtless a method that has much appeal to many others. For that reason I would welcome someone who in the future would start a new thelemic movement in California on an Lodge basis. In that case I think a new name should be adopted. Agape Lodge being defunct does in no way touch the O.T.O. as a whole. Nor has it any bearing on your personal activities of pushing 93, or of keeping the group together.

In this connections I think I better tell you that the FBI has been and is hot on my trail. You will probably remember their investigation of Agape Lodge in 1942 or 1943 where – as far as I know – Jack and WTS were involved because of complaints by neighbours. Have any other Lodge members been questioned at that time? I was called, or better, summoned to the F.B.I. H.Q. and severely cross-questioned. At least since that time (1943), possibly since 1942, my telephones have been tapped. A friend of mine was called to the FBI last week (they had recorded a phone talk) to tell them all about it (whether I am a Nazi, or a Communist, what he knew about A.C., whether he had been in California, whether he knew thelemic literature, etc. etc.) It so happened that I had not seen that friend for a year or two, and that he knew or remembered only vaguely about my talking or showing him *Liber AL*, and *OZ*; and that he is a loyal friend. He has been the first who – to the annoyance of the FBI – called me up at once and asked me what I had committed, and that they had a 200 page file on my case.

The whole thing is against A.C. and against Thelema (they knew that I had testified in 1934 for A.C. in his libel suit and that the British since then have consistently refused a visa to me).

I should not wonder now if they have not for a long time watched my envelopes to know the names of those with whom I correspond, in order to get data on the spy net that I control, in the USA and especially in California, but also abroad. For many years we have had the most peculiar, sometimes naive and childish experiences. The pieces only now seem to fit into a scheme. I presume they know the names and addresses of everybody in Cal. To what extent they check on them I don't know. The fact is that our phone at H.Q. is also tapped. As nobody can find the place the first time we have arranged for visitors to call us on the phone from the nearest town or phone, so that I can meet them and take them up to our house. We are quite secluded and it begins to be funny for us to see soon after a visitor has phoned that some lout passes near by to try to get the number of the License Plate or see what wicked plotters are there.

Of course, we have nothing to hide. We have no secrets. Nor do we try to do anything even in the slightest to the detriment of the U.S., or the Government. In fact, my friend advised me to frankly write to Edgar Hoover and ask for an interview (a thought I've had before). But I'm poor at talking, I could never expound 93, or, in case of attack, defend my or our position decently. The time, I feel ever surer, will come for things of that sort. I like a fight, a real fight. But it is the Gods who will prepare the day, and Patience can be a great virtue. One must know to wait.

I leave it to you to tell members of your group about this situation. I think Ray should curb his obsessions by certain fanatical, one-sided ideas and train his mind by definite effort to push through those clouds on his soul to the true light. I think Jean and Ero should be notified, and especially Georgia. They, the F.BI. must in some form keep a tag on Thelemites in California. I wonder whether anybody has perceived anything?

I wish I could have given that copy of "The Classic of Purity" to you. You have deserved it more than anyone. But you will understand?

I think your plans re *Liber Reguli* and the Mass is excellent. Let me know how things will go and progress.

The Burlingames place: The Pentagram regularly should be good. But if the odor has a physical basis it should be tackled from that angle.

IX°: all very good what you say; but if they want to share in the property of the Order, they must first help to create some. Therefore it says in the VI°[74] that any member of that grade is expected to deed some real estate to the Order. It has all been somewhat lax in the handling of the Constitution. But a time may come when some pep can be put into it. The main assets of the Order are the copyrights etc. – Joe Miller would not be a real IX° of the O.T.O. Remember that various schools in the West as well

---

[74] Germer is actually referring to the VII° of O.T.O., not the VI°.

as in the East possess and teach that secret and they do not belong to the OTO.

What did you find out about the $70 that you paid for the Temple equipment? I would like to get the record straight.

I'll write you about the Rituals again later. Meanwhile I'd like you to send me one set complete. – Meeka, of course, is entitled to a set of the Holy Books.

Love is the law, love under will.

Best of love from Sascha and yours,

Karl

K. J. GERMER
260 West 72nd Street
New York, N. Y.

Nov. 30, 1949

Dear Jane,

Do what thou wilt shall be the whole of the Law.

No further news yet about possibility of printing *Liber Aleph* in Germany. This has much attention from me.

Yours of Nov. 17. Don't forget to return "Enquiry" when through. "Changes?" I think next March will bring something.

Before I forget: a set of the Holy Book reproductions should be given to the Rancho RoyAL crowd, they may not have these books. – I hope the *LXV* with Commentary reproductions can be taken in hand shortly. May-be I can get a few to send out by the end of the year.

The Heart of the Master: yes, if some bookseller wants to buy one or two copies, sell by all means. I would ask $4.00 net per copy, they are so scarce.

Symonds has found a publisher for his biography of A.C. Of course, he sounds antagonistic. But we cannot expect more from an outsider. I'm sure the publication of his book will do some good.

No, the Receiver did nothing about *Liber Aleph*. It is simply that the Hastings printers did not answer letters and were generally unbusinesslike. Also we did not have the money to pay the balance. Wait about this before speaking to Paul.

I do not understand this sentence in your last letter: "There must be a medium in the group for one thing; that there is to be an addition to or emendation of his work for greater clarity, for a greater number of people." Well, I may understand now, But what has Hugh to do with this? – Do send me your notes on what you get through Hugh.

No: I have not received any copies of *Book 4*/I. They are hard to get by.

Nothing else that I can think of. I wish I had a typist to help. There is the set of "Letters" to complete. There are a number of "Letters" which you don't have, and there is now a new sequence to the list.

Yorke, as you know, had taken a vow some 20 years ago to collect all of A.C.'s material and store it ultimately in the British Museum.[75] He has kept sending me copies of all kinds of letters, documents, diaries, etc. etc. which he in his searches had either bought, obtained from the owners on loan. He wrote me asking me to write Californians to make copies of letters sent by A.C. to them. For the time being I have excused them as being too old or otherwise in jobs with little time to do this tremendous work. But I want him to continue with sending me his stuff. So if ever you should write him treat this with diplomacy.

Love is the law, love under will.

---

[75] The Yorke Collection is presently housed in the Warburg Institute, University of London.

Ever yours,

Karl

5169 ¼ Fountain Avenue
Los Angeles, 27, California

December 7, 1949

Dear Karl:

Do what thou wilt shall be the whole of the Law.

    I found the occasion to speak to Paul about the possibility of publication in Germany – that is, it flowed in naturally – of *Liber Aleph*. He said he would be unable to help because of the improvements he made to his beach property. I saw these improvements when there with Ero and Jean for lunch when they were down two weeks ago – the 17th November it was. Quite an amount of shoring, of an excellent type, outside additions to the cabin, etc., etc., bought last February.

    He has ordered a copy of "Enquiry" from a dealer handling this sort of thing, and would like to get a copy of the magazine carrying the Yorke article. Could you tell me the name and month of issue? The Symonds article left him speechless, dumbfounded, principally because of being a literary executor; but also because he found one paragraph belaboured A.C., then came another paragraph which spoke rather well of him.

    Hugh is the 'receiver' of, or medium for, what has come through. Strike out the word "emendation" in what I wrote formerly. It does not belong. Hugh seldom gives the exact words used. He translates through his own words for the most part. What seems to be impressed upon him. Also, my setting up of what he said was done a day or two later. There was the word "addition" and also "so as to reach a greater number of people". Our next meeting, December 13, will likely bring something. I will keep you well informed. Hugh is performing *Liber Samekh* and lately has received the King scale Hierophant's colour. The 777 correspondences are rather interesting.

Another item: Paul called when Jean and Ero were here, to bring me a new book, "In Search of the Miraculous", Ouspensky, posthumously published. During the talk between him and Ero I sat silently. There came a transition: Paul on another plane – I know not which or what. I gazed, and to myself said, "I have never really known Paul". Now Hugh always sits in the same chair when here, and in the same place. Paul was now in Hugh's chair, drawn out and away from its usual place. After the above realization, Hugh was sitting in the same chair, at his usual place; and I know that he, Paul and myself formed a triangle for something to be done. But what this work is I know not – at the moment at least.

I looked over at Jean and Ero, and they seemed far from me, and without any special contact, with perhaps a light mist between. Ero wants to come into town and go to school on G.I. funds. Electronics. To get anywhere 3 years will be necessary. While discussing the matter, I saw him out in large expansive country – trees, hills, etc. (Dams? Bridges? Canals?)

Please understand I do not immediately accept this 'medium' vision work as it comes. It must be rigorously tested. But as I said, records will be kept, and you will be informed.

Friday I posted 5 Rituals, plus procedure of Council – 6 in all. I took a chance on straight mail, when I discovered I could not register because of the scotch tape on my home-made envelope.

Ray B. finds himself unable to send his remittance before the 10 or 11; Therefore you will hear from me shortly, and I will then enclose "Enquiry". I have made up some notes, but want to go over the article again before typing it out for you.

What you say about Yorke's gathering of A.C. material for the British Museum, because of an earlier vow, is news. I have some interesting and valuable letters from Aleister. Does the B.M. accept typed copies of letters? Or does Yorke want such for himself? This for my information; I could not type them now, in any event. Also, I kept many things for Agape Lodge; but as I am now sceptical of an organization to receive such, what would you suggest? I enclose list of books. I had thought of sending Grady a list also. I am putting my things in some sort of convenient order, because my heart has been bothering me lately – somewhat. But I believe this is entirely in my hands. Ergo: Plenty of pranayama, or other deep breathing. I have a tendency toward shallow breathing, even holding my breath for a bit!

In this housecleaning I came across the typescripts made from Yorke's notes on Eqx 4 and 6. Four copies, plus his notes. Do you want Grady to have a copy of each? Ray B. can go over mine if you see fit. When you first sent me Yorke's various notes, I typed those on *Liber VII* and those on the New Testament. Over a year ago. As I do not find them anywhere I assume they were sent you at the time.

Two nights ago Monty phoned me from Sacramento 1) to ask about Roy; 2) to say that he was concerned about his A∴A∴ work, that he had written you but had not received a reply. I assume this is because you have been too busy, and I shall so write him in a day or two. If he were close at hand, where we came in contact, I might do something for him (if you saw fit), but outlining his steps as he proceeds may be quite beyond me. Understand, he did not ask me to step in! He asked nothing of me except to say if I could give him any information in the matter of – what to do, I think he meant; whether to sit tight and await the outcome, or whether you would help him. I feel it is not up to me to make a move. Does Grady handle any work like this? I sent a woman to him who had appealed to me, but have not yet heard what took place. I shall write her shortly and make inquiry. She thinks her interest lies in extra-sensory work. Yoga? Well, I will ask her a lot of questions.

I feel like telling you I have found it next to impossible to write Schmolke. My last to him was dated June or July so last week in November I finally got a letter put together somehow. I felt guilty. He had written 3 times in the meantime. Any reason for this?

Perhaps you know Jean has a case of bursitis? Her displacement notice was withdrawn and the attack came shortly after. Ero has not written since the 17th Nov., nor has Jean. I shall send a note asking how she is getting along.

Love is the law, love under will.

With love,

Jane

5169 ¼ Fountain Avenue
Los Angeles, 27, California

December 27, 1949

Dear Karl:

Do what thou wilt shall be the whole of the Law!

    I sent by registered mail this a.m. "Enquiry" and Yorke's article inside its covers, with the copies of Yorke's notes for *Equinoxes* 4, 5, 6, 7. Lines at the P.O. were so long before Xmas, that I held them over till I wouldn't need to stand in line.
    Your letter of Nov. 30. The small unopened parcel which I thought contained 2 copies of *The Heart of the Master* held instead 4 copies of the Pasadena prints of *Liber AL*. Therefore I have no copies of the 'Heart' for sale, nor do I have a customer. The copy I loaned was returned with "too unintelligible".
    So far I have not found the occasion to write Yorke.
    Monty has taken me into his confidence – with the promise not to mention it to anyone – that he proposes joining you for a period of study. Need I say this makes me happy – happy, indeed!
    This, of course, brings up Roy, who is now with Frances Ward in San Gabriel. He eats well, etc., but can only propel

himself when a sturdy shoulder is available on which to lean. I have not yet heard how the speech is progressing – if at all!

I saw Phyllis a week ago, and was shocked at the "pig-headedness" of the early Winona Boulevard days still showing up; i.e. in adopting wholeheartedly what Roy had told her regarding a few matters. She must confuse the agent with Adonai. This truth came just as I had started the care, and I was too shocked to stop and speak further. Too, it was late. But now I know how to reach her, I think. She will have bitter days ahead of her, but that too is all right, for I believe she has good material deep down. I now have the poems of her later period – that of suffering, and may type out one or two for you to see this afternoon, if all goes well.

I am enclosing a bit of Diary re happenings of the past two months. With some of this matter you are already acquainted, but here is the sequence. Hugh said beginning of November, "Don't be surprised at anything – Keep your eyes open – Take good care of yourself!" I don't know what it is all about, but to my conscious mind there have been a few bits of value.

> Have I left myself unguarded?
> Are they hurdles I had to take?

As I was last summer impressed with the necessity to breathe more in order to live, it would seem to me the "Battle to live" of Nov. 29 was the correct procedure.

The black waters of Oct. 25 made a deeper impression.

Of interest. As her English Course thesis Phyllis is writing her autobiography, and will use her Winona diaries. The whole to be submitted to me when she gets it, chapter by chapter! Jane will get some eye-openers, with some of which I already agree.

Love is the law, love under will.

"Enquiry"

p. 29   I never saw the "leopard skin", but did see photographs of its use in the performance of rituals. He himself mentions it in "Moonchild".

I knew Aleister in Cefalu and Paris, and never saw him attempt to hypnotize people.

"Eyes retained a fixed concentration" because of drugs. Is this possible?

The Jupiter robe, $7°=4°$ A∴A∴, had a hood which could be pulled over the face, and this had holes for the eyes to look through. He some times wore this with the hood always thrown back, however.

I know nothing about "Ruthah". He did like civet. Aleister performed a ritual, or rituals, some years before the Cefalu period to make himself more attractive so that he could always find partners for his thaumaturgy. His diaries are quite frank, as you doubtless know.

p. 30 The Italian climber. Crowley, being English, with their habit of understatement, might say he was bored with this Italian climber to conceal a deep agony over the whole misadventure. (If he said it!) Also as a method to rid himself of questioners.

p. 32 I understood A.C. wrote *The Book of Lies* in the Cafe Royale, while drinking brandy and black coffee.

Bottomly's weekly journal *John Bull*, a London rag. One of its flashy headlines for Jane Wolfe read, "We Trap the Temptress!"

p. 33 I thought the American sojourn the Gethsemane that produced the Magus. But Symonds would not know that!

p. 34 I never witnessed a temple ceremony such as described. "Horned One", branded witches, dancing naked, etc. And I am quite sure none such ever took place. We were always robed, simply, for that is all we had. A.C. on a few occasions put on one of his A∴A∴ robes, but he wore mostly his red Egyptian abbai shot with gold, which he also wore frequently around the Abbey. On a few occasions, a white abbai shot with silver; the one mentioned in the "Cairo Working".

"Thou Spiritual Sun? Thou Satan ", etc., etc. is from *Liber Samekh*, which is not a group ritual. How wonderful if all could have achieved samadhi at the same time! Such a day might come in the future? But it was not possible at Cefalu. We were not ready for anything like that.

(This all sounds quite dull and uninteresting to me, but I have been through strange moods and tenses this fall, unable to do anything creative. May I get myself straightened out as the Sun Moves Northward!)

Jane

K. J. Germer
260 West 72nd Street
New York 23, N.Y.
Endicott 2-6799

January 4, 1950

Dear Jane,

Do what thou wilt shall be the whole of the Law.

It will take some time to answer all the points in your letters of Dec. 14, 7, and 27. So I'll start of least somewhere. (I have been very busy lately and not very well.)

Thanks for M.O. for $47.00!

Yours of Dec. 7. That article by Yorke was in the 'Occult Observer.' I don't have number of issue here – is at H.Q. will make a note of it. – Generally speaking, we can't expect any of these writers to produce anything adequately appreciating 666. Yorke wrote me he has seen the MS. of Symonds's book on A.C. and said it will not please A.C.'s adherents or followers. Nor do I expect it. All these people (Yorke included) are shallow. Yorke should know better; but having fallen down in a critical magical stage turned his love into hate, the usual way (like Jones). The magical art is to acquire a point of view to use even the slaves for their proper job. Yorke was and still is instrumental in collecting masses of A.C. material from the most obscure sources, paying for these things phantastic sums and sending me typed copies faithfully. He just sent me among many other valuable material a copy of A.C.'s diaries of 1917-18! which he had bought from somebody. More will be forthcoming from him. He himself will pass his collection on to the British Museum in the end. – With Symonds the case is similar: he is still lower than Y., just a mere plain newspaper scribbler, with that outlook; his only interest is to make money with his book; and he writes it in that sense. But – the Gods are probably shuffling the cards, and we can't know what the final results will be. –

I did get the Rituals you mailed – but have not checked them yet. Will do so later. – Please do not bother at the moment about copies of A.C. material for the British Museum, though. Not Airmail, we only use 5¢ foreign postage! If you have time enough, it might help appease and encourage Yorke to send him some stuff from time to time. When you do, you might make copies for me too. If you can't type now – send Y. a note to encourage him. As to your own 93 stuff and files: I think you should make a Will to pass all this material on to H.Q. which will be the center for everything – not the British Museum or Yorke! What you have is stuff of the Order, and that must go to the Order again, not to outsiders.

I have the 418 comment notes which you typed: thanks! If you like, do send Grady a set.

Your list of books and MSS is surprisingly great; many books I have not read, but would like to read. One MS. puzzled me: "Atlantis" which I think is missing here. I have seen this years ago, but I'm sure I have not got it among the material from A.C. arrived so far. When you have a chance to verify, I wish you'd give me precise data! Number of pages etc., contents. If this MS. is lost elsewhere, as so much else, we'll need your copy for duplication.

"Enquiry" and Yorke's article: I think the latter was published in "Occult Observer", a sheet published by Michael Juste, who is of doubtful value. I can let you know later; I have the copy at H.Q.

Monte has written me: he must first settle his affairs. Spring would be a good time for his arrival.

About Roy I have not much to say. I wish I could about Phyllis, but it seems to me she will have to solve herself some problems or complexes. I agree: she has good material, I thought this always. I like those poems of hers that you sent. AND GENERALLY, she has a quality which is rare, something genuine; it is this that seems to have been exploited for selfish purposes by Roy. Phyllis will have to get her eyes opened, and cut the magical bond. Others have had to do similar things. *LXV* has something (though referring to a higher plane) on this: Chapter I, 7-9; IV, 16-20. – Also, the "Master is selfish!" She must learn to see in any physical manifested man (or woman) nothing but a means through which 65 tries to talk and convey instruction, and enlightenment. One step, and nothing else!

Re your diary notes: I must say frankly that there is not much that strikes me as on higher planes. I wonder whether this would be a fair criticism to make as to the actual facts. I remember that Max's diaries also seemed to 666 when he saw them to contain nothing of real value. And yet! Max proved by his life that he was way above those notes. Is it only that Jane, like Max, cannot bring down to paper the higher plane material that certainly is conveyed, if only before dawn during sleep, or during the waking hours. We must make an effort to catch those messages.

I'll go into your remarks re "Enquiry" when I have the copy at H.Q. You forgot to mention that you also lived with A.C. in Tunis (you say only Cefalu and Paris). To be complete would give more value or weight to your statements. Should I send your notes to Yorke or Symonds, I'll add this.

I do wish I knew what you know about the way Roy influenced Ph. – or others – against me. – Phyllis certainly does not play the role of 'outcast'! I believe being treated as such is part of the game the H.G.A. is playing with one's soul – the soul of 'chosen ones'. Sasha was an outcast all her life, despite all appearances. But that was necessary to bring out the pure gold. I could compose a long list of brethren and sisters in whose life this trait was paramount! And the loneliness! One must learn to become so intimate with one's H.G.A. that one gets a dislike for all other company. – I have never kept my eyes off Phyllis.

Let me now close, have too much to do. My love to you!

Love is the law, love under will.

Karl

5169 ½ Fountain Avenue
Los Angeles, 27, California

January 15, 1950

Dear Karl:

Do what thou wilt shall be the whole of the Law!

Enclosed M.O. for $70. Ray B: Dues $14, $5 Aleister A. Mildred $7.50 one-half annual dues for 1950. The Balance, $43.50 Dues, $14, and contribution - - for such use as you see fit to make of it, -- from Jane.

Phyllis. She has not known Roy very long before she noticed various characteristics which seemed awry, and at intervals mentioned them cautiously, or otherwise, with the result that she almost lost the one who to her at that time, was none other than Adonai himself. Therefore she deliberately chose the path of Devotion, abandoning aught else and accepting Roy in whatever guise.

These months since Roy's stroke have compelled much soul searching, and she came to know Roy was the instrument of and that she has a work of her own apart from Roy. She demonstrated the entering wedge by the purchase of a secondhand typewriter, to carry on her school work. Ergo: When $25 were given to her at Xmas, her first thought was to send it immediately to Roy. Now, she will be ready to do typing in the summer; but at present the school work is too heavy to help before the summer vacation. As she now thinks her future may call for writing, she has a heavy schedule in her English class, as her teacher is encouraging her much.

I asked Phyllis why she stayed away from the initiation you attended. She said it was because of Frances. Phyllis insisted on letting the group know of her relation with Roy, she "thought it only fair". Presently she dropped out of Lodge, etc. and I suspect Roy smacked her down pretty thoroughly. He spoke to me twice about the possessiveness of Phyllis (which I well knew) and told me he had to be quite drastic: i.e. stay away completely. In the early days this absence made her quite ill. I have witnessed the reactions to "solitary confinement".

Roy, it seems, resented your reference to "the Gods". "What does he know about the Gods!" etc., etc. I said: "What does Roy know?" She said, "Well, success is your proof! And we shall find out if Karl knows", closing the car door with a finality. This latter is what bowled me over. There is more than that, I think - - in fact I am sure there is more, but I did not go into the matter further than that.

I have been there since the above. The store is over, so I took up the matter where we left off, and asked her if she felt she would know what activities you might carry on as head of the A∴A∴ & the O.T.O. I also then told her what I may never have mentioned to you: that Roy expected to be made the spiritual heir of A.C. (this is intimated to me after A.C.'s death, and he was indignant that he was not cabled the news instead of Jane W.) – and that he was deeply jealous of you, even though he had come to realize that he did not want organizational responsibility -- only the individual.

However, Phyllis has now relinquished Roy to the extent of facing the possibility of another partner. Heretofore impossible, altogether impossible, even should Roy die. "But Roy will have to release me: not till then." I said, "But you now realize that Adonai functions where He listeth, and suppose He asks another partner?" Well...It will have to be greater than this; greater!" "Different, at least, shall we say?" And here the matter was left.

She has now asked about a copy of *Little Essays*. As you said $3 to members for *The Heart of the Master* I assume that is the price for the Essays? As any rate I am taking her, on my next trip, the first volume of the "Letters". And I mean to take advantage of this opportunity to give Phyllis all the Thelema material she can handle. There is a letter of your about 0=2 I want her to see. Also the *Commentary*, when she finishes the "Letters".

I should add, in case of and when a new partner it will have to be Aleph-Lamed, she said. She worked quite a bit on the Book of Thoth before Roy's days, also started astrology in which he later helped her. She has a good foundation, and the root of the matter in her.

Mildred has now a job – perhaps she has told you, and we all are quite happy about it. Ray has not had a day off for two years – possibly 3 – and that is one of the matters to be taken care of – an occasional rest, or possibly 2 days a week off – as he had with his former job. This affords some rest. Now before she went to work, she typed Yorke's play. I have it here, and will send it under separate cover to you – one copy. Then Yorke's original and one copy to him. This leaves two copies in Mildred's possession, one for them, and an additional copy should another be asked for.

Before receiving your last letter, it had occurred to me that possibly you might be interested in the build-up of my present book collection? And I have made a list of those presented to me, etc., etc. The Thelema books are as I reported some years ago. Nothing has been added there. Meantime Paul, since I have known him, has given me 11, Hollander 2, from Maym Kelso's books after her death came 7, Mrs. Sherrill 1, Mary Green 3 novels, Willie Green "History of Art" by van Loon, as a memento.

I have accepted all books offered me, with the idea of building up some sort of a Library for the O.T.O I am glad you suggest sending them to Headquarters - - experience out here has demonstrated the utter uselessness of giving it here. In the meantime, I have an unexpected use occasionally for a book little used – *When the Sun Moves Northward* by Mabel Collins about a year ago; it meant much. To-day *Secret of the Golden Flower* is filling a need – breath. Strangely enough, in this book I saw the first mention of "Kill the heart" – with an explanation that I can accept.

I have two newcomers in my loyal group of Paul and Hugh, and here is where these various books come into considerable use. I am not an extemporaneous speaker, and I adopted the plan of Max, reading from a book, interpolating a though that may suddenly enter, or stopping for a question or thought by some one, and then discussing at the end of a section. My main concern is getting their minds working, and opening the way for subtleties to creep into their hearts or spirit.

Love is the law, love under will.

All love to you and Sascha,

P.S. I saw Roy last week – skin clear and pink, looks splendid – speech poor, halting, and pronounced with difficulty one or two words. Must lean on a shoulder in order to move, cannot coordinate brain and fingers to touch the right piano key - - Frances hopes to reclamation (?) will stem from the piano.

K. J. Germer
260 West 72nd Street
New York 23, N.Y.
Endicott 2-6799

January 17, 1950

Dear Jane,

Do what thou wilt shall be the whole of the Law!

Your very informative letter, and your M.O. came to-day. Thank you for both! To take the latter first, I was waiting for it and sent off Ataturk's school fees through the bank in the afternoon. So you can see how welcome your increased contribution was. – Economically, things have not been too easy at this end the last year. Business slack; studio ditto; expenses and the responsibility for H.Q. a burden. The only contributions those I get from you and Jean. You can understand how important a role they had to play. But I hope 1950 will be better. I wish Jean were here. She could, I'm sure, make easy money if she were here now.

Phyllis is too valuable to be neglected, and I'm glad you keep after her. Roy told me that he had a way with women that his technique made all the women he had adore him. But this is an outer thing, a perfected technique which any rascal could utilize for enslaving them. Ph. must learn to understand. Her problem is her "possessiveness" which she has to sublimate to a higher plane. It stems from a good quality: the intensity of the devouring urge. But the tool (in this case the man) is not the object of the aim. She must not mix up Roy with Adonai. Nor her H.G.A.

Did you get a chance to read "Heavenly Bridegrooms" (by Ida Craddock), reviewed by A.C. in the *Blue Equinox* pp. 280-81? It is a very valuable book; I sent it to California some years ago, and it seems nobody understood it. Ida C. had her H.G.A. and gives quiet a lot of information about the K. & C. In her case the H.G.A. manifested as such after his physical death. As these manifestations pertain to four-dimensional planes, it seems that such a relation would be hardly possible if the two beings would happen to meet on the material plane, unless one has already advanced far above anything that can be called human. Fortunately, the influence of the H.G.A. from the higher plane, let me say as a discarnate being, is much more effective, provided the soul has once attained to the K. & C. It seems to me that Ph. did slide into this some years ago; that she had her communion with her H.G.A.; that she did not fully understand either his nature nor his language; that, like Elsa in Lohengrin, she wanted the intercourse to take place in the physical body, and that as a result he went back to the Graal from where he came.

What she says about 'Roy having to release her' is absolute bunk. It is she who has to release 'Roy' whom she "winds about with her close coils *LXV*, II," and then go back to her H.G.A. and apply the same process on Him. Through HIM is the only salvation, ALL other media are temporary, and, if persisted in, poison to the soul.

I will be glad to send her *Heavenly Bridegrooms*. May-be she will understand it. But you can do another thing: write a letter to Mr. Theodor Schroeder, Cos Cob, Conn. and ask him for a copy of the book. Enclose $2.00 and ask him if he can send you any other literature on the strange case. He is poor, and is looking for an "Angel" to finance his books on this and other material. Don't mention my name. He lives on the occasional sale of his stock.

Other "partners" for Ph. ? Why, she can have as many as she wants, if only she will remain true to her H.G.A. She hurt and offended HIM very deeply when she began to 'toy with old sweetnesses' by devoting herself, by worshipping, a mere man Roy Leffingwell in favour of HIM! I wish you would sear this complex of facts into every fibre of her soul. It can make me so mad!

It is allright for you to give her as much Thelemic food as you have. But don't give her indigestion; let her first learn her vital lesson; transform herself magically; eradicate 'Roy' for ever; and learn again to listen to the subtle voice of her H.G.A. In time, as she learns, this voice will become ever clearer. Then only, if she follows this voice, will she become calm.

I hope I have been complete enough about this matter, but ask or write me any time there is a question.

Roy? It is one of those sad cases of becoming obsessed by vv. of *Liber AL*, 220. He: expecting to become A.C.'s, 666's heir!!! The man must have been a lunatic. What has he done ever to merit it? Well, I have seen stranger things; no: of many strange things I've seen, this is one of the strangest! We better forget him! Why should any new partner of Ph.' be "Aleph-Lamed"? Roy's number of 111 is the number of several people connected with the work, in case she refers partly to this, Or does it only mean that he should be a Thelemite (because *Liber AL*)? But that title of the book is not complete, the full title is secret, anyway.

I'm glad to hear about your extension of your circle and your library. One never knows where a seed will grow up to bloom in a garden, and one must not care. As you well know, the tending of the garden is the sole object; besides, we ought to work in eternity, not in time.

I have no word about the progress of *LXV* with Comment; as soon as I get the first copies you'll get one.

Love is the law, love under will.

Ever fraternally and with love from Sascha,

Karl

PS. Y'day came a note from Jack Parsons; is coming to N.Y. for 4 or 5 days. I wonder! Once bitten, twice shy. He broke a pledge to me once (poisoned by Smith); he may yet be in touch with him. K.

5169 ½ Fountain Avenue
Los Angeles, 27, California

February 7, 1950

Dear Karl:

Do what thou wilt shall be the whole of the Law!

Phyllis has cleared up surprisingly where Roy is concerned; the school work drained off her energies and desires. She now has a rooted interest in her Art ground work, her English and Psychology. Roy has receded. She spoke quite frankly about his ego and its ramifications, for instance; how he catered to, and kept alive the "God Roy" he and his family had created, although complaining about their dependence on him, etc.

She says now, it does not matter whether Roy comes, or goes. And a fresh spate of happiness and joy is with her, In fact, I believe she is anticipating a new interest, and will be ready for it when it comes! So much has she changed since my former visit. I feel she could do much for J., who has so blindly blundered with women. His potential has always appealed to my imagination; the right woman could, I think, steady him. But S. is absolutely taboo with P. from all angles. It occurred to me that it was to ask her back to the household, wherever it is, that J. wanted to see her. Her field has expanded, she is building her own broader base to the pyramid, and at present she can find no interest in organizations.

As a series of strange dreams visited [and] ceased after Roy's illness, I feel like including three of them here. She calls them her "Cellar Dreams". They all had to do with her locking all doors and windows in the living part of a house because of fear, and going to the cellar, where there were horrible things.

1. An indescribable creature on the floor, which the first time she was able to pass though much frightened. She then entered a tunnel, through which she passed on hands and knees, encountering beetles, roaches, etc., etc. finally to emerge into sunlight, trees and flowers. What she wanted.

2. A Building with elevators. She went up; she went down and into the cellar, where the pipes were clogged by a dead body. She spoke: Don't tell me about this: I know it already." She felt but did not want to admit that the dead body taken from the pipes was that of Roy.

3. Smith. In a cellar, she and Mary (a friend living across the hall) were separately wrapped each in a blanket, and lay on the floor. Smith appeared & wanted P. to move away from Mary. P. said: No! Put me nearer Mary!" This Smith did, then sat down in a familiar chair, and impatiently tapped, tapped a cigarette on its arm, as though waiting....waiting...

She discovered on writing her auto-biography for school work, that there was a phase of her Winona life she could not face. However, she promised to dig up and write it as if about some one else. Will get the Autobiography in a week or two, and expect some interesting reading. Sara Dodge – Jane Wolfe. 'Nuff said.

No word from Jack.

Love is the law, love under will.

All love to you & Sascha,

Jane

New York 23

Feb. 17, 1950

Dear Jane,

Do what thou wilt shall be the whole of the Law!

Yours of Feb. 7th with M.O. for $57. Thanks!
I'll credit everyone.

Your report on Phyllis is most interesting. I'm glad she is beginning to see light. The dreams: I can do no better than to refer you to "The Wake World", *Konx Om Pax*, part II, and more particularly page 12, bottom paragraph. The No. 1 'dream' may well fit it. – Not knowing Ph. well at all, it is so hard for me to judge her problems, except in a general manner. I remember her vaguely from my talks on *LXV* in L.A. I was introduced to her, but she hardly left an impression on my mind. In fact I would not recognize her if I met her accidentally. Nor have I seen her diaries. – Sara Dodge? Who is that?

Should my theory be right, and should she be working towards an Tiphereth illumination, which I presumed her to have passed – I'd like her to keep her diary as complete as possible especially during the coming phase. She may understand it only long after fully. Impress on her also that those 'dreams' ought to be considered as messages, or warnings. I wish I knew more about her.

    I see you have not heard from Jack, nor anyone else. Nor have I. I'm beginning to wonder whether my first letter to you of Jan. 25 was not the correct view after all. However, I don't want to enlarge on this now except to warn you to be even more cautious. May-be there is activity in the Smith quarter. (There is for instance that 'dream' of Phyllis';) and then Jack's behavior if seen in perspective. In June 1949 he wrote me a long, decent, letter reviewing his past years. Then I heard S. was visiting him – may-be the tempter, to subtly wean him away from his new-won spiritual honesty, and integrity. And now he may well be again in subservience to S. Several of his remarks had the distinct Smith tinge.

    A question from Jean induces me to state my position with regards to H.Q. and contributions from Thelemites. - You know that I cannot get H.Q. registered in the name of the O.T.O. because the Order is not legally established here. For that reason I consider the monies received as in Trust for the G.W. While the bulk of the burden has been borne by Sascha – purchase of the property as well as maintenance, the simple position is this: When we bought the property there was a balance in the treasury of about $1000. I added this to the down payment, and have since applied income from 93 members (at least what was left over after paying freight, office equipment, A. Ataturk fees, etc. etc.) towards mortgage interest and maintenance. I also had to cable $400 to London in 1948 to pay for some urgent debts or funeral expenses.

Love is the law, love under will.

Ever,

Karl

PS. Re: several of your remarks on S. & J.: We must Doubt, Doubt & Doubt again & again. Spiritually honest people are always in danger of falling for subtle wish - phantasms of the kind as things should be, or would be nice if they were true! How often and bitter have A.C.'s disappointments & betrayals not been due to this tender weakness! K.

K. J. Germer
260 West 72nd Street
New York 23, N.Y.
Endicott 2-6799

March 7, 1950

Dear Jane,

Do what thou wilt shall be the whole of the Law!

    Before I forget: Last Summer I sent you the only existing copy of *THE LAW* by Mary d'Este (really A.C.) which Yorke loaned me to make copies and then return. He reminded me of it. What can you do?
    Paul acted very right in 'bawling out' Case[76]. Too long to explain. Paul (Congratulate Paul from me! Please.) is a Thelemite and Case a rat. It would be a 'sin' on Paul's part to get a feeling of guilt. – Besides, Case has a copy of *The Book of Thoth*; but he'll only steal from it; he is a deadly enemy of A.C.'s and of 666's, as the whole crowd through whom Jones works. A Thelemite is something dangerous anyway; only Achadites are the thing I know all this from contact with a number of these vermin, and I met Case too several times, and saw clear. 'Poseur' is one description of C.

---

[76] Paul Foster Case, prominent occultist and founder of Builders of the Adytum.

But I'd pass that by. What is more despicable is the dark small sinister soul that informs him.

That crowd tried to convert me to Achadism, to the Joneses! All Jones wants from me – as far as he is still of some sort of sane mind – is obtain some Thelemic discoveries, verses of AL, 220 on which his mind is ruminating like a white mouse in a cage.

If possible, let me have the March contribution as early as possible. It's that bad!

Love is the law, love under will.

Warmest love from Sascha and yours,

Karl

PS. *LXV* with Comment is complete on stencils; I hope to be able to send out copies soon. It is over 100 pages! 8 ½ x 14".

PPS. 666 is operative right along. His claim to have been appointed to rule the planet is a fact. It takes initiation and rise to high planes to realise this and see it clearly. There are people, gifted, who are able to communicate regularly with Him. Not I, for I am blind to a special degree. My knowledge derives from planes beyond Ruach etc. I think this category of people should not try frantically to get consciousness on lower, visible, planes, as through the lack of it implies failure. Read 1st Aethyr, where 'blindness' is a quality, not a defect. K.

P.P.P.S. Just received a letter from the pit from Frederic. Is half starving because the government who owes him about $1000 in back pay since he stopped working for them has not paid even yet!! He asks me for a loan of $100 or less.

I can't do it, or anything. I know Fred will pay back the moment his money arrives.

Would Paul be a dear and advance it? Act quickly. If he will do it, do it this way;

Ask the American Express Co to ask their Berlin representative, Mr. Gould – by wire to pay Frederic Mellinger. His private address is Berlin – Zehlendorf, Argentinische ALLEE 11.

I'll pay any expenses.

K.

5169 ½ Fountain Avenue
Los Angeles, 27, California

April 17, 1950

Dear Karl:

Do what thou wilt shall be the whole of the Law.

LXV arrived this a.m., per express. Slower than parcel post, which Watt said he would use. The binding is splendid.

My doldrums have disappeared, and I am giving the credit to *LXV*. And I now ask about the "Letters" yet to be copied, those not heretofore read by us. You said there were such. I could do them by easy stages. Also I am taking up pranayama again, in not less than 5-min. periods to start. Little enough, but when I wake at night I can take 10 minutes. "Your life depends on your breathing" meant to me, at the time, better and more full breathing than I was in the habit of doing. Could it also mean more than physical life?

A letter from Yorke, which I enclose. Please return. In sending *The Law* I made a short comment on Yorke's article in the little magazine, saying I could accept criticism of the man Crowley, as folks could not understand, but that I was disappointed in the *Sunday Supplement* reporter as I had expected a biographer.

I did not let out a squeak about his article, so now, as you see, I am trapped. I shall write Bayley – no more than a friendly note, however; mebbe I can start a bit of a thaw.

I am acknowledging receipt of *LXV* to Watt by this post.

Love is the law, love under will.

Love, health, and wealth,

Jane

P.S. Strikes me I've taken over the Jones act of pelting folks with letters.

K. J. Germer
260 West 72nd Street
New York 23, N.Y.
Endicott 2-6799

April 20, 1950

Dear Jane,

Do what thou wilt shall be the whole of the Law!

 Your letters of April 12, 16, and 17, with enclosure from Yorke which I return herewith.
 LXV: May-be perfect outsiders ought to pay $10? What do you think?
 Jack Parsons: Your explanation re his nature was new, but very enlightening.
 Liber VII: Only those few vv 20-29 in Cap. V?? To help you with one little angle: Cap. II, vv. 13-20 brings a close

description of the geography of the place where A.C. first met me in Thuringia; a close description of the scenery and the persons and the people (toads and cats, ye slimy things, the 'full moon'). Circuit of pines; tall yews beyond. When first reading the book I was bowled over, rejected it, until all the rest of the book began to give me real insight, and made me drunk. Some day, I'll have to write my Commentary, the one that A.C. never dared write, which can be published after my death. (Please keep this under your hat!) Similar remarks refer to *LXV*. The 'Preliminary Analysis' was written by A.C. in 1923. Since then very much light has been shed on so much of it. Again: it may be up to me to write a Commentary on the book some day. – No one else could do it. But you ought to be able to penetrate quite a lot from your knowledge.

I am under the firm conviction that we are heading towards very big magical events, or rather outer events of which the magical pressure on some Thelemites are but a forewarning. Still, one can say also that the whole period through which we are living is nothing but one big crisis, without beginning or end.

Women (your query on April 16). Read the 'Letters' concerning 'Woman', and some others whose title I forget now. They give the formula of her method of working. ('Family', in part also). – Contrary to the American conception which has invented the fact that American women are 'pure', resent 'sex', don't have any such 'dirty' desires, and that wicked, dirty, low, Man is only full of desire, sex, and therefore 'rape' etc. etc., the experience and the philosophy of other races and countries, are just opposite. The nature of Woman is to crave for fulfillment of her vacuum with an intensity that only few men can come up with her; so they use other means, in addition to normal, to prevent arising hysteria from lack of satisfaction. Why is Hysteria so prevalent in the U.S.A.? Why do women drink so much? Why can Americans only go to bed after having a load of booze first? It is all so funny. – But I think RHK is on the job to remedy this.

Sascha gets the most enlightening and frightening confidences from her U.S. female acquaintances. It took her years to obtain an understanding of this – to her – perfectly unknown behaviorism. She knows women who tell her to refuse herself to me and learn the American way, so that the husband pays a higher price!!! 'Oh! You European women don't know how to treat a man!!!' How abject all this is!

But it is the fault of the American men! They think they are very virile, because they fight among each other, think they are tough, and all the rest: but before their wimmin folk they crawl! The Sun has to dominate the Moon; the dog has to wag the tail; not vice versa. Right now you have these vice snoopers in L.A. A thing unheard of in a civilised country.

I hope Ero is going to write me about his reaction to Roy. He seems to have a surprising sensibility. – I hope Jean is getting through the phase in which she is. The trouble is no one can advise her.

"Letters": Let's wait a little. I have proposed to Watt to do them next, but being a very big job (450-500 pages), the resolution must grow slowly, I'm afraid he could only do it if we pay a good typist. The whole expense will be terrific. Typing – as you can only do 5 at a time, is unsatisfactory. Right now I'd need several sets.

Why do you feel trapped because of Yorke's article? Tell him straight that I sent you a copy, and say frankly what you think of it.

I leave it to you to act as you think best. He has help to make copies, so if you send him yours on loan to return them with a copy for me – well and good. – Yorke is doing a really magnificent job. Very much that I would never have seen were dug up by him and he sent me copies.

Try your best to get on the right side of Bayley, but don't mention me.

Keep your girl that'd do some typing on ice. One never knows.

My foot is healing very gradually; you must know that such a thing is merely a matter of patience. But it handicaps me awfully. I can't make progress in cataloguing the files as I'd have to go from file to file and from shelf to shelf. It requires much work to make one set of *Magick Without Tears* completely ready, collating, finding meanings mistakes, omissions, etc. etc. – and finally to make one or two copies. I think there are now some 85 'Letters' in all.

Love is the law, love under will.

Ever yours, with love from Sascha,

Karl

Is there still a possibility that you might be able to contemplate a stay here?

5169 ½ Fountain Avenue
Los Angeles, 27, California

July 31, 1950

Dear Karl:

Do what thou wilt shall be the whole of the Law.

 Since Paul was here, and read to me his letter to you, I have debated adding a few words. It may be unwise, but I shall do so.
 One afternoon while Ero and Jean were still in town, Paul told me that he had loaned Ero $100 – a sum asked by Ero when he changed schools so that he would not lose a month awaiting his Government check. Paul then added: "I wonder how soon Karl will get it." It was Paul's intention to have Ero send that hundred to you when repayment by Ero was offered.
 As Paul enclosed his check for $50 it would seem as if he wanted you to have another $50, from Ero – the balance then to be returned to Paul. Or was this clear in Paul's letter to you?
 At this same time Paul was concerned about the One and/or a merging with the whole. I read that portion of your letter to Roy L. of March 21, '49, concerning "0=2 --- 2=0." But there is

Ararita, Cap III – "Say thou that He God is one; God is the Everlasting One; nor hath He any Equal, or any Son, or any Companion." I should be happy for information and/or explanation here.

Monty is overwhelmed with debts and liable to lose all if he cannot make a loan. The "friend" who got him to Sacramento played him false by selling out his practise to Monty, inasmuch as a druggist there undermined anyone seeking Mexican clients. However, the druggist is not entangled with the Law, and may be Monty will pull out of his sorry mess. He stayed with the Burlingames when here two or three days, and Ray had long talks with him, for which I am thankful. He, by the way, thinks Monty's state may be Magical.

I had a yen to once again perform the Deacon role in the Mass, and so informed Smith. As it happened, Marie Prescott was at Lake Arrowhead over the week, so I enjoyed the doing of the role once more. And was glad to know some power was there. As we talked afterwards -- (I also had dinner with them out under the trees) -- I could not help but think he is on the Path once more. Or am I wrong in this?

Love is the law, love under will.

May the High Gods be with you both,

Jane

K. J. Germer
260 West 72nd Street
New York 23, N.Y.
Endicott 2-6799

August 4, 1950

Dear Jane,

Do what thou wilt shall be the whole of the Law!

Thank you very much for your M.O for $25. It is a great help, still, though Paul also sent me $50, this time it will be a narrow squeeze. And we are so terribly short at this end.

I had no notion that Paul had given Ero $100, nor that Ero and Jean were back in Barstow. I have written Ero c/o Georgia.

Sorry, I can't help too much with your question re 0=2 beyond that respective "Letter" in *Magick Without Tears*. Briefly, Nuit says "none and two...for I am divided for love's sake, for the chance of union". If the subject is united with the object (or any two opposites) it does not become "One", but Zero. If you divide an apple in two halves (as was done to the Universe, it appears, by the act of "Creation"), and let them lead separate lives for ages, aching each one half to unite with the other half, their getting together again, after vainly trying to find the exact opposite through endless ages, creates a blissful happiness, and they form a circle again, a Whole (apple) Zero. Substitute for each half apple a male and a female of any species, or plus and minus, positive and negative electricity, the result of the union is always bliss, heat, light.

We should not confuse this Nuit-cosmic conception, applying to a Law governing the whole cosmos which includes all nebulas, stars, all galaxies, etc. etc., with the local system of, say Ararita where 418 is a special case in the possible union of Hadit and Nuit. Suppose I would say that Ra Hoor Khuit is ONE child of Their union ruling this present Aeon. Then this is but One event while Nu and Had are eternal principles valid in this, the last, and the future Aeon.

This explanation, or attempt at an explanation, will certainly not satisfy you, nor me. Each chapter-verse starts with a 0, and descends in the attributions down from Kether to Malkuth, and then dissolves them again. You cannot transpose different systems, as you cannot do it with languages. The letters "RAT" in English means a rodent; the same in German "counsel, or Advice".

May-be on another occasion I can write better and sounder on this. I am no good at intellectual analysis or argument.

I have no definite judgment on Smith. If he is a true Thelemite he should accept 666's instruction to all Thelemites re Aleister Ataturk. Reactions in such primitive things are good touch-stones.

Frederic gets great praise for his lectures on Theatre matters; has published a book (in German) which is first-rate and deep. He tries to bring in Thelemic thought through his art. He has written some plays. 666 thought very much of him and expected more.

Love is the law, love under will.

Thanks for your good wishes which we reciprocate.

Karl

PS. Did you send for the copies of your letters from 666? Will I get a set of copies? K

PPS. No reason why you should not read the "Paris Working"! It should not pass into unauthorized hands. Jean should not have except through Max's death.

P.P.S. August 5

I have just answered Monte's letter of early last month and find his letter to you and your reply. From what you say that he has been in L.A. I fear he has been with Roy, and my conviction is firm that Roy has become a "center of pestilence" and is of the greatest danger to all who contact him. Because these demonic influences are so subtle and so pernicious, people pooh-pooh such remarks. But you should know better. Tell me what you know about whether Monte saw R. or not.

What brings me to this is your paragraph to him about the "teacher". Monte seems to have some peculiar fantasies about many such things. Why not have common horse sense? When you are in first grade you have another teacher than in 5th grade. Your school marm teacher would be unsuited to you when you have risen to a grade where a university professor or an Einstein teaches you. A. C. had innumerable teachers, he went from one to another to learn from each, to 'pick the brain' of each of them in their field. And then you reach the stage where each pupil is your teacher; when, understanding that every event is a particular dealing etc., you ought to accept 65 as your direct teacher through that particular event.

I would like to keep the copy of your reply to Monte of May 25 as it contains so much information that was unknown to me. If you want it back, tell me.

Love, K

5169 ½ Fountain Avenue
Los Angeles, 27, California

August 12, 1950

Dear Karl:

Do what thou wilt shall be the whole of the Law.

Yours of August 4, for which I thank you. I am sorry to have put you to the time and effort of writing re 0=2. You gave that pretty throughly in your letter to Roy of March 21/49, copy of which you sent me. It was in relation to Naught equals Two that I wanted the information re "Say thou that He God is One". It was the use of "One", and this you have now explained by calling my attention to 418 as one event while Nu and Had are eternal principles. Which is a help to me, and I am grateful.

I shall watch Wilfred re money matters. At present I take him at his face value because they are having a tough time holding on, and have gone hungry at times doing so. Meantime Smith is carrying out a consignment for his German friend -- Smith being an excellent cabinet maker. When the persnickety Chinese job is finished he will get some money, though not market prices. Also, as I believe I wrote you, he will apply for his Security Pension this fall.

I will present him with a copy of Baphomet's Instruction to the members re Aleister Ataturk, and wait for the Fall to demonstrate his willingness to contribute.

Yes, Yorke had the letters and returned them possibly six weeks ago - - maybe a month. I was surprised at their quick return. He said one of the three copies was to be sent you. At one time he left London during the summer. Perhaps he still does so? I have not yet answered his later letter, but must do so shortly.

Monty called on Roy. This he took up pretty thoroughly with Ray, and Ray just as thoroughly went over Roy from all angles with Monty in return. Ray thinks he has one new angles to consider – he, Monty. I was glad he stayed with the B's, because the Mexican can talk more freely with a man than a woman. I get at Monty much better through letters.

I would like to have the copy of my reply to Monty of May 25, but shall be glad to make a copy of it for you.

I rather think Paul has made a step forward.

a. He had been building up a tension for many days; until finally Dorothy suggested a trip. However, one day after breakfast at home he went into town to his office, where he possibly stayed till afternoon when he sallied forth to the Goodfellows' Grotto on Main Street, to mingle with old cronies and imbibers. This eventually got him into the hands of a Main Street character of no mean ability and accomplishments.
b. Paul brought this stabilized, poised, and simple fellow – having faced innumerable situations and solved them in his own manner, to call on me and tell me that at last he (Paul) would have another San Francisco experience, because "Henry" would pilot him thither and yon. I found this man of about 40 thoroughly fascinating, but all that is too long a story; but as I write I wonder if I was brought into the situation so that Paul should be guarded and finally put safely into a cab, and that this

man had to meet me so as to be impressed into a bodyguard. And he carried out his job to the letter.
c. They left, and headed straight for Main Street. The evening was a total flop, and for days Paul was in "a somber state." His words.

As a result of the above Paul reported to me eventually, I lost all my toys!" And further: "I know now I must get to the forces back of the symbol." (His toys: symbols) I take this to mean he is loosening the grip of Nephesch. And in all this I see the hand of the H.G.A., step by step as I have numbered the paragraphs above.

I understand somewhat at least the pupil being the teacher. Many are the times Hugh or Paul put me on the spot, and made me formulate the incoherent, for instance. And they have modified me in more subtle ways, Paul in one way, Hugh in another. H., it seems to me, gets nearer to actuality then Paul – the latter needs the maze of intellect. But what influence he could wield if…if…? I am not impatient; and in fact now feel encouraged.

Sunday, Aug 13.
John Ellers, former members of the Order, stopped by last night. He is foreman of a State road-building gang, which opens up new highways, north, south, east and west in California. Their family having all married, he and his wife Thelma live in a trailer and so have their own home wherever he is detailed. This by way of introduction.

They had called on Roy earlier in the day, having been brought into the work by Roy, and give me the following report.

A recent visit to the doctor disclosed Roy weakening almost perceptibly. Blood pressure now 170, pulse disturbance, legs and feet shaky. The doctor, it seems, is and has been curious about a persistent "mental block". A deep inner fear could cause this, no doubt, and from the first he was badly scared. The doctor said Roy might linger for some time, or go rather shortly. The Ellers also, as did Ero, Jean and myself Easter Sunday, think he is childish.

The Ellers promised to call again, and I will then have ready a copy of Baphomet's Instruction re Aleister Ataturk. They were always helpful, so now a foreman could contribute something.

Love is the law, love under will.

All LOVE to you and Sascha.

Jane

K. J. Germer
260 West 72nd Street
New York 23, N.Y.
Endicott 2-6799

August 17, 1950

Dear Jane,

Do what thou wilt shall be the whole of the Law.

    Thanks for yours of Aug. 5th with $50 M.O. – You must have received my thanks and confirmation of the $25 M.O. you had mailed me before?
    I hear Monte has visited Roy and I have seen fit to warn him. You, surely, must know Aleister's practice in such cases? He usually forbade all members of the Order to have any further contacts with a fallen candidate. The fact is that a candidate who breaks a magical oath loses his spiritual integrity. It is as if the Secret Chiefs Themselves take a hand and deal out the proper punishment. Anyway, the man loses any spiritualism he may have had; instead of his "Angel" he becomes obsessed and controlled by his "demon", his evil persona, and is a "center of pestilence" in the strictest sense of the word. For that reason sympathy visits on Roy Leffingwell and similar things are a magical crime to oneself. I feel sure that people who disobey such laws, feel themselves

sooner or later the evil contamination they were foolish enough to permit.

I do hope that Jean and Ero will have visited Roy for the last time. May-be I should have issued a stern warning a year ago. Anyway, may-be their removal to Barstow was a blessing.

It may well be that W.T. Smith should after all be put in the same class, and you should keep your eyes open. Do not imitate me when I keep in touch with him. I am gradually getting to see WTS's position. He is bitten by the same bug that bit and destroyed so many others.

Love is the law, love under will.

Will mail this in N.Y.

Ever yours,

Karl

P.S. N.Y
Found yours of Aug. 12 now.
Your information & news very interesting. but leaves nothing to add at the moment.
Love again from Sascha too.

K. J. Germer
260 West 72nd Street
New York 23, N.Y.
Endicott 2-6799

August 26, 1950

Dear Jane,

Do what thou wilt shall be the whole of the Law.

    Yours of Aug. 12, arrived after mine of Aug. 17.
    Did you send me a set of the letters Yorke returned to you? If not, please do!
    I enclose Monte's letter to you and your reply of May 25. Thanks!
    Your note re Paul and Hugh: the basis for the 'pupil being the teacher', I think is that through your training and growth you have Understanding on higher planes, unconscious planes. It is like a reservoir of water that is untapped. The moment someone taps it, the water runs freely. It may occur to you that when questions are asked ('tapped') you may answer and be surprised at what you say, and only understand later the meaning in your own conscious mind. I'd be glad if Hugh and Paul would make real progress.
    What is the latest from Phyllis? Thanks for your report on the Ellers. May something come of it.
    There is nothing else now. The cable for A.A.'s school went off: I'm awaiting the last shipment from London of A.C.'s material any moment now. After sifting it I can at last start on some sort of preliminary catalogue. The job is tremendous that ought to be done But I am confident that the time will come when I can work with some constant help. Ero and Jean remark on 'magical attacks' and I feel they are right. But I also think we have weathered the worst and that smoother sailing is ahead.

Love is the law, love under will.

Ever yours with love, Karl

K. J. Germer
260 West 72nd Street
New York 23, N.Y.
Endicott 2-6799

Sept. 13, 1950

Dear Jane,

Do what thou wilt shall be the whole of the Law.

Thank you for yours of Sept. 5 with M.O. for $40. Thank God Jean-Ero and Ray-Mildred helped for certain extraordinary expenses this month.

Yorke is quite allright; still, I have written him again to-day about your letters. I am sure he has sent the set of TS. copies with the cases of the remaining material which, he says, was picked up by the shippers Aug. 18th. I am waiting anxiously for the advice by the N.Y. Customs Brokers that the shipment has arrived here.

Ero-Jean: I believe you are right about your diagnosis of their mutual relation. It may well be that Jean may have completed her job with Ero and that the friction is the usual one when relations become stale. If not severed, the friction gets worse and grows into hatred. Both being Thelemites, they ought to face the situation and take the necessary steps. Ero, having learned so much from Jean may need another teacher; Jean having proved that she has learned the lesson from Max, may need to find another male that needs her wonderful pep-injection-treatment, and gradually grow a crop of promising Thelemites. Why not should both be chosen to find wealthy partners? Both are young and are well on the way of the discovery of their True Wills. Keep an eye on them. I like Ero very much and he has promise – and Jean!!

The Book of the Law preaches Freedom, real freedom, freedom from and freedom of, but always subject to Will. That means strict discipline of mind and body. In other civilisations such as Islam, or even France and Italy, your question re 'sodomy' would sound like a joke. But even in the U.S.A. the practice seems to have been common among the boys and men in small towns. I remember a married man who told me in 1927 that the repression of natural intercourse by the 'moral-immoral' codes of society and religious customs forced him, and his brother, but, as they found out later, other mature boys too, to take their pleasure from their pet cow in the stable, every morning. Both, boy and cow, enjoyed it extremely! This was, I think in Ohio or some mid-western state. Why should it be different else-where? I don't know what U.S. girls do in like situations?

Re Sun, 666, etc. "For He is ever a Sun, etc." The "He" is not A.C. but 666, who liveth forever, and runs the affairs of humanity. I wonder whether 666 has not been sending you messages.

Thanks for sending me the copy of your letter to Monte. – I wish Monte would see you more often now that he is going to be in L.A. again. He is also promising and is learning to transmute certain magical weaknesses. I enclose his latest, please return.

Love is the law, love under will.

As ever,

Karl

P.S. How is the new car going? What make?

K

5169 ½ Fountain Avenue
Los Angeles, 27, California

November 8, 1950

Dear Karl:

Do what thou wilt shall be the whole of the Law!

A report on Hugh.

For some time he has been practicing *Liber Samekh* -- indeed before he went away on his vacation in August, taken up again on his return, and continued five days a week since. As he uses the living room for his work, and the family are home over the week-end, work is impossible then. He has had these results: -

a. That the ritual is now a part of himself.
b. That it is necessary for the world that he perform this ritual, and that he perform it exactly as written.
c. That a "gold figure was manifested" before him at one time, but he could not diagnose the features.
d. That from the elbows up, and circling his head, was a strong vibrant emanation.
e. Again he comes into contact with power that is frightening, but he feels the day will come when he must use this power. At the moment there is no aim.
f. That his "inertia", which has distressed him, is to be disregarded. Hands off! Time will take care of that.

Meantime he is studying *Magick*. Before this book, *Abramelin-the-Mage*.

Our last monthly meeting – Hugh, Paul and myself (a strange animal is to join us in December) -- which was discussion from start to finish, led Hugh to say when here last that he was very disturbed over Paul's "confused" mind. Devious, I call it. A peculiar mind: that can nail him to the cross or keep him floundering in a morass. Or, again, fill him with a purring contentment. Possibly why he drank so freely.

Monty. He puts himself right in one's lap, with a "Here I am: teach me!" From Ray's remarks he is challenging when there, which pleases me. I have already told him that he will have to stand on his own two feet.

I can see now that I was all wrong with the dramatic ritual. My love of ritual brought this about. "Honorary" degrees, I understand, are bestowed with a reading of the given ritual; that Spencer Lewis got his seventh that way, a Degree that is necessary to function in an authoritative manner as he did. For full initiation the ritual must be acted out in open lodge. So I will go ahead as I understand is your wish; but start the work by taking up the Minerval first.

Love is the law, love under will.

Love,

Jane

K. J. Germer
260 West 72nd Street
New York 23, N.Y.
Endicott 2-6799

November 9, 1950

Dear Jane,

Do what thou wilt shall be the whole of the Law.

    Just a few lines to confirm, with thanks, your M.O. for $52.00. I don't understand your remarks on the M.O.'s; however, it does not matter to me.
    Please go ahead with the I° ritual. I have every confidence in you that you will make it impressive. The only O.T.O. initiation that I witnessed was that in the Minerval and it was a farce – I refer to Roy as G.M.
    My dear Jane: I think it is about time that you begin to realise that things like 'I have gone over in my mind' (your last letter) is possibly an impulse implanted in your mind by extraneous forces. If so, it comes from some one who knows better. It is not easy to check the actual source. In the meantime it is wise to remember that 666 has been appointed to act as Grand Hierophant.

His influence and direct inference upon activities has been plausible, or even evident, at this end in many instances. Sascha has been the recipient, and/or messenger in most striking experiences.

Generally speaking it is well to actually get it into one's minds and soul that "every man and every woman is a star" does mean what it says. For one thing then the incarnated man or woman is nothing but outmost the precipitation of a star on this earthy plane, in close touch on the higher planes with fellow stars, who may be incarnated or not, grown-up as humans or not; it does not matter. The actual impulses come from those high planes. It is by constant, or regular practices, with increasing intensity and ardour, that one makes oneself capable of understanding the language that those star souls are sending, especially in critical periods, or in answer to a prayer (which may well be an appeal for help or enlightenment without one's being aware of it at the moment); or in a state of deep worry about how to proceed, worry which automatically leads to deeper concentration, which in turn is heard, and: answered.

I'm writing thus to assist you in understanding the workings of the machinery in the extra-rational worlds. I am in touch with a lady of my age in Canada, who understands and lives this naturally, and who should be, or, may-be, is, a good Thelemite. She has been used as a messenger.

Now let me close my epistle. Do make your suggestions soon. – Monte wrote me yesterday. It is well possible that when he was led to you, (I'm speaking of his first contacting 93) he made the wrong choice. He chose to throw in his lot with Roy, which was a false choice. As a result he had to pay for it in hard and bitter experiences. Roy, at that time already had the sign of the fallen Thelemite on his brow. (If you reproach me for not having protected Monte during the time that I visited L.A., which I could have done) you would be perfectly right. I have learned much since then.) He was vampirised by Roy's aura, and sucked spiritually dry and led into the desert in the bad sense. May-be his leaving L.A. was a sort of protection by his H.G.A. to get him away from the evil influence. It cost him dearly, in material things, but he gained or has been given a chance to gain spiritually. He is of the right stuff, but weak. As you say, he must get a manly outlook.

I have one of A.C.'s diaries where he says that during the phase when he lived in the U.S.A. his problem was all the time to take the right choice between two women that were sent to him by the Masters. As though they wanted to test whether he was permitting himself to be guided by his right instinct, to choose the proper one. (You'll find a reflex of this in *Liber Aleph* chapter on Olun, I think it is, where he had to choose the right female.) But it seems to me that experience is really universally applicable. As we grow spiritually we learn to disregard external appeals, but listen to the internal. I mean by that: a candidate meets several, or, say, two people who could take an influence on his life. The one appeals to all his outer sense, eye, ear, sex, etc. It makes him fall in 'love' and he yields. The other party, turned up at the same time, and being the proper 'guide', is considered for a moment, but passed by in the uprush of the more immediate passion.

One has to pay for the false choice. For the higher grades it may be fatal; for the lower grades, one may get a second chance.

I'm writing this without premeditation. Think it over and let me know if it appeals to you. Could it apply to Jean's case? - With Ero?

Love is the law, love under will.

Love,

Karl

In a former letter Monte said he wanted to write me for advice re domestic matters. He never did & need not do so, as long as he sees the problem spiritually and does not refuse to act when the call and conditions for action comes. – It's all in "Magick W.T.".

K

5169 ½ Fountain Ave.
Los Angeles, 27, California

November 13, 1950

Dear Karl:

Do what thou wilt shall be the whole of the Law.

Because of Monty's reluctance to yield regarding all people as trustworthy, I gave him my copy of *The Mystical Qabalah* by Dion Fortune, asking him to read the chapters on Chesed and Geburah. These chapters, it seems, gave him a new outlook on humanitarianism, etc. He has a greater respect for Geburah qualities.

He has set up a book for the purpose of learning the Tree of Life, and plans to memorize some of the columns. Time will show. He said: "I am so happy to have a schedule of work, and I am glad to have foundation work. I have been given the deeper things, and I would like this other too." This particular way of looking at what he has to work on I will take up with him, so that he realizes they all are important. I quote him to you so that you have a fuller understanding of him.

It just how occurs to me that this Qabalah may be an intrusion at this time; that I should have written you before asking him to read Chesed & Geburah. I am sorry for this oversight; it stems from the fact that I have been accustomed to go ahead myself. I wish I had one of these books to send you; but I use it also at Burlingames. There is much of value in it. She uses *777* – states the H.G.A. is the higher self, which causes me to give them Aleister's description from MWT. He description of the Sephiroth are within the grasp of the lower grades.

He has gone over with me the Pentagram and Hexagram. These he performs 3 times a day. Also he will start a diary. I will watch that he does not neglect his medical practise, which is important for him magically, I think.

Family. All I can tell you is, that Monty's wife goes to a Protestant church; he had hoped she would follow him; that Adele, the 12-years old daughter, is in a Catholic school because of public school difficulty in his present locality. Adele has strict orders from Monty; also the Sisters were told not to indoctrinate her in the Catholic faith. To this they agreed, after being convinced of his desires.

He now has – *Magick Without Tears* (my first bound copy), Minerval & First Degree for study. We will go over these Wednesday.

Tree of Life - - if you approve.

I will have to get closer for further suggestions.

Incidentally, he told me he was to have been Krumm-Heller's successor, and this puffed him up and made him feel very good. Now he laughs at this.

Since receiving yours of November 7 I feel sure my first reaction regarding Monty's initiation was correct. Once more I was influenced by another mind. Having made the decision, I phoned Mildred what I proposed doing. She was delighted. I went to the B's Tuesday to conclude arrangements, but found Ray against my plan; and I permitted myself to be talked out it. He suggested sitting in the same spot throughout, the three of us reading, without dramatizing. To me this would have been fatal, inasmuch as Ray stumbles and stumbles in his reading. Also it would have robbed me of magical power, which I could have commanded (under these circumstances) were I robed and conducting an initiation. I get so mad at myself for listening to other people! Jean might have been willing, had I waited. Monty said with shining eyes; "How superior to Masonry!" when I had finished here at our bungalow.

Jean assured me on many occasions that she "loves" Ero. When I heard of her marriage, I exclaimed "Good God!... Well, it won't last!", but I must add I felt Ero would draw away. I asked her, at that time, why she married, and was told Ero was embarrassed by the easier arrangement – felt guilt.

What so upset her when they were down here, was that Ero did not function as lover & husband for quite a spell. And a bit of laxness in this way still goes on in Barstow, she told me when down here and in front of him. From the many many talks when they moved down, and since they have returned to Barstow, I got the impression this was the difficulty. A thought! They now drink together. Maybe liquor makes Ero a-sexual? It does some people. Let me add, however; They drank here, perhaps not in Barstow. Ero, I mean. Max put Jean through abstinence two or three times, because of her fondness for liquor. She I know drinks somewhat in Barstow – wisely.

Ero was in desperate need when he met Jean. She had suffered all those agonizing weeks and months with Max. They joined forces while Max was alive, to Max's agony of soul. Quite a situation: with Georgia also a knower.

Love is the law, love under will.

Jane

P.S. Please excuse all these typographical errors. I tire and my eyes some times bother. Monty, very hesitantly, asked if he could do something for me when here Wednesday – the trained medic realised my deficiencies. So I shall let him get after me physically. I need it.

K. J. Germer
260 West 72nd Street
New York 23, N.Y.
Endicott 2-6799

November 20, 1950

Dear Jane,

93,

Yours of Nov. 8. About Hugh. It strikes me that he is really a go-getter, that he is really passionately going for it! Impress on him that Abramelin the Mage's system has been superseded by the ritual in the VIIIth Aethyr. The idea is more or less the same. But it is more condensed. I believe I told you once that in my case the chamber in which one has to perform one's prayer daily, was my cell (#175!!! – only a German can understand it – it is the number of the paragraph of the German Code of Law dealing with sodomy or homosexuality, and this operation deals with the yielding to the rod of Adonai – 'I was pierced as a thief by the Lord of the garden', and other passages!) in the Concentration Camp. Let Hugh realise that it is always the essence of an idea that has to be observed; it's so romantic to read that Abra Melin was a rich man, could afford to buy a house, and then arrange circumstances to fit his description of the op[eration].

I hope he will be successful; if he gets definite results, let him send me a brief record. Meanwhile, let him also remember that he is after the intimate intercourse with someone who is more to him than any other human being. Let him not distract himself by too much need of talk, and discussion with others during this phase.

Yours of Nov. 13: I suppose you know that Dion Fortune was in close correspondence with A.C. – I have the file. But she demanded that his fact should be secret, as otherwise she would lose her standing. I can understand this, knowing the English system (it is the same here); she had not the stamina and moral courage of coming right out in the teeth of English Society.

When you can spare it, I'd like to see her Mystical Qabalah. I've never seen it. Regardie knew her well at one time and wrote her some of the most insolent letters, imitating A.C., and calling her names because of certain sexual irregularities. He possibly had an affair with her?

Of course, Monte should build up his medical practice again, and higher. He should be happy to have a profession in which he is more or less independent.

Why should I specially approve of your studying the Tree of Life with him? Give anything he needs and wants. – I am in touch with Krumm Heller's son Parsifal, but don't know whether he is any good or will be.

Let this be all for to-day.

Love from me and appreciation for you splendid work!

Love is the law, love under will.

Karl

P.S. I don't like this at all that Jean and Ero have begun drinking again. You have to protect Jean – and Ero. It shows that there is something spiritually wrong! They must check these first symptoms of going downgrade.

K. J. Germer
260 West 72nd Street
New York 23, N.Y.
Endicott 2-6799

December 9, 1950

Dear Jane,

Do what thou wilt shall be the whole of the Law!

  Thanks for yours of Dec, 4 with $60 M.O. I am pleased to see that $10 can be considered as from WTS and I'm entering it thus. – Monte sent me a nice check which helps for the A.A. fees.
  Hugh: I am gratified about the way he works. Do give him *Equ.* I, 8 to study. How A.C. on page 14 took his resolution which he let grow gradually, and then kept to the injunction "Invoke Often!" Let him go through that record and remember that the operation continued with clocklike regularity and intensity through those many months on horseback through the walls of Yunnan-China, with wife and child! In the course of such work all kinds of fulfillments seem to appear which must be rejected if it is not That

for which one undertook the work. I have confidence in Hugh to do it right.

I must repeat again and again that in all genuine work, inspired from on high, there are guardians who supervise the work. Nor must you or he forget that 666, The Beast, is operative all along and is silently testing worthy candidates.

Monty: the spelling is Memphis and Misraim. But what is the "Eastern Star" - it isn't Besant's co-masonry by any chance? I never heard of it. Is it an Order or a Lodge working under a proper legal charter? From what I know he would have to take oaths of secrecy. Will they not conflict with what he really stands for? Is the Eastern Star an Order that admits women? If so it would not be considered legal by proper masons.

I'm glad he is helping you with your health. I do hope you'll get really well again. You are indispensable. There is no one now who could take your place. – I'm glad Phyllis has come back to you. She is valuable. But it is up to her alone to kill the demon to whom she swore allegiance because he satisfied her sexually. I've said this before: that it is probably harder for a woman to drop a teacher that has served his purpose. A.C. had to drop such people as MacGregor Mathers, and several others, because his allegiance was ultimately to Aiwass; all others were but stepping stones. The same is true for all of us. We must learn that a visible human being cannot be the ultimate goal. We have to seek for that on the invisible planes.

Give my love to Mildred and Ray. They always are close to my thoughts. There is so much genuine loyalty in them and steadfastness! – I think there is no more danger for de-control of rents going into effect soon.

About your appearing in the Mass. Really, I don't know. If in any doubt, learn to send out SOS calls, and listen to the answer. On the whole it seems to me that WTS is showing signs of much improvement. Yet, as his mind may have a certain ascendency over yours, you may always have to be on your guard. But if he is going to do the Mass, it can only do good. If you should see that he is going straight for it, I don't think it would be wrong to appear in it.

I hope to be able to complete my catalogue within a few days. I will then send you a set, and I would like you to show it to

WTS. I want you to remain the custodian of the copy. – This catalogue will probably stand considerable improvement. It is the fourth that I have made. But always, when a new shipment arrived, I had to throw the old one overboard. My real catalogue is my Index card file. But that cannot be duplicated, or sent out.

I really don't know how I can get through with the work. I have quite a number of important letters which demand a lot of thought, and which have not yet been attended to. For instance, I have an application from a promising man from Ireland, born a German, who wants to become a Probationer of the A∴A∴. Do you have the Forms for the required pledges? If so, please send me a copy. I have never taken on any students. Nor were any formal Forms or pledges exchanged between myself and A.C. He had travelled a long way since building up his conception of the workings of the A∴A∴ grades or degrees. Do you have the various pledges and tasks? Please write by return. My man wants to start work on Dec. 21 and wants my acquiescence. All formal work is rather abhorrent to me.

I have not yet answered W.T.S.'s last letter of Nov. 5, but will do so within a few days. And his is only one of many!

There was something on my mind to tell, but I can't think of it.

Love is the law, love under will.

Love from Sascha and yours,

Karl

5169 ½ Fountain Avenue
Los Angeles, 27, California

December 15, 1950

Dear Karl:

Do what thou wilt shall be the whole of the Law.

Enclosed are 5 mimeographed copies of "Oath of a Probationer" of A∴A∴ and one copy of "Horned Moon" by Jack Parsons -- mentioned by him in the paper you sent me for identification. I regret the day's delay in getting these A∴A∴ papers to you, but I failed to locate my copies and so had to await the evening to get copies from WTS. He will send you samples of Examination papers of various sorts.

A.C.'s Probationer Oaths were on beautiful paper, with some gold lettering, and two seals, one red, the other black, with the appropriate ribbons attached. The Oath itself has full instructions on the back, but I will add that whereas a full Magical Diary for one year, after which came the examination paper -- in Cefalu the diaries were read rather frequently, and we were analysed on the blank sheet left for that purpose. I.e. We wrote on one side of the paper only, the other side was left free for A.C.'s notes re entries. The year would be a test for the applicant's really wanting A∴A∴, I assume; it also protected the Guru.

The Eastern Star is composed only of women – is no part of Theosophy – and was organized by the Masons, no doubt for their women folk; possibly at their request and to keep them occupied. They have rituals, hold offices, etc., as do the Masons, and are pleased indeed when complimented for good leadership in the Chair. Which is for one year, I suppose.

A letter yesterday from Jean tells me that it is impossible to put on an initiation at the Ranch. There ain't no roof on the aforesaid walls put up by Ero & Harold at Roy's request. Also there is the water shortage, and cold cold what is of it. We will talk things over when they come down for the Xmas holidays.

I plan to take part in the Mass the Sunday before Christmas, when the man and his wife have promised to come.

Love is the law, love under will.

All love to you and Sasha,

Jane

Hampton N.J.

Jan. 5, 1952

Dear Jane:

Do what thou wilt shall be the whole of the Law.

Thank you for your long letter with enclosures, which I return with this.

I'll write Paul soon. The school seems to have accepted my suggestions and are keeping Aleister. I'll need help and am sure Paul will do so as soon as I write him. It was a complicated correspondence to get the result, as Deirdre MacAlpine is not just what you'd call businesslike. And one letter never reached me from her. It was mailed to the former address.

I saw Ero shake his fist at me at the time of the accident, but never told anybody. The whole relation at H.Q. has been a mess. Joe, since Barstow, figured Jean was or would be his. There was a break between Ero & Jean practically when they arrived here, and once or twice Jean was on her knees before me (literally, not figuratively!!) imploring me to take her away from Ero. It foundered on the rocky iciness of my nature, my below-par libido, my slowness of reaction to obey directives from on high(which, I realised much later, it probably was.) But on the other occasions Jean played up intensely to Joe to such an extent that Joe went to

Newark and rented a 3-room apt. for the purpose. And nothing happened! It must have been a blow to Joe, and a magical lesson, which, I hope, he has learned and assimilated in a BALANCED WAY, by which I mean that I hope he does not carry a grudge against all women to having led him by the nose in such a humiliating way. Needless to say, I had nothing whatever to do with this part of the drama, except possibly unconsciously.

Then, Jean played a game in a primitive and a little too obvious way with Sascha, who, being so much more mature, saw through it from the start, causing antagonism. – My break with S. is ordained, I feel sure. May-be my subconscious wants me to make the break on my terms, when I think the time has arrived. Yet I know that all such considerations are bunk. Jean would be excellent as a partner for me in the Work which I need, but she needs one for other things too.

My prime consideration is to preserve the assets as much as I can manage, for the G.W. If we sell H.Q. there must be enough in my share to have something to operate with when I should arrive in Cal.

I like Jean. I like Ero. I like and respect Joe very highly. (He is a King.) He has behaved and acted royally, and poured out lavishly – I'm mot speaking about his transfer -- and Sascha alone has seen this deeply, while Joe seems to have been influenced intensely against the one person who Understood him, his nature, and his problems!) Add to this trio Frederic's presence, the Sascha-problem, and you get the Five-Body problem, which even mathematically is insolvable. Irrationally, yes, it can be solved, but that requires instant understanding of what your HGA counsels, and acting thereon without doubt, or arguing. I am still very low, I know. I am quite prepared to place all the blame on myself alone.

I have had the K.& C. since 1927 (Boston phase). 1931 was my 7°=4° period. Then 666 pushed me into the Abyss. (I reacted wildly, and smashed everything of A.C.'s plans with very tragic results for him. It was "danger and trouble" for him. 1935 brought the Babe of the Abyss. and 1938 A.C. acknowledged me as M.T. --- Now here is my incredible blindness: In retrospect I can see all this, now at least. But it was only in 1946 or 1947 that I began to realise what the HGA might mean, or had meant since

1927. I never realised that A.C. actually considered me a M.T. until he reminded me in a letter of about 1946 or 1947 that a M.T.' ought not to act or think the way I expressed myself' in letters. I could (now) give some striking examples of my blindness in matters of the HGA. A.C. thought I was faking ignorance, while it is the bitter truth that I was so totally blind. (In 1887 I had a serious eye disease and was for months in a hospital; had to wear blue glasses up to my 7th or 9th year. When I mentioned this to A.C. soon after I met him – he discovered my blindness quickly – he thought he could cure me magically. But the way I saw and see it, it is part of my T.W.)

May-be this explains some things to you.

Ritual: yes, indeed, I do not care for them but I do not loathe them! By ritual I mean any form of invocation or practice that implies dramatic performance. Nor do I understand such formulae as IHVH, or Geomancy- I would not call reciting the Holy Books ritual. I view it as a sort of mantra as once I start a chapter, it keeps running along without my being consciously aware of it. If I am interrupted – it continues at the exact spot where I was stopped, the moment when the interruptions have ceased.

The idea back of the term Ritual in AL, 220 is much more general and universal. Political, moral, ethical, religious conventions have a form or ritual as a basis. This refers especially to the ritual of law in this country. Anybody who has been the victim of legal, religious, or moral procedures – better persecutions – knows this. They are called "black"rituals.

Oh! I know well about Roy having played the "spark-plug" for Phyllis' growth to Tiphereth (I'm sure that's what it is!). But we must not mistake the tool for Adonai. You throw the tool away when used and keep on with the job. That's where Phyllis got on the wrong track. Incidentally, I feel sometimes as if Phyllis focused her imagination too much on me as an object of love. If you deem it wise to discourage this, do. I like everything about her. But I am not a lover!

Yes, we should have printed A.C. on the title page of 418.

I enclose the Texan Raymond letters. Please return after reading. The duplicate copies I sent you you can keep.

Candy[77]: this sounds truly astonishing. Can you get her birth date?

Love is the law, love under will.

Karl

Your Solstice gift for H.Q. came last week. it is a masterpiece in every respect, and a work of art. Thank you so much. Everybody admired it, also some experts.

K. J. Germer
260 West 72nd Street
New York 23, N.Y.
Endicott 2-6799

February 21, 1952

Dear Phyllis,

Do what thou wilt shall be the whole of the Law!

    I have a number of letters, older than yours, unanswered, for I am too overworked with mundane matters – if you like to call it – for every bit of mundane work is with me part of, and in service to, the G.W. Still, I want to say a few words in answer to yours at once.
    Thanks for list of books – more than I would have expected.
    I cannot follow in every detail your qabalistic combinations, though I admit they may have a deep meaning for you. But you keep harking back and on the number of 111 for

---

[77] Marjorie Cameron

which Roy Leffingwell claimed that it was his! Now, please let me tell you that there are many people in the order who at one time or other claimed this number as theirs. The proof in the pudding is that the claimant live up to that number. R.L. never did!

Roy Leffingwell never succeeded in reaching even the foothills of the mountain. He was up to the last full of vanity, self-importance, and, I must say it brutally to you, of dishonesty, by which I mean spiritual dishonesty. I can tell you now that A.C. perceived this many years ago before his death, and he warned me very especially not to be too trustful towards him.

What I admire in you is your beautiful purity of soul. Yet it is those whom the enemy (who ultimately is God Himself) picks out for His severest tests. They are tested in the very quality in which they excel, for every positive quality, if not balanced, can become a danger towards reaching those shores beyond where there is no preference either right or left. If you keep on seeing in the fallen R.L. that little bit of genuine spark that was so hidden under the mountain of impurity, with possibly dreams of "pure woman or maiden saving impure man", you remain simply obsessed.

The process of freeing oneself of such obsession is a long and hard one. Meditate deeply on *LXV*, III, the verses about Theli, Then, Lilith. It is only the appeal to Adonai that will help you get somewhere. And then finally, even that helps no more, and it needs the appeal to the Elephant Gods, as it is there expressed. I feel you are under guidance. But there comes a time where the inmost soul has to take a strong and voluntary step itself. - - -

There are millions of male stars in the universe. The French have a saying "un cou chasse l'autre"; one could transpose that and say: "one phallus chases the other away." The more male ideas, or points of view, a female soul marries, the wider becomes the horizon, the greater its universe; the less it can fall victim to one exclusive point. The more it finally is ready to marry 65 Himself!

Dear little Sister, I have watched you for a long time, since first you sent those sketches which revealed your genius. I sent them instantly to A.C. who saw them in the same light. Since then you have grown considerably, and I doubt not in the least that R.L. with his technical knack with women in a special field brought some things to maturity. But the attitude of each one of us, male or female, should be: now that's learnt; what next? There is no end to the Path!

Go see Jane. Show her this letter after having thought about it. She knows much of these things, having been around Aleister so long personally. May-be she can elucidate things that are dark. But for Adonai's sake: Go On!

Love is the law, love under will.

Karl

Re: typescript work.

We have come to the conclusion that it is not satisfactory to make a (small) number of carbon copies of this valuable material. There is so much to do, and it should be done properly. Carbons, if made in a suitable number of copies, must be done on thin paper, which is not good. The copies after #3 are not easily legible. Finally, there are not enough copies to go around. And, on top of all that, it takes such a long time to stick the carbons in every time. We are preparing steps to use another method, either the "Ditto" process, or Multigraph. In either case the typing is done on a Master, as thin as a carbon – only one single sheet! They will be sent to H.Q. and we will make 50 or more copies, the first as good as the last. The print will be on both sides, just like a book, and we will bind the finished book here, and then mail them out, so that distribution is over a wider area, in case of untoward events. This would assure preservation.

Frederic Mellinger is now working on the correction of the MSS., comparing with all available material from which we have to get a final version that has all the Greek, Hebrew, and Latin insertions correct from a literary point of view, so that when we finally send the TS. out for copying we shall gave the assurance that there will be no mistakes.

When we can start, we may require the help of everyone who has a typewriter. The Masters can be bought locally according to our directions. They cost from 4¢ to 8¢ per master, i.e. $4 to $8 per 100. We expect to be ready with the first job in 4-6 weeks.

260 W. 72
New York 23, N.Y.

March 1, 1952

Dear Jane,

Do what thou wilt shall be the whole of the Law.

    I enclose copy of a letter which Jack Parsons sent me. Show it to Wilfred, whom I wrote yesterday and mentioned it, saying that I was sending you a copy.
    This is another case of somebody promising trying to face a type of archdemon whose malignity he has not suspected. The accomplishment of the Abramelin operation is not as simple as that. The urge must surely not come from vanity, ambition, or other reasons such as lust for power. I sent Jack a short note, but I doubt it will help in any way.
    This is all for now. How did you like the Cammell book? I enclose copy of a letter written by Louis (Marlow) Wilkinson to Cammell. I replied extensively. – Oh yes: Wilkinson also mentioned that the son of his close friend John Cooper Powys is at the same school as Al. Ataturk, and they are good friends. He states: "and they seem to be friendly to each other. This Powys boy is evidently appreciative of A.A., tells me how unusual and how clever he is. I am glad to be able to get some news in this way."
    Wilkinson knows Deirdre MacAlpine well, has been visiting her in Scotland, but complains also that he cannot extract a word from her. "It is a peculiar obliquity on her part".

Love is the law, love under will.

From H.Q. in the midst of a violent snowstorm, I hope the last this year.

Ever yours, which love to Mary K.,

Karl

1071 S. Orange Grove Ave.
Pasadena, Cal.

2/11/52

Care F. [addressed to Germer]

93

No doubt you will be delighted to hear from an adept who has undertaken the operation of his H.G.A. in accord with our tradition.

The operation began auspiciously with a chromatic display of psychosomatic synchrons, and progressed rapidly to acute psychosis. The operation has alternated satisfactorily between manic hysteria and depressing melancholy stupor on approximately 60 (40?) cycles and satisfactory progress has been maintained in social ostracism, economic collapses and mental disorientation.

These attainments are mentioned not in any vainglorious spirit of conceit, but rather that they may serve as comfort and inspiration to other aspirants on the Path.

Now I'm off to the wilds of Mexico for a period, also in pursuit of the elusive H.G.A. before winding up in the guard finally via the booby hatch, the graveyard, on [illegible]

If the latter [illegible] you can tell all the little Practicuses that I wouldn't have missed it for anything.

93 93/93

Noone
Once called ∴ 210.
[Jack Parsons]

New York 23

April 1, 1952

Dear Phyllis,

Do what thou wilt shall be the whole of the Law.

Yours of March 22 arrived yesterday. Take your time to answer, I can well imagine that your time is fully taken up. In fact, I cannot see how you can cram all your personal, your school, and your children's' work into a 24 hour day!

Your letters always please me. I have often told you that I have watched you ever since you first sent those sketches and caricatures of Winona Blvd types in. I am very glad indeed to see how you follow your true guide, and how naturally all your thoughts and actions, as well as your whole life spring sanely from this simple root. It is so rare to watch some aspirant grow like this. I don't see where I'd have to criticize, or even to find a dent so that I could raise an interesting argument. I am glad to have you say that there is no magical bond any more between you and R.L. Surely, he served as a rung to a ladder at that time. And surely others ought to follow to get up to another rung. Does perhaps *Liber Ararita*, of which you must have a stereotyped copy (otherwise I'd send you one) help you to further understand this idea, of where the magician experiences all types of experiences, and discards them, because ultimately he dissolves all of them into the thirteen rays of the Crown, and that Crown is ONE.

Have you read *Heavenly Bridegrooms.* I once sent my copy to the West Coast, but I never heard whether anybody had really found much in that book: by an American woman who describes her intercourse with her HGA at length. The book appeared, I think, in 1917 and was very highly commented upon by A.C. in the *Blue Equ.* May-be Jane has a copy? This is only a suggestion to assist you in reading literature that can throw further light on that puzzling problem of the H.G.A., and Adonai. I tried to explain my point of view when I made those two lectures on *LXV*, and tried to show how *LXV* gives it under the two symbols of the Heart girt with the Serpent: there are two separate entities who together produce Adonai. The true contact of these two takes place on invisible planes. It is possible that in rare cases the twain meet in the physical body, but that is not necessary, for even if they do, they may not recognize each other as such, unless they both have risen to very high levels.

In the meantime the HGA sends messengers to train one in a particular job for which one has to become ripe, from time to time, who in themselves have no other purpose but just that, and should be discarded as the lesson is learnt. You understand this clearly, but it does no harm if I express the same idea in another form. You too understand that to "become normal, to become attached to one man etc." would, if satisfied, make you stagnant, and make a slave of you, rather than a Queen.

If it is true that you "love" now, I suggest you keep your magical diary all the more assiduously. For you never can tell when this may lead to a smaller or greater illumination when things are given to you and which you should carefully write down, even if they appear absurd at the moment, it may be years later that you begin gradually to understand the language. A.C. received *LXV* and *VII* in 1905, I believe, but it took years to understand the books. I had a phase of this sort in 1927 and while in the Concentration Camp in 1935. The power of the HGA is unbelievable to absurd details. For instance: in the C.C. I was in solitary confinement. When the operation came to a climax I was changed to another cell with the # 175 (which in the German code is the paragraph concerning buggery: and, as you know, it is the HGA who takes the active role in that operation, the magician has to become a bride, and the HGA takes the active role and the Magician "was pierced as a thief by the lord of the garden" (*LXV*, IV, 40; see the commentary to this.) For you as a woman this is easier, as you have the yielding attitude by nature. Also: paper, ink, and a pen, or pencil had been taken away from every one. But when it became necessary that I had to keep a diary, I had all of these; they came to me in the most natural way, without a plan on my part. And there are other instances of the foresight, wisdom, and power of those four-dimensional beings. Trust them! Study this book with the Comment deeply, or, better, if you find the time, learn one chapter, and gradually the whole book by heart. You will thank me some time for this advice.

Do you have a copy of *Liber Aleph*? If not Jane can loan you hers.

Now to some prosaic things: - The Commentary to *The Vision and the Voice* consists of annotations, made by Frederic in the copy of Vol. V of *The Equinox* to each verse or line, typewritten. I have one copy sent me at the time by Yorke typed straight through, marking each marginal note with page, and line from top or bottom, numbered. It is a tedious way of finding a particular note, unless one adds the notes into one's personal copy of the *Equ.*V. volume. The whole should be about 45 pages typewritten.

Typing on Multigraph Masters is a simple matter. I enclose one half of an actual master. All one has to do is to type straight on the blue side (they have 2 types; one yellow, one blue; we shall use the yellow masters, as we will not have to make more than 25 or 50 copies; the yellow master can be used up to 250 copies!) You would also have to use a special ribbon, sold by the local Multigraph-Addresograph distributor, which does not smudge and keeps the keys cleaner. Costs $1.50. A special eraser, costs 9 cents. and the master cost about 6.5 cents each if bought in lots of 100. Before you should do anything about this, ask me for the particular number of the masters, for they differ for different machines available.

All you have to do when you have finished is to send me the masters, and I'll get them run off here. (Unless there is a cheap local party available; it can be done anywhere in the U.S.)

As you see this is much easier typing than with umpteen carbons. Tell Jane about this plan. She may be able to enlist help from other parties who have sound suggestions. Our plan is only to get a goodly number of copies of A.C.'s works in as many hands as possible, to preserve them from any catastrophe.

I wish I could see you again. We would have much to talk about. And I'd love to do it.

Love is the law, love under will.

Karl

K. J. Germer
260 West 72nd Street
New York 23, N.Y.
Endicott 2-6799

May 5, 1952

Dear Phyllis,

Do what thou wilt shall be the whole of the Law.

    Yours of April 27, received to-day. I want to answer now, else I don't know when I'd get to it.
    It is hard to try to explain in a letter what my ideas are about the HGA. You'd ask me again and again. Nobody explained it to me. I believe every one has to find out for him/herself. You've got to start from another beginning. You are Phyllis on this plane, but you are also a Star from time immemorial and you have had innumerable lives, and represented different types in their course. If you imagine yourself for a moment (to use the imagery of *LXV*) as a Serpent, in which function you would not be operative as Phyllis, but on quite another plane: then there must equally be a Heart around which the serpent has to wind itself (*LXV*, II, (I am the Heart and thou the Serpent; wind thy coils closer about me...) which Heart may at this moment be manifest as a human – or not. It is not very important, because it is not Phyllis that is doing the winding, except as, by initiation she gets a reflection of what is going on in her soul as a human being. The Heart (on its plane) will constantly be doing the tickling, if you allow me to say so, the stimulating, the urging towards that goal (the union of the two) which It is longing to accomplish. Once you know the various vv.

of the 5 chapters of *LXV* by heart you will find innumerable passages that keep springing up in your soul and mind to illuminate you. (I wonder whether it is wise to memorize several books at a time. I suggest to stick to one, and that is *LXV,* and get the whole of it into your blood; *VII* can follow later; it will not mean or teach you too much now.)

You should not worry at all, at all about finding a human partner on this plane to accomplish that union, for it is a mystical union, and a human being would only distract or destroy. Take A.C.: he was looking through all his life for the real Sc[arlet] W[oman]. It was only at the end of his longing that he found what it was all about. And yet, every one of the Sc.W. had to convey a message, a lesson to him: but they were nothing but messengers; as soon as he took them to be more, they were torn away from him, and ended wretchedly.

Keep affirming in your heart your longing, your devotion, to 65, or the HGA: He is constantly around you, once He has found ingress to your soul. He is watching over you, and the more you begin to perceive His signs, that He is giving you, the more subtle will become your senses, and get attuned to His language.

Even the apparent difficulties in your life are part of His plan. One thing that all of us forget is that the clock on higher planes does not go by hours, days, months and years: the periods are different; the crime is impatience. The moment you stop desiring, in comes 65. Easy to say, huh? It is the simple things that are hard!

Moreover, it is the HGA Himself who will set the proper day and hour for the union. Then all will be prepared beautifully and fall in its place. The leisure, the aspiration, the Yoga, the surrounding, the silence, and all the rest. Did I not tell you that He arranged everything for me in the solitude of the Concentration Camp? Learn to abandon yourself with utter confidence to Him. Yet, as it is said: Invoke often! Learn the whole of *LXV* by heart!

Par. 1 on page 2 of your letter: I cannot judge. But here is a thought: some women, (also men) are able to enjoy in the physical union with such an intensity that they fall into a samadhic state. I envy them. May-be what you try to describe was this? If so, there was no union with your HGA. He only used some physical body to bring, what He wanted to give you, about. The thanks must not go to the body that was only used as a tool, an instrument. There should not be any 'backtracking'. If there is, it should be in the direction of false conceptions about the interpretation of the phenomenon, or phenomena, if the experience occurred frequently.

False entities or voices: yes there are plenty. And I must confess to my shame and regret that I have not solved the problem of how to distinguish in every case.

Diary: yes, there are often things or thoughts one is given or urged to write down, that seem outrageous (at the moment). Have you checked such thoughts 3 years later to see whether you do not discover that there is very deep material in them? Don't forget that Truth on the higher planes may look quite different from the conventional truth in which we have grown up.

Have you now in your possession one of the *LXV* reproductions with A.C.'s "Preliminary Analysis". Let me know, and I'll send you one. It may help in a way to get some rational understanding of many passages. Still, it was just a "Preliminary" analysis; there's much in the verses that has been discovered since; much is yet to discover.

Yes: we will have to copy *The Vision and The Voice* with the text, complete and the Notes under each page. It makes it hard work; true. but there are not many who have vol. V of *The Equinox*. Next time I'm out at HQ I'll get a volume ready, so that you can start to work. I think we shall have to use close (single) spacing, otherwise It would be too lengthy. I will see Jean who knows all about the Master typing, for the exact number of the masters. – Israel Regardie, while he was yet a Thelemite, typed a copy out for himself with the Notes under each page to which the note belonged and had it bound up. I had to return it to London. We found that there were innumerable mistakes, and I shall send you a correct set.

You will have to keep the keys of your Woodstock very clean; they are now very blurred.

I'll close now. I hope I have brought a little light into your doubts or questions.

Love is the law, love under will.

All the best to you.

Karl

PS. "Elephant Gods": see *LXV*, III.
In the Prel. Analysis this is surely explained. (Yes, it is!) Yet, in my experience, a sort of virago, or termagant arrived on the scene to break the obstruction by force.

K. J. Germer
260 West 72nd Street
New York 23, N.Y.
Endicott 2-6799

June 24, 1952

Dear Jane,

...The Greetings of the Equinox of Summer!

Do what thou wilt shall be the whole of the Law.

    Your short note re Jack of June 17, came y'day and your full letter with (incomplete) clippings, to-day. Thanks very much. I have sent letter and clippings to Jean-Ero and now answer from memory.
    I am deeply sorry. I had pinned great hopes on Jack, as the type of man he represents is badly needed in this country. But, I must confess, I remained sceptical about his attainment, of his having crossed the abyss. And when I heard from you about Candy I feared the worst. The trouble is that his education was not

rounded off; the American system does not favour the classics; We are so far beyond them: we are Americans! The deep all-round education which Europe gives, even if one does not go to college, which one breathes there, protects promising students of Jack's type from making a certain type of mistake.

However, this is past, and my sorrow remains. When I received your first note, I instantly had the conviction that you say Helen expressed: that the Gods saved him from a worse fate. – I find Phyllis' statement a definite message, to be heeded, as I have been doing, or trying to, all along. You know that I have a high regard for P.'s attainment. I'm sure she has gone through $5°=6°$, some time ago. I'm sure she is under guidance. I'm sure the typing of *Liber 418* will help her a lot. I wish I knew her better; when I was in L.A. the first time, I met her, but her image is indistinct. I don't think I exchanged one word with her. It is not my way. And yet I had followed her magical career since when first I saw those caricatures, which made a similar impression on A.C.

I'm glad you held that service and that so many were present. And Georgia too! - - I'll let you in on a thought which so far has to remain a secret. There is the spec to sell this house, and, if we get enough, to move further West. It is all vague as yet. It need not be California; there is Utah, for instance; centrally located; possibly a population not inherently hostile, as fanatics are and are always likely to be. I'm sure that all here would welcome the move. The problem will be to have something to make a living. – The climate is dry and may be more favourable; and high altitude is better, for me, at least. It is a decision involving many angles.

I had no idea Helen had so much experience; her observations re ink come very timely as Jean is coming to H.Q. with an expert on Saturday to run the machine and show us tricks. I can then ask him. Please thank Helen for her advice!

Your 'Mirror' clipping was incomplete, one page was missing. Please get me two sets of clippings of all papers discussing the case for myself; and send one set direct, by ordinary mail, to Yorke. If ordered quickly, they charge only the regular price for re-edition. He has been sending me duplicates of all clippings, and I have to reciprocate.

I must write to Wilfred soon; his letter and copies are still in the unanswered file. I'd have to write about the O.T.O., and dislike doing that.

Let this be all for now. Probably if I had not sent your letter off at once to Jean, I would have some other points to take up from it.

Love is the law, love under will.

Yours, with love,

Karl

P.S. Can you give me literature on the 'Oedipus complex' in English? It is a problem Joe has to solve, and though I've understood it for ages, I am a poor explainer. I wish I could advice him a book, or books, in which this deep-seated urge is made plain. Dianetics should have done it, but, apparently, there is nothing in it.

K

1701 Pico
Santa Monica

Dear Karl,

Do what thou wilt shall be the whole of the Law.

The Azar experience happened last July 1, 1952. I was awakened by a brilliant light coursing up and down the spine. It was the most intense light which I had ever experienced, although a little work has been done on this up to Tiphereth. This light did not light up the Anahata center, but seemed to be confined to the spinal region. Along with it there was some instruction and some explanation which left my mind as soon as I wakened. All I was able to save from the sleeping state was the word Azar. I was able to keep this because I was told very strongly not to forget it. I was admonished to write it down, which I didn't, but remembered it until the next morning. The word was in Hebrew and was to be enumerated, kabbalistic correspondences worked out, etc.

This happened after an evening which had been disturbing to me. W.T.S. and Helen had been over, and I had felt it necessary to do a banishing ritual after S. left. I did this both before and after my nightly ceremony directed to the Angel. The ceremony had been greatly lacking in concentration because of the aforesaid disturbance. I think Smith has this effect on me. I must continually find answers to his twisted reasoning and on this evening I was still thinking about what he had said as I went through my ceremony.

When I awoke I thought it had been the Angel, but reason also told me that it might be wishful thinking or pure intuition.

The proof of the pudding seems to lie in the word Azar, but I don't seem to make this fit into the past events. What does it have to do with 276? I think I am 276, for the enumeration fitted a certain period so well. The future is unknown, perhaps the word will fit in there somewhere. Meanwhile I am puzzled.

As you know, there was a period when I was involved deeply with Love. At the beginning of this period I felt the time had come to step out of my neophyte purpose or formulated motto "Firm of Purpose" and take on something else. I took on "I will to love". The first part of this, using every letter, enumerates to 165. Also P.E.P. added up to this. This latter were my initials when I was using my maiden name and I invariably signed all artistic works with those initials. The second half of this motto added to 111. The word love was a key. Also Roy was using this number, as you know. The whole of the motto added to 276, or spelt kabbalistically, ROV. Put a tail on the V and see a name. Now all letters having 2 in them are Beth, Kaph, and Resh. BKR in English. All letters having 7 are Zain, Ayin O and Nun final. So far, BKRZON. Is it not funny that my Dad and brother and son all carry the name Bickerton? 6, of course are the letters Vau, Samech and Mem final. These do not fit in obviously, but may through correspondences. Vau, for instance corresponds to Taurus, my rising sign. I'll not go further afield for there is danger of delusion.

The problem before me now is to find the significance of Azar. I have several ideas but think I might delude myself if I take them too seriously. That is why I asked you. Here are a few of my delvings. The letters ZAA are used for the 27th Aethyr. Moon is the symbol I get for this Aethyr. R is added to this, a number corresponding being 200 and also meaning the Sun. Now 276 written in that funny way which I took up before this dream? Starts with 2 looking like the moon and ends with 6 looking like the disk of the sun. Zain seems to fit very well as it corresponds to Gemini, in which sign I have four planets. Also I seem to work by intuition, a Gemini trait.

A propos to your suggestion to put a point in the sun! I do not at this time think I have attained to that point! Of course I shall not use it.

Now I'll leave this subject and go on to something removed from my self. Have you noticed in *The Book of the Law* how the words Ordeal X seem to suggest Aleph, the fool? OX from the initials of this. OX is Aleph. Aleph spelt out in full equals 111. Love enumerated with every letter used adds to 111. The Fool signifies both Nuit and Hadit. etc.

No, I have not heard further about AZAR. But I did have another experience where I realized the nothingness of pure existence and the power which made outward events. It all came on very easily, no light, no blinding sense of vision. It was just like stepping quietly from one room to another. No fanfare, no surprise. No Angel. I was That which made my life, and former lives and future ones. The That was nothing, just pure power. Creative power. It had no form, only the outer events which It (I) created had form. They appeared as a network of points connected by red lines and I was the center. A center of nothing without even the existence of light. I think this was probably very important and I am still astounded how easily it happened.

I had better stop right now before I pour out my black mood of the present on your shoulder. Will I never gain the Knowledge and Conversation? It seems such a waste of time to study on the silly college courses when I would rather study

Astrology or write poetry or paint, etc. But I know it is good discipline and I shall stop this lament this minute. Excuse please.

I've not forgotten that I have promised to show you some more poetry. It's not that they are much good, but they are a reflection of emotional and sometimes intuitional reactions to events. I can't write unless I am inspired, and inspiration has some value. Trouble is, the instrument of expression is not refined enough.

I hope you are well and are still planning to come out to Calif. I send all my best wishes.

W.T.S. knows about that bookstore combing London for Crowley's books. Jane told me that he told her.

Love is the law, love under will.

Love,

Phyllis

New York 23, N.Y.

July 7, 1952

Dear Phyllis,

Do what thou wilt shall be the whole of the Law.

Yours of July 1 reached me to-day. I answer at once so as not to keep you in suspense.

I cannot check on what I have written you about *Liber 418* and its arrangement, nor do I have any copy of it here to consult. I think the whole is arranged in the following parts: -

Introduction (this should have Roman numbers, I, II, III, etc.)
The titles of the 30 Aethyrs
The Call or Key in the Enochian and the translation
The Synopsis

I think in this order. But use your own judgment if in doubt. May-be in one letter I have made another suggestion? This may have come from doubt as to the validity about the "Synopsis" for which I had to write to London. This has been clarified. The "Synopsis" remains, and we leave out the : what is it called? at the end of the printed Vol. V, as the Synopsis replaces or improves it.

I suggest you start with page 1 for the titles, and we do not give a page number to the title page at all. It won't do to start with 1 and then have the Introduction begin with I (Roman).

Your machine shows a very clear type, and I'm glad we were mistaken about it being elite. I'm glad Helen was of help. I must write her and WTS. I'm also glad you've won another scholarship. Here is a request I mean very seriously: should you run into financial difficulties DO NOT hesitate to write me; I'm perfectly entitled to send you help from the fund that has been put at our disposal. Do not feel any spiritual qualms; it is your work, your sacrificing any possible vacation you probably need badly, your help, that count infinitely more than a small check that I can so easily send you, and which is lying in the bank for just such a purpose!

Now about your queries! What you say was very interesting. Do not forget that I have been asked to, but have not formally lifted that old injunction by A.C. against WTS. Why not? I don't know. I did not get an urge, that must suffice. Dear child: your questions go to the bottom of one of the deepest problems that have puzzled and tortured all initiated men and women from time immemorial, as you could find out from reading the records of the Saints (men or women), the great men of genius and so forth. I suppose it is the conflict with being human, with a body of flesh, and the fact that you have risen to or above Tiphereth where the voice of the Secret Guide is gradually taking over and begins to speak to your soul. The 20th Aethyr, I think it is, initiates this phase. I am a very poor teacher along these lines. I had this experience in 1927. But I am so dull and dumb (have you seen my horoscope? If not I'll send you the main data.) with so much Earth weighing it down, that I paid no attention to the guide, and its voice, until, let me say, 1947-48!!! This may sound unbelievable to you. But then, my case may be different. My connection with A.C., the man, was so close and intimate, that I all the time thought that the impulses came from the man A.C., and, thinking so, I obstructed. The moment the man died, the interpretation changed.

Do not follow me; obstruction to the impulses and the Voice has become second nature to me, through so many years, and I may have suffered for this obstruction badly, very badly, and made my life miserable without need. Learn to follow the voice instantly, without questioning unduly. Did I quote that old saying of Mystics: "Perinde ac cadaver!" If not, I repeat it and explain: the idea is that once one has heard the Voice and of the H.G.A. one must learn to follow INSTANTLY, even to the perishing of the "Cadaver" which is the mere body, and the rational mind which reasons against it.

I believe it is the hardest lesson to learn. I shall be happy if I can make one human's life happier for teaching a lesson, which I have too much failed to learn!

As you progress in they typing of *Liber 418*, you will discover that the H.G.A. grows ever more and more. In other words the path is unending. Your views and your understanding at this moment will not be the same as years hence. Do not think for one moment that A.C.'s conceptions about this problem were the same when he was 50 as at 70!!! "Strive ever to more..and if thou art truly mine..." etc.

All you can do is to remain in the intimacy of your H.G.A., train your finer senses and your soul to receive ever finer and subtler impulses; sometimes they appear, or may appear, atrocious (as you grow). Never mind. Your HGA looks farther ahead than mortal can. The only danger is that there are other beings in the invisible universe who are sent to (test or) thwart your true path; that is where constant inflaming yourself in prayer is so important, by the method that your HGA will indicate you.

Yes: one is alone in this task, it seems, as long as one does not fully realise the intimacy with one's constant companion. (See *LXV*, 1: "There was a maiden...and therein she forgot her sighing and her loneliness!" That particular verse, in that form, may apply to a special case, but it is universal in the general way.

Some day, if it comes about, and if we should move the documents to the West I may be able to show you some of A.C.'s records on similar matters, and how he disregarded messages which were give to him. We should all learn to do better and not make the same mistakes. – Yes: but *Liber VII* is my favourite; do learn it. – Curiously enough to-day when I got your letter I had another from London, urging to print Liber Aleph. We will. – Do you have a copy of *Liber LXXXI, The Tao Teh King*? If you want, I'd like to send you one. It also should be reproduced.

I always like to answer your letters. I should have amplified on your special questions re WTS. You will find that your Guide if constantly around you, especially when He knows that you need his advice. He begins with subtle inspirations. If he perceives that you are not trained or fine enough to heed them, understand them, he fires heavier artillery, though He dislikes the need for it; I have found that in cases where action was important, He had to almost materialise Himself, which is an effort, and takes away from your own nerves, I believe. So He had to almost shout at you.

93 93/93

Yours,

Karl

1701 Pico
Santa Monica, Calif.

July 16, 1953

Dear Karl,

Do what thou wilt shall be the whole of the Law.

    I can hardly write this letter for the touch is so different from that used on the electric typewriter. The latter is really a marvelous machine but it has taken some time to get fixed, and held up my progress with the masters.

    I am now trying to make up for lost time, doing from 10 to 15 masters a day, and have reached p. 52 of the manuscript (old masters). I expect to have these done by the end of this week and a start made on the letters in the box.

    My plan and hope is to finish M.W.T. by August 5 and then to take the vacation, some 700 miles North, to see my sister for two weeks.

    We are all planning on it and looking forward to the trip. We hope to leave Aug. 7 and go by Greyhound bus.

    When I come back I should like to start immediately on *Liber Aleph*, if I may. This is the Book I really wanted to do this summer, I want it very badly. I could get a good deal done on it before school starts on Sept. 20 or thereabouts, and probably finish it off before the school work becomes absorbing. What do you say?

    I hear that you plan to fly to Calif. this summer. I can only hope that it won't be while I am away, for I think I have much to say to you.

    Your last letter was very helpful. Asar spelling did assist to explain Azar. The latter spelling had to be so in order to connect the thing with me. Otherwise I should not have wanted to claim it. I showed Jane your letter and she immediately quoted "Let Asar be the adorant". That was it, right that moment, what I had wanted for a long time. I had been working a little on the Third Chap. of *Liber AL* and had not looked at the first. But the time of her quotes and letter fitted into place beautifully, I probably should not have been ready for it sooner.

When I got to the place in the Introduction of M.W.T. where it mentions the values of the Greek letters (numerical), I was deeply disappointed to find this information left out. I have only been wanting those values for 10 years, about! Are they the same as the Hebrew equivalent letter with its value? If not, where may I find the Greek Qabalah? I know no Greek, but I see I must learn something about it. The Qabalah and its tie-up into Tarot and Astrology fascinate me greatly. Already parts of it have sprung into life. There was even a stage with R. when I was able to name the card which pertained to the particular Operation.

"Qabalistic counting of words in English" – A.C. did it for the word 'Love' in the Introduction to M.W.T. Maybe it is wrong in all cases to so do, I don't doubt. I thought A.C. did discover the English Qabalah? by finding the correspondence of the English letters to the Hebrew? No? Not even part of it?

I have just read through A.C.'s letter on Astrology and find no fault with it. I have been laughing at what Mellinger wanted to cross out though! Shall I say I think he is Pompous? Now I am being devilish, and it is against my principals to make personal remarks in a letter. Bad girl! And that after I got my initial training in Astrology from him, too! I should tell you a story on this score some time! More devilishness!

I adore doing M.W.T. I have fun with it. And in many cases I am so in sympathy with what A.C. says! I guess I shall have to grant you what you said about Tiphereth, for what A.C. writes about that stage has sprung into meaning for me. When once one has known that burning joy - - - - -

> "Ah, little world, must you still be crawling
> When I am flying?
> Come and fly with me!"

Can one meet the Angel on another plane? I have never been any good at Astral work and don't really understand it. But one can still have a conscious mind going on and taking note of things and still be somewhere else, all the while in a position in the body. Is it not so? Does not all these things take place in the brain? Are not the higher planes merely other states of consciousness? All this sounds so confusing. I shall try to explain.

One lies in a certain position and is in the body, one knows so all the time. The mind may be subdued but still hums along and notes down happenings, sort of like a scribe. It may even be surprised all by itself at things that happen, but still not be in the place where it happens. And some other part, let us call it the aspiration, is on an entirely different plane and is conversing there! There is even landscape which it experiences! There is the vastness of space inside the brain!

Ah, this is enough for tonight. It is almost midnight and I must go to bed. So I can type tomorrow, of course.

Love is the law, love under will.

Fraternally,

Phyllis

1411 So. Federal
West Los Angeles 25, Calif.

July 20, 1952

Dear Karl,

Do what thou wilt shall be the whole of the Law.

Thank you so much for the offer of a little financial help at this time, both in your letter to me and in one to Jane. She told me about it. Of course I refused. I appreciate this gesture very much but you have all the burden of managing the books and their distribution, and, if, as you hint, you are to come out to the west, there is the problem of moving all those materials. I really could not, in all seriousness, and for the sake of my own sense of honour, accept anything at all. We are in this business together, all of us, about the books, that is. My small contribution of typing is not enough as it is, without my accepting any money from you. I always make ends meet, no matter how things get tight. So do not worry on that score. However, I would like to say that I am very grateful for this generous gesture.

    I have been looking over your chart and I notice that the Dragon's tail is in the seventh house. According to my method of interpretation, this would mean that the seventh house, partnerships, marriage and sociability would be the sphere of least resistance, possibly the point of self undoing. On the other hand, the Dragon's head is in the first house, in conjunction with Uranus. This would give an unusual and surprising personality. Uranus in the first house gives you that New Aeon slant, so to speak. The curious thing about this planet is that it is one angle of a grand trine. Pluto is trining it from Gemini, and Sun and Mars from Aquarius. This could almost be unusable and too fortunate for occult expression if it wasn't for your Jupiter in the twelfth house of confinement and of the soul's growth in darkness forming a square to Pluto. This helps to release the energies of this fortunate grand trine. You probably know that the Uranus and Pluto in the configuration are excellent for occult work. The fact that Pluto is retrograde makes its effect on you an inner growth of this power, instead of outer. It is a planet of rebirth, as a retrograde planet it would seem to indicate in our chart a protest against the old order of society. You probably know all this, I am wandering on through the various aspects of your chart, as though you were here to listen to my thoughts. Also, Pluto in the ninth house is connected with Philosophy and far-reaching thoughts. A master of the Royal Art is what comes immediately to my mind. Pluto quincunx to Venus and Mercury seems to indicate an adjustment and self-improvement of this power in the house of the home or of the soul. The home and fourth house matters of the subconscious and soul, etc. are sometimes upset by the effect of Uranus squaring them from the first house. Here is a challenge and a problem for you to work out at times. You may get a violent discord in the home because of your Uranian personality. Decisions are forced upon you which you must meet. Quiet and confinement will at times smooth all things down, for Jupiter trines this fourth house Venus and Mercury. Your planets are so interwoven with each other, it is very remarkable. This would seem to indicate that one department of your life is extremely wound up in another. Nothing is cut off and left out, all works together in the wholeness of your nature.

This fact also makes it difficult for me to get a good picture of your chart. Well-integrated is my decision. You say Earth weighs it down. I don't quite think so, I think it is more this trine effect. Yet your challenges from the squares would make the trines go to work for you. Anyhow, with the addition of Pluto to your chart, this makes five planets for air or intellect. But it strikes me that there is sometimes difficulty in expressing the intellect, or to get it to work for you. It is as though you had to build up some kind of steam pressure to make it go to work, and you would not always feel like doing this. It would be an effort. Given quiet and peace, free from the pressures of the Uranian personality and need for action, the intellect would probably flow more smoothly in its workings.

Uranus in conjunction with the North Node, or Dragon's Head has made you develop the personal self and has made this personal self extremely fortunate. Things drop into your lap like plums so to speak. Also this Uranus position in the grand trine and with the Node indicates your Destiny or position in occult matters. With this configuration is becomes a natural thing that you should now be in your present position as executor of A.C.'s will and as the gentleman we all look up to as our present leader here on the west Coast. It is a matter of Fate or Destiny. The growth of this destiny takes place in confinement or quiet. Again back to Jupiter in the 12th, you see.

Now I am going to be very frank, which I probably shouldn't be in a letter, but as I talk to you. However, I hope you will forgive me. I see in this grand trine of yours extremely great energy for the Royal Art or for a Magick approach to life. Do you know what I mean? Why do I say great energy? Because Mars and the Sun are conjunct. This gives great energy tied up with the individual Self, they trine Uranus, the inventive and explosive planet, and again trine Pluto on the other side, the regenerative power of Sex in its highest form and working. But this power does not work out through the house of marriage satisfactorily because of the Dragon's Tail in that position. It is challenged by the 12th house Jupiter and by the fourth house Venus and Mercury and is forced to work through these channels by their very nature of obstacle set in the way. But Venus and Mercury are quincunx to Pluto, an aspect of adjustment and expansion and self-improvement. Again pointing to the fact that this growth has a lot to do with the fourth house of soul and home, etc. Sun and Mars make another quincunx to Jupiter in the 10th house. Self-improvement with confinement and through fifth house matters of outward expression, loves and children. Children? none of your own because of the powerful Sun and Mars in the fifth. But an interest in them.

Saturn makes and quintile aspect to Jupiter, which gives mastery over your affairs and great creative power. Moon is sextile, giving harmonious action from the 7th house of legacy through women. Moon – woman. Also emotional life harmonious with the practical affairs, and their settling, also moon forms a sextile to Mars, which makes a harmonious aspect to help further the fifth house martial energy. Which energy is tied up in the grand trine with Pluto and Uranus. Moon square Mercury, another obstacle to using the intellect. Intellect challenges the world of emotions and vice versa.

This is by no means all, I have just begun to scratch the surface so to speak. Perhaps my analysis has gone wide in some places. If so, please let me know. I am such a young Astrologer, I like to know if I get it correct. It is a check on my mode of working. But I am going to have to stop this reading of your chart, for it is taking up so much of this morning and I know very well I should get to work on the *Vision*. I haven't even gone into the position of Neptune, nor into finding any parallels, if there are any. Will you forgive me if I stop and if you like I will continue with this in future letters?

If you are really coming out to the West I think it would be a very good thing. W.T. has become a problem to me, at least. I very much feel that a person with higher knowledge than mine should analyze the situation and act accordingly. I don't think I aught to tell you my thoughts on the matter, for they might bear some influence, and I may not be really qualified to judge. Further, the problem is up to someone above my position and above his. It really has nothing to do with me except that having met him again there is an equation to work out on this score, but not so far as the Order's decision is concerned. This sounds terribly involved, I hope you gather what I mean.

You mention "the fact that you have risen to or above Tiphereth". And you surprise me exceedingly. I had never thought of it this way. If anything, I thought my position would be indicative of aspiring towards Yesod. To me there is a path stretching before and behind with no landmarks on it. A judgement saying I have risen to Tiphereth belongs to the outside world and not to me at all. If it is really true, then perhaps it is only an emanation on the outer of an inner state of soul. I can hardly describe what has happened to me, but something has, that is certain. I have changed from what I was in the past. There is an "unheard voice". But there are no visions such as one would expect with Tiphereth. It is like going to sleep and dreaming and gradually growing, and then waking up when somebody throws cold water in your face and says "Tiphereth". One wonders which is truth and is inclined to believe in the quietness of the dark more than the cold water.

As for the voice, in this way I reason about it. One can act in one way or another, one can go this road or another, and in the end it does not matter in the least. One is a mote of sunlight dancing in the sun and all that matters is that Light which is one's source and one's object of love. How can one road or another possibly make any difference then? So why not follow that unheard voice? If intuition speaks, one might just as well follow its dictates. For any direction is the same, as long as there is the Sunlight. The spiritual Sun, that is. All experiences are necessary in the long run, they are emanations of Nuit, they are the possibilities of Nuit experienced by Hadit or the point of light that each one of us is. The only thing necessary is the Love of Nuit's possibilities. I am apt to call it passion for experience, or for existence. But passion anyway, no matter what happens.

I am appreciating the "Vision" very much. It is unbelievable how several years ago I could not understand it, and now so much becomes clear.

Yes, I have a typewritten copy of the *Tao Teh King*. Mildred gave it to me not so very long ago. I thank you for your offer of one. I hope you are serious about coming out West. The feeling is personal, I must confess. I do not know whether this is really the best thing for you financially or otherwise. I do not know the first thing about how good for the Order it would be, or for such matters as storage and distribution of copies of the books, or so on. So you see I can only say that I hope you will come out here from a personal angle.

Now I must really stop, I have been all morning and the children have been milling around for something to do. Kwen is visiting us this week. I like him very much and think he has possibilities.

Love is the law, love under will.

Fraternally,

Phyllis

1411 S. Federal
West Los Angeles, 25, Calif

August 13, 1952

Dear Karl,

Do what thou wilt shall be the whole of the Law.

I was very sorry to hear from Jane yesterday about your accident. Three broken ribs, and a punctured lung are nothing to make you feel very joyful, I am sure. But I should think, from your natal horoscope, that this is now the confinement in which you make great forward strides. You will be having the peace and quiet which you so much need. A change to get away from your Uranian personality commitments, *n'est-ce pas*?

The horoscope analysis by Surya was received by me and I have been very interested in reading it. I have let Jane see it, and we enjoyed it together. She can be trusted to let its contents get no further. For myself, I feel honored that you have seen fit to allow me to read it. I had a feeling that you must have many horoscope analysis that were much better than mine could be at this moment of time, when I wrote you my very short beginning of an analysis. That is why I plunged immediately into aspects, and tried to get an over-all picture first. I happen to think much of all the aspects, even the little ones like semi-sextiles because they have worked for my method of analysis in the past. But I don't use wide aspects which are over 10 degrees distance in the case of the sun and the moon or which are over 7 degrees distance in the case of the other planets, and I notice that this horoscope you sent me does use these wide aspects. That is the difference you will find between astrologers. And this is why it is best to have as many astrologers as you can find to help you work on your chart. The very best interpretation of a chart which can possibly be made is the one you do for yourself. No astrologer can possibly know all the contents of your personality because the multitudinous aspects and other factors make the task an impossible one. Also no astrologer can know just what you have done with the original birth factors. How your will has changed the appearance of certain tendencies, for instance. There is always the principle of indeterminancy in a horoscope as there is in trying to know just what an atom is like.

But this is probably all too much heavy stuff for a person in bed, even though his mind is going while his body rests. You mean much to us all so I hope you will make the rest a good one and become more Whole through it. You have all my sympathy, and good wishes for a quick recovery and good health afterwards.

The book is well along and I have ploughed through the Tenth Aethyr to date. You probably remember the character of this one. Needless to say I was greatly impressed with the horror of the Vision, but also glad to know that there is a method of handling it.

Silence and concentration is the only answer to the working of the Ruach when it gets to such a contradictory stage at the Abyss. This is very good to know. Now I am going on into the 9th Aethyr and love to hear about the blessing which it deals with. This book is doing me much good; many years ago I could never have dreamt it would mean so much.

I have a friend staying with me for two weeks right now. I have known her for a long time and she is a wonderful sport and very generous. We have often called her the fairy godmother of the children. She sees to it that they get the most wanted gift on Christmas and birthdays, etc. It was she who supplied Sunny with his electric train and Lisa with her doll buggy. We have fun together too, for she has a marvelous sense of humour. So you see that life is not all work, I manage to enjoy myself.

Just now I had to settle an argument between the children about an old box. One never knows what will be precious to them next. One day they may help to throw out the junk and the next day they will try to rescue it from the wastebasket and fight with every one they think has had a hand in throwing it out. Life is never dull in my house. Also one wouldn't dare have nerves. Jane has often remarked about how I am able to shut out all the goings on and get work done such as studying and typing and letters in the midst of a rampage. I have had to develop the quality in self defense. The best thing about it is that I can use the humour in the situation and so can Jean, the friend I describe above. We have a lot of moments when the laughter bursts the walls.

Now they have all gone off to the store and I sit here, unable to think because it is so quiet.

I shall not go further into your horoscope at this time, for it would only be unwelcome at this moment, I feel. There comes a time when no outside word from any other person has any bearing on a situation. I feel that you have now such a time. Intuitionally, I confess. If the intuition is wrong, you can let me know sometime. I like to check up on them. One must try to be scientific even with such illusory matters.

There is one thing which I hope has not changed in aspect with your stay in bed and your convalescence. And that, of course, is the idea of coming out to California. But then this is your decision and one must keep hands out of it, or even wishes and hopes. You know, often I may seem very indifferent to things, and sometimes I wonder if I am inhuman. But it is all brought on by an extreme desire to influence another in his will in no possible way. "Do what thou wilt", one says to the other person and my silence often means only this. So now I have scolded myself for saying "I hope", and have tried to explain a positive type of indifference to myself. The sort of indifference that operates when Brotherhood (the true kind) is in the thoughts. One keeps hands off (and hopes and wishes) because one cares for a brother and wishes to apply the Law. One does it with Love under Will. Am I getting involved again? I had better stop and let you get your rest.

Love is the law, love under will.

Fraternally,

Phyllis

P.S. Jane paid for the mailing out of contributions, so please don't concern yourself with such matters. I mailed another load of masters to your address in N.Y. last Mon., the 11th. Shall I continue to do so?

General Delivery
HAMPTON N.J.

September 5, 1952

Dear Phyllis,

Do what thou wilt shall be the whole of the Law.

I enclose a few lines for you with the letter I'm sending to Jane of yesterday. I'm short of envelopes, have not been in the N.Y. apartment for over a month to replenish stock, as I have had no chance so far to get it to the Post Office. No car; no mail delivery; and the P.O. is a mile and a half away, a distance I don't dare walk as yet.

As to astrology: I quite agree with your limitation to the orb of aspects to narrow limits. But, you see, there are different schools, and this particular lady in question has reached the state of clairvoyance to a remarkable extent. In such a case the chart itself is a mere medium of concentration. The actual interpretation of its meaning comes then from other planes. A.C. had a similar gift: he would look at a chart for a little while and say; no good! without actually analyzing aspects etc. It is a sort of psychometry that goes to work. You say you are a beginner: you can never know where you end.

You have been working marvellously at 418; we expect to finish what you had sent (up to pp 84) to-morrow, and, when we get the rest, can reel it off quickly as Jean and Ero have now got the knack.

I am sure the book has benefited you much on planes you are not consciously aware of. It will grow on you as time goes by. What we all have to realize deep in our heart is the fact that conscious life is just an appendix hanging down on this physical plane from a Universe which is so incredibly vaster, richer, and fuller.

Let me congratulate you on your work and thank you for your help, and use this opportunity to send you even now the

Greetings of the Equinox of Autumn!

Love is the law, love under will.

Yours fraternally,

Karl

HAMPTON N.J.

October 14, 1952

Lt. G. J. Raymond, USAF
3715 Alverta St.
Houston 21, Texas

Dear Lt. Raymond,

Do what thou wilt shall be the whole of the Law!

This is the Greeting with which the late Aleister Crowley began all his letters, and closed them with the formula at the end. They are some of the fundamental injunctions taken from *The Book of The Law,* of which I will send you a copy herewith. As time goes on you will hear a lot of this, and I advise that you get acquainted with it by first reading it.

Thank you for your personal data. They do not suffice, of course for the setting up of a horoscope. If you can get an approximation of the hour or, better, minute, let me know.

Can you let me have more information of what the Satanists, you mention, teach? There are conflicting systems. Satan is, of course, Saturn, the oldest and most distant of the planets in the traditional system, who is Chronos with the Greeks, the Lord of Time, with all the attributions that go with him. How did Aleister Crowley's name get in? There is a certain connection, but it requires a high degree of initiation to understand it.

John Symonds, to be frank from the start, is a pure newspaper man, who happened to meet A.C. shortly before his death and seemed suitable to write his biography for the outer public. He has amassed a wealth of data, but proved incapable to delve deeper and does not understand Crowley's teaching at all. But I'm glad he put you in touch with me.

There is a group in California with whom I could put you in touch and with whom you could discuss matters personally when you are there, which is, after all, a better approach than by correspondence alone. From there on we could proceed more quickly.

You will have seen what a vast Crowleian literature exists, and to get acquainted with it there is no other way but to begin to study some of them. Many in California have quite a large collection of Crowley's books, and occasionally you can pick them up in Los Angeles book stores. It is true, they are hard to get by, and the book dealers ask often very high prices. I have compiled a list of those items of which I could send you a copy, with the prices at which I would let you have them. However, the most important, as a foundation for the study of Crowley's works and thought, would be for you to try and obtain a set of *THE EQUINOX*, Vol. I, Numbers 1 – 10 and Vol. III, No. 1, called "The Blue Equinox" in the trade. If you like, I would try to locate a set. They are rare and may cost $50 or more. But they are a good investment, and can easily be sold again. Sometimes one can get a set cheaper in London.

What you probably need first of all is an intense course of reading and study to round of your knowledge. *Magick in Theory and Practice* (which is my list, below) and *The Blue Equinox*, mentioned above, contain a list of books for general reading. Among them are such books as *La Bas* (Down There) and others by Huymans that have some bearing in the Black Mass, and the Satanists, I think.

The address in California, you could contact is Miss Jane Wolfe, 5169 ½ Fountain ave, Los Angeles 27, Cal., who can put you in touch with others.

Here is the list of books of which I have a few spares: -

Eight Lectures On Yoga	$5.00
Little Essays Upon Truth	4.00
The Heart of The Master	4.00
Moonchild (which should appeal to you v. much	5.00
OLLA, a volume of Poetry	4.00

The Fun of The Fair	1.50
The City of God	1.50
The Equinox of The Gods	10.00
The Vision and The Voice with Introduction and Commentary *)	3.00
Magick In Theory & Practice	12.00
The Book of Thoth	50.00

The item marked *) has just been published and I have given you the dealers' price. It is a reprint of one of the most important books by The Master Therion (Aleister Crowley) which was first published in 1911 but without the Introduction and the Commentary.

When I am next in New York I will give your address to one or two book dealers who sometimes handle Crowley items, or able to get them if they have your name on their list. I could also, if you wish mention your name to some London book dealers who often have Crowley books, or can get them. I shall always be glad to advice you on any book that should be offered to you.

Love is the law, love under will.

Sincerely yours,

Karl Germer

Hampton N.J.

November 25, 1952

Dear Jane,

Do what thou wilt shall be the whole of the Law.

Your letter of Nov. 21 is one the like I have not had from you in ages. How can anyone, or you yourself, say you are getting old and all such things? Should your hospital stay have rejuvenated you, mentally at least? Your letter handles subjects that are not easy, yet you set them down in a clear, coherent way!

No: there is no gossip, and all that you tell is very valuable to me. I have no further word from Monty. Should it be possible that he only got this idea of wanting to become a real doctor for vanity's sake? If he made good money, and a good living, in L.A., I wonder what got into him to chuck it? – It is absurd to think that in Latin countries men have no mistresses, or girl friends etc., unless he has no knowledge of the world. – Your data give me a much better picture. I had little idea of the man, psychologically speaking. The few times I met him in LA. brought only superficial contact. It takes ages to get close to anybody, if at all, for me at least.

Louis and Meeka. I had made up my mind to watch my step before your letter came.

I much regret that I had given you Mrs. Bachrach's name and her yours. Sascha says that if she had known I was doing this she would have advised emphatically against it. She says: "Mrs. B. can and may only make mischief." I hope it will not be too difficult for you to shake her off. - -

We had to get the Multilith machine repaired (cost $70 !!) but we did 23 masters Sunday, and they are perfect. It is now only a matter of how quickly Ruth can send us masters, we can run them off quickly and publish *Liber 888*. The next, I think, ought to be *Liber Aleph*, though I would have preferred to have this book printed by a regular publisher.

How are your relations with WTS now?

Phyllis sent me her poems. They came yesterday. I am deeply moved about her art, the depth of her feeling, the purity of her soul and everything. What she does not know – or may-be she knows now – is that what she considers her weakness, is her strength. I wished she would plunge into new experiences. The scars are but those of the heroine. I'll write her. What she lacks is adequate vocabulary, and be able to find better words to match the rimes.

You have trained a fine successor.

Love is the law, love under will.

Love,
Karl

Encl. letter for Phyllis.

***

Hampton N.J.

November 25, 1952

Dear Phyllis,

Do what thou wilt shall be the whole of the Law.

Your poems, mailed November 1, came yesterday. They were a revelation in many respects. They are fine, genuine, lofty. They show a great depth of feeling, they come from deep down in the well.
Did you want me to criticize? Of course, you are an artist soul, I must have written this to you or Jane long before. As I can hardly be called an artist myself, with little knowledge of literature, especially in English, I can only make some general remarks.
It seems to me that there is development: the form, rhythm, quality of rime varies, or has improved. The sentiment is always clean and pure, but you do not have attained mastery in riming, rhythm, wealth of vocabulary, (that is number of words, often strange, short words not in ordinary use). How to improve this? I don't know. You surely know the classics in the English language? I might say that I know of A.C.: he knew all English poetry almost by heart; he studied the established meters and science and rules of poetry, set up by the ancient Greeks and modern writers. You have got to

know the various poetic "feet" (dactyl, Iambus, trochee, etc. etc.) and master them. Etc. etc. etc. Otherwise your poems, however beautiful, cannot become gems. Sometimes I notice that you want to express something almost inexpressible, and appear to fail. To express subtle, difficult thoughts or conceptions, in language is one of the hardest lessons to learn. It is not a matter of length, quite opposite! It is the art of using what I might call magic words, little used by the common crowd, or by the newspapers, but impregnated by meaning by authors and poets of old. Do not fall into the common American error, that American women are different: they do not have to study the classics as they do in Europe. They are a new race. They can take an airplane and fly right up to the top without having to go through the drudgery of the Europeans.

Don't overlook that it is your genius who inspires you to write poems. If you don't have learnt to write and read, even He cannot make His scribe write masterpieces. It is for that reason that all great artists learnt the trade first; then learnt facility and get experience. Then at last can the genius get busy, inspire thoughts and forms knowing that a little masterpiece will come out. –

A.C. made a deep study of why it is that sometimes poems which don't have a rational meaning, make the deepest impression on soul and mind? – I wish I had the time to go through your poems one by one and indicate what I mean. - - - If you rime future with nurture you get a painful effect; similarly with innumerable other cases. A.C. had made lists of words for which it was hard to find a rime: the problem of increasing his facility was everpresent in his mind. Not otherwise can you reach beyond the average scribblers.

Your later poems seem to show that you have begun to Understand: why? this sorrow has to be (caused by separation, I mean); why we must not in despair or disgust at facts of life throw down the lute and refuse to sing. Some day I hope I can let you see A.C.'s diaries where you can see that he never became blasé; that he always, to the end, remained young; kept his impressionality and sensitivity. The oyster can only produce one pearl, caused by the squeezing out of protective material around a piece of foreign matter in its body that causes great pain. We should be different. Most human beings, and especially women, harden their soul when once it has been hurt to the quick by some experience in love. But "Exceed! Exceed!" means among other things that you have to let your soul grow to ever loftier heights. The next break or separation ought to be faced courageously. After all there is always "that which remains". All great poets have suffered intense pain in their sensitive soul, and it was that phase which produced their immortal pearls.

This is a universal law. Even "heroes" that have their work marked out for jobs in the outer world, do their greatest deeds after their deepest disappointments. Their iron has to be tempered by intense heat, and hardened and shaped by cruel blows.

Have you read the stories of female Saints? If not, it would not be loss of time to try to unearth some and study their lives. Or male saints if easier to get by. Only: the women describe often enough their sexual relations with what they call "Jesus" or some other name.

One word about "loneliness". As you are Hadit in the final analysis, you are alone; from your point, your look-out on the universe is different from any other, without exception. What A.C.'s diaries showed more than anything else was his loneliness. The higher you rise the more this becomes intense and acute. See *VII*, iv, 43 "... rare and far and utterly lonely, even as Thou and I, O desolate soul my God!" And "Into my loneliness comes–" What? A being, or a human being? On no! It is "the sound of a flute". He did not appear as a human companion, though it could be argued that later she or he did, for a short phase, so that "the dreadful issue could be fought out".

It is a curse to the soul to strive after something unattainable in nature. It is a boon to the soul to understand at last, how nature, or life are, and not waste any more time to pursue a phantom.

It is quite a different thing to satisfy your physical nature and sip the honey of flowers where your HGA sends them your way, and take your fill, as long as you always keep in mind "But always unto Me!" When your sorrow and need are really serious, and you appeal to your H.G.A., be sure He will send the proper parties, and smooth the opportunities. You have got to attune your senses to His ways.

Sascha, who is an artist's soul as delicate as yours, read your poems and was moved to the very depth. She planned to write you herself. Whether she does it I don't know. But she has long seen your outstanding qualities.

Let this be all. It is almost too much.

Love is the law, love under will.

Fraternally with love,

Karl

I'm sending this again through Jane, and hope you won't mind if I leave it open.

Hampton N.J.

December 7, 1952

Dear Phyllis,

Do what thou wilt shall be the whole of the Law.

Yours of no date.

Inspiration comes, I believe, to different people from varying causes. Love is one. In general I believe one can say a phase of high pressure is needed to make one sit up, and be stirred to one's very depth. At least so it may be for people like me. My Concentration period brought me great rewards. There is a German author who wrote a 2 volume book with details of how he experienced a state of Samadhi: he gave the full case history, how he fell in love with a woman, how that woman betrayed him, which shocked him deepmost, but as he forgave her from the bottom of his heart the Samadhi set in and he had the most amazing experiences which he set down in detail. I had the book in my library, but it is gone.

Yes: by all means, when you have the time, send me the rest of the poems. I'd like to read them. They will be safe in the steel files, unless you want them returned. Sascha, who understands your soul so well is the only one who has seen them – and admired them.

"The dreadful issue was fought out": How shall I explain? "As above, so below" – every love is a war between opposites that strive for union. (If Hydrogen and Oxygen want to unite they create the hottest flame known in chemistry.) A genuine love has got to have passion in it. The greater the opposites, the greater the difference is between the two parties, the more passion will probably be created – or call it heat. "With the violent appetite of the beast I hunt thee through the universe". Every fibre must be inflamed to produce the greatest results. You see, it is a natural phenomenon. There are natures who can inflame their souls through their own imagination. Not me. I have none. Each has to discover his or her own faculties and means of getting out of their shell – the word is ecstasis. – Back to the dreadful issue: that war, I said above, may last for years with suffering to both sides, as long as the mutual passion is kept at red-hot heat. Then the Ibis-fellow may appear, in order to bring Understanding and mutual recognition.

It was wrong of me to talk about the problem as I did in my last. These things each one has to "mull over" for years and years and years, otherwise it may not be possible for the flash of sudden illumination to ignite the dry tinder. I mean: if there is not enough of the latter, it can't be done. You must work it out for yourself.

Yes, please return the books you have to this address, Registered. What is the sign you put ahead of your signature?

Love is the law, love under will.

All the best to you, fraternally,

Karl
Dear Karl,

Do what thou wilt shall be the whole of the Law.

Thank you for your wonderful letter. I found it very encouraging. Sometimes I would like to believe I am an artist, but I am beset with doubts more often than I can I can believe it. There are so many Failures, and unpolished works as a result of my brush or my pen; and there is so much daily drudgery to get out of the way before I can devote any time to an expression, that I feel I could do; that I haven't allowed as much inspiration to work out in art as I would like. Consequently, when I do paint or write a poem, the result is very imperfect owing to lack of application to the matter. The poems you have read were inspired by love, as you know, and that fervor helped to fill in a gap of a lack of good solid study. Now, of course, college is helping fill in that lack to some extent. Next Spring I shall also be taking a course called Introduction to the Study of Poetry. This will help polish off my style, should I ever write poetry again. You see, right now, I even doubt that I can. One walks in the shadows at times, and this is one of those periods. I know the quiet periods are necessary and a part of my pattern. I even long to have peace at odd moments. But when these moments come, I resent them, and long to be producing again. Talk about contrary human nature!

Poetry, or art, is only a by-product of something else, and well I know it. It is an effervescence or a spilling over from a capacity for "extraordinary love" as Schmolke puts it. The next time I love, who knows what will result? It may not be poetry at all!

Yes, I know about loneliness too. It has been my companion ever since my early teens. I no longer fear it, for it is as you can say, "there is something that remains". Whenever I wish, I can reach out and be assured of that "something". This certainty becomes stronger with each great event or lesson. But your letter may be the needed prod to do some more serious work.

You are right, I swing to the oyster effect, the attempt to cover up a hurt with a hard coating. But I am also very naive, and jump in for another experience which I know will not be happy. And I also know there is no certainty in life except the H.G.A. I sometimes get the queer effect of pain while at the same tie knowing it is only a shadow and temporary. Perhaps it is only negating one attitude with another. I have outgrown the emotions expressed in these poems and I doubt if I shall ever think that way again. Or rather, if I shall ever love that way again.

I feel as though I were struggling to put down ideas again, and am becoming involved. Well, I shall leave it. I am only glad you got some enjoyment from the poetry.

My new address is above and I am finally settled in and the worst of the work is done. My schoolwork has suffered some from the upset, but fortunately, most of my classes have been easy this semester. I doubt if I shall come off with as many A's as I had thought, though.

It strikes me just now that I haven't sent the whole lot of my poems, only about ¾ of them. Would you like to read any more? Yes, I have copies of them. I only asked for their return, because of a nagging worry that they might fall into the wrong hands and be misunderstood. They reveal too much. To tell the truth, there too much of a tendency among some of our Thelemites to poke into another person's business and gossip. Or at least I found it so some years ago. I withdrew from contact with some of the worst offenders since then. There is always the possibility that some of them might have improved, but a few will never do so. There, I don't often make comments like that. I don't like to remark about others very much. Also any remark Jane may say doesn't come under this category. That goes without saying. She has my fullest confidence. Jane is balanced and straight, which can't be said of many others.

You mention "the dreadful issue" from *Liber VII*. I memorized this section but was puzzled about just this phrase. What connection does it have with the appearance of the H.G.A. in the guise of another human? Also, when this sort of thing occurs, can not one lay it down to a projection of the H.G.A. onto another, and consequently worship it as such? One later may withdraw the projection and then the other human ceases to exercise the same magic and the affair is ended. Sometimes I think the H.G.A. is very effectively contacted in the projection image. It is a foreshadowing of His nature in the realm of matter and in an understandable form. This is something of the idea lying behind the poems.

How else can one explain the fact of human love? But have I talked about these things before and am I repeating myself? I often mull over these matters, trying to extract the utmost of meaning from love. For after all it is my expressed will.

Now I think I have been confusing enough. I had better stop. There is only one course that remains unconfusing, that is action. It is doing. All thoughts upon it are mere tools, stepladders to Understanding, but in the end thoughts do not bridge the gap.

With all the best to you.

Love is the law, love under will.

Phyllis

Shall I send *Equ.* 5 and *Liber Saturnus* to your present address?

1701 Pico
Santa Monica, Calif.

Jan. 3, 1953

Dear Karl,

Do what thou wilt shall be the whole of the Law.

Greetings of the Winter Solstice.

Please do not remark that you shouldn't have written the way you did on your first comment on my poems. You certainly should write first impressions. That is what I wanted from you and your comments were very helpful. I was also very interested in that first reaction in various of its facets, for it revealed Karl. I sensed in your first letter that the poems had moved you very strongly emotionally, imperfect as I feel them to be. The emotions are, it is true, an imperfect manifestation of existence. But if controlled they can lead one into high realms of inspiration. They can also mislead. The trick is control of and detachment from them and their effects at the same time the effects are working for one. "There is that which remains." They are a tool the same as is the intellect, and a much more dangerous tool, because not rational. Among the emotions one faces some of the most horrible demons known to human thought. But harness their powers, and one may reach empyrean heights.

I might add further, that I keep constantly before me your admonition of study of other poets. This I shall certainly do, in one way or another, in the hopes that I may write again, and write better.

Yes, I know about that opposite effect. It does not make peace, but it makes the best art.

The sigil you ask about comes from my number all run together – 276. Moon on top, then the cross of existence (incomplete), followed by the sun. I believe I wrote to you once how I came by that number and its Kabbalistic enumeration.

Did I tell you about the time I got the name of an Angel who had made of the spinal column a column of brilliant light? It reached as far as Tiphereth and the name was AZAR, which I was to write according to the Hebrew and find the Kabbalistic enumerations and correspondences. I did so, but the true significance has not yet struck the labors of my brain with the lightning bolt of truth. I mention the thing in case you might possibly have an enlightening comment.

Jane remarks that a certain bookstore in Hollywood is eager for Crowley's books to sell and has combed London for them. They seem to be in great demand. From this information would it not seem feasible that some publisher over here might be interested in publishing at his own expense and risk in hopes of a good sales of the volumes? Would not the royalties add up in time to pay for the publishing of the more difficult and abstruse works? In short, have you approached any publishers? It is possible that the time may be here when the public, or at least a portion of it, is awakening to the value of his writings.

If you want another book typed by me, I am very willing to do it next summer. How about *Liber Aleph*?

Schmolke says in the first sentence of his letter – "Thousand thanks for your parcel which I received by Br. Saturnus in Hampshire." Now I did not send any parcel, can he mean one from you? He must have made some mistake and should perhaps be set right.

He asks if I can read German as he would then send me a book on the new Astrology, the system he himself uses. Imagine my chagrin to have to answer that I can't read German, only French. I am almost mad enough to take up the study of German on my own.

I sent the books, registered, shortly before Xmas. I trust you have received them? I also sent a piece of ceramics done by Jane and myself for Headquarters.

May the New Year bring success!

Love is the law, love under will.
Fraternally,

Phyllis

5169 ½ Fountain Avenue
Los Angeles, 29, California

January 20, 1953

Dear Karl:

Do what thou wilt shall be the whole of the Law.

I am glad indeed to have your letter of January 5. It is a great help. Frankly, I have been puzzled on occasions, to the point of "What ails the men!" But who is Jane to ask questions? She who could today be as active as Candy had she accepted the bit. Two or three years ago, Schmolke gave me a wisp of cheer when he wrote that Mars in midheaven meant delayed action – until "late in life". I thank you for giving me this knowledge of yourself. And I do hope the property will soon pass along so that you can come out here.

Now for Candy. And I find it hard to put her together. First let me give Jack's description. Discernible as an air of fire type, with bronze red hair, fiery and subtle, determined and obstinate, sincere and perverse, with extruding personality, talent and intelligence. I regret to say I forgot to ask the birth date when she was here yesterday. But I now have it marked down – written. So I enclose copy of her first letter to me. Also a second handwritten one, which please return.

You knew, no doubt, that A.C. asked Jack to perform a Working, for the manifestation of one seeking (?) incarnation. Candy gave me Jack's records to read. They lack, of course, the orderliness, clear sight, and knowledge A.C. brings to his records. Too, I don't feel competent to judge them, for I am always mindful of Jack's interest in Witchcraft and Voo Doo. But he got results of sorts, worked hard on daily practices with partners and alone, also two spells on the desert. He took it seriously, at least. Candy thinks the June Solstice will bring the culmination of the Working, when the "child will be born".

One of Candy's small band - - now three, but "destined to be twelve" - - being a Jewess canvassed a number of Jews in Beverly Hills out of her enthusiasm. I do not know the method of approach as such, but it is based on AL and the Tarot; which is the foundation of her work, plus what she got from Jack. But it was not until after Jack's death, when she was in Mexico, that things began to unfold. First, through her relations with a Mexican, then an English woman now living there (both sexual partners), and lastly a woman in Malibu (the Jewess) that her knowledge, her forces came to a workable focus at last. She would like to come to me if or when she needs help. And one of her requests is an afternoon with me to talk about Crowley, who "she fought desperately" for about five years.

I realize that one reason why I am interested in Candy is her activity. But could it – could it be a part at least of "The unveiling"? This has just occurred to me! She feared I might not be able to follow her in the New Aeon.

Love is the law, love under will.

Jane

Hampton N.J.

January 22, 1953

Dear Jane:

Do what thou wilt shall be the whole of the Law.

    Yours of Jan. 20 with enclosures from "Candy" – a peculiar birthday message of stuff!

    This whole Candy stuff coming to me so all at once, after I had always considered the very name as absurd and worthless, comes a bit as a surprise, and I don't know yet what to make of it. It can be utter madness, genuine hallucination, or – the very contrary. Reading her material could give me a sort of hunch of what she is driving at, or working on. But I'd have to know a lot more first.

    You did not send me her birth data. Please do! What is her maiden name? What are all her first names? It would be needful to go a little deeper into this. – If she has an air of fire nature, with a fiery sign rising, and otherwise many fiery planets prominent, she may have a natural capacity of being attuned to the worlds of Fire.

I am earth, way-down earth, with an 50 or 60 year-old thick crust of earth around a core that is at least able to evaluate natures so diametrically different. The more I'd know about her, the more I like. I remember that she was supposed to go to Europe years before Jack's death, and visit A.C. Why did she not do it?

Is she referring to the "Paris Working" when she says that A.C. gave birth to her three years before she was born? That was in Jan.-Feb. 1914. - - She says "seven years ago Jack began an opus he called Babylon". I remember him on one of his visits here to try to draw me out on who 156 was. He may have been obsessed by the thought of finding out and continued ops. – I did not know that A.C. asked him to do a working in the sense you state. I wonder when exactly this was? It seems Candy (the name makes me always think of "Happiness Candy", can't help it! She surely must have been born with a more magical name or names!) has very valuable material in her guardianship, which I hope she will preserve! – Is that wonderful lover C. mentions Jack? - - Your letters do not make clear who the names, places, and persons are, such as "the Mexican", "an English woman", "a woman in Malibu", "Booth", are; the role they play in the drama, so that I could get a clear picture. It's fine to be brief, but not at the price of vagueness. – But please do not make an effort to amplify!

What I don't understand is why C. expects June to bring the "birth" ? What period is at the back of the reasoning? 9 months? Not possible! unless it would be her own continuation of a given work, an op. done, say, in Sept. 1952. June is the time when the Green Man comes.

I can send you 11 copies of AL, cheap London ed. if you want them for Candy. – What is the "Book of Babylon" she refers to? – I return this letter herewith. It is quite remarkable. -
I enclose this with a Hymn to Pan issued by Alex Watt. May-be this Pan is what Candy is waiting for? She can have one if she likes. –

Culling wrote me a long, very sane and good letter. He must be one of these Uranian people who is easily misunderstood. He sent me $5.00 in cash. Please notify Mildred.

Love is the law, love under will.

Love to you,
Karl
5169 ½ Fountain Avenue
Los Angeles, 29, Cal.

February 7, 1953

Dear Karl:

Do what thou wilt shall be the whole of the Law.

    Margery Elizabeth Cameron, born April 23, 1922, between 8 and 8.15p.m.
    This is the best she can do on time.
    I gave Candy 11 copies of Liber AL obtained from the B's. I do not know why she did not see A.C. when in Europe. Possibly because she "fought him tooth and nail with Jack." Now she wants to know about the man, at least.
    No, she refers to her "magickal birth". She speaks of "1003" as the birthplace of both herself and Jack. I have a copy of Jack's report on the "Working", but do not know where it is at the moment, and I now want to get this letter on its way.
    Perhaps Phyllis has told you she expects much from June? Could it be that Candy also has felt something of importance for June, for she thinks there is a further enlarged combination of her work, which she called "the child". This is based, too, on the quarterly meetings (ritualistically) of the group - - hence "a child". She was glad to get Hymn to Pan.
    Candy takes kindly to suggestion or question, though I have gone carefully here, and has asked me to take over her people for instruction. One of them, a woman six feet tall, came to l003 and knows somewhat of the O.T.O. The change in her appearance since Jack's death and her return from Mexico, is astonishing to me. Before she was lackadaisical (when here at least), her skin looked dull - - now it is clear and her eyes are alive with interest and energy. Jack means much to her but she expressed herself as happy that he had gone, and said he had lost her fear of insecurity.

She offered me the Word of Power mentioned in the enclosed letter, but I remained quiet. The more so, as I had seen her but once.

She says that in the New Age in the U.S. negroes will be equal with whites, and that then would begin the absorption of the two into one race. I heard this sort of talk when I was in London.

Enclosed M.O. for $64.

Ray B.	19.00	
Mildred	15.00	3d Degree
Meeka	5.00	1 "
Hugh	5.00	
Paul	1.00	
Jane	19.00	
	$64.00	

Love is the law, love under will.

Jane

Hampton N.J.

February 9, 1953

Beloved Jane:

Do what thou wilt shall be the whole of the Law.

Thank you for the M.O., signed by Mildred. I hope she is not mad at me that I confirmed receipt the last time on a curt postcard only? My life is hectic – not so much from actual work, though there is too much correspondence to attend to, and important, too! – but I am mentally, or should I say, spiritually, in a crisis. Coming events throw great shadows ahead, as the Germans say!

I return Candy's letter. It is amazing! She may be crazy, but I doubt it. If she is not, if her work is directed from some higher intelligences, we should do well to heed her messages. Yet it may well be that she may be quite disappointed when June comes and nothing physically visible turns up in her presence. Unless the birth of that 'child' coincides with the manifestation of the Warrior Lord with was and with vengeance, which could well be.

All this from Candy has made me sit up and get quite a different view of Jack. I was so disappointed that you did not send me Jack's report on the "Working". Do please send it. This, together, with what I see in Candy's notes may clarify very much that I have known but had no verification. Do get that "word of power". One never knows. It may be insignificant. But it may also throw light on some verses of *The Book of the Law*.

In Southern Italy, as you should know, the mixture of white, black and other races (such as Phoenician, Saracen) has gone on for 2000 years. It may take that long until the fusion has come to pass in the USA. Visions of that sort (same as that of the "child") have their own laws of Time and Space.

No: I had no idea that Phyllis expects something for June, too! She has not written me.

As to Jack. Some years ago when he began to write me frequently for advice, he was glad when I gave him "child" as a key-word, which, he wrote back, was just what he needed. His working with Ron Hubbard was always of the greatest interest to me; he wrote very sparingly about it, not even to A.C. When I met him once in 1942, it was I think, he wanted to find out from me about the Scarlet Woman, which I evaded. Even then the problem fascinated him. It seems so hard to understand that the S.W., as well as The Beast, are the name of offices, not of human beings in the flesh. In the case of A.C. his work was in the outer, still, his work as 666 was secret. In the old times he proclaimed each new Moon as his S.W., it is true. He learned, I believe, only much later what the truth is, as one Note in *418* shows. – Please keep me abreast of any new development re Candy's work. –

I drew up a tentative chart of C., for – where is she born? L.A.? or in the East? It makes much difference. She has a number of excellent aspects for illumination. She has Scorpio rising, Neptune in the Ninth (philosophy, religion, finer regions), sextile Jupiter (illumination) Sun exact conjunction Mercury (she must have an excellent intellect. I get Mars in the Second, but if the birth were, say, 20 minutes later, her Mars (in Sagittarius) would be in the First, which would give red hair, or blond with a tinge of red. Is she of an aggressive type, vivacious, full of ideas, plans, initiative?

I see you have given her 11 *AL*, 220. If you need any, tell me. I do not like that we distribute the editions with the Church of Thelema address, if we can avoid it. At least the address should be torn out.

This brings me to a passage in Lt. Raymond's last. He writes: – (the man from Texas) "A few days ago, in some new magazine on the newsstands, I chanced to read an article on Los Angeles cults, an article which laid it rather thickly on the Church of Thelema, playing on the sensationalism, but mentioned not word on A.C. and his serious doctrines in connection with Thelema. The self-styled "journalist" expressed horror at some of the rites, which he was in no wise qualified to understand, even supposing he had the facts correct, which I doubt."

Do you know what this refers to? Could you get a copy for me?

Tired to death. It is midnight. I must close and make my midnight adoration!

Love is the law, love under will.

My love to you, always,

Karl

Hampton N.J.
February 19, 1953

Dear Jane:

Do what thou wilt shall be the whole of the Law.

Thank you for your letter with those from Candy and the record of Jack's.

I want to read Candy's letters once again; I have not had time to decipher Jack's first, so would like to to keep all of it for a few days. On first perusal I must confess that Candy appears to me a little off the beam. I doubt whether she has adequate facts to substantiate the flying saucer story. Whether she actually saw one at 1003 – how? In the sky, or in process of fabrication? It has long been supposed that they are secretly manufactured by the U.S.A. But: I have never been on Catalina Island, and from all I had heard it certainly would not be a given spot for secret experiments or tests.

The danger to people with a vivid imagination is that they yield too easily to, and become the prey of, obsessing thought, unless you chase the fog around them away, or have a helper to do it all the time for you. Else you might walk at dusk in the fields and suddenly see a ghost and run away, when a less imaginative person walks right up to it, and proves that the "Ghost" was a lamp post, or a pole in the mist of the landscape.

Please do make an effort to locate those records of Jack's. They may be too valuable to be in danger to get lost. I would like to find in them the details of exactly what 666 instructed him to do and work on. He never told me – as he usually did. There must be important letters extant which throw light on the matter. I have read the Aleister: Jack file through again and cannot find anything that looks like an instruction to do a certain opus. That is from 1946 on. - - - -

I am sending you to-day by parcel post 12 (twelve) copies of *The Gospel According to St. Bernard Shaw*. Please notify the following to pick up their copy, or get it to them as you find easiest. They are for yourself, Phyllis, Hugh, Mildred-Ray, Georgia, Meeka, Wilfred, Louis and Paul Millikin. This is 9. I put in three extra for use as seen fit. – As an afterthought I stuck in 25 copies of the completed ERRATA slip, for 418. Please give them to those that have a copy. Give an extra supply to Louis, as he sold or bought several copies. - - - I have sent copies to Barstow separately.

I am hellishly busy.

I've written Raymond to tell me the name of the magazine about the Church of Thelema. May-be Louis or Wilfred know? Will tell you if I find out.

Love is the law, love under will.

All the best to you and love,

Karl

Hampton N.J.
February 22, 1953

Dear Jane:

Do what thou wilt shall be the whole of the Law.

I have taken more trouble and care about the Jack/Candy material you sent me than usual, and have come to the conclusion that they are very possibly genuine. Jack's record of the Babalon invocation is not written, and condensed and clear as A.C.'s

inspired or dictated librae are. A communicating entity is, after all, limited by the perfection and transparence of the diamond or crystal available for transmission. Some of the verses in the book are unnecessary and irrelevant, I think. May-be the work is not even complete. May-be the magician was not considered mature or initiated, or pure enough? Who will judge?
Questions:

§ 14 "Le Dane" ? Is this correct or the best you can get?
§ 2. So far I cannot see it. Does it say HE or the Hebrew letter? Are you sure it says Ra-Hoor-Khuit? Or: …. KUT?
"Fourth chapter of the Book of the Law" is so far doubtful to me.
§ 5, 6, 7, 8. A pity that that page is missing.
§ 10, I can't find the word "pendulous".
13. Is "it may be unto death" crossed out and substituted by "fullsome" ? yes
33. "that she may have capraine and adepts at her service" - - - Captains?
(The date of the delivery of this book is not given. So that one cannot guess whether Verse 25 refers to Candy or another.)
§ 39 …"chisen" ?? Should it be "children" ? or "chosen" – "I shall p"?? Is this justlike that?
61. Do you know what "publish the secret matter…" refers to?
67. "sname" ??
68. Could "none" be "no one"?

    I will want more distance and more information. There is not much I'd wish to ask in detail, but think I should first wait for the further documents you want to send me. What year of February 27 was this communication given?
    I regret that Jack never opened up to me. Had he done so he would have found in me not a rival – as WTS made him fear – but would have welcomed him as a greatly needed brother who might have become a continuator of 666's work in the magical field. I would have told him with complete frankness that I cannot do this type of work at all
    The data given in Jack's "Analysis" are wrong. Venus is neither rising nor retrograde. Nor is Sun rising. I would hardly call

Saturn in aphelion, but at a stretch, one could. But his Saturn is rising, in his detriment in Cancer, close conj. with Pluto, and there are many strong and fine aspects. The poor Saturn may have prevented big success.

We needed a man of his youth, his calibre, understanding, faculty for mastery, so very very badly! Now that I see proofs for that it makes me sad.

I return the original "Analysis" to you, with a typescript copy. If you can decipher the words which I have left out, please fill in return the copy.

I also return Candy's letter.

I think you should keep all this material with great care, or, if you like, send me all for safe-keeping.

I hope you have not let WTS look into all this? Or anyone else? I am keeping it tightly shut. Sascha has seen some of Candy's letters and is amazed at the flame.

Love is the law, love under will.

Love,

Karl

P.S. *Liber 49* and the number of vv. "77" are possibly good enough in themselves, but have no magical or qabalistic relation to 156 or the word "Scarlet" woman. The name "Beast" has in the various transcription in Greek and Hebrew. The same applies to Babalon, or should. 49, and 77 are two rational numbers. They don't appear inspired. Only then will they yield new light. There are certain secrets which, I think, have been discovered since printing of *The Equinox of the Gods*, in the qabalistic appendix, of which Jack had not heard. Some numbers must have been given him by 666, but I doubt he discovered their meaning. I found them in a P.S. to the typed copy of "Emblems and Mode of Use", which Frederic years ago showed me. He had the copy from Smith. Smith had it from Jack. And Jack got it from me - - - without those qabalistic numbers: You have that document, have you not?

Encl. Original of Jack's Analysis.
       2 original letters from Candy.
       Copy of Analysis.
P.P.S. Have just copied Candy's enclosed letters. I must say, they stagger me by their evident madness! K.

Hampton N.J.

May 5, 1953

Dear Phyllis:

Do what thou wilt shall be the whole of the Law.

Yours of May 1. I wish I could be of help in Qabalah. But I can't. I have no imagination whatever, nor the technical knowledge. I have gone through the magical names in Abramelin squares, and can't find any that are like Azar. If you take Aleph, Zain, Aleph, Resh you get 209, 11 x 9, one half of 418, on which you might speculate, or seek light. If you spell ASAR (with its obvious meaning) you get 262 = 2 x 131 The name Asra, Azra, seems to me biblical (or Ezra) – but I have never read the bible. Ask Jane, who knows more about it.

Please understand that I make no claims whatever on Qabalistic (or technical) magical knowledge or interpretation. I am the very opposite to 666 in every respect. Once you get your copy of *Magick Without Tears* you may get some practical help in learning yourself.

However, I will say this, that I dislike your qabalistic counting of words in the ordinary English language, such as "I will to love", etc. English Qabalah has not yet been discovered; besides, English does not lend itself to it, anyway. With the older Greek and Arabic and Hebrew, or possibly much older name. I just find, for instance, that Ezra is a biblical name, if you take the letters as here written, they would add to 213, if only EZR = 212 =; but in Greek EZR would be 112 = 2 x 56. You'd have to consult *Equ.* I, viii for fuller meanings. I'm too busy now!

I like your spiritual growth, Leave yourself to your HGA and you can find no better guide for further progress. –

As to WTS: Never forget: I have never lifted A.C.'s old injunction re dropping all dealings with him. I must say I have looked with disfavour and suspicion on the chummy atmosphere that seems to have gradually developed. I made an exception with Jane, because of the Mass. But what has grown out of this is altogether different. From what you say, WTS argues; he has failed to cross the abyss; and so is eternally damned to the clutches of reason and 333. I had thought I could get WTS todo certain things to help, that's why I went along again; I'm afraid I have to reconsider. Please show this to Jane.

I have been, and still am, feverishly working on M.W.T. The typist has been working on the loan machine we have had last week, and it turned out that the work she did was meticulously done – BUT it is the wrong roller, the rubber is too soft, the impression is uneven. We have to scrap the masters once more! It is tragic. I won't get another roller before Thursday. And the new machine has been delayed. We need it badly because of the special types, such as ' ' ^ * ! =, the plus sign, and several others needed. I don't know how far we shall get. If necessary we shall have to print as far as possible, then send the Typewriter to California when Jean-Ero leave and you'd better finish this most important book, and we'd print it in Barstow. I'd ship the Multilith there. We'll see in a week or two, I hope.

Forget about my horoscope: we have so much to do!! And I am far behind in what I have to do! M.W.T. will run to about 400 pages if not more.

May 6. I'll add a few lines.

In the early stages our primitive natures require actual, visible, sensible, proof of an outer being contacting us. I remember in my early period I sometimes asked for a definite sign in order to

(a) reassure me in a sort of weak phase (b) to give evidence that I was on the right track. Yet: (this is important in my case!) I never connected such signs as coming from a definite outer being, I just took it as from 'God' or such things. My conception of the HGA has probably only been condensed after A.C.'s death. Funny? Unbelievable? It is so! The HGA has been taking almost violent, desperate means to bring me to the realisation of his existence and presence, and operation. But my hide was, and still is, too dense, so that A.C. once in the 1927 period wrote: "instead of a skin you have a carapace!" And this not as a joke, but rather in despair.

Be, and feel, happy that you are better constituted! Later, the messages become more subtle, and so that one cannot distinguish them from what we call 'conscience' in many cases. There are people who carry on definite conversations, they hear voice - or other type - messages; the difficulty remains, however, to verify the source.

Achad got messages to the last; but they were, since his turning away from 666, not from his HGA, but its shadow, the Evil Persona. As it is hard to follow the voice of the HGA in later stages, because often things are demanded that seem outrageous, against all morals and ethics, there is a danger of falling prey to the sweet whisper of the other guy (cf. Jesus and the high mountain; in Achad's case it was the promise that he was to be the bloke of *AL* III, 45 (the child), and A.C. seduced him, and fortified this conviction (a magical test!) by writing *Liber Aleph*.

"Neglect not the Dawn Meditation"! is one of the most important injunctions of A.C. (I only repeat: I don't do it myself! I can't meditate.) It is well to practice this as a routine, so as to prepared when the HGA arranges a phase for one of the – let me call it – technical initiations or illuminations. Why do I mention this here? Because you write you were deep asleep when you got that one message and only wrote it up, partly, after waking. In my Concentration Camp phase I was alone in my cell (when the crucial weeks same). I worked with hardly any interruption; sleep was broken up so that I never slept more than 3 hours at a time; and that "sleep" was light, and I snapped instantly back into work. If you read "John St. John" in *Equ* I, you have the same idea; except that A.C. did his op. by an effort of will and in 12 days.

What I want to say is that such high water marks are secretly arranged by the HGA: then the conditions are right and will bring the result about. But the training of one's mind to waken instantly and fully at a touch, is always helpful. - - -

    Well, I better stop now. This is running into a sermon! It is so easy to talk to you.

Love is the law, love under will.
Fraternally,

Karl

R.F.D.1, C/o Shivonen
Barstow, California

August 27, 1953

Dear Karl,

Do what thou wilt shall be the whole of the Law.

    Thanks for your letter of the 7th. No, it's not that I mind being corrected if it is objective – detached from other types of observation. It is true, I am perhaps abnormally sensitive to criticism – I've had it ruin my artistic output for long stretches of time. I know all this, know its sources, but I have not been able to develop a thick skin towards it yet.
    Today I am wondering about the burden Jane is struggling under – am worried to, to tell the truth. You know, of course, that her income is tiny – pension – and yet she sends her monthly contribution. Maybe she wants to – and might be offended at this presumption on my part – indeed I am presumptuous! But she is nearing quite an old age – and is spry and bright – but somehow I feel she needs a lot of consideration. I really am stepping over my

bounds! I hope all and sundry will not think too harshly of me! Not only does this sum go out from her for H.Q., but Mary K. is not as spry – needs a lot of attention – drains Jane's energy until I become alarmed! Needlessly? No! I don't think so!

But there it is – and I feel, that if possible, there ought to be help somewhere, somehow, for this situation, even if we can only lighten the burden here and there?

Now then – that subject is extremely delicate – and having unburdened myself, I turn to another matter.

You mention: "The enemy is waiting at the gate to disrupt it." (as you refer to M.W.T.)

What enemy?

I am perhaps singularly short-sighted to make this statement but I firmly believe there is no enemy unless we let him exist. In other words, the enemy would be ourselves! Are we not strong enough magically, to keep all such ideas at bay?

And now to explain this position I am going to quote from my diary.

Sun. Dec. 21 1952
Strange – vision? No! Experience.
Was reading Jung's commentary on *Secret of Golden Flower.* As I turned out the light and settled down to sleep I was suddenly in the center of things – and that center was an unmanifest Nothing. It was the true me, but it was nothing.

It was as though I were in the center of a ball filled with air or nothing visible, and all events appeared on the outer shell, connected by a network of red lines, like a cell structure, I imagine.

This experience made me laugh. One lives in the outer shell so much, and becomes involved, and thought processes tell us it is reality, but it isn't not at all!

The real reality is Nothing! Hence the joke!

Also, when one is the center, the Nothing that allows the outside shell of events to happen, one tremendous power over them. I had the feeling I could choose to experience any event, or not, as I liked. I could make anything happen.

This is because one event is as good as another and just as unreal.

The Nothing is the "diamond body" or the non-striving of Tao. And what a joke the whole experience was!

It was as though life as I know it had gotten turned exactly inside out and was the exact reverse of conscious thinking processes. Why, the thoughts themselves are the unreality!

I could go on and quote several lines here and there to see if this experience has any verification elsewhere. I think it does!

Crowley puts it in the Mass:

"Thou that art I, beyond all I am
Who hath no nature and no name"
                                        Etc.

You know was well as I do –

Also, Liber AL, II vs. 12, 13. "Because of me in Thee which thou knewest not." (Notice the not! nothing?) for why? Because thou wast the knower, and me."

A direct statement that Hadit was in Crowley – "the core of every star" Also is nothing or not – as in verse 15.

But then the shrine is to be veiled in verse 14. Is the truth too strong to bear? It would seem to me that these verses, my experience, probably other sources, would point to the fact that we are each one of us responsible for our own environment and that throwing the blame for not getting a piece of work done on "magical attacks" or "forces of disruption" or, or, etc. might be terribly dangerous thinking.

It is quite another thing if one knows that the particular work is not to be done now, because the Angel orders it.

It is not that I think you do this type of thinking, (or do I?) but I have seen others around me indulge in it when it was plainly weakness, mere speculation on their part, had no references to the K. and C. of the H.G.A, but was an excuse to excuse their own mistakes, or laziness!

So, though you (and Crowley) have a high degree of initiation, and could perhaps tell me these forces exist, and that I am too inexperienced to know, etc., etc., still, these remarks about "disruptive forces", "the enemy", "the gods" are sometimes dangerous to the weaker ones in our Order. I think a lot of them need a little stiffening of the spine by an attitude which says, "What's the matter with you?" All that is, that exists for you, was made by you!" Are we not our own enemies? Or otherwise?"

By now you probably want to throw me out the door! O.K., I'll go, but I'll waft you an impertinent kiss, dear brother, to show I mean no harm!

Have you asked yourself lately what your own enemy is doing? We all have them, usually conveniently out of sight in the unconscious.

With this parting shot you'll want to kick me out of the Order!

Who does she think she is?
Nothing! Nothing at all!

Love is the law, lover under will.

Love,

Phyllis

Hampton N.J.

August 31, 1953

My dear and beloved Phyllis,

Do what thou wilt shall be the whole of the Law.

Yours of Aug. 27, received this moment. First then: I shall not kick you out, but if I do any kicking at all, I shall kick you in! By which I mean, back again into the center of that Nothing!

But first, some things from outside of that Ball, the unfortunate periphery.

I am very glad that you write about Jane! I shall act accordingly, though maintenance of H.Q. becomes an increasingly difficult problem. And I don't know yet how to solve it.

Next: you don't say a word about progress on M.W.T. Please do only send me a few scratches on a postcard once a week, to alleviate my worries.

Next: PLEASE do not try to improve on Aleister's English. He learned it in Cambridge and elsewhere. I cannot do better than enclose a note and list from Jean, which please return. All these "improvements" are wrong. Dead wrong! --- I have written Jean and she may have shown you my remarks. In future, please beware!

Do you think it is possible to finish M.W.T. in time before you go back to College? All I want is to see clearly, have the facts!

I hear from Jean that the "o" is giving trouble, If so, the Remington service man should be called.

Now to your vision. It is very good. Also you have had the vision of the Universal Joke. Read the chapter "Laughter" in Little Essays!

But: we must go back to the periphery, as we have to do our work on that plane, and fight the conditions existing there. I think any Trance lasts only a rather short time. It refreshes, brings illumination, is a sort of proof that we have gotten there, gives comfort to the doubting soul. And then back again to the periphery and do our dull, dirty work again! Till next Sunday or holyday!

On the periphery we have to contend with hostile forces. A.C. himself often noticed and warned of magical attacks. Every time he started on the publication of a major magical work, he knew in advance that he had to face and brace himself for violent opposition. (When *Magick in Theory & Practice* was published he was kicked out of France where the printer was; with superhuman strength he delayed his departure, with all kinds of subterfuges, became sick, etc., so that he could stay on until he was sure the work would be finished.) So I don't believe we must ignore or ridicule such terminology. I dislike it myself, but rather from the point of view, that I hate to admit its efficacy: it hurts my vanity, or sense of strength to think that those blokes of the opposite number should have the power to cripple or delay our work. "The War of the Ages" goes on on all planes. The Gods Themselves have their (almost) equal enemies. I wish I could translate for you "Der Aeon des Horus", an inspired work by Ishrah on the story of Isis, Osiris, Seth, Horus, etc. in the Egyptian formulation. But the old Scandinavian legends (see Wagner's music dramas), and in the legends of King Atrus or Arthur cycle you have the same opposed forces. Tipheret and Kether are in the center column, but right and left are the Sephira that in themselves are unbalanced.

I have typed out the text of your vision, with your permission, I hope. It might come useful sometimes to weaker [brothers and sisters]. Your "Ball" brings to mind the "crystal without one speck" in *LXV*, iiv. But there are many other vv. in the Holy Books from which you can make verification.

You sweet little girl!

Love is the law, love under will.

My love to you,

Karl

Hampton N.J.

Jan. 20, 1955

Dear Jane:

Do what thou wilt shall be the whole of the Law.

I return Cameron's two letters herewith. Thank you for sending them. I wish you would preserve all of C.'s letters, and, better, send me all she writes to you. They are a sort of diary. Who knows whether some day "all the puzzle may not become clear".

But I believe you should warn her in the sternest language to heed the strict injunction in the Comment to *AL*. That blasted

Book is so terribly dangerous and tests its students a thousand times, in a thousand subtle ways; "deeper ever deeper" do its demons that run with it try to seduce the few worthy with every manner or means to bring them to fall. Do warn C. again and again. She it too valuable and you seem to be the only one to whom she looks upon with a certain respect or even awe.

That one letter of Oct. 22 seems to show that C. was not behind that A.C. film. But may-be she can find out its details.

I, too, see my body ransacked by all sorts of troubles now that I'll be 70 in a few days. Mostly feet, toes, and general. It is lack of circulation, as I have suffered from very low blood pressure all my life.

I do hope you'll find a place in Barstow soon, and I trust I'll be notified as soon as you have done so. In the meantime I remain anxious.

H.G.A. ?! I did get Him in 1927, but did not realise what had taken place until some 5 or 6 years ago, and even now rays don't penetrate properly, as I have a hide (or a carapace, as A.C. said) instead of a skin. But Cameron should try to make further progress and actually have verbal conversation in the way Ida Craddock had (see *Heavenly Bridegrooms* -- does she know the book?)

666 should certainly be behind you if you invoke Him. He is actually operating!

Love is the law, love under will.

All the best and love,

Karl

Hampton, N.J.

Feb. 5, 1955

Dear Jane:

Do what thou wilt shall be the whole of the Law.

Your letter of Feb. 2 came to-day, Saturday, when I have no means of getting this posted before Monday--two important days lost. I enclose copy of my letter to Ray-Mildred. Please give me, each of you: Jane and Jean, as complete a report on what transpired, with all details: number of times you saw this individual, what your impressions were, what questions or topics were discussed, what he tried to find out. Etc. Etc.

Of course, he said he was a friend of mine and all that. Fact is that he arranged a meeting with me, had a secret microphone installed to record the conversation. This was 15 months ago. I really wanted to get your reactions first, but time is short. -

Re that film by Engers[78]: Is this film actually running in L.A. now? Under what name "The Pleasure Dome"? Is it expected to reach here? Yorke has by this time seen the film, I suppose in London, heard details about the script, wrote "I expect to get and immoderate laugh out of it"; will meet Engers at his house shortly, or has by this time.

What Company was the producer? I want to trace it in New York.

Cameron and her gang can play all the roles she likes; that is unimportant. What counts is: where does she stand? It may well be that she has actually gone through certain initiations, but fell into the clutches of some Archdemon, and now is obsessed by it, while all the time thinking it is 666 - for, as you know - "the devil can take the shape of any God".

---

[78] Germer is referring to Kenneth Anger, as is obvious from the context.

I should really, have full details of all that happened. I would like to set Louis Culling on her trail; it seems to me that he is the only one with adequate knowledge and subtle strength to tackle her, and destroy her - should that become necessary. At this distance it is hard to judge. And she may have been on the White Path, and a true Thelemite. But when the forking of the roads comes, the deviation is at first almost invisible; it turns only slowly, imperceptibly, from the North Pole; but once the demon sees he has succeeded, there is no way back, and the curve draws away rapidly. Then they become Black Brothers.

Sorry, if this theory is correct, I cannot advise positive protective steps except intensified rituals which you know, and invocations.

Please write by return. I should like as much as possible before this villain Schlag[79] turns up. As he doubtless will.

Love is the law, love under will.

Fraternally with love,

Karl

February 20, 1955

Dear Karl:

Do what thou wilt shall be the whole of the Law.

Cameron. Aggressive and masterful – Yes! Because of these qualities, she accepted from Jack the role of Babalon, with all the hordes of followers with waving banners. This for about a year. It took another year to slowly drop the mantle. During this period

---

[79] Oskar Schlag, an occultist and medium.

she had an enthusiastic following. When she ceased to see herself in the role she needed ballast, and used marijuana for a time, which caused the followers to withdraw. She has had experiences that would have paralyzed most people, or driven them insane. (Her mother thought she was insane at times, and wanted her put in an institution.) She battled through, however, using the Hexagram on the plane on which she was working.

These experiences come at intervals. She lives a "normal" life for a time, then feels the necessity for a Retirement. And takes it, wherever she finds a place to carry on. And one always turns up! Lately, she found refuge with a man who belongs to and artistic group. He prepared a film of Cameron wherein she descried her pictures, which are or were on exhibition. I have seen them. Very, very striking. I would like to see them hung in a splendid timbered hall. Only in a considerable space could one live with them.

And she is articulate. Which I always note, and enjoy, due to my own lack. Cameron told Renee she would have to find another habitation. She never takes a salaried weekly job. She says she cannot do it.

If Engers could put in subtle nuances of value to the mind, soul, or Spirit, he could be valuable with A.C.'s writings. But I am skeptical. However, does one always know? Rhea suggests a fantasy for *Moonchild*.

Schlag. I waited to write you the following; first, that I might analyse matters somewhat; secondly, I wanted to hear from you. Your letter has arrived, so I go to my diary and give some notes.

I met Schlag Sunday, January 23. At Burlingames, after dinner in a restaurant. During the conversation I felt a vibration between S. and myself. Mildred also felt it. Later I said to myself: This man has something for me.

Tuesday afternoon, January 25, the B's, S. and myself, spent three hours with Phyllis and Marcia in Santa Monica. Phyllis, Jane and Schlag sat on a divan, Jane in the middle. Phyllis went out to make coffee – attention was centered elsewhere – S. said to me, "To aid you is now my task."

Monday, January 31, during the half hour S. and I were alone at the B's he said: "They have been watching you for some time." I did not ask who 'They' were, assuming 'they' were from the Switzerland coterie with whom you were in contact when I was back at H.Q.

At some period of the nights of Saturday and Sunday, I was slightly, slightly aware of Schlag and assumed it was my thoughts.
Monday afternoon he said "You crossed the abyss. I helped you." This stumped me completely. I stared in stony silence, my mind saying "but it cannot be." He noticed my reaction, and said: "There comes a curve in Time which changes its course somewhat, and it was because of this curve that you could cross."
And it was in this connection that S. spoke of the Great Angel Hua and the Unicorn, But, as I wrote, I could not recall his words, possibly because his statement gave me a shock.
Perhaps it was Jane who was vampirized?
You mentioned the 1st Aethyr. In footnote 2, A.C. writes "This angel was the Higher Genius of the Seer" And I have been thinking A.C. referred to Aiwass.
I give S. credit for one thing: "You will be told what to do" – from my own being at the time. Maybe it could be otherwise than my own Angel? No; I think not. But I shall watch.
I understand that S. teaches Psychology and Yoga at the Zurich University.

Love is the law, love under will.

With love,

Jane

P.S. I am using the Anthem from the Mass for my invocation and adoration of 666. "Thou who art I beyond all I am", dedicating the Anthem to 666.

PP.S. I know that Karl comes first with me. He is my link with 666 and Thelema. And he stands in his own right also.

1203 Inchon Avenue, C/o Sihvonen
Barstow Gardens, Barstow, California

March 5, 1955

Dear Karl:

Do what thou wilt shall be the whole of the Law!

    We are perched in a new home, as you see. Once more I have changed my address - my driver's license; and we may flit once more in two or three months!
    Now let me take Schlag. I want to put things before Papa Germer, so I will go along, paragraph. I had it all jotted down yesterday, in nice order; but the sheet went into the discard, no doubt, when Jean got busy cleaning up this a.m. At least I cannot find it. However, it was roughly as follows:-
    You mention Shin-Lamed-Gimel equals 333! Has this anything to do with me? I am not at home in tarot to that extent -- I mean, of knowing. No; Schlag did not impress Phyllis or Marcia -- except that Phyllis wondered if Schlag could not be helped to the right path. I forgot to mention this trip. Marcia and Phyllis went to San Francisco during vacation time, so as to register with the State Teachers' Association. They both graduate as M.A. in June, and are therefore eligible for College work.
    He told Ray he would like to find a Guru. Perhaps he is now looking for help from you or us? He know some Sex Magick, of course. Did you find where he stands on the Tree? I wrote re his O.T.O. stand, and he no doubt has told you his objection to *The Book of Thoth*.
    Now for my diary.

    Feb. 13. (After receipt of yours of 10.) I invoke the Yi re Schlag; and receive 12, Lingam of Yoni. The great gone, the little come.

I have felt for days that I did not want to write to Schlag. I cannot accept "crossing the Abyss." Jane must know. ... I now am responsible for my actions.

Feb 16. The result of my meeting with Schlag was stimulating. I flowed out to people; energy came to me, I was prepared to function in my field. Now everything seems blocked.

Some understanding has come. I must take hold of my moods - myself - and prove sovereignty.

Feb. 23 From August 1954, and continuing throughout Aug., Sept., October, I was torn up by the roots....Nov. 7 I moved to the desert near Barstow with Ero and Jean Sihvonen, practically stripped of my possessions; and I feel like a wanderer in the Wastelands. ...

Feb. 28 Lying awake after midnight I felt "alone, all alone on a wide wide sea."

Mar. 1 In L.A., the house guest of Hugh and Barbara Christopher -- walking up and down the room, waiting for Paul, I was confronted with the thought: "No one can put me across the Abyss. I must be the doer. It is my responsibility, my task!" (You may recall that in the former letter I quoted Schlag thus: "You have crossed the Abyss. I helped you." So I was hasty.) So I wrote down the statement: "I shall accept every phenomenon whatsoever as a personal dealing of God with my Soul. So Mote it Be!" I felt at the time Schlag forced this Oath upon me.

I do not know, of course, whether this Oath applies to Women; for Woman the Mystic (?) goes up the Middle Pillar. But as I see it an Oath must now be taken, to maintain sovereignty.

Mar. 4 Returning to Barstow. Between San Bernardino and Cajon Pass, near 3 o'c p.m. the Stephen Foster song "Beautiful Dreamer" kept humming through me. Then there permeated me what I called "The Ache of Man." About an hour later - on a milder way - there came an understanding of Man's bestowal of money to/on Woman. There was feeling with these two experiences - especially the first. Some time ago I heard the Wail of Woman (Women?) but there was no feeling. All this seems strange.

Phyllis tells me Neptune has entered my orbit(?) This is cause for happiness, but it is some of the above of the dangerous side of Neptune?

By the way, I burned Schlag's card with his address. He asked me to write him.

I hope this does not bore you too much. Writing it out to some one brings it to the surface, where it no longer troubles me. As my mentioning once more Fiat Yod. That can now be laid aside.

Love is the law, love under will.

Love to you,

Jane

PP.S. Waking slowly from sleep this a.m. came "Do nothing. Wait for the Lord."

DO my rituals, and a few other things. Pranayama, etc.

Hampton N.J.

March 10, 1955

Dear Jane:

Do what thou wilt shall be the whole of the Law.

Your letter just knocked me flat. It shows the way Schlag has dripped his poison into your blood.

Schlag = 333 by simple Qabalah; as I explained; Shin 300, Lamed 30, Gimel 3. You must surely know that 333 is Choronzon? Dispersion, the wickedest of all the Demons of the Abyss?

The only man who was contacted was Ray; and he was soon suspicious, and - so he says - when he asked too much about IX°--simply told him "it is in *The Book of the Law*". Yet, I'm afraid, Ray talks easily and freely.

I have no word from Mildred, on what transpired. And Phyllis remains suspiciously silent. Nor do you say anything, when you surely must have seen her recently.

This is the blackest of all the black attacks on the very core of the Great Work itself. I sent you excerpts from a correspondent in Europe yesterday. But there are many more ramifications which I know, on which I cannot speak.

Every Thelemite must now deeply cleanse him- and herself of this subtle poison. This refers especially to you, Mildred, and Phyllis. ANY, even the slightest correspondence with Schlag, by anybody, direct or indirect, must not take place. Should I hear of it, they must be shunned absolutely, and finally. Please send me a statement on this, and on what else you know or hear. Especially I want to know about Phyllis and Mildred, who are the most susceptible.

And you? How subtly Schlag played on your 8°=3° preoccupation! Being a medium and very clairvoyant, he could spot it instantly. You happen to be the one and only one who on the West Coast represented 666 himself, having known him personally; so he worked on you specially. But, I believe, you have crossed the Abyss, even though not on all planes. Why worry further?

Let us all do the little bit what each one is able to do under present conditions: that IS the G.W. A.C. is super-duper uranium mine that will require a hundred thousand minds to explore, catalogue, print, etc. for the next several hundred years. All we have to do, each for himself, is to plod along and do his little share. I am too weary to write properly; will send this along with a letter to Jean about Masters and the Commentary. For once I am deeply perturbed. If only Ero had been present and met the man!

Love is the law, love under will.

Fraternally, with love,

Karl
Hampton N.J.

June 27, 1955

Dear Jane:

Do what thou wilt shall be the whole of the Law.

 Thanks for yours of June 22. And for Cameron's letter. Her dream-vision does not mean too much to me. Yet it has, but she has to find out for herself, I think. *)
 The name of the city in Mexico is Guanajuato, not too far away from Mexico City, anyway, in the South, the civilized section of Mexico. I wish I could go there. I expect to go to Mexico some day, anyway. –
 Before going there you might suggest to her to make a careful list of all thelemic or literary files etc., and if she does not take it w with her, to deposit it safely.
 Has she replied to Kenneth Grant's Manifesto, whose equation is

$$\text{Isis} = \text{a planet} = \text{Nuit!!}$$

It is utterly crazy, as a planet is a mere satellite, then part of the Sun. The Sun with all its planets, is a mere mite in the system of our galaxy of stars. There are thousands or millions of galaxies. And Nuit embraces them all. To make Nuit a mere planet reduces Nuit to something insignificant. – Besides, I have made inquiries about this new so-called planet Isis, and there is no record of it anywhere I have asked or written to. It's all very silly, though Grant does have qualities. – However, we all of us, if sensitive, can go off the beam occasionally; main thing is to get on it again.
 Personally, I cannot get a mental picture of her, as I lack all imagination. Could you not send me some snapshots to help? Only after knowing her personally could I make up any opinion of her.

I'll mail this to-morrow by air so that you should get it before you leave for L.A.

That letter you mention to have seen where A.C. gives some instructions to Jack about the Babalon working and to keep it absolutely secret, keeps puzzling me. I do not question its truth, as I know that 666 sought to help efficient magicians towards a certain manifestation. But if so, I cannot understand that Jack should show it to you, if to you, possibly to others. I know from personal experience that Jack was that way. I hope some day you will find a record of the matter in your files or your diaries with dates and details, and that record.

Love is the law, love under will.

Love to you,

Karl

*) "...that drunkest never wine but to life..." *Liber VIII*.

P.S. Oh yes, there was something on my mind and now I remember. Cameron must have quite a file of letters sent by 666 to Jack (also of course others). It is these personal letters by 666 that must be safeguarded under all circumstances. As you know everyone that we could get a hold of, has given us a chance to copy those letters which were then returned to the owner, if desired. Is C. afraid to let me have them?

1203 Inchon Avenue
Barstow, California

October 16, 1955

Dear Karl:

93

The Holy Books. Some 30 Years ago I memorised *Liber LXV* to the middle of the last chapter; and repeated it over and over. But as I think of it now, much of this was for the benefit of the rhythm.

Liber VII, except for Cap IV, because of the strange hieroglyphs. It was my selection, but for an intellectual response, I think;- having no means of getting at these hieroglyphs. Cap VI I omitted entirely, although there were items and still are which please me very much.

I am once more memorising Cap VII- this time to get beyond the words Olalam! Imal! Tutulu! Touched me interiorly, and I am now using it was a mantra. Three words from that book give life to a new aeon.

Prologue I like immensely, and repeat often. Cap I is practiced for a dance while at Winona. Cap II is beautiful - but how can one describe them after all? Cap III was the one I chose after turning down IV. Later on I turned to Cap VII; and this now is my daily food. One night recently, between sleeping and waking, I found myself going over this chapter with grace and love flowing through me.

This in answer to your mention of repetition of the Holy Books.

[Kenneth] Anger. Why this preservation of the Abbey in Cefalu? It apparently fulfilled its purpose. And has now turned to hate. 1746 Winona Boulevard was torn down after we left and later a modern apartment building of two stories put up. 1003 was pulled down - so far as I know nothing has been built there. Anger mentions paintings left there? Canvasses apart from the house? If so, why were they not stolen. In our days everything was stolen by the Sicilians, right under our noses.

I painted the Magical Circle on the floor of the Temple room -- you may recall it-- after A.C. told me what to do and where to place the proper colours. I also did a bit of the Cauchemares. Perhaps you know these walls portrayed Heaven, Earth, and Hell. "Heaven" is on the outside wall, and the "grotesque blue foot" belongs to Aiwass, the central figure; the Scarlet Woman is on the right side of Aiwass. I do not recall the third figure, which is to His left. The three figures in swift motion.

What a pity Kenneth Grant has a copy of the diaries! Or, is it? Who knows? The "Cyclops", and a few other items, must have been added after my going to London. I should like to see the photos. Shall you be given a set?

By the way: I first used *Ararita* as a daily reading, every night on retiring while in London-- not all the I was there. At Winona Boulevard, and again at Fountain Avenue, I used it in a Ritual. Some of it I remember, and items here and there from this set of books, but in a more meditative way.

Love is the law, love under will.

Glad to hear the news of A∴A∴.

Jane

1203 Inchon Avenue,
Barstow, California

January 19, 1956

Dear Karl:

Do what thou wilt shall be the whole of the Law!

What is the origin or history of Abiegnus? What Race? What Occult Line? Is Abiegnus indicative of Tiphareth – the Home of Adonai? Or beyond that?

I recall Mont Salvat, the home of Lohengrin which seems to have originated in Spain? The Knights of the Round Table evoke Montsalvat. Or is Lohengtin solely a dramatization of Wagner.

I now feel like resurrecting these Symbols or Peoples; study them, and bring them to life. Why have they been dormant in my mind all these years? My greater interest is in Abiegnus.

There was much I wanted to hear from you, now you will not be here!

Helen Parsons warmed the cockles of my heart this a.m. when in a letter she told me to let her know when I can spend several nights with them, and really learn to know the place.

To strike a different note, Cameron's latest is enclosed. Perhaps it should be returned when next you write – rather, some time, to keep the sequence.

"Send behind the iron curtain for data of Maria" is rather surprising. But you may get good news from someone, some place.

Have had a shocking cold – doctor bills and examinations. Not yet quite over, but on the mend.

Love is the law, love under will.

Love to All,

Jane

Hampton N.J.
P.O. Box 581

Jan. 23, 1956

Dear Jane:

Do what thou wilt shall be the whole of the Law.

    I answer yours of Jan. (NOT June!) 19 at once. – You did not enclose Cameron's letter which I will return when it comes.
    Your questions: I'm afraid I cannot be of much help. However, here goes for what it is worth.
    Abiegnus is, I believe to remember, the Latin for Pine trees, the Mountain of Pines. But not positive, and all my reference books being packed, ask Wilfred who must have some, to check. It is the old Rosicrucian term. Its meaning? Refer to Mount Olympus, the seat of the Greek Gods; Meru, that of the Indians, and others. Briefly the place where high Inspiration comes from.
    The fact that you are so preoccupied with these terms may mean that you should look for the ONE who inspires you with these thoughts, and why? It is surely 65 or your H.G.A. who has long followed your path, sees your worry and anxiety, wants to talk to you but this is only possible in symbolic language. Possibly He knows that you are mature on some high plane and that you ought to become aware of what has taken place, there in your conscious, rational mind.
    People with constitutions like A.C., Jack Parsons, and, possibly, Cameron (also e.g. Sascha) can get direct messages, can actually talk with higher entities, either on the astral or higher planes. I, for one, am totally blind and deaf. In such cases there are other ways. What you have to learn is (1) the assurance that it comes from your HGA; and not is just an idea that pops up accidentally in your own mind; (2) that He wants you to walk up through the symbol, word, or idea, to what it stands for on those higher planes where images no longer exist ("Be not content with the image; I, who am the image of an image, say this", etc. *LXV*, I.)

(In 1927 I passed through what I call my Boston experience. I was being pushed through severe tests; the culmination came in June. I had just lost my well-Heeled job; had been sending $100 every fortnight on the dot to Paris; I got my last check, had not even the money to pay my ticket to New York; I sent the check all the same. There was a female in the ordeal. I was pushed to read up on the Parsifal legend; was walking in a park in Boston when a white dove suddenly sat down on my shoulder; I went home and got the Trance of the Universal Joke; coming home to the female involved hid in a closet, pointing to Kundry hidden in the bushes, then coming out and washing the feet of Parsifal (as in other legends). The candidate must learn to interpret such hints and urges so as to become firm and unshakable in the realization that, as human, earthly beings, we are but marionettes on the wire of higher forces; and learn to do THEIR WILL. This has to become so automatic that one does not even is conscious of it any more, or has to make an effort.

Yes: Montsalvat is another of those Mountains mentioned above. Your error is that you want to pedantically analyse the origin of any particular thing; it is always the same, just another name in the Hindu, Christian, Chinese, Bolshevik, or any other language. Do you think the Russian candidates are despised by God because they are living under another system? The American smear-slogan of Atheism, is just a competitor's envy and jealousy. The Thelemite makes no difference between any one thing and any other thing.

So, forget about tracing origin and meaning; try to see with your spiritual eye what it stands for.

I sometimes really think I understand what A.C. frequently said about me, that I am "spiritually ahead of him;" that I am the bloke who could never travel on the astral plane, because my mind instantly passed through all these lower planes and dwelt where images no longer exist.

I don't know if all this is being helpful to you. I'm afraid that it is hardly suitable for discussion with Wilfred.

No change in the position here; still waiting for report from Germany, where they are working on search and investigation. I must just be patient. But I can see clearly enough that the delay is for a magical purpose, and will cease the moment the purpose of the delay is solved. Be sure that I shall notify everybody at once. Incidentally, the longer the days get, the more we'd like driving!

Love is the law, love under will.

Fraternally,

Karl

1203 Inchon Avenue
Barstow, California

February 12, 1956

Dear Karl:

Do what thou wilt shall be the whole of the Law.

A long time since I wrote you!
First: Flu, which lasted some time. Part of December and ended in January. Then somewhere along the line came the ordeal – which I call "The battle with the Desert." Alone, alone on a wide wide sea, and never a soul to take pity on me. This included Mary K. and her agony.

Feb. 4 back to Barstow, and my deep gripe is over.

Feb 8 Power. A conscious awaking in my spine (?), back of the heart.
Power started. It eventually projected toward an objective, and united with the objective, in what I can only call a sparkling

"love". I feel like saying, atomic in some way. This has to be used in order to retain it in strength. Though it is not so vital at the moment.

Feb 9. This a.m. I became conscious of being one of the forerunners in the birth of the New Aeon; and took part in its activities.
OLAMAM IMAL TUTULU !

Feb 10. I picked up the Introductory page of the Commentary and found ideas, etc., which thrilled me – made me shake with joy. Ero and Jean floated into the picture and I communicated my joy and reactions to them. Heretofore I did not know what was on that sheet of paper for me.

Abrasax – a name which has interested me for a long time – has given some light. *Liber VII*, III, 4-42, showed itself faintly to me in the Temple at Winona Boulevard.

It is now time for Jane to look to building up the physical. Feb 8 should help this – plus shots in the bloodstream.

….. I just got one. Lying in bed, purposefully breathing Karl entered I sat up in bed, I got out, and have felt heaps better all morning.

Thanks.
I shall try to get to Phyllis in a few weeks. And I thought my time had come! I was so slender and weak.

Love is the law, love under will.

Love to All,

Jane

Hampton N.J.
P.O. Box 581

Dear Jane:

Do what thou wilt shall be the whole of the Law.

Yours of Feb. 12. It seems the Gods of initiation have been dealing with you. I am glad your health is better and that you have new courage.

You quote *VIII*, iii, 40-42. There are so many other angles that I could quote, such as *VII*, ii, 18, or 49 – and, again, so many others. What a book!

You did not, however, mention some practical things. Did you stay with the Smith's, and what impressions did you get? It would interest me, if you care to write about it.

Meanwhile, you will have heard from my brief letters to Ero that it may be that I can get through with this house deal after all. In a week or two I will know more.

Tell Ero and Jean that I have got their letter about the purchase of their house. I hope they had a bargain and are getting a house that is decently built and will not require immediate repairs and improvements the moment they begin to occupy it. Just in the last few days radio and newspaper were full of warnings and congressional investigations on abuses of that sort, especially where G.I.'s were concerned. If they can take the house over in April, I expect to be there by that time to make plans for help in manual work where the printing is concerned. – The arrangement of the house and general set-up just made to order. I still have not decided where to store the archives – Barstow, Phyllis, Malibu (though that seems the last place for me to choose), or Mildred's Storage place as a temporary place.

In case you go to visit Phyllis, please write me your impressions and give her my love and the news; she wrote a month or two ago I haven't answered her for lack of positive news.

Love is the law, love under will.

Fraternally,

Karl

Hampton N.J.
P.O. Box 581

February 29, 1956

Dear Phyllis:

Do what thou wilt shall be the whole of the Law.

I still have a letter from you lying here unanswered, dated Dec. 4 (1955, not 1954!) and having just seen the letter you sent to Jane, I had better tell you the latest from here.

As far as the sale of the house goes, it appears I am in process of removing the last serious obstacle. But it will surely last till the Equinox until I shall be able to leave from here.

As far as the sale of the house goes, it appears I am in process of removing the last serious obstacle. But it will surely last till the Equinox until I shall be able to leave from here. That is three more long, oh, so long!, weeks at the least.

Now for you: I was distressed to hear of your car accident and can only congratulate you that it was not worse, and you or your kids were not seriously injured. You refer to Uranus passing over your Saturn as a possible cause. I don't know the date it occurred. But watch the opposition of Saturn to your radical Mars. Mars loves to cause accidents of that sort! And he will visit you again this year.

However, from the spiritual point of view such aspects, especially Uranus conj. Rad. Saturn, should have a strong, lasting, and repeated influence on your magical growth. Have you had dreams or visions these periods?

I am not in a mood to write long letters these crucial days, weeks, or months. I just attend to routine. Almost all has been packed in cases, made ready for shipment, and I have been living like in a camp for over three months now. Quite trying, as you can imagine. Even now I have not made final plans as to where to ship and store all my stuff. I hope the Equinox will bring an indication and an urge, and settle many things radically. It was a hard Equinox this last for me.

Whatever happens I am looking to visit you, provided all goes well. Meanwhile best of luck to you and your children!

Love is the law, love under will.

Fraternally,

Karl

Barstow, Cal.
601 Frances Drive

October 4, 1956

Dear Phyllis:

Do what thou wilt shall be the whole of the Law.

Yours with interpretation of Meeka's nativity. I must really admire it. You are more than an ordinary astrologer. Having, with hard work, mastered the fundamentals, you have risen above it, and probably will more, so that you almost become prophetic. Frankly, I was amazed, the more so as it was surely done rather quickly, as you must be overburdened with work and daily routine.

But I have seen earlier carefully worked-out analyses from you; it seems that you have reached a stage where you contact powers that inspire, instead of the more rational interpretation. Anyway, I remember I had taken your interpretation of my chart, done with care years ago, as a message.

Here is "Henry" Coon's chart, the real boss of the show. Despite your heavy load, if you can do it, look into this chart which seems quite interesting. If the time of birth is correct, what I generally never like in a horoscope is the Dragon's tail in the First. Smith has it, and a number of people in my life, who all had some spiritual defect. A German lady-astrologer once told me: "watch out for such; you must be careful".

4 planets in Taurus gives extraordinary strength and firmness, and all in the 12th, too! And Taurus is an imprisoned sigh, i.e. has no place on a cusp. Similar to yours, all planets, except in Uranus are in the East, 7 houses without planets.

The woman is an "early-ripe". She began a business of her own, successfully and operated it at 16. Then studied Mechanical engineering at Columbia, has degrees, and can take up study of any scientific subject at will. She has extraordinary will power, firmness; can hold her own in strenuous discussions with several cagey people; is 6 ft tall; worked her scheme with great success up to 1941-42; then had a severe accident, also her husband died, and in despair or frustration chucked the whole thing, retired to a beautiful spot in Arizona. Meeka had had business dealings with her while M. had a job in an industrial company and knew her product. Took endless pains to trace her, with success after 3 years of search. Then set about to infuse new hope and courage into her. The result is mostly her own work. "Henry" had another accident where she broke her back, and can no longer drive about, so Meeka does all the outer things for her. (I suspect that a much closer relation existed between them at one time.)

Now my position is this: my exclusive concern is with being able to print many books beginning 1959, Spring. I am not interested in "millions" of anything, except printed words.

Another aspect: Sascha came to Las Vegas, because there is a Savings Bank that pays 5% and she had invested her money there while she was still in the East. I saw her Sunday, because Meeka (her mother also is a voice teacher in L.A.) had trained a man in Escondido, who set up a voice studio there, and is so busy that he needs an assistant. Besides, his wife is pregnant, and Meeka told me y'day on the phone that he wants to give up (sell?) his studio. I think this is a godsend for Sascha who is now eager to begin again. Should she be able to make a living, she would like to invest her cash into this Mine-Metals venture. It is for that reason also that I feel a responsibility. But on general terms I accept this thing as arranged by the Gods for the sole purpose to enable us to do what has to be done shortly – and no more. Others can make the "millions" if they care.

I wish Grady, before meeting Dorey, would be able to do a little practices, so as to subdue somewhat his all-too-strong intellectual approach, which hits me always in the eye. May-be I'm wrong, and you are better judge of him. Incidentally, did I, or did he, send you his birth data? If not, here it is: Born Oct. 18, 1918, Oklahoma 7 a.m.

I get 3°49 Scorpio rising, [Neptune in] 9° Leo in X. Sun is in 24°20 Libra exact trine Uranus. A.C. always expected much from him. That trine gives that particularly fine aspiration that A.C. liked. His Sun also has a sextile to Saturn in 25° Leo in X,

Enough now. Too long already.

Love is the law, love under will.

Yours,

Karl

Rt. 1, Box 122
Livermore, Calif.

Oct. 9, 1956

Dear Karl,

Do what thou wilt shall be the whole of the Law.

    In answer to your letter re: Grady (no date). I am very sorry to hear that he has been in arrears. Did he promise to start payment on the first of Oct. or November? I hope by now that he has done something. Meanwhile, I shall try to get a moment to mention it to him next Sunday. He is bringing 3 other people interested in the Tarot and Astrology as well as himself and wife and Dorey's will be here to meet them. That makes 9 guests - wow!

    I am also sorry to hear that you are in need of cash. Enclosed is $10. For the beginning of my payments to you. I shall be able to do this much quicker when I finish paying off one of my bank loans in May. In other words, in June I can double or more my payments to you on your loan to me of $200. If this still keeps you in arrears - I could take another loan - and pay all off at once?

    Now, Foxie.[80] Here are my strong impressions -- and practically verified by what Grady has said. It was jack and W.T.S. who make the mischief with her. She is mortally afraid that she will lose Grady and the above two as you know imbue everyone with their license (but not freedom) towards sex. If Foxie is averse to Thelema, I am sure it is only because of the above fear. She adores Grady - more than he loves her. She would fear as much for the strength of their ties that she would act strangely if she thought they were threatened. But as to the money they owe you - I am sure they will both treat it as an honorable debt and pay it off. It might be that some financial emergency arose. I will try to find out.

---

[80] Born Claire Halleck Palmer. Foxie was an O.T.O. initiate and the wife of Grady McMurtry at the time.

Now, Grady himself. Yes, you were absolutely right. G. misses that warmth of nature, the HEART, that every master must have. I have no chance to talk to him about this. My hands are curiously tied both in his case and in Dorey's because of the respective wives. Dorey needs help, too. Is probably planning to make some sort of retirement to in the Spring to contact the Angel. But I seem to be able to do nothing for him. Back to Grady - if the emotional nature is so weak -- is it not doubly difficult to make progress because that the spheres of Netzach and Yesod are too much slighted? How can he control the emotional forces (basis of so much energy) if he has never experienced what they are? Does he not, as yet live in the heart of things, does not penetrate the core of life.

Anyway, the purpose of that picnic was to help Foxie adjust to Thelemic principles, and the same will be stressed once more next Sunday. There will be three wives here at the same time.

Now for your letter of the 4th Oct. Thanks for your kind words on the nativity of Meeka. Yes, it was done in a hurry and without reference to a single book. So I know I missed a lot - but thought you would be interested in what the horoscope said to me directly. I will send you something on Henry's chart next time as I have only time now to get this off with the check. Can you check her time of birth? You have a doubt if it is right. Yes, the relationship between the two women was the closest it could possibly be. Yes, I have Grady's chart and will send you a note or two on that when I do something on Henry's.

Grady - No - it is 28'51" of Libra rising. If it was Scorpio he would not be so cold. Mercury on the Asc. - there is your intellect. Sun trine Uranus; Neptune, Mars, Moon in a Grand Trine. The Saturn makes him desire to be at the head. Remember your Saturn is also in the 10th. So if you two lock horns over matters of authority you can lay it to that. Saturn in the 10th is a sign of a dictator type. I have already laid him low on various ideas (such as another House - like Jack and W.T.S.) which would lead straight to his being in charge. He ought to be initiated by the Forces that be to fit him for some leadership in the Order and he ought also to be held in check. I think that Uranus opposing his Saturn will do it. He is much more sensible on some points that Jack ever was. Also

Sun sextiles Saturn - almost exact. And he does have a head on his shoulders and common sense as well.

The Neptune in grand trine aspect makes spiritual things easier - to easy - and is so good that he becomes lazy. He needs stirring up where Neptune and Moon are concerned. It will come through sex - Moon is squared to Pluto. Squares in a Grand Trine are what loose the energy. But all this may have to wait until his drive towards the Ph.D. are satisfied. Tremendous force to get things done - 5 planets in Fire and 5 in Cardinal signs. Ah, but he does need the heart. Jupiter in Cancer might do it but is square to Venus. Here is his peculiar self-indulgence. And explains why he tells me of 3 extra guests on the spur of the moment - and other little thoughtless acts. There, I have done more than I thought - and I must teach tonight.

How wonderful to have someone like you to talk to - even if with a letter.

Love is the law, love under will.

276 [Phyllis Seckler]

Barstow, Cal.
601 Frances Drive

October 12, 1956

Dear Phyllis:

Do what thou wilt shall be the whole of the Law.

How delightful your letters are, thought they are of need written always under time-pressure. This, incidentally, you should will to change; I have been reading in Newsweek issue of last issue which Jane gets, how overworked American school teachers are; it is more than a shame.)

I must send this note off at once, so as to reach you before you see Grady. He wrote me a long letter with a $10 check. I don't press him; all I want is that he say a word so that I know where I am.

In my reply a few days ago, I urged him to thelemically prepare himself for the meeting with Dorey, and NOT MAKE IT A SOCIAL AFFAIR, which will only lead to a gossip session.

Naturally, you protect your sex, when speaking of Foxie. Her very fear of ever losing her man creates a sinister magical aura. I wonder how it is that you do not see certain magical facts which are dealt with in *LXV*, iii, first part in dealing with Than, Theli, Lilith; each one of these phases has to be dealt with by the aspirant; each is an ordeal of severe nature, according to the awareness, past karmic experiences of an aspirant in that particular field. I don't for a moment view Foxie as the Lilith; even; she'd probably be only the Than or Theli type or function. Grady will be of no use to the Order unless he masters these demons.

Keep all this to your bottom self!

I won't go into your astrology re Grady at the moment. May do so another time.

It may well be that Dorey's attachment, as long as it is not broken, will hold him back until he can do it. It is in that field that I am obliged to admire W.T. Smith's clear vision; though, I believe, he fell into another exaggeration, and so another abyss.

One could write a book on the subject, but Wagner in Parsifal, describes the Kundry problem clearly enough, with the "flower maidens" serving as the first assault on the weaker Knights to the Grail. Parsifal, though successful, was the slow poke; instead of the path of Raja Yoga, the royal, the direct, he went probably the Karma Yoga which permitted him only after endless wanderings and experiences to reach the Grail. He had a pure soul, that saved him. Grady, I hope, has that purity of aspiration; only his appeal to his H.G.A. can save him. He has a long way to go, I'm afraid.

Enough now, I begin to gossip.

Love is the law, love under will.

Yours,

Karl

Oh, I forgot: thanks for the $10 check. Please don't worry. I am sure times will improve for you.

Rt. 1, Box 122
Livermore, Calif.

Oct. 15, 1956

Dear Karl,

Do what thou wilt shall be the whole of the Law.

    I have read with interest you last letter and find much to comment on which seems to be bursting to get out. You caused quite some thinking.
    Now - on the problem of Kundry. At first what you seemed to say seemed to be an insult to my sex. It is true I am getting (no have been) very tired of the old Aeon ideas concerning the feminine half of the world which I encounter at every turn. They are so deeply entrenched because of the fact that the last aeon was paternal and it may take a few hundred years to get over them. Meanwhile I shall strike a blow or two for liberty.
    It does seem to be an observed fact that a woman now and then turns some aspiring Aspirant away from the true Path. Why does this happen? Who tells us the root of the matter? Why? Why?
    Dion Fortune in her book *The Mystical Qabalah* gave me a clue here. Correct me if there is a better source which can refute what she says. She says that the true occult tradition is that man is positive on the physical plane, feminine, or negative on the next

plane - that of the astral, or emotional; positive on the next- the intellectual; and negative again on the spiritual. Conversely, a woman reverses this; she is negative in the physical; positive on the astral or emotional; negative on the intellectual; and positive on the spiritual plane.

So then, if this be true she is already stronger than the man spiritually and so could sway him though this fact. The old fairy tales seem to point to this when the Prince goes seeking for the Princess. She is meant to represent the Soul or the spiritual part of life and once he has united with that principle he is happy ever after. *The Book of the Law* also points this way when Nuit says "To love me is better than all things." Nuit represents the feminine principle of nature and she promises all riches in her worship. Through various other passages the Aspirant is exhorted to "come ever unto me" and "if the ritual be not ever unto me: then expect the direful judgement of Ra Hoor Khuit!" and many other passages which indicate the above matter. We are not exhorted to worship Hadit - but only as referring to his relationship to Nuit. Hadit is the point within us that goes - that accomplishes the act of Union.

Now back to man and woman. Any woman might possibly be placed by the magician on the throne of Nuit - spiritually, that is, and worshiped as one manifestation of that Great Infinite. Or other aspects of Nuit might be worshiped "I am above you and in you", for example. If She is worshiped there is no danger. Where then does the danger lie? Not I woman - for she could be the representative of Nuit. If the magician is powerful enough he could make her so. The answer then lies in the magician himself. Nuit says - "There is no bond that can unite the divided but love." We are divided from realization of her omnipresence by taking a mortal body.

If a man can still love his wife and put her on the Throne - as is done in the Mass - she represents to him no danger of stumbling on the Path. To do this he must have controlled sex - must have controlled the Astral - or the emotional life within himself and must put every action to the service of the highest of ideals - the love of Nuit. Can woman help it if he does not do all these things? If he stumbles because of his inability should she be vilified, avoided, enslaved, reduced to the lowest animal life as she has been in a past Aeon?

Women have enough of Nuit in themselves to rebel against the man who is weak. She will turn and devour him because he does not love her enough. He can't - if he has no control. She knows this intuitionally. Many a woman dreams of the strong man - the Knight on a charger - the King among men. She would give all she possessed her soul even, to be associated with such a man. But she is sometimes merciless if he is not spiritual. She is positive spiritually - and that causes her reactions to the weakling. A man must strengthen his spiritual and emotional side.

Kundry does not like her position. The Magician she serves is at least strong - even if a Black Magician. She waits for the real Strong Man - and she tests every comer. She hopes she will find one who can exert real control - who has the real strength to love. No weakling (she knows) can really love. And when Parsifal leaves his wandering - when he grows up into the Magician - she becomes allied with him and, as a representative of the most spiritual in life she becomes invaluable.

Again - as to marriage. "There is no bond that can unite the divided but love. All else is a curse." Now if the marriages we have discussed do not come up to this rigid standard they should be abolished and he or she involved is particularly weak to allow such a situation to go on. We are in the Aeon of Horus - the child - and no longer can we blame one sex or another exclusively for what happened. Both are responsible - but each within his or her function. This throws further light on the passage "Oh lover, if thou wilt, depart." The middle stage deals in particular with love and so all passages in *The Book of the Law* which talk of this subject ought to be referred to.

The very heart of the Lilith problem is that the Magician is bound to her through moral love. He finds it sweeter than anything else in the world. But he has failed to put Lilith on the throne of Nuit and so she remains Lilith and the very nature of mortal love has the fact involved in it that must die and fade out. It has a systole and diastole, also a death and rebirth and is subject to all the laws of duality that everything manifest on is subject to, and in the same way.

However, should this First Matter be transformed into the pure matter of the soul and its aspiration - in definite instructions as given by Nuit - the curse is lifted from mortal love. In actuality it is really a reflection of the love of the mortal for the Angel, or for the Divine, and the love of the Angel for the mortal which he has created.

What a sin then, that love should be put to such uses - as happens and is the temptation in marriage. One partner may seek to use or enslave the other. One of the two may hope to hold and keep something which by its very nature is not stable. One could may seek to own another. And yet love is the bridgeway to Nuit - she says so herself. But it can't be restricted nor retrained in any way. "The word of sin is restriction." Probably 90 percent of marriages are rifled with this sin.

There - it is very sketchily presented. If you have any pros and cons I would be glad to hear them. Some of my own confused thoughts on the subject are finally falling into place - only to be stirred up by the next event. Jean will witness that I have been interested in the problem for a long time. You perhaps can guess from my history why it should be. But woman was not made to be a shadow of man, nor a slave, nor an Osiris woman - a helper. She does it, true - but it is not her only function. She is herself and too few men know or realize it. You are the only one so far that I have met who had an inkling of this simple fact.

My letter is too long and has taken too many days to finish. I shall close and sent it you.

Love is the law, love under will,

Fraternally,

Phyllis

Barstow, Cal.
601 Frances Drive

Nov. 1, 1956

Dear Phyllis:

Do what thou wilt shall be the whole of the Law.

    Your letters are different. They force one to go a little below the surface. I'll do what I can, though I am at the moment too much preoccupied with decisive and cranky problems. (The most important is that of Sascha, which seems to be near a first solution.
    Dion Fortune's book was sent to me by Jane, but, I'm ashamed to say I did not read it. If what you quote is her theory, it seems plausible to me, or could be; I would not say now. That some sort of such a relation exists has long been known to me; may-be she has it from Blavatsky or elsewhere. But why do you say you have to break a lance (or however you express it) for your sex? Look at the Stélé: is not Horus worshipped by the Beast? Do never misconstrue the fact that the Head of A∴A∴ is the Silver Star, not the Golden Star. I have an idea that a Star can take a male or female body in any particular incarnation. It don't make no diff. But if it takes a female body it just cannot function as the creative genius; yet, even as a female incarnation its accomplishments can be overpowering: compare Semiramis, Cleopatra, Katherina the Great, Elizabeth, Blavatsky, Jeanne D'Arc, and so many others. I could say more, but can only whisper it into a silent ear. Besides I'm yet a learner.
    Kundry: the way Wagner shows her I agree with most of what you say. Is she smaller because she functions as a woman? Would you prefer a reversion to the matriarchal age - because you say the last aeon was paternal?
    The root of the matter? (your § 3). I don't know, but here is an aspect. Most men and women are primitive, in an early stage of magical evolution; they have not begun the lesson of control of different functions. But even if they have a long past behind them,

if they have skipped one or two incarnations, have forgotten, they have to re-learn the relation between woman and man. So, they have to go through the Than, Theli, Lilith experience slowly, painfully, until they reach the Snake of Emerald stage. (One thing in passing: as you must have found in *418*, A.C. commented, was it in the 3rd Aethyr, that may-be Alostrael - Leah Hirsig played the role of Lilith? in his life? You see, Lilith has marvelous qualities which baffle even the Magus. Though in this instance I won't be too positive at all. Just food for thought.

Another aspect: why should men and women not have to face and pass similar problems and ordeals? Oswald Spengler had a word about women who, independent stars, master sex, and rise above the usual type of men. This, of course, only when they ripen magically, and are no longer slaves. I think many movie stars belong in that category, also "grand amoureuses" of the French type. I believe it all boils down to the need for a woman to know as many males as possible and for a man equally. In fact, I think a woman has the edge, for she can always, a man, not. --- No: we must not worship Hadit! It is He that worships.

'Danger' ? That exists for both alike. It may be generally to fall into a rut, to refuse or have to make new experiences, to be afraid to face the unknown, to become a habit-human, a bourgeois, to love comfort, to yearn for 'rest'. Every relation between two tends to be habit forming; stimulus ceases; passion ends; I doubt if – as you write – "if a man still love his wife …". If you live too long with one man it becomes drudgery, even he be great. If you are a Queen in your own right and can match his stature, there will come a point when tension stops; that, I believe is the time for her to strike out towards a new mountain peak and climb it.

In other words, my thesis is not yours, that the old Aeon is to blame. The law is for both alike, has ever been. May-be not so in America where matrimony is sanctified by law, habit, economics, and religion. But take the prominent Americans, men or women: they break through this bondage. Except that in other countries marriage need not be dissolved specially, each simply goes her or his way; there is no heart-balm, or ostracism, to make it impossible, difficult, or profitable.

Kundry: § 3 p. 3. It is a matter, it seems, of what genus or magical family she or Kundry belongs to. Klingsor belonged to what we call the Black tradition. Kundry essentially to the White. She fell under the power of Klingsor, true, because he was strong. But I say: strength is not the criterion, not alone. Kundry became the servant of the G.W. not because Parsifal was, possibly, strong, but because she was from time immemorial sworn to serve the G.W. If you seek long enough with infinite patience for your Parsifal, he will turn up some day, I'm sure.

Why your constant outburst against, or defense of, your sex? I have no such thought of finding fault with it. There is no mention of "marriage" in *Liber Legis* anywhere. Only love.

Lilith: I wonder whether she can ever be put on the throne of Nuit (your § 1 p.3). I believe she belongs to the demonic world, at least in her temporary function. As such, the magician has nothing to do but to learn and understand her function, then destroy her in that function. The Universe is so vast, there are always, phase; and the number of these phases is endless; on hundred years even for one "who does run forward so fast" as A.C., are not enough to go through all of them.

In closing let me say that my philosophy in all of this is, that the goal for every one is to become a Sanyasi, or Sanyasina; where worldly aspirations have ceased or been overcome, so that all personal needs are confined to a rice bowl, a spoon and shoes and dress for walking. Then let the spiritual light shine. Marriage or the lust for living with a companion do not exist; they may be taken up as a temporary burden for one particular job to be done.

Do over come your inferiority complex re women. There are some women around who have reached, or are near, the Sanyasina stage, I believe, if they would only begin to realise it and live like it in full consciousness, then disquiet of mind and false seeking will drop off automatically.

Love is the law, love under will.

Stimulate more letters where one has to dive deeper!

Yours, Karl

Rt. 1, Box 122
Livermore, Calif.

Dec. 21, 1956

Dear Karl,

Do what thou wilt shall be the whole of the Law.

    Greetings of the Winter Solstice.
    The silence isn't quite complete - though I must say my letter in answer to your last is too terribly delayed. Work, and nothing else. I have completed enough ceramics and put a sign on my gate that they are for sale, but there has been not time to place them in a decent shop and so have sold nothing. I would be getting out of debt if I had. It is slow to build up a side line like this especially when school takes so much out of me.
    Got a couple of interesting instructions via intuition which I am also trying to carry out. We will see - of course nothing can be said now. But if I told you that I was ordered to "establish a headquarters in my name"? Ye Gods, how do I know? If is to be so, things will work out. I keep it in mind and do what I can.
    I have started the ball rolling for a Jr. College job but as yet do not know the upshot of this either.
    Meanwhile I felt like writing two poems and enclose them for you. Also sent copies to Jane. I really believe you two are the only ones who can appreciate them. They are not perfect and one ends rather clumsily but there it is until I can get an inspiration which would polish it. Also made a stride or two in painting. People say I should begin to sell those. Maybe, some day.
    Thank you so much for your long answer to my remarks on women. It is true women are working out from the yoke of the past but the Sanyasina stage is far. How does she accomplish it? I would like to venture a guess that it is though love. It is a much maligned type of word, is it not? But there comes a time when one operates on a type of love which is not upset by personal idiosyncrasies of whoever is the loved one. And the love may be so impersonal that several people are loved wildly all at once. It is

a kind of extension of the love for the Angel of for Life or for God, or however you want to put it. A very delicate subject and not good words for it.

Well your letter was good, but divorced from actual conditions. It is those conditions I am always seeking to answer in my mind. I know they are not good - but they are a part of the illusion of life with which on must work. And rising above them - for me - comes through understanding. Why marriage? etc., etc., and sometimes answers come through devious routes. I am a very curious person. I once asked - "why life?" and it took years to answer that one halfway satisfactorily.

The children are all well and I too. But strapped for money. Eye glasses and shoes and everything. Spring will be better - some of the debts paid off. Meanwhile we scrape through the season. How is Aleister? And all the rest? And you?

Love is the law, love under will.

Fraternally,

Phyllis

Rt. 3, Box 479
San Jose, Calif.

Jan. 27, 1958

Dear Karl,

Do what thou wilt shall be the whole of the Law.

Yes, I have been busy, terribly so, and trying to gain back my old pep and energy, too. It wasn't cancer but the Dr. did remove 2 lumps. This depleted my strength. Then I had exams and grades to conduct in school and every weekend spent in looking for a new house.

We may move to Santa Clara – not too far from here and about the same distance from school. We are losing this house because of the income tax – old – of Bill's[81]. But we may have a chance to sell on our own and so meet the down payment on a new place.

I was saddened by your letter about Jane, and deeply shocked that senility had really set in to that extent in so short a time. It is tragic – but you and Sascha are better off out of all the work and care involved.

Also – I will say, too, that your last letter was in very strong tones. I know I provoked you – but I feel we are old friends and I meant it in a friendly spirit. I am too critical – yes? No – please do not misunderstand – I am not suspicious of Sascha as you suggested. I am only trying often to see if each person can understand himself. If he can – then he can control himself. If he can control himself he has a fair chance to control the world and events like magical attacks. On this latter I have much in mind I want to ask you.

Tonight the children reminded me I had to say a banishing ritual over a year ago when I received a stupid communication from Culling. Was this an attack? I had forgotten the incident in my usual happy way. Anyhow – perhaps I usually have no trouble because no one knows about me. Well – let's leave the whole subject until we can talk about it for a few hours. It is complicated.

I received a letter from Mark telling me about his new baby and asking for a horoscope but he sent no return address. Very stupid of him. Do you have an address for him? He really doesn't deserve a horoscope at that rate but it you write to him please tell him he had better send me an address and apologize because I have done something about the horoscope after all. Also I would like to tell him he is very young and may have to suffer unless he grows up. Isn't that just like me?

I must close – too much to do. The best to you and Sascha.

---

[81] Bill Wade, Seckler's second husband.

Love is the law, love under will.

Fraternally,

Phyllis

West Point, Calif.

Box 258

Feb. 3. 1958

Dear Phyllis,

Do what thou wilt shall be the whole of the Law.

It is with pleasure that I confirm receipt of your unsigned letter of Jan. 27, received to-day. I want to say a word or two at once so as to make you assured that there is no cloud on our spiritual horizon. I was a little mad on one occasion, when your professorial manner was too evident. But, as you say, to be outspoken is the privilege of friends.

We were much relieved to hear that there was nothing serious. I am not relieved to hear that you are so overworked. Sooner or later your great gift for work must be available for things like literary help, preparation for publications, better, for help at headquarters where there is so much to do. You are the intellectual type, which I am not, I regret to admit it. What I want to say is that I'm sure you would find great pleasure and happiness in managing the literary material and organizing it. I always must force myself, which is not proper. If work is in the line for which one is fitted, one never tires of it; the best test is that it makes one happy. For me it is drudgery.

Magical attacks: I think one can say that there are many levels of these. On lower levels it may be hostile waves sent out by another, acutely felt by sensitive persons. Jones (Achad) once tried to open my mouth forcibly to make me reveal certain secrets. This was seen clairvoyantly. Then he put a curse on me, as a result he died one year later. (I did feel the effects very acutely at the time of his attacks. But wounds and scars are an honour in battle.)

Then you can go higher and higher, to larger, more general spheres. Why, for instance, could not the phase of acute crisis in which you find yourself with Bill (your operation, tax troubles, change of domicile, search for house, etc.) be the result of magical hostilities whose source is as yet unknown to you, partly because you have not trained yourself in this field?

You can go still further and speak of a magical climate which is not favourable at the moment, for any of us. The Three Schools of Magick give pointers of what I drive at. The other schools know just as well what we want and plan. So, if they cannot prevent they can at least throw sticks into the spokes and make trouble.

Banishing ritual: I think I told you that I have never in my life done anything of that sort to protect myself. Being ignorant of your relation with Culling, and what he wanted from you, I cannot judge whether there was a magical attack involved. Hardly, I should say. Yet, Culling was possibly one of the more important types I had come out to the West for to test. Did I tell you that, after cultivating his intimacy for many months, I have found him bad, and dangerous for the Work, and for genuine seekers. His magical atmosphere is charged with a sinister poison. I have dropped him completely.

When exactly did Culling approach you? Month or date? What was his object?

Marcelo Ramos Motta's address is P.O. Box 6165. L.S.U., Baton Rouge, La. You are so right: he is so young! Life will trim his cockiness – provided the Gods take an interest in him. I think he has a knack of irritating the female sex especially. He behaved with ill manners to Sascha, too.

Do you remember that I gave Meeka $2,500 as a loan in Sept. '56? She has, with another gangster woman this so-called mining scheme near San Bernardino. It looked promising, and she baited me with her pledge that the millions that were expected would to a great extent go to set up a big H.Q., with printing press, etc. etc. In short, she solemnly pledged it for the G.W. What is the truth? That she and her spiritual master mind, that other female, are out to defraud investors. Well, anyway, I gave her $2,500 against the promise in writing of a second trust deed on her house in the Canyon – never given – and am now unable to get it back. The lawyer whom I consulted asks $250 cash down and 33-1/3 of the net proceeds, if we win, thus a loss of $1,000, always provided that I can raise the $250 cash.

Then I gave, as you know, over $630 to Grady. I have asked him for the return of the money of which he still owes some $400 to 450, as I need it really badly now. Is there a chance? Hardly, under present deplorable circumstances. He even takes my giving him that money for granted. I have my grave doubts about his magico-spiritual status, and am wondering whether he can be 'saved'. He is a man. He has gone through college. He should be able and entitled to a good position and income. He is a born American with all the privileges and facilities. Why is it that he is in such a sad state? He has worked as a salesman for cars, failed in San Francisco and lost his last job. This is not a case of magical attack. He has sunk into the bourgeois mentality of his un-Thelemic family. There is one danger greater than any for a Thelemite: to have in his circle an impure element, particles which are hostile to Thelema. It will breed scorpions and poisons.

I must say one thing most emphatically to you: you might construe the above two cases as an un-subtle hint to pay me back the paltry little balance you may still owe me. I say in all truth that this is not so. You have been a shining example of working and succeeding against obstacles and holding up the flag. It has been a pleasure to help you at a time when help was needed.

I believe that my own frustration-period of the last years was cause by passing through a period described in *LXV*, III, vv. 6-16. If that is so, the cloud should gradually lift, and the Work go forward again. We need it if March 1959 is to initiate a 5 year period of Speech.

Love is the law, love under will.

Fraternally,

Karl

Rt. 3, Box 479
San Jose, Calif.

March 26, 1958

Dear Karl,

Do what thou wilt shall be the whole of the Law.

>The Greetings of the Equinox of Spring.
>Ever since the Equinox I have wanted to write this letter. Even before – but strangely enough – not only is the teaching a strain so that I let everything I ought to go – but events have been simply fantastically bad for a long while. Even now I can hear you question – what has been wrong?
>And I do not want to speak of it as it involves other people – hit me indirectly – but still badly enough. Suffice it to say that Lisa must now be boarded with my aunt near San Luis Obispo and I must pay the extra for the board.
>That's not all – debts on Bill's business have been staggering and we are at our wits end to figure how to meet everything. The sale of this property will bring some relief but meanwhile to do that we must secure a quit-claim deed from his former wife and that we are not able to do for the last several months. So we will realize nothing on this if the Bank forecloses.
>All of which makes me doubly curious about your magical attacks. All These happenings seem to have a basis in Astrology. Transiting Saturn is going across Bill's Sun and is now conjunct his Moon in Sagittarius. At the same time this same Saturn is opposing my own Sun and Moon. Best thing to do – as I can see it – is wait out the storm as best one might.

But I must confer with you about magical attacks and learn all that you might be willing to teach me. Why don't you use banishing rituals and so on? This is a long involved subject so I intend to try to get up there some time during the summer to talk about it.

Have you heard any news about Jane? I've heard nothing since you told me you took her back to L.A.

Please let me know how you and Sascha are. Did you have snow there this winter? Were the roads difficult to get in and out of when it stormed? I've thought of you often.

We must get rid of all the animals as it costs too much to feed them. I would like to know if you still have a fancy for Coco? It will break Sunny's heart to part with her but it might not be so bad if she is with someone he knows. What do you think? She is now older than when you knew her and obeys much better. He has done quite a bit of training on her. Thank you for your little note with the greeting of the Equinox. I would answer your last letter if full if I could find. it. I thought I knew exactly where I put it but my files badly need cleaning – so it has been misplaced.

Love is the law, love under will.

Phyllis

West Point, Calif.
Box 258

April 7, 1958

Dear Phyllis:

Do what thou wilt shall be the whole of the Law.

    Your letter of March 26, which reached me days later as we have been snowbound for a while and I could not drive to West Point.
    Jane died Saturday, March 29, at 12:20 p.m. from sheer exhaustion in the Home where she had been, (and where Mary K. has also been transferred, I believe.) Mildred has been attending to matters there. We all considered it as a great blessing to her, as her life had become continuous torture of late, and she had expressed it to me several times that she wished for the end. She has been cremated.
    I am sorry to hear of your difficult situation. It must not necessarily be "magical attacks" for which one must look. Sometimes there is something subtly, magically wrong in one's life and the H.G.A. speaks to you in His language to make you sit up and take notice, and search yourself.
    (Remember when I was in a stagnant situation some years ago, when I searched for a new partner, because I thought that was what I was ordered to do; I was wrong, though, I was punished, had to pay dearly.)
    The harm is not permanent and final when one recognizes the errors, and appeals to the HGA to help one rectify the situation. People like Achad did persist, and went insane, and became a traitor. Ra Hoor Khuit punishes direfully those that are not chosen for "regeneration of the world".
    Banishing rituals: I have never used any in my life, in fact, would not know how to work them; but this is individual; you must not follow. However, such rituals do not work, or have the opposite effect, if the root of the trouble has not been detected, and one remains on the wrong path. –

Please do not overrate me. I have never claimed technical knowledge in things magical. Still, all I could tell you will be at your disposal when you see or call me.

Coco: too late! We now have a bitch, a wonder dog, only 6 months old, but you should have seen her to-day when there was a herd of cows, she got mad, jumped out of the car, and chased them when they had been blocking the road. We could not take two females.

Do stick to your plan to visit us in June (your vacation?). We should love to have you to stay; you can have the bedroom that Jane had and which is empty.

They all say that this was an exceptionally bad winter. Until Jan. 23 (when we drove Jane to L.A.) we had almost constant sunshine. Since then such rain, and for the last few weeks much snow, though never more than 8", and it melts more quickly than in the East. We never were really marooned, only I loathe to put on the chains.

Love is the law, love under will.

Love from Sascha,

Karl

18862 Casa Blanca
Saratoga, Calif.

Jan. 1, 1961

Dear Karl,

Do what thou wilt shall be the whole of the Law.

I looked through all Jane's papers to find the Banishing Ritual you asked for. All that came up was the enclosed copy of

A.C.s notes on it. I really looked with a fine tooth comb, too. As a result, I have been wandering around in the past. Some of the correspondence here and there took my eye. Well it was a great show while it lasted. Wish I had time to write a book on Jane.

Financial matters are gradually improving with us. With my tongue in my cheek and a large hope that this can be kept up - I enclose $5.00 to take care of some of the incidental work of H.Q. Stamps and envelopes and all that. My hope is to increase this sum when we finally struggle out from the mountains of debt. But it is a hope! Now if we don't get a landslide of other Dr. or hospital bills or what not we will be lucky indeed.

I feel too much is left unsaid over the past 3 or 4 years but there is nothing I can do. You complain in your letters about how things disappear but I have seen you mislay things under my very eyes and not know where they are.

Once when there with Bill you asked me three times if I had returned a book I was reading. Each time I indicated to you just where it was and each time you forgot and went on worrying about it. I strongly suspect that you send forms to various people with no note on whom or where or what was sent. Or if you make notes, you probably forget where the note is.

But you see, all this is a ticklish subject. You have it in your mind that certain Govt. depts. are responsible. I listen to you in sympathy but in my head I think that Karl is getting forgetful and is the unfortunate victim of a persecution complex. Then I try to figure why the High Gods have made him so and whether it must be that way because it is perhaps more of a safeguard to the books he is caring for. All this races through my mind as you complain of spies. At the same time I know that if I protest Karl will only lengthen and broaden his state of mind to include me. For such is the nature of neurosis with which you are inflicted. Everyone must be suspected. If fear this has done a great deal to your various contacts with aspirants and perhaps all kinds of people. Perhaps it must be so, who knows?

Now you see, a heavy burden is off my mind and I have also hit at a barrier which lies between me and the only other true Thelemite which I know. I hope that this letter does not raise the barrier higher in action of self-defense on your part.

Love is the law, love under will.

Fraternally,

Phyllis

P.S. There may be a missing part in Magick for I was always taught to do it this way.

i. Touching the forehead say Ateh (Unto Thee)
ii. Touching the solar plexus say Aiwass
iii. Touching the genital region say Malkuth

All else is the same.

West Point, Calif.
Box 173

Jan. 3, 1961

Dear Phyllis:

Do what thou wilt shall be the whole of the Law.

    Thanks for your letter (and enclosure!) and the trouble you took. What you sent me is not what I am looking for, that I have. It is a re-arrangement of the ritual itself.
    I am glad to hear that finances are improving, at your end, anyway. I join my best wishes to your hope. Is it that Bill has now permanent contracts for his product?
    As to forgetfulness, you are right; despite an extraordinary memory A.C. in respect to loan of books, MSS., TSS., etc. had the same failing. I see a spiritual basis for this. About your further

criticism, I cannot blame you. You have evidently not gone through experiences such as *LXV*, II, vv. 4-6. A.C. had. Jack Parsons had some experience. McMurtry had a brush with them, yielded, and sold himself. Neither have you been a trained Freemason into higher grades. The very basis of their doctrine-training demands some mastery. So does the O.T.O. – but where, outside of Smith, was or is there anybody who has experience? So, let's forget it.

No, dear Phyllis, you could not possibly raise a barrier against me. Not now! Not as long as you keep you true aspiration aflame. The way I see it, you have mundane work cut out for yourself before your H.G.A., who hides under the name of Asar (Azar) will arrange your outer life in such a way that you can devote yourself exclusively to Thelemic work.

Love is the law, love under will.

Fraternally,

Karl

18862 Casa Blanca
Saratoga, Calif.

March 20, 1961.

Dear Karl,

Do what thou wilt shall be the whole of the Law.

Greetings of the Equinox of Spring.
Thank you for your last letter - it was just what I needed. One sometimes feels terribly alone, even though doing something for the furtherance of Thelema.
Yes, I do have a tremendous task. Much of it has recently materialized in fact, has been going a year. I hardly dare mention

it for fear it might fall through. With Jane's death there was no longer anyone to talk to about matters which were common knowledge among us Thelemites or others striving for spiritual growth. So what used to be an outlet got pretty well dammed up. Now there is an outlet again. I am writing a series of letters to Bill's son Bruce, now stationed in Japan with the U.S. Navy. The letters are designed to shake young people out of the current materialistic beliefs. Mostly because Bruce and many others in my immediate family are such victims of materialism.

Of course the letters allow me to express the thoughts, ideas, and modes of behaviors which have existed in me for so long. I hope they will lead many young people to an appreciation of Thelema - for in time I shall see if I can get them published. Meanwhile they are a tremendous work. I already have a small book of them but much world need to be edited.

Well, I don't think I mentioned it at any time in the past but a peculiar vision occurred some years ago which still has me guessing. I spoke to the Angel - while meeting with him - one sentence. "Let me be Thee". Now this, I think is really peculiar. Anyhow, if true, I may be in the process of becoming and so see Him in visions no longer. But, as you say, there is plenty I have not been initiated into and so plenty escapes me.

Yes, at some time I must devote myself to Thelemic work and sometimes I can't understand why not now. Perhaps I am paying a Karmic debt. But I also feel that this absurd teaching of adolescents will end in another year or two. I do have to earn a living at the present and it is for me an easy and rather pleasant way out, but scarcely the Real thing that I want to do.

I still make discoveries, though, and wish I could talk them over with someone. I am reading *The Mystical Qabalah* by Dion Fortune and find much in there worth discussing. Someday I should also like to ask questions about my own Qabalistic figurings but must needs shelve all that until the right expert comes along.

Love is the law, love under will.

Fraternally,
Phyllis

West Point, Calif.
Box 173

March 24, 1961

Dear Phyllis:

The Greetings of the Equinox of Spring!

Do what thou wilt shall be the whole of the Law.

It is always a pleasure to hear from you; being all alone, isolated, speaking Thelemically, is a test for you in itself. I feel wonderful for you that you now have what you call an "outlet". I trust it is only a beginning.

The Great Work of Ra Hoor Khuit is visibly progressing. I must have it expressed often to you that the periods of Time in which They live are different from ours. It is so hard and agonizing for us humans to accept Theirs and to learn to (a) see and understand Theirs and (b) learn to adapt our vision of *Liber Legis* to it as well as our life. It would be nice to see L.L. established in the world in our time, to see all the prophecies fulfilled – those of Chapter III, and those of I, 61, etc. No wonder that so many whom I know and have known have fallen by the wayside because they began to doubt the Book. Even after A.C. had spells, for in the early days of 93 it seemed so fantastic that He should be chosen for such a tremendous job; even in the 22 years that I was more or less around him he suffered from being able to bring about the acceptance of the law. Oh! How he suffered!

Where are helpers to-day? Where the generation of men and women that will accomplish the next step? Much has been done in Germany. I see small and delicate plants trying to spring up here and there. So it encourages me to hear of your new venture. One can never know what sequoia will grow out of it. And one should not care. All you can do is heed the impulse from your H.G.A..

I like what you call your vision that you mention. Recently I have been led to read over *A Dweller on Two Planets* by Phylos, edition 1920. I had this from the collection of Jane. It is a very remarkable book, and I am going to read it again. Do you know this? It even throws light on the doctrine of Nu and Had on the large world and the individual entities in the human world. The book demands careful reading. If you have or know it, it may be useful to read it again; if not, there is now a new edition available; but I shall be glad to send you my library copy on loan.

It seems I have been led or ordered to these 'outermost places' and that I have to stay here for the time being, though I often itch for a change. But the events have to pass and blow over first, apparently. You will always be welcome to visit here and talk problems over.

Love is the law, love under will.

Fraternally,

Karl

West Point, Calif.
Box 173

Dec. 26, 1961

Dear Phyllis:

Do what thou wilt shall be the whole of the Law.

Thank you for your letter of Dec. 18 and for the circular of the Mystic Book Club. I had heard about them, but did not know their address.

We were both distressed to hear about your health, and your financial straits. With your income, you should really never have worries to buy eye glasses, or similar necessities. Is it possible that you are unduly sacrificing yourself?

Thelema is a whole job. Its guardians watch the few disciples that show promise closely, and may I say 'jealously'? – that they do not share Thelema with lower pursuits, or old sweetness. You must, I suppose, have many conflicts – in your professional work, your home, your children, and what not, and, combined with the general state of disruption of the atmosphere – magical and spiritual – in the whole world, it would weigh heavily on you sometimes. Especially now when we may be driving towards a climax in the affairs of the world, and then you in particular fell the opposition of our friend Saturn, as I notice.

Such periods demand from us that we listen intently to the 'Voice' of the H.G.A.

Well, I cannot go deeper into all this, I have to drive to the post office with matters concerning *Liber Aleph* which are important and want to take this letter with me.

Liber Aleph is printed in Brazil, I have just on Saturday received and advance unbound copy which goes to a possible Distributor. The Publishers are Thelema Publ. Co., West Point, Calif. As soon as I get copies I shall send you one. If you are still in touch with any of the old Smith group of so-called Thelemites, you might distribute the copies of the prospectus which I enclose. I am not in touch with any at this time.

I very much should like to read what you have up to now written. I am the champion slow reader, but if you would send me what you have Registered, I promise to return it Registered within one week. I'm sure close study of *Liber Aleph* will be of great help to anything you will write.

All the best to you from myself and from Sascha who takes great interest in everything.

Love is the law, love under will.

Fraternally,

Karl

188162 Casa Blanca Lane
Saratoga, Calif.

March 11, 1962

Dear Karl,

Do what thou wilt shall be the whole of the Law.

Thank you so much for *Liber Aleph*, which I received yesterday. Enclosed is a check for $10. to pay for it and also for an extra copy if you have one to spare. I would like to give the extra as a gift to Bruce if he would like it. Please note that the check is dated for April 1, 1962. The budget is always in a sorry state after the 5th of the month for Bill and I are engaged in paying off debts too numerous to mention. I hope this postdating of the check won't inconvenience you but I would rather you had it right now than wait for April 1.

Also you will find enclosed a circular from the Mystic Arts Book Society. Do you suppose they might be useful in publishing some of Crowley's works? The Editorial Director - John C. Wilson - has said some of the most sensible things about Crowley that I have heard in some time. I almost sat down to write to him to comment him on his common sense but thought that perhaps I had better not. What do you think?

Who wrote the description on the book jacket of *Liber Aleph*? Was it Marcello Motta? Bickie has been fascinated for a long time by Marcello and would like to have his address. Are you still in touch with him?

My health is 100% improved since Saturn transited out of an opposition to natal Saturn. I knew this would happen and deeply regret having consulted a Dr. about it all. However, maybe his medicine did have an effect on the virus I was suffering from, who knows?

Your last letter set me deeply thinking so that I didn't know quite how to answer it but I think perhaps I ought to clear up a few points. Yes, Thelema is a whole job as you suggest. I have always thrown myself heart and soul into the spirit of *The Book of the Law* and have gained much supreme joy out of the guidance received therein. But your sentence made me wonder if you meant that I had not enough time for Thelemic matters. There is always enough time in the thoughts even if not in the daily life. I must work for I have no independent income. If I am married there is a chance that outside work may some day cease. If I am single there is no remote chance of this. My attitude towards marriage is a funny mixture but please to remember that the Angel ordered me to do this. However, all my love comes through and to the Angel and Nuit - or that is where the intensity of it lies. Quite different than when in the poetry writing stage. Love for other people, for my work, for the garden, for painting, for beauty, then spills out of the main concentration. Needless to say, many things can happen now without upsetting me too much. I find life is truly joyful. I sing paens of praise in my interior every day. Kind of mystical, isn't it? I guess I am just that type.

Now you say that "Thelema is a whole job. Its guardians watch the few disciples that show promise closely, and, may I say 'jealously?'- that they do not share Thelema with lesser pursuits, or old sweetnesses."

Here you have me stumped. Lesser pursuits? One does what one has to and does it with praise and joy. I have Saturn in the 4th house so this has always given me very heavy home burdens. I expect this configuration will always behave this way. There is probably some deep soul lesson in it for me. Now that the children are grown and all in college this burden still continues and actually I can't let any of them down by cutting off money or similar things. Then Bill has needed assistance so that the business can develop and some day may yield considerable returns, who knows? If it does I have a certain percentage of the profit marked for Thelemic books only. The whole thing is a gamble but then so is much of life. So those are my bones in that department. Then comes the necessity to help others - hence the letters to Bruce and the training of Bickie. Who knows where all that may end?

It is true I spend much time creating beauty for I love life so much I can't live without it. I must paint and garden and weave and all the rest of it just so beauty is created in the surroundings. I have not been fitted by nature to create it in great public works - as

Frank Lloyd Wright did. My efforts have always been domestic and personal. Some day I might possibly support myself a little by selling ceramics and paintings and weaving but it would never be possible to make as good a living from it as I do now from teaching. That is due to the structure of the modern world and also to some of my own shortcomings.

The word "old sweetnesses" I thought applied to the Scarlet Woman. Here I do not understand your use of this thought out of context, as it were. It certainly mystifies me and I scarcely think using those words applies in my case. Unless you have something else in mind which you do not explain.

If I ever am in a position where I don't have to teach I would certainly like to write. But I must have absolute quiet to do it for the family says one sentence to me and the whole chapter flies out the window. I am crossing my fingers that this quiet time will arrive some day.

All my best to you and Sascha. I think of you both often.

Love is the law, love under will.

Fraternally,

Phyllis

West Point, Calif.
Box 173

March 17, 1962

Dear Phyllis:

Do what thou wilt shall be the whole of the Law.

Yours as of March 11. We are both glad that your health is better, Sascha joins me especially in this wish. – Thanks for check, April 1 is quite allright.
I am sending you to-day two more copies of *Liber Aleph*. One is for Bruce. The other was (first) intended for you to send to the Mystic Art Book people, but I have since heard that they are a sinister outfit as far as the work of Thelema is concerned. The books were packed, so use the second copy for some other purpose or keep it.
You send me that prospectus which shows on the front A.C.'s picture together with the arch-enemy of all things Thelema, the Jesuit Montgomery Summers. – They are also connected to a fraudulent group that wanted to re-publish *The Book of Thoth*, luckily Frieda Harris refused to hand over her paintings, and did not fall for the swindle. You know possibly the surface of the ocean, but have no notion of the monsters in the Deep. – Anything you may hear of these people, let me know.
Motta: yes, he lives in Rio de Janeiro and did all the publishing, editing, correcting, printing, and binding of *Liber Aleph*, including the blurb, etc. He is promising, but has yet to pass the cataracts, the Niagara and many other ordeals.
That passage which seems to have upset you: don't take it too seriously. It certainly has no reference to the Scarlet Woman. Try to understand my situation. Here I have (by order) to live in what you might call 'the outermost places', review from here the many so-called Thelemites that are in California, and have to watch one after the other go to the dregs. It is sometimes a little heartbreaking, if I have a heart to break. This is concerning the little world. In that above the clouds it is different, though nothing

seems to happen as to the progress of the Great Work. – That passage was probably also a reaction to your long silence. You are, remember, the only Californian, still attentive to your H.G.A. and obedient to His voice.

You may be called to do much for Thelema yet, when the time is ripe. You would be ideally fitted for work for which I am lamentably ill equipped. But what will you? We all have first to so fulfill and put in order the mundane things, before we are permitted release, to do higher things.

Love is the law, love under will.

Fraternally,

Karl

West Point, Calif.

May 25, 1962

Dear Phyllis:

Do what thou wilt shall be the whole of the Law.

My deepest sympathy for your accident. Be glad that it was not a real fracture. Sascha had this some years ago when she broke the wrist. I suppose you had great pain, but it is surprising that you could go so quickly to school again, even drive!

Ero: yes, Jean has been his vampire in the same sense that is shown in chapter 100 or *Liber Aleph*. I freed him once, he broke, they divorced; but he fell back under her spell. The usual thing.

I think it is a good thing for Bickie[82] to memorize *AL*. I suppose you have given him the necessary perspective, so that he grasps the conceptions of Nuit and Hadit. As against the Christian heresy or parochialism of the vision of the Universe. Briefly: there are (progressing) egocentric, geocentric, solarcentric, galactocentric, visions of the Universe. And then beyond our tremendously huge knowledge of our (relatively) small galaxy, the conception of the millions or billions of galaxies in space as known now by our modern astrophysics.

Christianity is Christocentric; it sees Jesus, at best as one local Yogi, as the focal point in the Universe around who the Universe has to turn; it still clings to the view that the Earth is 6,000 years old, with the Jewish Bible record as the only tradition, while Hindus, Chinese, Egyptians etc. go far beyond that in time; and modern science takes the age of the Sun and Earth and the solar system as at least 4 billion years, probably 6. Man has lived on this planet for over 1 million years. That is why the church has always fought and hated and persecuted Science. In short: Christianity is a ridiculously parochial religion, to-day suited to the minds of the lowest tribes.

I was lucky to grow up in a circle of my older brothers who, at the University, studied math, physics, biology, etc. etc, all hostile to Christian teachings or conceptions. In the U.S.A. it is still tabu to express enlightened views on this subject. So Bickie would be well advised to open his mind, but keep silent, especially when he should go into the Army, where Free Thought is not tolerated. –

Beatific vision: some of your recent letters made me think that you were experiencing a sort of its lower forms – quite natural for you as the born artist soul. Remember, there are many stages of this.

Thanks for writing me – with you left hand – I envy you that you can do it, and mine and Sascha's best wishes for your complete recovery.

Love is the law, love under will.

---

[82] Seckler's son, Paul Bickerton Seckler.

Fraternally,

Karl

Marcelo Ramos Motta
Caixa Postal 15, Tijuca
Rio de Janeiro
Guanahara, Brasil

30 May 1962

Care Frater:

Do what thou wilt shall be the whole of the Law.

I wish to re-phrase my last letter to you, once the hose of personal feelings is over: under no circumstances would I ever start an "O.T.O. movement" in Brazil without your permission. If by any chance O.T.O. documents come to my hands, I will inform you at once, and will hope to hear from you on the subject. If you request them, I will forward them to you. If you tell me to keep them, but not to start anything, I will most surely comply. If you tell me to start a movement, I will start it not in my name, but in yours.
    The Order of Thelema is another matter. I claim jurisdiction over it, complete, by right of appointment.
    The Manifest of the O.T.O. in my book never stated, nor does it now, that I, personally, intended to start an O.T.O. movement. I have never claimed to represent the O.T.O. at any time. However, my jurisdiction extends over the use of Thelemic material -- or rather, its mis-use by fools. It was on these grounds that I wrote to the Swiss. I never claimed to be their superior. I earnestly wish you would write and request a photocopy of my

letter to them, so you can see for yourself. I did, in my letter to them, demand that they stop misquoting *AL* and renew contact with their rightful superior -- but I meant you.

I am not writing this letter with second intentions. I have been so deeply hurt by all this O.T.O. entanglement that I wish to have nothing to do with the order. Your lack of trust has wounded me more than I can possible say, and was the cause of my violent letters to you. Understand I am not withdrawing or retracting one word. My knowledge of the circumstances may be at fault; on such a case, and in a case only, I would say that my attitude was un-called for. But I doubt it. Only time will tell.

You have, all this time, been expecting or demanding that I behave towards you the way you behaved toward A.C. That, if you would only think, is absurd, unfair and un-Thelemic. "One law for the lion and the ox is oppression." You are not A.C., I am not you, and our relationship and circumstances are never and could never be the same. I cannot mold myself by you--and would not even if I could. Until the Abyss--if that day ever come--I am I. After, I Am That Am. Meanwhile, I am doing my best at a rough tough job; my best may not be up to your standards, but it is the best I can do.

I beg of you to keep in touch, not for my sake, but for the sake of the Work to which I, at least, am pledged, and which must be above any personal differences between M.T. and an Adept.

About two weeks ago, since you were not, obviously, going to write Mrs. R. again, I wrote her myself. She answered about that subject I will rather not mention in a letter when it is not necessary. She said she had delayed answering your letter because she has been expecting every day an answer from the S. librarian, but it hasn't arrived yet. She said she was in no hurry, and that she would let me know about the decision.

I am telling you this so you can, if you will, write her and tell her not to consider me as a prospect, and indicate somebody else more to your liking.

I cannot think of any other way in which I may try to prove to you that this letter is not an attempt to fool you, beguile you, or trap you.

Incidentally, I offered her the original price she had asked, and offered her a contract and all possible guarantees.

Love is the law, love under will.

Fraternally,

Adjuvo

P.S. I called myself an Adept--or rather, Adjuvo. My estimate of the situation is, Adjuvo is, if all planes are considered, merely a Neophyte, and could not be more. But on a certain plane, there is Adjuvo $6°=5^{\square}$ who is a Major Adept performing the administrative task of a Major Adept: that is, trying, working absolutely alone, to keep discipline among the people all on their separate planes, and to transmit clearly the utterance of his immediate superior, O.M. $7°=4^{\square}$. As for my "beasthood", that has to do only with the Order of Thelema and matters of Thelemic import; such as I already said, the profanation or distortion of A∴A∴ publications in Class A-- and more specifically, *AL* and the spreading of the Law. Whatever confusion I may have experienced and am still experiencing in this account must be put down to the schematic nature of the arrangement of my vehicles, and only time will take care of that--if it will. I do not underestimate for one moment the dangers and risks inherent in my position; but I am, as I said before, trying to do my job the best I can, and there was nobody else doing it, and besides--I have been appointed, since the Solstice of Summer 1960, to do precisely this. That if you remember, was a time of my Initiation when I claimed the Grade of Neophyte, and was very puzzled that you did not know that I had been appointed the Beast. The reason was probably that the whole thing is on a plane below the Abyss, where you are not aware of what is going on--and, as far as I can sense form the nature of your Will, you don't particularly care.

As for Marcelo Ramos Motta, he is the ape of Thoth--not even the Ape; and he tries to keep it in mind as best he can, which he will humbly admit isn't saying much. But then, you haven't been exactly helpful yourself, have you?

As for the O.T.O., being sane, at least at the moment, I will say that never in my sane moments did I think that I could do a better job than you. I don't have what it takes.

West Point, Cal

June 9, 1962

Care Frater Adjuvo:

Do what thou wilt shall be the whole of the Law.

If one tried to go into refuting or arguing your recent letters one would run the risk of getting contaminated by the demonic forces that have got a hold of you. What I will do is give you the benefit of my experience. It has been my privilege or misfortune to have to watch at least a score of "experts of delusion" in the last more than thirty-five years of my connection with Thelema!)

What you claim – the title of BEAST – is only minor, i.e. a repeat of another title. (Yet Crowley assumed the grade only 15 years after he had become M.T., while you are at best a Neophyte!)

Others are, or have been, infinitely more ambitious. One was an Ipsissimus (long before 666 himself took the grade) claiming such high initiation that he had received the oracle of the Aeon following Thelema, so that he disposed R.H.K. and made Him obsolete. There have been and still are several Babalons, one of them is mother of the "child to become mightier than ...etc.". Several are "the child". I have suggested to them to form or enter "Babalon clubs" or "Child Clubs". One was Ra Hoor Khuit Himself. One lived with a grey cat and had passed beyond Chokmah the way beyond. Then there was the obsession in California by the prophetic vv. At the end of *LXV*, iv. One implored 666 (the First) to take him along on that trek. Some actually prepared that "journey after into a land of pestilence and evil" – after's A.C.'s death. Needless to say what happened to them.

To add to the Ipsissimus Achad, he became a good honest Roman Catholic, went back to Jesus and Mary; once, when I laughed and refused to acknowledge his authority, he laid upon me the curse of *AL*, II, 60. It bothered me a little, true. He died soon after.

I could quote more, but enough of this! You can take this warning or leave it.

I want to hear from you about *LIBER ALEPH*. Have you dispatched 50 copies of the book to me, in parcels of 5 each, for which I asked after sending Weiser the books I had there?

Also: are you making preparations to get the 300 copies on the way to Weiser? After your long evil-inspired letter to them, I have not written them. I wanted to lay a plan before Donald Weiser to solve this matter. Instead of hearing simple facts, you bombard me with reams and reams of extraneous things. Remember: magically you have taken upon yourself to get *Aleph* distributed. If you should fail in this, I hate to think what would happen to you.

Love is the law, love under will.

Fraternally,

Karl

Calixa Postal 15, Tijuaca
Rio de Janeiro
Guanabara, Brasil

5 July 1962

Dear Karl:

Do what thou wilt shall be the whole of the Law.

    I am sending you today by air mail, as per your instructions, two exhibits of my shame and guilt, just come out of the press. I labored three months to avoid precisely many of the irregularities of printing that you will be able to notice, specially having to do with left margin squaring. For the next book, if any, I will be changing my printers...
    I am under continual, subtle and insidious attack, as you probably know. Have also a seriously infected tooth which is affecting all the left side of my cranium with strong headache. Will try and see a specialist about this today. May have to pull out several teeth—vanity, vanity!
    I am also sending you today, by sea, registered, ten copies of *LIBER ALEPH*. Others will follow regularly until they complete the fifty you ordered.
    I don't know if it is necessary to say this, but I have abandoned any claims to anything whatsoever, including leadership or even membership of the "ORDER OF THELEMA"; furthermore, I shall not write or publish any more books, nor answer any queries about the present one, without your permission, and the benefit of you advice, watch, and criticism.
    I have also abandoned any claims of "being", or representing, under any form, 666.
    I do not even claim the grade of Zelator, either, until I hear from you if you accept my pledge.
    This is not humility, mind you, or if it were, it would be false; I have very little human humility in my make-up. It is simple common sense, or better yet: instinct of self-preservation?... Or, survival?...

The ego runs around in circles, as usual...

Let us put it this way: as long as I must be a slave, I'll rather be the slave of the A∴A∴ as represented by Karl Germer, than both slave of 333 as represented by Oskar (please notice I had written Karl!...) Schlag, my father, and anybody else who may come up!

Love is the law, love under will.

Fraternally, your unworthy pupil,

Adjuvo

ABOUT THE EDITORS

Dr. David Shoemaker is a clinical psychologist in private practice, specializing in Jungian and cognitive-behavioral psychotherapy. David is the Chancellor and Prolocutor of the Temple of the Silver Star. He is a long-standing member of O.T.O. and A∴A∴, and has many years of experience training initiates in these traditions.

He is the Master of 418 Lodge, O.T.O. in Sacramento, having succeeded Soror Meral (Phyllis Seckler), his friend and teacher. He also serves as the Most Wise Sovereign of Alpha Chapter, O.T.O., as a Sovereign Grand Inspector General and Bishop of Ecclesia Gnostica Catholica. David was the founding President of the O.T.O. Psychology Guild, and is a frequent speaker at national and regional conferences. He is also a member of the U.S. Grand Lodge Initiation Training and Planning committees, and he is a member of the Advanced Initiation Training presenter team.

David was a co-editor of the journals *Neshamah* (Psychology Guild) and *Cheth* (418 Lodge). In addition to his essays in these publications, his writings have been published in the journals *Mezlim* and *Black Pearl*, and his chapter on Qabalistic Psychology was included in the Instructor's Manual of Fadiman and Frager's *Personality and Personal Growth*, an undergraduate psychology textbook. He was the compiler of the T.O.T.S.S. publication, *Jane Wolfe: The Cefalu Diaries 1920-1923*, and a co-editor of the T.O.T.S.S./Teitan Press collections of the writings of Phyllis Seckler, *The Thoth Tarot, Astrology, & Other Selected Writings*, and *The Kabbalah, Magick, and Thelema. Selected Writings Volume II*. His popular *Living Thelema* instructional segments have been presented regularly on the podcast of the same name since 2010, and he is the author of the books *Living Thelema* and *The Winds of Wisdom*.

In addition to his work in magick and psychology, David is a composer and musician. He lives in Sacramento, California.

Andrew Ferrell is an IT professional specializing in deployment of large scale semiconductor design centers across the globe. In his formal education he studied Cognitive Science at UC San Diego, with a focus on techniques of Artificial Intelligence modeling. He sits on the Board of Directors of the Temple of the Silver Star as Librarian and Archivist and serves as Praemonstrator for its San Francisco Bay Area local body. He is an aspirant to A∴A∴ and as a member of O.T.O. he has worn several different hats as a local body officer.

As T.O.T.S.S. Archivist he is dedicated to preserving and sharing the printed legacy of Aleister Crowley, Karl Germer, Jane Wolfe, and Phyllis Seckler.

Outside of professional and magical interests, he enjoys travel, pushing culinary boundaries, training his dog, playing tour guide, and making multidimensional puns. He lives in San Francisco, California with his husband and beloved hellhound Axel.

Stefan Voss is hydrologist and chemist studying isotopic age-dating of groundwater and anthropogenic effects on water resources in California. Currently in graduate school, his research focuses on analytical method development for the analysis of wastewater tracers in surface and groundwater. His academic interests extend to ethnobotany, psychopharmacology, and all things pertaining to the study of consciousness.

He is a senior member of the the Temple of the Silver Star, and an instructor at its Sacramento Campus. As an aspirant to A∴A∴ and a practitioner of esoteric Taoist martial arts, his focus is on the development, training and mastery of practical magick.

He currently lives in Sacramento with his partner, three dogs, two cats, six chickens and dozens of house-plants.

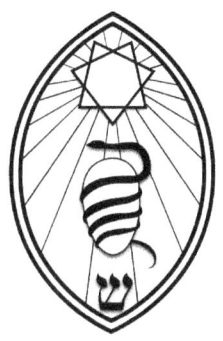

Temple of the Silver Star - Academic Track

The Temple of the Silver Star is a non-profit religious and educational corporation, based on the principles of Thelema. It was founded in service to the A∴A∴, under warrant from Soror Meral (Phyllis Seckler), to provide preparatory training in magick, mysticism, Qabalah, Tarot, astrology, and much more. In its academic track, each student is assigned an individual teacher, who provides one-to-one instruction and group classes. Online classes and other distance-learning options are available.

The criteria for admission to the academic track of the Temple are explained on the application itself, which may be submitted online via the T.O.T.S.S. website. The Temple has campuses or study groups in Sacramento, Oakland, Los Angeles, Reno, Seattle, Denver, Boston, West Chester (Philadelphia-area), Toronto, Japan, Austria and the U.K. Public classes are offered regularly; schedules are available on our website.

Temple of the Silver Star - Initiatory Track

The Temple of the Silver Star's initiatory track offers ceremonial initiation, personalized instruction, and a complete system of training in the Thelemic Mysteries. Our degree system is based on the Qabalistic Tree of Life and the cipher formulæ of the Golden Dawn, of which we are a lineal descendant.

Our entire curriculum is constructed to be in conformity with the Law of Thelema, and our central aim is to guide each aspirant toward the realization of their purpose in life, or True Will. In order to empower our members to discover and carry out their True Will, we teach Qabalah, Tarot, ceremonial magick, meditation, astrology, and much more. Our initiates meet privately for group ceremonial and healing work, classes, and other instruction. We occasionally offer public classes and rituals.

Active participation in a local Temple or Pronaos is the best way to maximize the benefits of our system. However, we do offer At-Large memberships for those living at some distance from one of our local bodies.

If you are interested in learning more about our work, we invite you to download an application from our website and submit it to your nearest local body, or to contact us with any questions.

totss.org

Do what thou wilt shall be the whole of the Law.

The A∴A∴ is the system of spiritual attainment established by Aleister Crowley and George Cecil Jones in the early 1900s, as a modern expression of the Inner School of wisdom that has existed for millennia. Its central aim is simply to lead each aspirant toward their own individual attainment, for the betterment of all humanity. The course of study includes a diversity of training methods, such as Qabalah, raja yoga, ceremonial magick, and many other traditions. A∴A∴ is not organized into outer social organizations, fraternities or schools; rather, it is based on the time-tested power of individual teacher-student relationships, under the guidance of the masters of the Inner School. All training and testing is done strictly in accordance with *Liber 185* and other foundational documents.

Those interested in pursuing admission into A∴A∴ are invited to initiate contact via the following addresses:

A∴A∴
PO Box 215483
Sacramento, CA 95821
onestarinsight.org

The Student phase of preparation for work in A∴A∴ begins by acquiring a specific set of reference texts, notifying A∴A∴ of the same, and studying the texts for at least three months. The Student may then request Examination. More information about this process is available via the Cancellarius at the addresses given above. Please use only these contact addresses when initiating correspondence. NOTE: While our primary contact address is in California, supervising Neophytes are available in many countries around the world.

If you are called to begin this journey, we earnestly invite you to contact us. Regardless of your choice in this matter, we wish you the best as you pursue your own Great Work. May you attain your True Will!

Love is the law, love under will.

INDEX

A∴A∴, [xi], 3, 5, 7, 9 n.9, 16 n.15, 27, 32, 42, 58, 79, 89, 90, 91, 154, 155, 157, 158, 172, 193, 194 n.69, 210, 213, 242, 253, 255, 256, 263, 338, 357, 385, 389, 391-393, 395
Abramelin, 14, 96, 245, 251, 263, 317
Adonai, 122, 130, 151, 182, 190, 192, 212, 217, 219, 221, 252, 259, 261, 262, 265, 266, 339
Æon of Horus, 161, 324, 355
Æon of Thelema (*see* New Æon of Thelema)
Aethyrs, 191, 277
Agape Lodge, [vii], [viii], 3 n.1, 4 n.4, 8 n.8, 16 n.14, n.16, 22 n.19, 26 n.21, 35 n.24, 37, 38, 40, 42, 44, 48, 49, 51, 52, 57, 59, 62 n.39, n.40, n.41, 64, 65 n.43, 67 n.45, 73, 75, 77, 78, 83, 86, 87-88, 99 n.50, 104, 106, 117 n.52, 118 n.53, 120, 124, 142, 144 n.59, 149, 153, 155, 158, 163, 166 n.64, 167 n.65, 172, 176, 181, 183, 193, 202, 203, 204, 210
Aiwass, 254, 330, 338, 371
Ajna, 129
Aldrich, Meeka, 117, 118-119, 124, 146, 206, 295, 310, 314, 346, 347-348, 350, 364
Alexanderplatz Prison, [x]
Alfred Herbert Ltd., [x]
Allene, 162
American Express, 229
Anger, Kenneth, 327, 337
    Inauguration of the Pleasure Dome, The (film), 143 n.57, 327
Aquarius, 283
Arthur, King, 325
Asana, 60
Astrology, 26, 49, 62 n.39, 120, 160 n.62, 161, 171, 183, 219, 276, 278, 281, 285, 288, 289, 291, 292, 305, 318, 346, 347, 349, 350, 352, 362, 366
Ataturk, Aleister, 135, 182 n.67, 184, 193, 194 n.69, 203, 221, 226, 236, 238, 239, 263

Azar, 273, 274, 275, 280, 304, 317, 372

Babalon (Babylon), 308, 314, 316, 328, 336, 386
Bachrach, Mrs., 295
Barstow, CA, 22, 155, 235, 241, 250-251, 257, 314, 318, 320, 326, 331, 332, 337, 338, 342, 344, 346, 351, 357
Barth Publishing House, [x]
Bax, Clifford, 152
Bayley, 154, 230, 232
Beethoven, Ludwig von, 27
Belgium, [x], [xi], 19, 20, 164, 169
Bell's Palsy, 141
Berlin, Germany, [x], [xi], 9, 148, 229
Besant, Annie, 254
Beth, 274
Black Mass, The, 293
Black Pearl, 391
Blavatsky, H. P., [x], 27, 357
    Voice of the Silence, The, 27
Boleskine House, 96, 129
Bonaparte, Napoleon, 15
Book of Abramelin the Mage, The, 245
Book of Babylon (*Babalon*), 308
Book of the Dead, The, 120
Bottomley, Horatio, 213
Bremen, 173
Bremen Theater, 156
British Museum, 207, 209, 215
Buddha, Gautama, 67, 70
Buddhism, [x], 67, 70
Builders of the Adytum, 227 n.76
Burlingame (Graham), Mildred, 53, 65, 69, 70, 72, 74, 84, 85, 87, 94, 142, 143, 145, 146, 147-149, 170, 172, 173, 175, 176, 178, 179, 180, 185, 198, 201, 202, 203, 217, 219, 243, 250, 254, 287, 308, 310, 313, 327, 329, 334, 344, 368
Burlingame, Ray G. (Frater Aquarius), 53, 65, 69, 70, 71, 72, 74, 83, 84, 85, 87, 92, 94, 101, 103, 104, 113, 115, 125, 143, 145, 147-149, 169, 171-175, 176, 179, 184, 185, 201, 205,

209, 210, 217, 219, 234, 238, 243, 250, 254, 310, 313, 327, 331, 333, 334
Cabala/Cabalah (*see* Qabalah/Qabbalah)
Cameron, Marjorie, (*aka* Candida *or* "Candy"), 143, 260, 271, 306, 307, 308, 309, 311, 313, 314, 315, 316, 326, 327, 328, 329, 336, 340
Cammell, Charles R., 263
  Aleister Crowley: the Man, the Mage, the Poet, 263
Cancer, 315, 351
cancer, 361
Canright, Barbara W., 54, 112, 113
Canright, Richard B., 53, 79, 112, 123
Cartwright, Barbara, 85
Case, Paul Foster, 227 n.76
Catholic Church, 57, 58, 158, 250, 387
Cefalu, Sicily, 3, 14, 16, 29, 30, 60 n.37, 74, 90, 92, 93, 124, 132, 161, 213, 214, 216, 256, 337, 391
Chiswick Press, The, 80
Choronzon, 138, 333
Christian Science, 32
Christopher, Barbara, 332
Christopher, Hugh (*née* Max Rosenau), 62 n.40, 67, 92, 93, 96, 112, 168, 177, 181, 184, 185, 186, 197, 207, 208, 209, 212, 220, 239, 242, 245, 251, 252, 253, 254, 310, 313, 332
Chronos, 292
Cleopatra, 357
Collins, Mabel,
  When the Sun Moves Northward, 220
Columbia House, [xi]
Co-Masonry, 254
Communism, 178, 204
Cooper, 103, 112,
Cooper, Jean, 181
Craddock, Ida, 221, 326
  Heavenly Bridegrooms, 221, 326
Crowley, Aleister, [vii-xi], 3 n.1, 7 n.5, n.6, n.7, 9 n.10, 16 n.15, 17 n.18, 18, 19, 20, 21, 23, 25, 27-29, 32, 33, 34, 36, 37, 38, 40-41, 46, 48, 49 n.29, 51 n.30, 52, 58, 60, 61, 62, 63-64, 66, 68, 69, 70, 73, 74, 76, 77, 78, 80-81, 82, 83, 84, 85, 86, 87, 90, 91, 92, 94, 95, 96, 97, 98, 99, 100, 101, 102, 103-105, 106, 107, 108, 109-111, 115, 116, 121, 126, 131, 133, 135, 136, 137, 141, 142, 144, 145, 147, 148-149, 150, 151, 153, 154, 156, 157, 160 n.62, 162-163, 168, 176, 181, 182, 183, 186, 187, 189, 190, 191, 192, 193 n.68, 195, 198, 201, 202, 204, 207, 208, 209, 213, 214, 215, 216, 218, 221, 222, 227, 229, 231, 237, 242, 244, 248, 252, 253, 254, 255, 256, 258-259, 261, 265, 266, 267, 269, 270, 272, 276, 277, 278, 279, 281, 284, 291, 292-293, 294, 296, 297, 298, 304, 306-307, 308, 309, 311, 312, 314, 318-319, 322, 324, 326, 329, 330, 334, 336, 338, 340, 341, 348, 358, 359, 370, 371, 372, 374, 377, 380, 384, 386, 387, 392, 395
  Master Therion, 9, 139, 172, 173, 174, 179, 294
  Beast, The, 3, 4, 5, 6-7, 8, 11, 12, 13, 15, 129, 177, 181, 182, 254, 311, 316, 357
  Baphomet, 57, 58, 110, 158, 238, 239
  works:
    Artemis, 66, 69
    Atlantis, 215
    Berashith, [x],
    Blue Equinox, The, 120, 173, 221, 293
    Book 4, Parts I and II, [x], 120, 168, 169, 207
    Book of Lies, The, 120, 213
    Book of the Law, The, 3, 58, 108, 149, 152, 181, 182, 183, 190, 243, 275, 292, 311, 315, 334, 354, 355, 359, 374, 377
    Book of Thoth, The, 101, 105, 115, 118, 119, 193, 219, 227, 294, 331, 380
    Cairo Working, The, 213
    City of God, The, 79, 80, 189, 193, 294
    Collected Works, The, 132
    Commentary on H. P. Blavatsky's The Voice of the Silence, A, [x], 27
    Confessions of Aleister Crowley, The, 58, 138, 203
    Eight Lectures on Yoga, 120
    Equinox, The, 51, 120, 168, 191, 211, 267, 270, 293
    Equinox of the Gods, 149, 183,

294, 316
Fun of the Fair, The, 80, 189, 193, 294
Goetia, 120
Golden Twigs, 151, 163
Gospel According to St. Bernard Shaw, The, 313
Heart of the Master, The, 9, 181, 183, 185, 189, 197, 207, 211, 219, 293
Holy Books of Thelema, The, [xi], 41, 74, 91, 111, 150, 199, 206, 259, 325, 337
Hymn to Pan, 308, 309
John St. John, 14, 319
Konx Om Pax, 171, 225
Liber AL vel Legis (see *Book of the Law, The*)
Liber Aleph, 69, 112, 134, 148, 151-152, 163, 169, 206, 207, 208, 248, 267, 279, 280, 295, 305, 319, 376, 377, 380, 381, 387, 388
Liber Ararita, 67, 177, 181, 185, 234, 235, 265, 338
Liber LXV, 5, 185, 337
Liber Samekh, 127, 167, 209, 214, 245
Liber Trigrammaton, 181, 185
Liber Tzaddi, 178
Liber V vel Reguli, 17, 205
Liber OZ, 51, 112
Little Essays Toward Truth, 9, 120, 165, 186, 193-194, 219, 293, 324
Magick in Theory and Practice (*Book 4, Part III*), 11, 193, 293, 294, 324
Magick Without Tears, 137, 144 n.58, 198 n.73, 232, 235, 250, 317
Message of Master Therion, The, [x],
Moonchild, 212, 293, 329
Olla, 126, 189, 193, 293
One Star in Sight, [x]
Paris Working, The, 236, 308
Report on the Great White Brotherhood, A, [x]
Rodin in Rime, 169
'Science and Buddhism,' [x]

Sepher Sephiroth,
Sword of Song, The, 169
Tao Teh King, 120, 279, 287
Temple of Solomon the King, The, 58
Three Schools of Magic, The, [x], 364
Vision and the Voice, The, 67, 267, 270, 294
'Wake World, The,' [x], 28, 147, 171, 225
Winged Beetle, 169, 181
Culling, Louis, 99, 106, 143, 146, 164, 166, 308, 327, 362, 364

Dante Alighieri, 190
Dawson, 32
Dee, Gabriel, 17
d'Este, Mary (Soror Virakam), 227
Dharana, 60
Dhyana, 60
Dianetics, 273
Dodge, Sara, 225
Dorson's, 79
dove, 341

Easter, 239
Eastern Star, Order of the, 254, 256
Egyptian mythology, 129, 325, 382
Einstein, Albert, 237
Elberfeld, Germany, [x]
Elizabeth I, Queen, 357
Eller, John, 22, 167, 239, 242
Eller, Thelma, 22, 239, 242
Esterwegen Camp, [xi]
Ewing, Fred, 79

Federal Bureau of Investigation (F.B.I.), 26, 204
Firth, Violet (*aka* Dion Fortune), 198, 249, 252, 353, 373
Mystical Qabalah, The, 249, 353, 373
Forman, E. S., 53, 56
Forman, Phyllis J., 56
Fortune, Dion (*see* Firth, Violet)
Foster, Stephen
'Beautiful Dreamer' (song), 332
Franklin, Benjamin, 15
Fraternitas Rosicruciana Antiqua (F.R.A.), 153 n.60

Freemasonry, [x], 250, 254, 256, 372
Fuller, J. F. C., 91

Gardner, Mary, 158
Gemini, 275, 283
Gene, 146, 149
Geomancy, 259
Germer, Cora (Eaton), [x], [xi], 4, 14, 19, 20, 23, 27, 38
Germer, Karl (Frater Saturnus), [vii-xii], 1-389
Germer, Marie (Wys), [x]
Germer, Sascha (Sasha) Ernestine (Andre), [xi], [xii], 61, 87, 100, 105, 118, 129, 131, 132, 133, 135, 136, 140, 144, 149, 156, 162, 164, 165, 176, 184, 186, 187, 195, 197, 198, 200, 203, 206, 216, 220, 223, 225, 226, 228, 231, 233, 240, 241, 247, 255, 257, 258, 295, 299, 300, 316, 340, 347, 348, 357, 362, 364, 367, 369, 376, 379, 380, 381
Gnostic Mass, 16 n.16
God, 6, 18, 58, 67, 99, 114, 118, 137, 142, 177, 190, 192, 198, 199, 202, 234, 237, 261, 318, 327, 332, 341, 361
Goethe, Johann Wolfgang von, 190
Golden Dawn, The Hermetic Order of the, 17 n.18, 49 n.29, 165, 394
Graham, Mildred C. (*see* Burlingame, Mildred)
Grant, Kenneth, 164, 335, 338
Great Brotherhood of God, 120
Green, Mary, 120, 219
Gurs concentration camp, 19
Gwynn, Margot (Margaret), 118

Hadit, 114, 183, 235, 275, 286, 298, 322, 354, 358, 382
Harding, Dr. M. Esther, 177
Psychic Energy, 177
Harris, Lady Frieda, 148, 151, 380
Hartmann, Dr. Franz
Rosicrucian Lessons, [x]
Hayes, Jeannette, 74, 75
Hell, 6, 338
Heru-Ra-Ha, 182
Hinduism, 185, 341, 382
Hirsig, Leah (Alostrael), 7, 358
Hitler, Adolf, 52, 58, 126, 127, 128, 129

Holy Bible, The, 7, 76, 191, 317
Holy Grail, 352
Holy Guardian Angel, [vii], [xi], 5, 6, 10, 14, 110, 134, 169, 170, 174, 189, 190, 191, 199, 201, 202, 216, 217, 221-222, 239, 247, 249, 258, 259, 264, 265, 266, 268, 269, 278, 298, 302, 318-319, 326, 340, 352, 368, 372, 374, 376, 381
Hollander, 194, 219
Hoover, J. Edgar, 205
Horus, 46, 161, 324-325, 355, 357
Hubbard, L. Ron, [viii], 64 n.42, 123, 127, 311
Huysmans, Joris-Karl
Down There (Là-bas), 293

ibis, 300
Ireland, [xi], 123, 255
Isis, 161, 324, 335
Islam, 151, 243

Jacobi, Jolande
Psychology of Jung, The, 102, 112
Jeanne d'Arc (Joan of Arc), 357
Jesus Christ, 9, 298, 319, 382, 387
John Bull, 213
Jones, Charles Stansfield (Frater Achad), 7, 12, 15, 30, 36, 75, 95, 138, 150, 159, 171, 174, 176, 202, 215, 227, 228, 230, 319, 364, 368, 387
Jones, George Cecil, 395
Jung, Carl, 102, 112, 177, 178, 185, 199, 201, 321, 391
Jupiter, 213, 283, 284, 285, 311, 351
Juste, Michael (*aka* Michael Houghton), 216

Kabbala/Kabala (*see* Qabalah/Qabbalah)
Kahl, Regina, 16, 31, 53, 71, 73, 103, 112, 121
Karma, 70, 174, 352, 373
Katherina (Catherine) the Great, 357
Kelso, Maym, 67, 219
Kirchner, Mrs. Vernon, 153, 154
Klingsor, 359
Krotona, 165
Krumm-Heller, Arnoldo, 153, 251
Kuentzel (Kuntzel), Martha (Soror I.W.E), 9, 125, 126, 142

Kundry, 69, 341, 352, 353, 355, 357, 359

Lady in the Dark (film), 79
Lao-tze, 185
Laver, James, 152
Laylah, 69, 72, 85
Le Vijean concentration camp, 19
Leffingwell, Rhea, 22, 94, 101, 135, 137, 138, 139, 140, 143, 158, 176, 180, 188, 200, 202, 329
Leffingwell, Roy, 22, 25, 31, 34, 42, 47, 64, 84, 90, 94, 96, 98, 99-100, 101, 115, 123, 124, 135, 136, 137, 138, 139-140, 143, 144, 145, 146, 155, 157, 158, 159, 161, 163, 167, 171, 176, 180, 186, 188, 190-194, 196, 197, 198, 199-200, 210, 211, 212, 216, 217-218, 220, 221, 222, 223-224, 232, 233, 236, 237, 238, 239, 240-241, 246, 247, 259, 261, 265, 274
Leipzig, Germany, [x]
Lekve, Friedrich, 172, 174, 175, 179, 184, 201, 202, 203
Leo, 67, 348
Lewis, Spencer, 245
Liber Saturnus, 303
Liber Thisharb, [x]
Libra, 67, 348, 350
Lilith, 261, 352, 355, 358, 359
Lincoln, Abraham, 15, 27
Lindbergh, Charles, 11, 15
lion, 384
Lohengrin, 221, 339
Los Angeles, 4, 14, 16, 21, 26, 65, 66, 71, 75, 78, 82, 84, 86, 88, 92, 97, 102, 111, 117, 119, 123, 127, 132, 159, 165, 171, 176, 184, 196, 199, 208, 211, 217, 223, 229, 233, 237, 244, 249, 256, 282, 287, 293, 305, 309, 312, 393

Maat (Maut), 39
MacAlpine, Patricia ("Deirdre"), 151, 182, 193 n.68, 257, 263
McCoy, 81
MacGregor Mathers, Samuel Liddell, 48, 49, 254
Magick & Yoga Confronted, 165
Mars, 3, 283, 284, 285, 306, 312, 345, 350

Mary, 387
McMurtry, Grady, 53, 63, 65 n.43, 66, 123, 149, 152, 153, 155, 195, 196, 210, 215, 348, 349-350, 352, 365, 372
Mellinger, Frederick, 53, 61, 62, 63, 82, 86, 87, 88, 89, 91, 93, 95, 96, 112, 115, 126, 127, 128, 135, 148, 153, 156, 161, 171, 174, 228, 229, 236, 258, 262, 267, 281, 316
Mercury, 283, 284, 285, 311, 350
Meru, 340
Mexico City, 335
Mexico, 234, 238, 264, 306, 308, 309, 335
Miller, Grace, 157, 194
Miller, Joe (Joseph D.), 53, 62, 67, 70, 73, 87, 194, 205
Millikin (Milliken), Paul, 155, 163, 166, 169, 170-171, 176, 177, 184, 186, 188, 189, 197, 199, 200, 207, 208, 209, 219, 220, 227, 229, 233, 235, 238-239, 242, 245, 257, 310, 314, 332
Mirror, The, 272
Mohammed, 151
Montenegro, Dr. Gabriel, 167, 183, 185, 195, 196
Montsalvat, 339, 341
Moon, The, 231, 232, 275, 285, 288, 304, 311, 350, 351, 366
Motta, Marcello, [viii], 364, 377, 380, 383-386
Mount Olympus, 340
Mudd, Norman (Frater Omnia Pro Veritate), 7, 12-13, 14, 15, 30, 74, 95, 150, 174
Müller, Max (ed.)
    Sacred Books of the East, The, 120
Munich, Germany, [x]
Mystic Arts Book Society, 375, 377

Nazism, [xi], 20, 125-126, 142, 204
Gestapo, [x], 26, 58, 193
Schutzstaffel (S.S.), [xi]
Neptune, 161, 285, 311, 332-333, 348, 350, 351
Netherwood, Hastings, 106, 148
New Æon of Thelema, 283, 307, 343
New Year's Eve, 66
Nirvana, 185

Northrup, Betty (Sara), 64, 66, 68, 69, 72, 78, 79, 84, 104, 117, 123-124, 127
Northrup, G. E., 53
Nuit, 104, 182, 183, 235, 275, 286, 335, 354-355, 356, 359, 378, 382

O'Connor, Mrs. Frank (*see* Rand, Ayn)
Oath of a Probationer of A∴A∴, The, 256
'Oath of the Abyss, The,' 5, 32, 138
Occult Observer, The, 214, 216
Oedipus complex, 273
Oliver, Frederick S. (Phylos the Thibetan)
Dweller on Two Planets, A, 374-375
Osiris, 161, 324, 356
Ordo Templis Orientis (O.T.O.), [vii], [xi], 3, 4 n.4, 5, 8 n.8, 9 n.9, 12 n.13, 27, 32, 42, 45 n.27, 48, 51 n.30, 54, 56, 57, 58, 59, 65 n.43, 66 n.44, 67, 89, 107, 113 n.51, 153 n.60, 157, 158, 159, 172, 173, 175, 176, 179, 181, 193 n.68, 204, 205, 218, 226, 246, 273, 309, 331, 349 n.80, 372, 383, 384, 386, 391, 392
ox, 384

Palmer, Claire Halleck 'Foxie', 349, 350, 352
Pansophia, [x]
Parsifal, 15, 252, 341, 352, 355, 359
Parsons, John (Jack) Whiteside, [viii], 22, 26, 31, 38, 40, 42, 44, 45, 46, 48-49, 50-51, 52, 53, 54, 55, 56, 59, 63, 64, 66, 67, 68, 69, 70, 72, 74, 76, 78, 79, 80, 81, 82, 83, 84, 86, 87, 88, 89, 92, 94, 95, 96, 98, 101, 103, 106, 107, 109-111, 112, 113, 116, 117, 119, 120, 121, 122, 123, 124, 126, 127, 130-131, 143, 145, 150, 158, 188, 204, 223, 225, 226, 230, 256, 263, 264, 271, 272, 306, 308, 309, 311, 313, 314, 315, 316, 328, 336, 340, 349, 350, 372
Horned Moon, 256
Pasadena, CA, 21, 22, 31, 32, 41, 46, 67, 68, 70, 71, 72, 75, 77, 85, 88, 103, 119, 166, 211, 264
phallus, 261

Phylos the Thibetan (*see* Oliver, Frederick S.)
Pickfords, 13
Pluto, 283, 284, 285, 315, 351
Pope, The, 57, 58, 181
Portinari, Beatrice, 190
Powys, John Cowper, 263
pranayama, 60, 165, 196, 197, 210, 229, 333
Prescott, Marie, 124, 127, 234
Psychomagian Society, 75

Qabalah / Qabbalah, 71, 165, 177, 249, 252, 274, 281, 304, 317, 333, 353, 373, 391, 393, 394, 395

Ra-Hoor-Khuit, 315
Raja Yoga, 352, 395
Rand, Ayn, 111-112, 113, 114
Fountainhead, The, 111
Raymond, Lt. G. J., 259, 292-294, 314
Regardie, Israel, 17, 120, 198, 252, 270
Reuss, Theodor, 12 n.13, 153 n.60
Rodin, Auguste, 169
Ruach, 228, 289
Rudhyar, Dane
Pulse of Life, The, 177

Sagittarius, 312, 366
St. Cyprien concentration camp, 19
Sammasatti – Analysis of the Mind, 165
Satanism, 292, 293
Saturn, 3, 285, 292, 315, 345, 348, 350-351, 366, 376, 377, 378
Scarlet Woman, The, 7 n.7, 30, 74, 182, 311, 316, 338, 379, 380
Schlag, Oskar, [viii], 328, 329-330, 331-332, 333, 334, 389
Schmolke, Herbert (Ishrah), 160, 170, 200, 210, 301, 305, 306
Schmolke, Mrs., 170
Schneckenburger, Ruth, 100, 136, 143, 188, 203, 213, 295
Schneider, Georgia, 67, 73, 74, 84, 87, 94, 100, 104, 105, 120, 135, 138, 140, 141, 144, 149, 155, 157, 162, 182, 188, 194, 205, 235, 251, 272, 314
Schneider, Leota, 17, 18
Schneider, Max, 8, 17 n.17, 18, 20, 21, 22, 23, 25, 27, 32, 34, 38, 47, 64, 66, 69, 71, 72, 73, 75, 76, 77, 83, 84, 85,

87, 94, 100, 101, 103, 133, 138, 141, 144, 145, 146, 149, 152, 153, 155, 163, 172, 182, 188, 195, 199, 216, 220, 236, 243, 251
Schroeder, Theodor, 222
Scientology, 123 n.55
Scorpio, 311, 348, 350
scorpion, 365
Scotland Yard, 26
Seckler, Paul, 60, 79, 112, 155 n.61
Seckler, Paul Bickerton ('Bickie'), 377, 378, 382
Seckler, Phyllis (Soror Meral), [vii], [viii], 32, 53, 63, 65 n.43, 67, 81, 89, 120-122, 129, 167, 171, 194, 212, 216-217, 218, 219, 223, 225, 226, 242, 254, 259, 260, 265-267, 268-271, 272, 273-291, 295, 296-305, 309, 311, 313, 317-325, 329, 331, 332, 334, 343, 344, 345-382, 391-392, 393
Secret Chiefs, The, 191, 192, 195, 202, 240
Secret of the Golden Flower, The, 220
Semiramis, 357
Sephiroth, 28, 249
serpent, 129, 182, 190, 266, 268
sex, 14, 231, 248, 251, 252, 254, 285, 298, 331, 349, 351, 354, 358
Shakespeare, William, 15, 27
Sherrill, Mrs., 162, 165, 219
Shoemaker, David, 391
Sihvonen, Ero, 144, 166, 332, 144, 166, 184, 194, 202, 205, 208, 209, 211, 232, 233, 235, 239, 241, 242, 243, 248, 250, 253, 256, 257, 258, 271, 291, 318, 332, 334, 343, 344, 381
Sihvonen, Jean, 144, 166, 332, 144, 166, 194, 202, 205, 208, 209, 211, 232, 233, 235, 239, 241, 242, 243, 248, 250-251, 253, 257, 258, 271, 291, 318, 332, 334, 343, 344, 381
Smith, Helen Parsons, 26, 42, 49, 50, 53, 55, 64 n.42, 77, 78, 79, 85, 88, 95, 97, 99, 100, 101, 111, 121, 272, 274, 277, 339
Smith, W. T., [viii], 4, 5, 9, 10, 13, 14, 16, 22, 25, 26, 30, 31, 33, 36-37, 39-43, 45, 46, 47, 48, 49, 50, 51, 53, 54, 55, 59, 61, 62, 63, 66, 71, 77, 78, 80, 84, 94 n.48, 96, 97-98, 99, 106, 106-107, 109, 110, 111, 116, 117, 120,

121, 127, 138, 145, 150, 163, 174, 223, 224, 226, 234, 236, 237, 241, 274, 316, 344, 347, 352, 372, 376
Liber 132, 94, 95 n.49., 106, 107
Solstice, 101, 120, 132, 150, 176, 182, 260, 303, 306, 360, 385
Sorbonne University, [x]
Stele of Revealing, 184, 185, 357
Summers, Montague, 380
Sunday Supplement, 229
Symond, Vernon, 106
Symonds, John, 151, 152, 164, 207, 208, 213, 214-215, 216, 292
Great Beast, The, 207, 214-215, 292

Tarot, 32, 40, 79, 80-81, 92, 94, 95, 96, 97, 101, 105, 112, 115, 281, 306, 349, 393, 394
Taurus, 275, 347
Teitan Press, 391
Temple of the Silver Star, 391-394
The Qabalah – Best Training, 165
Thelema, [vii], [viii], [ix], [xii], 3 n.1, 19, 36, 58, 60 n.37, 67, 71, 73, 81, 128, 140, 143, 148, 160, 174, 175, 178, 179, 180, 193, 201, 204, 219, 312, 314, 330, 349, 365, 372, 373, 376, 377, 378, 380, 381, 383, 385, 386, 391, 393, 394
Thelema Publishing Company, [x], 376
Theosophical Society, 40, 165, 256
Thoth, 385
Torah, 382
Traenker (Tränker), Heinrich (Frater Renatus), [x], 12, 90
Tree of Life, The, 28, 85, 129, 185, 249, 250, 252, 394
Binah, 129
Chesed, 249
Chokmah, 30, 36, 129, 386
Geburah, 249
Hod, 132
Kether, 129, 235, 325
Malkuth, 235, 371
Netzach, 132, 350
Tiphereth, 158, 169, 225, 259, 273, 277, 281, 286, 304
Yesod, 286, 350
Tunis, 74, 216
Uranus, 161, 283, 284, 285, 345, 347, 348, 350
U.S. Navy, 124, 373

University of Cambridge, 11
University of Leningrad, 111
University of London, 207 n.75
University of Oxford, 11
University of Southern California, 22
University of Zurich, 330

van Loon, Hendrik Willem
   History of Art [sic], 219
Venus, 283, 284, 285, 315, 351
Vernal Equinox, 47
Vivekananda, Swami, 120
vulture, 197,

Wade, Bill, 362
Wade, Bruce, 373, 377, 378, 380
Wagner, Richard, 325, 339, 352, 357
Warburg Institute, 16 n.15, 207 n.75
Ward, Frances, 211
Washington, D.C., 24
Washington, George, 15
Watt, Alan, 308
Wellinger, Frederic, 173
Wilder, Thornton
   'Our Town' (play), 156

Wilkinson (Marlow), Louis, 151, 152, 153, 263
Wilson, John C., 377
Wolfe, Jane (Soror Estai), [viii], 3-39, 40, 42, 44-98, 100-102, 106-118, 119-139, 141-146, 150-171, 172, 175, 176-189, 192, 193, 194-260, 262, 263-264, 265, 267, 271-273, 276, 280, 282, 287, 288, 289, 290, 291, 293, 294-296, 299, 302, 304, 305-316, 317, 318, 320, 323, 325-344, 345, 352, 357, 360, 362, 367, 368, 369-370, 373, 375, 391
Wolfe, Mary K., 92, 97, 115, 131, 132, 160, 162, 165, 182, 200, 263, 320, 342, 368
Wright, Frank Lloyd, 379

yoga, [vii], 28, 59, 60, 120, 162, 165, 191, 210, 269, 293, 330, 352, 395
Yorke, Gerald, 16, 17, 155, 164, 207, 208, 209, 210, 211, 214-216, 219, 227, 229, 230, 232, 238, 242, 243, 267, 272, 327

www.ingramcontent.com/pod-product-compliance
Lightning Source LLC
Chambersburg PA
CBHW071647160426
43195CB00012B/1377